Endorseme

"When we got married there was no manual, when we started a family there was no manual and when we became a territory manager there was no manual. We looked at our new territory like the stars in the sky. Millions of opportunities, but which one do we concentrate on first? We started our journey taking that first unknown step. But today Richard Harshaw has given us a guide to help us with that journey. We will all have our successes and mistakes. Harshaw's manual will minimize those mistakes. I wish this book was available forty years ago. It would have helped me with my journey. May your purse always hold a coin or two; may the hand of a friend always be near you and may you be in heaven a half hour before the devil knows you're dead."

Bill Knox, Territory Manager

"Every successful Territory Manager in the HVAC industry knows the value of industry experts and the training they provide. Richard Harshaw has an amazing insight and understanding of our industry and the challenges we face as TMs. I know this book will be an invaluable resource to me and to you for many years to come. Thanks, Richard, for all you have done to help me be successful!"

Billy Johnson, Territory Manager, Aces AC Supply North

"In the forty-seven years that I have worked in this industry, the technology today is unbelievable. It will continue to change as the years go by. The thing that has not changed is that this is still a people business. Your relationship with your customers is vital for your success. Harshaw's advice will help you be the Territory Manager that your customers look forward to seeing."

Ralph Ingebritson, Territory Manager

"Albert Einstein said: 'If you can't explain it simply, you don't understand it well enough.' Well, Dick Harshaw explains it 'simply' while making it fun in the process, and he understands it well enough because he has lived it. Much of my success is because of the many things I have learned from Dick. This book will certainly add to the success of any TM or Sales Manager."

Art Guilmet, Guilmet & Associates, Training Consultants,
Norcross, Georgia

The HVAC Territory Manager's Field Guide

Richard Harshaw

The HVAC Territory Manager's Field Guide

Published by:
Intermedia Publishing Group, Inc.
P.O. Box 2825
Peoria, Arizona 85380
www.intermediapub.com

ISBN 978-1-935529-90-3

Printed in the United States of America

Dedication

This book is dedicated to those who went before me and helped make me the person I am today. Some of them are no longer with us, but their memory and legacy live on in me and will transfer to you as you master the principles in this book.

I wish to thank my wife, Loretta, for putting up with me as I labored for several years in writing this book. Her patience and steadfast belief in me helped me give birth to this baby!

I want to thank my editor and publisher, W. Terry Whalin of Intermedia Publications in Peoria, Arizona. Terry and his team helped trim the edges and bring a truly professional product to market.

I also wish to thank those who poured some of their heart and soul into me as I learned the ropes: from my time at Missouri Public Service Company, William Van Dyke, Larry Letzig, Tom Coleman, Wes Westmoreland; from my General Heating and Cooling days, Bob Coe, Bob Quackenbush, Ron Gully, Don Rickman, E. F. "Cass" Cassing, Bill Knox, Ralph Ingebritson, Larry Skorupan, William "Bud" Tholen, W. Terry Tholen, Calvin Price, Mike Hall, Bill Kaiser, Rob Morton, John Kallenbach; from my career at Carrier, Loraine Ball, Mike Hartlieb, Rick Roetken, Joe Schoener, Bill Stewart, Anthony Ranieri, Art Guilmet, Wayne Morrison, David Taylor, Bob Livingston, Margo Freewalt, Derrick Marris, Elio Andreatta, Jack Tobik, Brad Johnson, Dave Reinstra, Randy Black, Don Johnson, Bob Ramp, Richard Roley, Terry Calder, Scott Walker, Robert Madden, Stewart Docter, D. C. Surface, Gordon Powers; from my dealer portfolio in Missouri, Charlie and David Rogers, Jack Reed, Jim Woodman, Roger Davidson, Jim Beerman, Gus Steiner, Bill Smith, Eldon Jenkins, Jerry Boschert, Don Hilgedick, Don Fritz; and from my clients, Rhamy Morrison, Billy Johnson, Mark Korte, Greg Johnson, Jay Gordon, Lee Hendrickson, Terry Whiteley, Ron Clark, Richard Specht, Bobby Leggett, Ted McDonald, Andy Armstrong, Natalie DeRousse, Mike Simpson, Mickey Smith, Gary Mummert, Mark Nelles, Doug Widenmann, Diego Stefani, David Trautman, Andrea Dopp, Carol Baker, Tommy Taulbee, Tom Diab, John Bart, Eric Griffen, John Wright, Dan Keck, Scott Ansley, Michelle Wilton and Kevin Hehn.

I am truly grateful to you all!

Table of Contents

Foreword

When Dick Harshaw asked me to write a foreword for this book I was stunned. I had never done anything like that nor thought I would. I accepted on the spot. I have always been a person that would venture out and then find out how to do the job. It was then my mind started sorting out all the things I knew about Dick, the time line of the past thirty plus years that was involved, and what in the world was I going to say. Slowly it started to take shape. The more I thought about it the more I got enthused about doing it and from then on it seemed like a slam dunk… it just flowed.

I think there are many territory managers in this country that owe a lot to Dick. I will never know. But I do know that if they will take his training and apply it they would be more profitable and enjoy their business more. Dick doesn't teach a trouble free business. He teaches how to stay as trouble free as possible and how to handle the problems that come along… something like life I think. I entered the HVAC industry in 1960. There were many changes going on at that time with new high speed compressors (3600 RPM), R-22 refrigerant was just starting to show up in condensing units, and quick connect tubing was just coming out. You should have heard the complaints from the dealers. Some threatened to quit the business if these changes went on. None did quit but you could tell it wasn't welcomed.

At the time Dick entered the industry these changes had already taken place and most dealers were settled in… complacent would be a good word here. Up until the 1980s the demand for comfort was greater than the supply of goods from the manufactures. That was about to change. As manufactures were enlarging, ramping up with more capacity, and merging, the supply outdid the demand. Prices started to fall along with profits. Dealers that used to have it their own way most of the time, were finding it harder and harder to "compete" with all the new dealers with low prices. Most dealers had forgotten how to sell. Most were too lazy to try to learn, but the dealers that understood this were doing fine. Enter Dick Harshaw into a topsy-turvy business field.

Dick could have chosen any industry and that industry would have greatly benefited, but he chose the HVAC industry, and it is still benefiting. It was especially good for GH&C (General Heating & Cooling). That's where I met Dick in the early 1980s when he signed on to be the Service Training Manager. Dick put together a dealer/contractor training program and facility that hasn't been equaled by anyone in the Midwest. It was a real draw for our company.

As he did his job, Dick knew he couldn't stay as a training manager and get ahead so he sought a sales position within the company. My territory was rearranged so we could make a new one for Dick and he started a branch sales office in Columbia, MO in 1984. Little did I know that Dick would look to me to help him get started.

I had been in sales for almost twenty years by then and starting relaying all that I could to give him a jump start in his territory. He was an extremely fast learner and I don't remember having to go over anything more than once. It didn't take long till I knew he was now on his own and didn't need my help anymore. It's fun to take credit for a guy like that but I know different. Dick took what I had to teach and made it soar. He started introducing computers to his dealer/contractor network in the territory with sales analysis data and projections etc. and before long had surpassed my sales levels.

It wasn't long after that I recognized that Dick was unique in many ways. He had that sense that all good salesmen have about their dealers and was then able to help them achieve bigger and better things for themselves. Whenever you can help someone else achieve more, with more profit, you have reached a delicate balance between salesman and customer. My boss told me once that you really didn't have to like a person to do business with them, but it sure helps. Dick was that kind of guy. He had a way to cause you to like him. This isn't a natural thing with anyone… you have to work at it.

Someone told me once that they had never had an insurance policy knock on the door and try to sell them insurance. I don't think anyone has ever had a car pop up in the parking lot and say… "Here I am, come buy me." In fact, I think it's safe to say that probably nothing ever gets sold without ***someone*** behind the sale doing all the things necessary to help a customer.

That's what Dick learned early. He learned that when you work harder on yourself than on a product you'll grow faster and better. After a product line has been learned and is intact, the difference is in people. It's always the people that make the difference. That's what Dick learned early and what he began studying early. That's what made the difference for him. Sure, all the nuts and bolts count but it's always the people that count the most.

Dick learned early on that the dealer that has the correct attitude towards his business and his customers will be more profitable in his business and more respected in his community. Dick teaches in his own manner but he does get across the difference between the "purpose" of a dealers business and the "aim" of it. Most dealers would answer that the "purpose" is to make a Profit. When asked what their "aim" is they get confused thinking that they are the same. The explanation is easy. Dick proposes to the dealer the following: The "purpose" of his business is to solve the customers comfort problems in the most economical way. When the dealer has that purpose in mind he asks different questions of the customer in searching for an answer. The customer now has a sense that the dealer REALLY wants to help and not just sell something.

If a dealer truly has the correct purpose for his business established then he will prosper. His profit will take care of itself and he will grow. Along with his personal training he started putting together financial training programs for his dealers. A lot of the background for all he was doing came out of the dealer financial training program that Carrier started in 1970. He soon learned that most dealers didn't know how to run a company. Analyze a financial statement??? Are you kidding? Why do I need a monthly statement? I have my accountant do that stuff at year end so I can pay the taxes I owe. It didn't take long for Dick to see what the road ahead was going to be like, and he had to adapt. Now he knew he had to develop a sales strategy along with the financial management programs to really show dealers what they needed to know to survive and be profitable and to be able to change when necessary.

I think that is where Dick saw another light. I think he asked himself that if I can teach the dealers in my territory, and they can improve and prosper better, why can't I do it on a larger scale?

Enter a fiasco that cost GH&C the Carrier line. A lot of things happened because of that change. Dick left GH&C and started working with the new factory owned Carrier distributor CPD (Comfort Products Distributing).

About a year after he started with CPD he left and went to work for the Carrier training department doing the type of training, through the distributors, for the dealers, that he had been doing in his own territory. It was a match. Now Dick could spend all his time refining his skills in an area he knew well.

After a couple of years of holding financial and sales training meetings for the various distributor's dealers, Dick left Carrier and started out on his own.

This was the birth of Lodestar Consulting. This is what separated Dick from the crowd. Now he didn't have to bend to anyone's whims or directives. If he knew a new idea was right, and a change was needed, it was implemented. He would live or fail with his own initiative.

HE HAS BEEN RECEIVED WELL. Dick's vigilance in the sales arena, particularly the HVAC market, has kept him abreast of the ever changing demands that the new and younger crop of customers want. He understands that a customer will keep looking until he finds what he wants. The dealers better be ready to deliver if they want to prosper.

Dick is unique as I said earlier. His hobby is Astronomy. He has even written a book on the subject which I don't think I would understand. He is the President of his local Astronomy Club in Phoenix, AZ. He moved there over two years ago so he and his wife, Loretta, could be closer to family. Since Dick flies to most all his engagements, he can live almost anywhere, so living in the Phoenix area where the sky is clear and beautiful almost all the time was a natural move.

I know Dick still calls me his mentor so I will take what credit is due. However, it is I that will now, and forever, be in his debt for all that I learned from him. I couldn't ask to have a greater friend and confidant. He is a great Christian friend and I value his friendship. Maybe more then he knows.

Bob Coe
Retired Territory Manager
Kansas City, Missouri

PS: THIS BOOK IS A MUST FOR ANYONE IN THE HVAC INDUSTRY

Chapter 1: What Is Your Job?

Territory manager!

The title can seem a little overpowering sometimes.

So just what is a "territory manager" (TM) ?

> ***A territory manager is a person whose job is to work with the contractor accounts that have been assigned to him or her in such a way that he or she makes a profit off the work done in the territory they are assigned to cover.***

That's the "book definition." But I would like to extend that definition a little. **Think of your territory as if it were your own *private business.*** Imagine that *you* have made the investment to create and build this business, and now you are responsible *to yourself* to operate that business in such a way that it returns a strong profit for *you.*

Granted, you work for someone else. Someone else's signature endorses the front of your paycheck, not your own. But if you will think of your territory as your own business to run profitably, you will go a long way toward being a Tier One Territory Manager, the top echelon of a four-tier pyramid! (We'll talk more about the tiers later.)

Why a "Field Guide"

Perhaps when you were younger you participated in a Boy Scout or Girl Scout troop, 4H, or some other youth activity. Most of these groups publish "field guides," booklets on the philosophy of the group and helpful tips on how to gain new skills, like hiking, camping, fishing, canoeing and so forth. Browsing the shelves at a full-line book retailer can lead to the discovery of hundreds of field guides in virtually every form of human activity there is! There are field guides for bird watchers, wild flowers, planets and stars, deciduous trees, reptiles, stamps, Corvettes—and the list goes on and on.

The idea behind calling this book a field guide is in keeping with the idea behind field guides. In this book, I will be sharing with you some of the philosophy of being a Tier One Territory Manager as well as giving you helpful tips and ideas on how to become a Master of the art.

But I do promise this—there will be no knots to learn to tie, or merit badges to earn. Your merit badges will be in the form of your commission check stubs!

Why Should You Listen To Me?

More than likely, you have no idea who I am. Yet here I am stating that I am going to share with you valuable tips and insights that can make you a Tier One Territory Manager. Can you trust me?

For most of my adult life, I have been in the HVAC industry. I graduated from college in 1973 with a degree in Mathematics Education with a minor in Physics. I taught high school for three years and then went to work for an electric utility as a district sales supervisor. At the time, I knew nothing about sales, but then again, when you work for a monopoly, how difficult is it to sell?

Actually, I had stiff competition. My job was to promote clean, efficient electric heat to people who were building new homes or remodeling existing ones in my territory. In our market, that meant heat pumps. At the time, natural gas was almost as cheap as dirt, so it was difficult to convince people to go with a heat pump when they could install a gas furnace and an air conditioner for much less money and have lower operating costs too! Of course, in the rural areas, where the alternative was costlier propane, the battle was much easier to win.

In that line of work, I met hundreds of HVAC contractors and got to know several of them quite well. After all, if you are going to refer a homeowner to a contractor for their new home, you don't want some idiot botching the job. So I carefully cultivated relationships with about two dozen of the area's best contractors.

One year, one of those contractors offered me a job. He wanted me to spearhead a new replacement sales division and get the service department into good shape to support it. (At that time, he was almost 100% new construction. This was the late 1970s, a time when interest rates were in the double digits and home building almost ground to a complete halt. This contractor saw wisely that to survive, he needed to move more and more into the replacement market, but to be successful there, he'd have to have a strong and profitable service department.) I thought about it for a few days and agreed to go work for him.

Rocky Start

And *that's* when my real sales "education" began. I sold practically nothing for my first three months! I would go out to the customers' homes and do my measurements and examination of existing equipment and try to determine their needs, and then give them a price, and almost always they'd use someone else. And it did not seem to matter where my price was—I lost jobs when I was the low clown on the totem pole and I lost them when I was the highest. I did not see a pattern tied to price.

So I figured that selling must involve things besides price and determined to start to learn this new craft.

Selling is a Skill You Can Learn

I went to the library and got a book on selling. (I don't even remember now who wrote it or its title.) I began to read and take notes, and started to put into practice what I was reading. Gradually, things began to improve.

Then I got a book by Zig Ziglar and found myself having a jump start to my sales development. Looking back on those years now, I must admit that many of the things I did from Zig's book I no longer do as I think there are now better ways to do some of the things he writes about, but 90% or more of what Zig says is still relevant and useful and you could probably help your own growth as a sales professional by reading some of Zig's books.

Eventually, I learned how to *differentiate* myself and my company on sales calls, and

Sales People are NOT Born

Look at the obituaries in most papers in any given week and you'll see where some person who died was a sales executive for some company when he or she was alive, or they sold insurance, or managed a sales force, and so on.

Now, look at the birth announcements in that same paper and note that Mr. and Mrs. John Doe are the proud parents of a new 7 pound 5 ounce baby boy or girl.

I have yet to read a birth announcement that said "Mr. and Mrs. John Doe are proud to announce the birth of a 7 pound 5 ounce salesman!"

Sales is a learned skill, not one we are born with. No doubt some people have a better intuitive sense for the subtle behaviors and statements that lead to powerful sales, but anyone who wants to can learn how to sell better, if they are willing to admit they don't know it all and then apply what they learn, adapting it to their own personality as they go.

then things began to really improve. I learned, for instance, that I really did not have a snowball's chance in the Netherworld if the customer was a price driven person.

The Shape of the Market

Modern market research reveals a basic fact that every HVAC contractor needs to know. Depending on which source you read, you'll find that *about 24% of the market is driven by* ***price***—they only want the cheapest price for the thing they want to acquire. Quality is not that important so far as the product is reasonably good and you can get it for them at the price they are willing to pay.

Another 17% or so of the market is not price driven, but rather **value** *driven.* These are the folks who will pay more money—sometimes a *lot* more money—to acquire a thing if they think the quality is there to back up the price differential. With these folks, I would not say that price is not an issue (because price is *always* an issue)—it is just not *the* issue.

The balance of the market—roughly 59%—can go either way. And this is where the research gets juicy: they tend to end up in the part of the market the sales person *comes from*. In other words, if the sales person works for a price oriented contractor, he or she will more than likely make a sales presentation based on price. If the customer buys from this sales person, they are actually buying on the basis of price. But if the sales person comes from a quality-driven contractor, the customer will probably end up buying on the basis of quality with price being farther down the list of concerns.

In practical terms for me working at that dealership, this fact opened up a whole new world to me. Our dealership handled two lines at that time—the two largest lines in the United States, Carrier and General Electric (which was sold to Trane in the 1980s). Neither brand at that time was cheap, and to add to my misery as a sales person, we were a union shop. So our labor costs were about 30 to 40% above the norm versus non-union shops. So here I was trying to sell some of the most expensive products in America with some of the most expensive help.

Right away, I realized I could never win with the 24% price driven segment. And since, by odds, one call in four would be a "pricer," I could waste a lot of time and effort chasing work I would never be able to get.

Conversely, I also realized that 76% of the market was **not price driven**. So I had a larger field to play in than I realized… if I could just determine where the boundaries were.

And that lead me to create a qualifying script.

Qualifying Prospective Customers

I am not a big fan of memorizing and reciting scripts on sales calls as that can start to sound mechanical, and most people see right through it anyway. (And let's not even start to talk about the ubiquitous "robo-callers"!) But scripts can and do work well on the telephone if they are done without using a "reading voice." So I wrote and started using the following script to screen out those people that I probably would not be able to sell to anyway.

> "I am so glad you called our company today for a new unit quote. I would love to work with you, but before I do, there are a few things I want to tell you about and then a very important question I want to ask you. Is that okay with you?"
>
> [Customers always said "Yes" at this point.]
>
> "Great! When Bill[1] started this company nineteen years ago, he had to make a tough decision. He had to decide whether to offer his customers the best products and services money could buy and install and service those products with highly-trained and skilled people, or he could cut corners and offer his customers a cut-rate job. But Bill decided then, as he still insists today, that quality is the most important thing he can offer. And all of our customers are glad he did. So we handle America's two best—and frankly, most expensive—lines and we use highly trained and skilled Union labor to install them. Our labor costs are well above those of non-union shops in our area. As you probably know, quality is not 'cheap' but it costs less in the long haul than junk.
>
> For that reason, I will tell you up front and without apology that I am going to be high priced. In fact, I may be the highest price you receive from those you call. But I know that once the job is installed, you'll be happy with it for years to come, whereas if I cut corners somewhere, eventually it would come back to bite me, and you.
>
> Now for the question I want to ask you. I realize that there are times when price really is an important issue—in fact, the most important issue on the table at the time. For example, you have just learned that you are going to be transferred on your job and so you'll be selling your house soon, and you figure you won't be able to get out of the sale the money you'd put into a top-notch system. Or some unexpected expense has arisen and you need cash to take care of that issue. Now knowing that I am going to be high, let me ask you this key question: Is your primary concern at this time the price of the job, or are you willing to carefully weigh higher quality against the difference in price?"

1 Not his real name.

[I wait for the customer to answer. About 25 percent of the time, they would reply that price was their greatest concern. If they did, I would then say this: "You know, Mrs. _____, I appreciate your candor. And you have saved us both some time, because frankly I cannot help you. I cannot offer you the lines that I carry and install them for the kind of price you think will be fair. If I were to meet your price, I'd have to cut something out of the job, and that is not okay by me, and it would not sit well with you either, would it? So let me suggest you contact John Doe of Doe Heating at 555-7878. John offers jobs at the kind of price level you may be seeking, and he can better help you than me at this time. I do appreciate your call, and if you decide later on to change your mind, I'd be glad to visit with you."

At this point you could hear a pin drop. By the way, about a third of those who would call John Doe would call back in a day or two and say something like, "I talked to John Doe, and you're right. He offered us a very good price. But there was just something about him that did not sit well with us. Would you still come out to see us and help us out?" Would you believe that I got about three out of four of those second-time calls?]

If the customer said that price was not the driver, I'd set an appointment, and then had only to do one thing—quote a high price during the sales call. In fact, if I am not high (or the highest), they may be disappointed in me.

Yet I got about two out of three of the calls I went out on, and I was, on average, about $700 higher than my competitors. That's roughly $2,500 in today's dollars.

The Grass is Brown on Both Sides of the Fence

It's funny, but while working for the electric utility I saw Bill as a resource I could recommend to customers. When we met together, I always saw his good side. But working with Bill day to day let me begin to see how he handled stress and strains, and it was not a pretty picture.

After a little over a year at that business, I decided to leave.

Through a sequence of events that is incredible (and not worth going into detail here), I landed a service technician support/trainer job at the distributor who sold us our Carrier equipment.

I soon became the technical school leader as neither of the other two technical engineers had any educational background. With their help, we put together a strong curriculum of basic service skills classes, advanced courses, improved an eight-station fully rigged training lab with bugged units to practice on, upgraded our training center's media capabilities, and so on. In 1983, I began doing some of the sales and business training for our contractors and territory managers too.

Apparently I made an impression on the right people because in early 1984 I was offered the opportunity to move to one of our outlying locations and open a sales branch.

For the next six years, I was either first or second in gross margin dollar generation month by month among about twenty-four sales reps. And this with the smallest territory in our company (in terms of population and disposable dollars).

I learned early on—and believe to this day—that *by providing the value-added services and advice most young and growing contractors desire, a Tier One Territory Manager can leverage knowledge and experience for margin dollars and live well even when the territory is small.* This field guide will share with you many of the things I learned then as a territory manager, plus things I have learned in the years since from other Tier One Territory Managers in the United States.

Fast Forward

In 1990, I went to work for one of the largest manufacturers of air conditioning equipment in the world.

I worked for that company until February 2003, when I started my own company, Lodestar Consulting Systems, Inc. During my time with that manufacturer, I was responsible for dealer training of a non-technical flavor, producing workshops on management, financial analysis, job pricing, labor control, and sales, among other themes. I also headed up a consulting team that at one time had four consultants who could make calls on individual dealers to help them grow their businesses. And I started working at the next level up, consulting with some of that manufacturer's distributors, helping them improve their performance in their markets too.

My company's name is derived from three interrelated facts. First, Lodestar is an old name for the North Star (Polaris). Being an avid amateur astronomer, I always dreamed of a company name with an astronomical twist to it, and Lodestar seemed perfect. (You see, in the days before Global Positioning Satellites, or GPS, people would navigate ships at sea by using the stars; in particular, Polaris was of vital importance. So the idea is that even as a navigator can use Polaris to plot a safe course for the ship, so Lodestar can help a business plot a safe course for growth and development.)

The Consulting part of the name tells what the company does. I consult. (As I explain to clients in workshops, “Those who can, DO. Those who can’t, TEACH. And those who can’t do or teach CONSULT.”) In particular, I draw upon my extensive experience in this industry to help my clients become more efficient and prolific at making money. I am one of the few people I know of in this business who has been on all three sides of the fence—contractor, distributor, and factory. I can speak the language of all three lands!

And Systems belies that fact that I use a systematic approach to consulting. I often rely on process maps I have developed over the years to help me unravel a client’s issues and prepare a blueprint for success.

So now, you be the judge. Based on what you’ve read so far, either I am qualified to teach you some new things that can help you grow and become a more effective Tier One Territory Manager, or I’m a nut and you can throw this book away right now.

But no refunds.

The Physics and Biology of Being a Tier One Territory Manager

In my college days, I majored in Mathematics and minored in Physics. I love Physics to this day (I usually capitalize it out of reverence!). To me, there is an elegance to Physics that perfectly marries the abstract power of Mathematics to the daily realities of our world (even if those realities are not always intuitively obvious, like in Relativity or Quantum Mechanics).

Physics has a hardness to it, a certain well-defined cause-and-effect chain that enables us to build predictable models and testable theories.

For instance, if you put a golf ball on a tee and hit it with a 3-wood, the ball will leave the tee at a velocity and angle that can be precisely calculated based on the speed of impact with the club, the club’s face angle, and the power behind the swing. One can then calculate with high precision where the ball will land after allowing for wind, temperature, humidity, and other factors. Now in everyday life, no golfer I know of—not even Tiger Woods—does these calculations. They “do” them in their muscles, which have been trained by hitting a ball off the tee with a 3-wood tens of thousands of times. But the point is that Physics allows us to predict cause-and-effect chains with great precision if we have the patience and skill to do the math (within the confines of Heisenberg's Uncertainty Principle).

Likewise, there are certain skills a Tier One Territory Manager must possess that are "hard" like Physics, things that are fairly well established in a cause-and-effect chain. So in this book, *the first section will be on the Physics of being a Tier One Territory Manager.*

But the world of Biology is entirely different. If I hit a golf ball with a 3-wood, I can predict with a fairly good degree of accuracy what will happen. But what if I hit a passerby on the shin with that 3-wood shot? What will he or she do?

There is no way to predict! Oh, to be sure, they will have some sort of hostile reaction. They will probably yell, "Ouch!" or something stronger. They may grab their shin and massage it. But beyond that, what might they do? Run? Find a policeman and report me? Take a pistol out of their purse and put three slugs into my chest? Claw my eyes out?

I cannot predict.

So the second section of this book is devoted to the Biology of being a Tier One Territory Manager. Here we'll talk about those "softer" skills where the cause-and-effect chain is not so obvious, or where there are no clear-cut or hard-and-fast answers to the questions.

What's Your Tier?

To see what tier you may be in as a Territory Manager, use the CD that came with this book and open the "Tier Assessment" Excel file. Answer the questions as honestly and as accurately as you can.

What's your tier? If it is Tier One, you really don't need this book. You could have written it.

But if it is Tier Two or lower, this book can do you some good. Read on, if you have the drive!

Chapter Construction

In closing this chapter, let me share with you what you can expect of this book in terms of format. Each chapter will be written like this one, with a chapter title, and major sections set off by blank space and heavy boldfaced and underlined italicized headers (like "Chapter Construction").

From time to time, I will include interesting information that helps illustrate the text material. This will be enclosed inside a light gray side-bar box, like the one on page 3.

Finally, each chapter will end with a set of Questions. If you are reading this book on your own, you may wish to do them to check your understanding of the material. If you are working through this book with other territory managers under the leadership of your Sales Manager, they may become homework assignments from the Sales Manager. The answers to the exercises are available in a sales manager's CD-ROM that can be purchased separately.

Recommended Reading List

As A Man Thinketh, James Allen. Brief classic by a nineteenth century English essayist. Excellent treatise on how your self-talk translates into what you are on the outside.

At America's Service, Karl Albrecht. What great service leaders do to earn their market positions. Good lessons for the Tier One Territory Manager here!

Innovation and Entrepreneurship, Peter Drucker. Rather heavy work but a classic on cultivating the small-business mind-set.

Leadership is an Art, Max Dupree. Included in this chapter because, if you think about it, a Tier One Territory Manager is actually nothing more than a Leader of Leaders.

Moments of Truth, Jan Carlzon. How one airline's visionary strategies for customer service made it a leader in its category.

Secrets of Closing the Sale, Zig Ziglar. Classic book with about 100 "closing scripts." Whereas I don't advise a scripted approach, the book is excellent material to help you grasp the subtle psychology of bringing a sale to conclusion.

See You At the Top, Zig Ziglar. Classic book on how your success as a sales person must flow from what is in your character. Excellent reading material!

The Soul of the Firm, C. William Pollard. How a servant mentality in business is not only good philosophy; it is also a great way to build sales!

Steps to the Top, Zig Ziglar. Sequel to *See You At the Top*, with more examples and thought-provoking ideas.

Total Customer Service, William H. Davidow and Bro Uttal. A six-point plan to gain sales through service strategies.

Review Questions for Chapter 1

1. A territory manager is

   A) responsible for developing an assigned customer list or building business in a de fined geographic area

   B) responsible to make a profit for his or her employer

   C) the owner and operator of a "private" business

   D) all of the above

   Answer: _____________

2. A field guide

   A) guides you through fields when you're on a hike

   B) is a book of folk lore about the customs of a given area

   C) contains practical information on how to accomplish certain tasks

   D) is a book used by guides on wilderness adventures

   Answer: _____________

3. In the context of this manual, Physics refers to

   A) "hard" skills that are basically cognitive in nature and tend to produce predictable results when applied

   B) working a territory with the least amount of energy

   C) getting more done with less effort

   D) making money through brainpower, not brawn power

   Answer: _____________

4. In the context of this manual, Biology refers to

A) the maggot nature of some contractors

B) how contractors evolve over time, like life on earth

C) "soft" skills that, though vital, are not always easy to predict an outcome when used

E) the complex nature of being a Tier One Territory Manager

Answer: ____________

6. Complete the pie chart below to show how the market in general is comprised (price-driven, value-driven, either way). Label each slice.

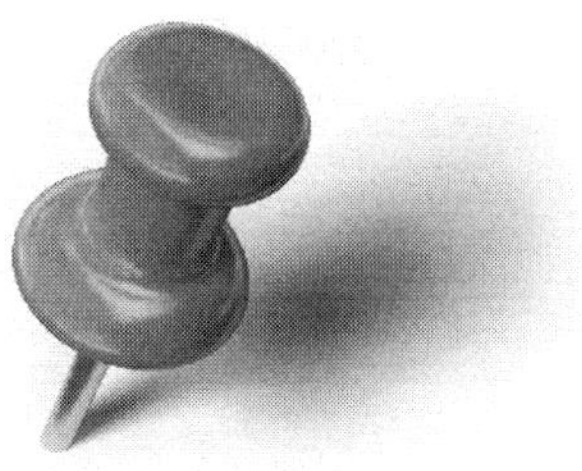

Chapter 2: Maximizing Your Income

Now why would the second chapter in a manual like this be about maximizing your income?

Because ultimately, to succeed in this business, you must do what your boss wants of you, and that will be clearly spelled out in the way you are paid.

How Much Fire Is In Your Belly?

How much do you want to have a good, rich life? How big a house do you want to live in? What kind of car(s) do you want to drive? What kinds of toys do you want to play with? What kind of travel do you want to do? What sorts of restaurants do you want to frequent? What level of insurance do you want for yourself and your dependants? What kind of retirement do you want to enjoy? And when?

All of these questions point to a single answer—how much do you really want the brass ring on the merry-go-round? I have seen all types of sales people in my life, and I must honestly say that those who are content to live mediocre lives with mediocre accouterments are rarely Tier One Sales People. They may be nice folks, but they won't set the sales world on fire.

Usually, those who have a burning desire to live well (in terms of possessions, at least, and money) tend to make better Tier One Sales People.

This is not to say that life is all about pursuing things. I don't believe that it is. But it does say that those who tend to be the best of the best of the best are driven by a desire to win and show off their winnings by the way they live.

So look at yourself in the mirror and ask yourself the questions that started this chapter. What is driving your forward to succeed in sales? If it is not the trophies, then what is it? Does your motivation have enough power to take you to Tier One status?

People Do What They Are Paid to Do, Not What They Are Told to Do

There are about as many compensation plans in the air conditioning business as there are brands! And like the different brands, each plan has its strengths—and weaknesses. In this chapter, we will briefly review the different types of plans that are common and explore how a territory manager paid under that plan could maximize his or her income.

One of the common complaints I hear as I consult with distributor sales managers is, "I just don't get it. I want my guys to set up new dealers like crazy, but they just don't do it. They call on their old accounts all the time. Or if they do set up new accounts, they set up losers who fizzle out in the second year!" I then ask to see the compensation plan, and in almost every case, I can spot the problem immediately. The territory managers are not being paid to recruit new dealers or the right *kind* of new dealers. They are being paid to make the easy sales. And when I point that out to the sales managers, they often are stunned to see it, and then want to know how to create a plan that achieves their goals.

Plans Must Be Linked to Strategic Goals

In 1999, William A. Schiemann and John H. Lingle co-authored a book with the formidable title *BULLSEYE! Hitting Your Strategic Targets Through High-Impact Measurement.* Although not a book I would recommend for territory managers, it should be a must-read for any sales manager.

The premise of the book is that most companies do a very poor job of creating strategic plans in the first place, an even worse job of creating simple but accurate measures to check progress toward the plan, and an even worse job than that of tying this all together into a compensation plan for the sales force! The book is well-written and full of examples of how to do the process.

Suffice it to say for now that ***any compensation plan put out by a distributor should be tied directly to its strategic plan for the year.***

If you don't see a clear linkage between your pay plan and your distributor's strategic plans for the year, you should ask your sales manager for clarification. In some cases, you may not even know your distributor's strategic plans for the year. If you are responsible to bring in sales to fulfill a strategic plan, you have a right (and a responsibility) to know that plan and make sure you do all you can in your territory to make it happen.

Most compensation plans involve at least two pieces: base pay and incentive. The base pay is the fundamental amount a sales person is paid, while incentive refers to additional income that can be earned based on meeting specific behavioral or performance objectives.

What Motivates You?

One of the most important questions to answer when it comes to compensation plans is to know what motivates the people who are going to be paid by them. It should come as no surprise that money is *not* a universal motivator. It is a universal *satisfier*—everyone likes to get it. But money in and of itself does not always spur all people on to greater efforts and achievements.

In particular, research shows that different types of people prefer different types of motivators and rewards. Consider, for instance, what is valued by these two groups:

Low value sellers: working hours

High value sellers: total compensation and pay differences

Here are some other striking differences:

30 years and younger: total pay, mix between base and incentive, stock options, career paths, skill development, flexible environment

40 years and older: retirement plans, independence, job security, location, travel, vacation

Young high value sellers: total pay, pay differences, independence, responsibility, career paths, quality of co-workers

Young low value sellers: health benefits, retirement plans, product quality, job security, location, hours

Men in general: total pay, independence

Women in general: health benefits, travel

However, a striking find is that high-value men *and* women both have the same things on their radar: ***total pay, pay differences, independence, travel, and manager quality!***

The way a compensation plan is structured will determine what sort of talent a company attracts. If your distributorship wants to attract and keep high value sales talent, it needs to focus on creating the opportunity for its sales force to make a ton of money, especially in contrast to those who are not viewed as high in contribution value, and give its sales force a strong sense of autonomy, overseen by top-shelf managers!

The Simplest Plan: Salary Only

The simplest pay plan for a territory manager is the salary-only plan. In this plan, a territory manager is paid a fixed sum for the year to do his or her job.

After considering the traits that high value sellers prefer, you can probably see the problem with this compensation approach. It will not attract high value sellers. People who don't like taking risks, people who like things steady and predictable, will *love* this type of compensation plan, but the sales managers in such organizations should not expect any Olympic efforts by the sales team.

Base Plus Incentive Plans

The most popular form of compensation is a mix of base plus incentive. In these plans, a seller is guaranteed a minimum income (the base), but it is not enough to satisfy the physical and psychological drivers that energize a high value seller. The incentive is where the high value seller can rise as high as they wish in terms of value and income.

But there are several ways of doing a base and incentive plan. Let's look at them in order of increasing complexity (and potency).

Base Plus Commission Plans

This is the most common pay system in sales today. It is easy to administer and the math is straightforward. It communicates clearly to the sales force what behavior gets rewarded.

On the down side, it can also pay for the wrong results. But more on that later.

(1) *The simplest base and commission plan* is where the sales person is paid a base salary plus a commission based on total sales dollars. For example, the base might be $20,000 and the commission might be 2% of sales.

> **Example 1**: Jane is on a plan where she has a base of $24,000 and earns 1.75% commission on all sales, regardless of the gross margin. If she sells $4,000,000 this year, she could make $24,000 in base plus 1.75% of $4 million (which is $70,000) for a total of $94,000.

To maximize your income on a plan like this, you need to sell, sell, sell. It does not matter whether or not you make those sales at a profitable gross margin for the company. You just need to sell. And that probably means you'll become known as the low-price supplier in the area. There's nothing wrong with being dominant in the price segment of the market if you can keep your other costs in line. Huge volumes with low margins and even lower overheads can generate enormous profits! But this kind of sales plan does not reward the territory manager for account development, and distributors who go to market with this approach often lose customers to suppliers who can effectively scratch the itch of customers who lean more toward value than price.

(2) A variation on this plan is where the commissions are paid only on sales *above a minimum gross margin level.* (This is sometimes called a *floor* in compensation plans.)

> **Example 2:** Jane has a base of $24,000 and earns 2% commission on all sales over 16% gross margin. This year, she sold $4,000,000, but $400,000 of those sales were below 16% gross margin. Her qualifying sales then are $3,600,000, of which she gets 2%, or $72,000, plus her base, for a total payout of $96,000.

Here the secret is making sales at or above the floor as much as possible. This type of plan will discourage the territory manager from pursuing commercial plan and spec work (where 99 times out of 100 the lowest price gets the job) and it will also discourage the territory manager from going after residential new construction, which is notorious for being hyper-sensitive to price. If the local market is strong in the replacement sector, such a plan could be very workable. But it is often unwise to ignore the commercial and new construction markets in an area!

(3) A third variation on the base plus commission theme is the *draw* plus commission. This is a little more subtle. An example would be best.

Example 3: Bill is on a draw plus commission plan. His draw is $24,000 ($2,000 a month) and his commission is 1.6% of sales. Last year, he sold $4,800,000. What was his income?

His income would be computed as $2,000 minimum per month with this monthly base being deducted from commissions. So, Bill would earn $24,000 in base pay and 1.6% of $4.8 million in sales (which is $76,800), from which the company deducts his base of $24,000, leaving him with commissions of $52,800. His net pay would be then $76,800. However, in slow months, Bill still makes his $2,000 minimum, but may have a future commission check reduced by the shortfall between his commission and draw for that slow month. For instance, if March came in at only $100,000, his 1.6% commission would generate only $1,600 in pay. Since he is guaranteed $2,000, he makes $2,000 for March. The $400 "overpayment" is deducted from a future commission check which is large enough to cover his base plus the overpayment. If, for instance, his April generated $200,000 in sales, he would have a check of $3,200 coming, less the $400 overpayment he received in March.

The program is basically a commission-only plan in reality. The monthly minimum guarantee of $2,000 however is a great comfort blanket for territory managers who are just getting started in the business and don't yet have a lot of confidence in what they can do. Seasoned veterans would probably find this kind of pay plan to be de-incentivizing.

(4) A very powerful version of base plus commission is to offer a base (either as a salary or a draw) and *base the commission on the gross margin dollars generated* by the territory manager. Since the gross margin dollars are going to be smaller than the raw sales dollars, the commission earnings rate must be higher. Here's an example:

Example 4: Paul is on a plan where he can make $18,000 base and commissions of 9% on all gross margin dollars generated. Last year, he sold $5,000,000 at 23% gross margin. What did Paul earn?

He generated a gross margin pool of $5 million x 23% or $1,150,000, of which he gets 9% (or $103,500), plus an $18,000 base. His total pay would then be $121,500.

Such plans are very attractive to aggressive, self-motivated sales people who realize that the only thing that can block their earning potential is their own drive. Such plans are very effective where the territory manager has considerable control over the pricing the dealers receive from the distributor, as well as some control over commercial quotes. But in an operation where the pricing is set by management and not adaptable by the territory manager for the local market, the territory manager may feel boxed in or limited by pricing that he or she feels is not realistic for the market.

On the positive side, a territory manager who is skilled at bringing value to his or her dealers can usually leverage that value for extra margin dollars and make a great deal of money in the process. The down side is that territory managers on this system will usually avoid low margin work, such as large plan and spec jobs or residential new construction (especially multi-family work).

(5) A powerful variation of the base plus commission themes is to make the commission scale variable based on a combination of sales versus quota and gross margin percentage averaged. For example, consider this matrix:

Revenue vs. Quota							
110%+	1.00	1.04	1.06	1.12	1.16	1.20	1.24
107 -110 %	.96	1.00	1.04	1.08	1.12	1.16	1.20
103 -107 %	.92	.96	1.00	1.04	1.08	1.12	1.16
100 -103%	.88	.92	.96	1.00	1.04	1.08	1.12
97 – 100%	.84	.88	.92	.96	1.00	1.04	1.08
94 –97 %	.80	.84	.88	.92	.96	1.00	1.04
90 – 94%	.76	.80	.84	.88	.92	.96	1.00
	90 – 94%	94 – 97%	97 – 100%	100 - 103%	103 – 107%	107 – 110%	110%+
	Gross Margin vs. Quota						

In this plan, management has worked with the territory manager to determine two vital targets: total sales ("Revenues") and gross margin. The numbers in the grid tell the territory manager what to multiply his or her commission rate by to get the commission for that combination of volume and gross margin.

Example 5: Mike is on a plan like the one shown above, and where his base is $20,000 a year and his regular commission rate is 8% of the gross margin dollars.

Mike ends up the year at 112% of the gross margin quota and 105% of sales quota. What will Mike earn? His gross margin dollars amounted to $920,000.

The multiplier for 112% gross margin and 105% sales is 1.12, so Mike's commission rate for the year is effectively 8% x 1.12 = 8.96%. He earns $20,000 base plus 8.96% of $920,000 or $82,432 for a total of $102,432. Note that had Mike come in below plan (say, only racking up 86% of sales quota and 92% of gross margin quota) his effective commission rate would have been 8% x 0.76 = 6.08%. His commissions would have been based on gross margin dollars of $756,000. He would have made a lot less—in this case, $45,965 in commissions plus the base, for a total of $65,965.

An Aggressive Idea

The most aggressive compensation plan I am aware of comes from a distributor in the United States who pays his territory managers with an awesome package.

The territory managers are on a commission *curve*, where the more they sell and the higher the gross margin they sell at, the higher their commission rate climbs. (If you can picture a ski jump as viewed from the side, you have an idea what the graph would look like; rises slowly at first, then gets steeper and steeper very quickly.)

He has some territory managers making almost $300,000 a year in income.

He also does not provide car allowances, cell phones, or expense reports. He tells his sales force words to the effect, "I am setting you up as an entrepreneur in your territory. Run it like your own business and make a profit with it. If you think you need to entertain a client to make more business, do so. That's why I'm paying you obscene wages in the first place. Don't burden me with your territorial expenses. Just make money for me, and I'll cut you in a sizable chunk of it. Otherwise, you'll become A. T. I." (A. T. I. means "available to the industry.")

Commission-Only Plans

There are really only two variants of commission-only plans: commissions are paid on the total sales, or on the gross margin dollars generated. If paid on gross margin, the commission rate needs to be higher than the gross sales rate.

This is a controversial way of paying a sales force. A lot of people in sales are afraid of being 100% commissioned. "After all," they say, "what happens to my income if I have a bad year? I could be wiped out!"

Yet my experience in talking with the few commission-only territory managers I can find has been that these people never really have a bad year! When the year starts getting soft, they go out and find ways to make it happen and end up with a good year!

They also understand that for a person with a large amount of drive and self-motivation, this is the *best* compensation plan in town. Most commission-only reps know that a base and commission plan means the company has shaved the commission rate to pay for the base. These high-drive reps will often tell their companies, "Keep the base. Give me a higher commission rate instead and don't put a lid on what I can make! Then get out of my way and let me bring in the sales." And bring them in they will!

But What About This Year's Strategy?

So far, we have reviewed common compensation plans that probably 98% of all distributors use in one form or another.

But do these plans really move the distributor forward with regards to his annual strategic goals, as discussed earlier in this chapter?

In most cases, no.

For instance, suppose that next year, the distributor has the following strategic goals:

- Each territory manager will recruit four new dealers with a minimum net gain in aggregate sales of $300,000
- Territory managers will aggressively promote the new furnace lines, with each territory manager reaching a minimum of 20% of all furnaces being the new line
- Each territory manager will convert a minimum of four dealers with aggregate sales of $600,000 to our elite dealer program
- Each territory manager will achieve 40% or greater participation by his accounts in our pre-season stocking and advertising programs

I could list many, many more, but these are typical and represent solid, well-stated strategic goals.

Now, go back over the plans on the previous pages and ask yourself, "Which of these plans, if any, will help this distributor achieve these four strategic goals for this year?"

Give up?

The answer is: none of them will.

Remember, people will do what they are ***paid*** *to do, not what they are* ***asked*** *to do (unless what they are asked to do and paid to do are the same).*

So we need to consider that in some cases, a distributor will need to modify the compensation plan to achieve critical annual strategic goals.

Getting Specific With Compensation

The adjustments to compensation that we will now look at can be used right along with the plans described earlier. In all cases, however, I recommend that the distributor management team carefully calculate the impact each enhancement could have on the company's finances before announcing the new plan. (It would be a disaster if it cost more to pay out the bonuses than the sales results they bring in!)

(1) Enhancement 1: Bonus Pot for High Performance

In this system, a bonus pool is set aside for each territory manager. A performance table like this one is then generated for each territory manager:

Revenue vs. Quota							
110%+	$7,500	$9,000	$10,400	$11,900	$16,300	$20,600	$25,000
107 -110 %	6,900	8,300	9,800	11,300	11,400	16,300	20,600
103 -107 %	6,300	7,700	9,200	10,600	12,500	14,400	16,300
100 -103%	5,600	7,100	8,500	10,000	10,600	11,300	11,900
97 – 100%	5,400	6,500	7,500	8,500	9,200	9,800	10,400
94 –97 %	5,200	5,800	6,500	7,100	7,700	8,300	9,000
90 –94%	5,000	5,200	5,400	5,600	6,300	6,900	7,500
	90 – 94%	94 –97%	97 – 100%	100 - 103%	103 – 107%	107 – 110%	110%+
	Profit vs. Quota						

Here, a territory manager has the chance to earn up to $25,000 over and above his or her normal compensation based on the combination of revenues and profit he or she generates. (We could also base this table on revenues and gross margin, or any other two related and measurable quantities.)

If the territory manager just manages to hit quota on both scales, he or she would make a bonus of $10,000. If they come in above quota, though, they could make up to $15,000 more than this, depending on the combination of revenues and profits they generate.

(2) Enhancement 2: Product Mix Bonus

In this option, the sales manager creates a menu of product sales goals for the territory manager to achieve in the coming year. It might look like the one below:

Number of Product Quotas Achieved	Multiplier
7+	1.50
6	1.00
5	0.67
4	0.40
3	0.15
2	0.00
1	0.00
0	0.00

For each territory manager, a bonus bucket is established (say, $10,000) and measures are kept for each product quota achieved. For instance, the quota could be a raw number: "Sell 800 compressor-bearing units with SEER of 16.00 or higher." Or it could be a percentage measure: "20% of all compressor bearing unit sales must be ductless split systems." Since this table shows seven quotas, the manager could write different quotas for up to seven product groups or categories, or even specific models.

Now, if at the end of the year the territory manager has achieved the quota on four of the seven goals, he or she earns a bonus check of $4,000 (by taking the $10,000 bucket times 0.40).

(3) Enhancement 3: Strategic Initiatives Agenda

Similar to enhancement 2 above, the seven tiers of the chart could refer to seven specific non-product results to achieve. For instance, some of the seven criteria could include: 1) convert four dealers to our brand with a net gain in aggregate sales of $400,000; 2) get Jones Heating to sign up for our elite program; 3) get three builders set up on our builder upgrades program, and so on.

Okay, So What?

Wow, that's a lot of different ways to be paid! Can we boil this down to a simple matrix to capture the highlights, pros and cons of each plan? Look at the matrix below.

Plan	Simplicity	Ease of Administration	What you must do
Salary only	Simple	Easy	Just show up
Base + Commission on sales	Simple	Easy	Sell your socks off at any gross margin level
Base + Commission With a floor	Simple	Moderate	Sell your socks off above the cut-off GM% level
Draw + Commission	Simple	Easy	Same as Base + Commission (above)
Base + Commission on GM$	Simple	Moderate	Sell your socks off for as much GM$ as you can get
Base + Variable Commissions	Moderate	Mod-Difficult	Maximize performance in the two areas being measured by the matrix
Commission only	Simple	Simple	Sell all you can any way you can
Base + Commission + Bonus to quotas	Moderate	Mod-Difficult	Surpass quotas on both axes of the matrix
Base + Commission + B onus on agenda	Difficult	Difficult	Fulfill as many of the objec- tives that are assigned to you as possible

What If Your Manager Does Not Give You Specific Objectives?

It may be that your sales manager has not given you specific objectives, that he or she has only said to you to sell, sell, sell!

If your relationship is solid enough, you may want to have a private chat with your manager and ask him or her what specific things do they want you to do this year? If they simply say, "Sell, sell, and sell some more," chances are that they don't have a clue themselves about the company's strategic goals. Don't come down on them for that—they're just as much in the dark as you are because apparently upper management has not communicated clearly to middle management what the company's strategic plans are, either because they don't know the plans themselves, or they have chosen to not divulge those plans to anyone. That was a popular management style fifty years ago. It's a bit risky in today's fast-paced market!

Chances are, though, that if you ask your sales manager what sort of things he or she wants you to focus on for the year, they will respond with thoughtful and significant ideas. If you respond well to those suggestions, your future in that company should be as good as you care to make it!

Funding Bonus Pools

A final thought about bonus pools (like the last two examples we looked at): many companies deduct the bonus pool amount from the territory manager's normal commission pot and let them earn it through specified behaviors.

For example, if you normally make around $60,000 in commissions and your sales manager wants to create a bonus pool for you that will motivate you to exceed your quotas for volume and gross margin, he or she may say to you that the company is adjusting your commission rate this year so you will make $50,000 in commissions if you do what you normally do. The other $10,000 will go into a special bucket. If you perform to quota for volume and gross margin, you will receive this $10,000 bucket at year end. If you exceed your quotas for volume and gross margin, you could earn as much as $25,000 (in our example) additional. You could also end up making less this year if you severely undershoot your quotas.

Suggested Reading

For sales managers (and, for that matter, upper managers), I would suggest the following books:

BULLSEYE! Hitting Your Strategic Targets Through High-Impact Measurement by William A. Schiemann and John H. Lingle. Creating powerful metrics for solid strategies.

Winning Score: How to Design and Implement Organizational Scorecards by Mark Graham Brown. How to communicate powerful metrics in simple but clear ways.

For territory managers, I recommend these books and papers:

The Game of Work by Charles A. Coonradt. How to make work as much fun as fun.

The Great Game of Business by Jack Stack with Bo Burlingame. An inside look at Springfield Remanufacturing Corporation and their approach to employee involvement.

It's Your Ship by Captain D. Michael Abrashoff. A look at how one U. S. Navy ship's crew sees their jobs.

The Open-Book Experience by John Case. A collection of vignettes about companies where employee initiative rules.

Open Book Management by John Case. The ground rules for open book management.

The following are monographs published by The Corporate Executive Board, a think-tank of major corporations headquartered in Washington, D. C. Monographs are made available to member companies and may be difficult to find on the open market.

Beyond Volume: Aligning Sales Compensation With Corporate Strategy. How to link long-term strategy with this year's pay plan to achieve superior results. February 1999.

A New Dashboard: Next-Generation Metrics for Diagnosing Sales Performance Problems. Several new metrics are considered. April 1999.

Review Questions for Chapter 2

1. Suppose you are the sales manager for a distributor and this year, the manufacturer you represent has come out with an entirely new product line for high-efficiency equipment. Your distributor sees great promise in this line and wants it to get off to a rocket start. What sort of compensation plan would be best to use in the coming year?

A) Straight commission

B) Base plus commission computed on gross margin percent

C) Salary only

D) Base plus commission plus a bonus based on exceeding volume and gross margin quotas

E) Base plus commission plus a bonus based on reaching specificgoals in terms of new product sales

F) None of the above

Answer: _______________

2. Suppose you are on a base and commission plan with a bonus pool for exceeding volume and gross margin targets. (See the table on page 22.) Your base is $21,000. Your commissions last year were based on 8% of the gross margin you generated, but with the new bonus, they will be 7% of generated gross margin with a $10,000 bonus bucket waiting for you if you hit volume and gross margin goals. Your quota for the year is $3,000,000 in sales and $630,000 in gross margin. At year's end, you post sales of $3,680,137 and gross margin dollars of $806,123. What will be your compensation (to the nearest whole dollar) for the year?

A) $85,490

B) $77,429

C) $102,429

D) $89,829

E) None of the above

Answer: _______________

3. Suppose your sales manager comes to you and says, "I want you to come up with five specific things tied to new dealer recruiting that can drive a bonus plan for you this year. They should be clear, easy to measure, and tied to dollars. After we can agree on the list of objectives for recruiting, I'll set up a bonus pool for you of $10,000. You'll earn the proportion of that bucket that you meet the objectives on. If you meet four of the five objectives, for instance, you'll earn 80% of the bucket. Any questions?" In the space below, write five well-stated and clearly measurable objectives for recruiting new dealers for the coming year.

1. ______________________________

____

2. ______________________________

____

3. ______________________________

____

4. ______________________________

____

5. ______________________________

____

4. Suppose you have a special "elite" dealer program that combines factory programs with distributor programs at the local level to create a powerful marketing team between member dealers, the distributor, and the factory. The base package for this program is the same for every dealer—for instance, special pre-season advertising co-op rates and special enhanced marketing funds earnings rates—but other features are *ala carte* and may be used by the dealer if wanted, and then the dealer pays an added fee for the feature. Here is a list of some of those *ala carte* features:

Neighborhood post card mailing for twenty homes around every replacement job location

Special spot buys for dealer-tagged commercials on The Weather Channel (local cable)

Special billboard program for metro area dealers

Reduced tuition for distributor-sponsored schools (technical, business management, and sales)

Access to on-line ordering and warranty processing

Access to the manufacturer's special dealer intranet where a storehouse of tools awaits the dealer

In the space below, write three objectives that could be assigned to a territory manager who is tasked with getting more dealers to use the *ala carte* programs.

1. ______________________________

____

2. ______________________________

____

3. ______________________________

____

Chapter 3: What Is Your Time Worth?

Knowing what your time is worth as a territory manager is crucial because it can help you set the boundaries on what sorts of activities will get your attention—and which ones should not.

One method would be to take your annual compensation (including benefits) and divide by the number of hours you work in a year. But that's only a measure of your hourly cost, not your hourly value. And the two are very different!

Instead, let's focus on what research shows us to be the key driver in the productivity of a territory manager—*the time you spend in front of customers*. There is no better predictor of performance than this one simple metric.

Let's begin by figuring out how much time you spend on the job each week. One survey of high output territory managers a few years ago showed that the average high output TM spent an average of 52 hours a week on the job. Of that time, the average TM spent 11 hours a week on paperwork; 8 hours a week on the telephone; 2 hours a week in internal meetings; 3 hours a week in other office time; 10 hours a week in travel time; 2 hours a week recruiting new business; 2 hours a week of other out of office time; and only 14 hours a week in front of customers! A pie chart of this data is shown on the next page.

Research reveals that it is those 14 hours a week in front of customers that are the key to a TM's success. If a territory manager can spend just a few hours more a week in front of his or her customers, sales can rise dramatically. For instance, going from 14 hours a week with customers to 16 hours a week (2 hours a week more time) is an increase of 2/14 or about 14% more time. Coincidentally, sales would rise about 14% too! If a TM could spend 20% more time with customers, his or her sales would probably rise at least 20%. Get the idea? (This assumes, of course, no change in the weekly sales call routine. Later in this field guide, we'll talk about how a change in the sales call routine can have an even more dramatic effect on performance.)

So the critical factor becomes spending time with customers, not doing other things (that may be necessary but don't directly contribute to sales).

Time bandits are those little things that steal your time and keep you from being with your customers. To get an idea of what types of things may be posing as time bandits in your daily routine, fill out the worksheet below to the best of your ability. Be honest with yourself. You have nothing to gain by kidding yourself, and you could lose a lot by self-deception.

How Territory Managers Spend Their Time

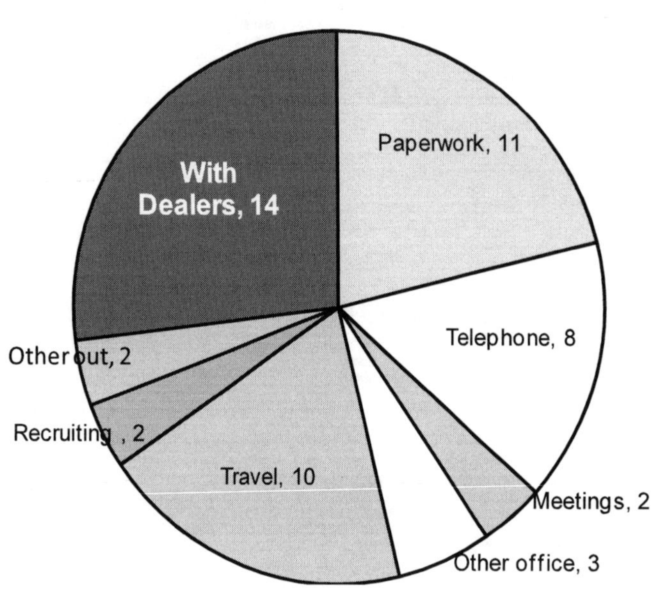

Weekly Activity	Hours Now	% of Time Spent Now	Hours Desired	% of Time I'd *like* to Spend
Paperwork		%		%
Telephone		%		%
Meetings		%		%
Other office time		%		%
Travel		%		%
Recruiting		%		%
Other out of office time		%		%
Face to face with customers		%		%
Totals		100%		100%

To spend more time in front of your customers, you will either have to work more hours per week (I don't normally recommend that, unless you are well below the fifty-two hour a week average), or you must take hours from non-customer time activities and devote them to customer time.

Some distributors have resorted to hiring support staff to do some of the paperwork and telephone work that TMs have had to do in the past, freeing their TMs up for much more field time with dramatic results. But if you work for a company that has not seen that glorious light yet, you will have to find a way to do it yourself.

When I was a TM, that's the position I found myself in. Realizing that to see more of my customers meant automating my processes as much as possible, I pestered my boss to get a laptop for me until he finally gave in. I was the first TM in our company to have a laptop (1987), and the thing was a museum piece by today's standards. It weighed sixteen pounds, had 64 KB of RAM and a 10 mega-byte hard disk drive (can you believe it!?). I soon realized there was no software for TMs on the market so I had to write my own programs for job quoting, order entry, and other functions, all using Visicalc (a forerunner of Excel) and Dbase II (an early database program). Automating my routines let me spend about five hours a week more with my dealers and still get my other tasks done, with a corresponding jump in my sales.

Knowing what I know today, I would say to you that if you do not yet have a laptop, get one. If your company won't supply it to you, get it out of your own funds. You'll more than make up for it in extra commissions in a few months.

Time Management Techniques

Normally, this would be the place to put a series of time management techniques, but I am devoting an entire chapter to that (Chapter 27). If you feel a need to go over that material now, feel free to read Chapter 27 out of sequence when you finish this one.

Computing Your Hourly Value

I opened this chapter with a question about what you were worth. It is now time to compute that number. You'll need your last year's sales records and a calculator to do this, or you can use the CD that came with this book and open the Excel worksheet titled "What I Am Worth."

STEP 1: Write your annual sales goal here: $____________________

STEP 2: What gross margin percentage did you average last year? ____%

STEP 3: What is your company's average overhead percent? _______%

STEP 4: Compute your net margin (Step 2 minus Step 3): _______% NM

STEP 5: How many working days are in your average year? _________

STEP 6: Working weeks in your year (Step 5 / 5): ______________

STEP 7: Hours you spend in front of customers per week now: _______

STEP 8: What are your sales weekly dollars? (Step 1 / Step 6):

$______________________

STEP 9: What are your daily sales dollars? (Step 8 / 5):

$______________________

STEP 10: What are your hourly sales dollars? (Step 9 / 8):

$______________________

STEP 11: What are your sales dollars per hour with customers? (Step 8 / Step 7):

$______________________

STEP 12: Let's now compute the same data for your gross margin dollars. Your weekly gross margin dollars are (Step 1 times Step 2, then divided by Step 6):

$______________________

STEP 13: Your daily gross margin dollars are (Step 12 / 5):

$______________________

STEP 14: Your hourly gross margin dollars are (Step 13 / 8):

$______________________

STEP 15: Your hourly gross margin dollars with customers? (Step 12 / Step 7):

$______________________

STEP 16: Your weekly net profit dollars are (Step 1 times Step 4, then divided by Step 6):

$______________________

STEP 17: Your daily net profit dollars are (Step 16 , 5):

$______________________

STEP 18: Your hourly net profit dollars are (Step 17 / 8):

$______________________

STEP 19: And your hourly net profit dollars with customers are (Step 16 / Step 7):

$______________________

Let's pause and capture the key points before moving on. Find the results from the steps and write them into the summary table below:

	Sales	**Gross Margin**	**Net Profit**
Weekly	(Step 8) $	(Step 12) $	(Step 16) $
Daily	(Step 9) $	(Step 13) $	(Step 17) $
Hourly	(Step 10) $	(Step 14) $	(Step 18) $
With Customers	(Step 11) $	(Step 15) $	(Step 19) $

Notice how I have drawn a heavy line around the "With Customers" line. Focus your attention on those numbers for a moment.

Now ask yourself this question: "What interruptions and changes to my normal routine are worth more than these numbers per hour of my time?"

Ponder that deeply for a minute or two. Put this book down and close your eyes as you think about this. When you have thought it over, pick up this book and resume your reading.

Most TMs will find numbers in the $4,000 per hour range in sales, about $800 to $1,000 per hour in gross margin, and $200 to $500 per hour in net profit. Are your numbers in that general range? Better? Weaker?

Now let's assume for a moment that you have a pickup truck and that your dealers are in the habit of calling you some mornings and saying, "I sold a job last night but don't have the unit in stock. Can you bring me a three ton model X this afternoon?" As may have been your normal habit, you load up your truck and deliver the unit. A two-hour unexpected trip, but it was worth it, right? After all, you saved a sale for your dealer, right?

How much net profit per hour are you worth? Does a special delivery service charge that much to make that same delivery that day? Probably not. Wouldn't you be dollars ahead then to hire a special delivery service to take the unit out to the dealer and spend your two hours finding someone else to see doing a productive *sales call* and not a *delivery?* (I get a lot of TMs fighting me on this one. Go ahead. The numbers defeat you. And they will every time!)

When Styles Collide

I once worked with a Tier One territory manager named Bob Coe. (He wrote the foreword to this book.) Bob was a superb TM but complained once that he had a few dealers who were driving him nuts. He agreed to let me help him run an X-O Survey on himself and his dealers. I then compiled the results and showed them to Bob.

Instantly, Bob said, "I see now where my problem lies!"

Bob was about as value-driven as any TM I have ever seen, scoring 98 on the X-O Survey! The four accounts that were driving him nuts were all very low on the score—12 or less. The rest of Bob's accounts all scored 50 or higher.

That block of four price-driven accounts was a hard group for Bob to deal with—until he learned why he always clashed with them, and then made the conscious decision to change how he called on them and to revise his expectations. (That's why he was a Tier One TM!)

Once he had made these adjustments, he went back to having a good time in his territory.

He has since retired, but his lessons remain true for all of us.

Or suppose a co-worker sees you in the office on Tuesday morning and says they need your help in doing a load calculation. Three hours later you are done. The co-worker has achieved his or her assignment, and they are grateful to you, maybe even getting an order. Feels good, doesn't it?

But was it the best use of your time that day? Only you can say, but this is a numbers driven business, and if your numbers are weak and you are spending time being the water boy for the team, maybe you need to be reassigned?

And Now For Something Really Different!

Let's now compute what might happen if you spent just five hours a week (only one hour a day) more in front of customers than you do now. (This means that Step 7 would be increased by 5.)

Let's do the math:

STEP 20: Net hours per year you'll be adding to your time with customers (Step 6 x 5):

______________________ more hours

STEP 21: Probable increase in sales volume (Step 10 x Step 20):

$______________________

STEP 22: Probable increase in gross margin dollars (Step 14 x Step 20):

$______________________

STEP 23: Probable increase in net profit dollars (Step 18 x Step 20):

$______________________

If your sales grew by the amount in Step 21, how much would your sales be next year (Step 21 plus Step 1)?

$____________________

What would your gross margin grow to? (Step 22 plus [Step 1 times Step 2]):

$____________________

And what would your net profit rise to (Step 23 plus [Step 1 times Step 4]):

$____________________

Are you beginning to see the point?

More Donuts and Coffee?

So what do you do with your extra time in front of customers next year? Do you bring out *more* donuts, or spend *more* time on the golf course, or go out for *more* lunches?

Not if you want to see a change in your numbers.

You must change your routine. The extra time you spend with your customers must be time that results in the growth of their business in some way—either in the overall physical growth of the business if they are already pretty loyal to you, or getting more and more of their business if they are not. And both approaches require something more than "business as usual." You have to be prepared to bring a lot of added value to the relationship.

But that's what the rest of this field book is about, so we'll take those steps as we come to them.

Review Questions for Chapter 3

1. When you consider what you are worth per hour when measured by time in front of customers, do you find yourself re-evaluating how you use your time day in and day out? How do you see yourself differently?

2. One of the hardest things for successful people to learn how to do is say, "No!" Does your value per hour make it easier to say "No!" now?

Chapter 4: Rules of Thumb

Every trade has rules of thumb—quick and general guidelines for what should be normal for a business. Knowing some of the basic rules of thumb in the HVAC business can help you become a wise and intelligent vendor of business growth strategies, something most up-and-coming HVAC contractors are seeking.

Rules of Productivity

A publication of the U.S. Department of Commerce, in cooperation with the Census Bureau, is a gold mine for statistics about the HVAC business. Their report is issued every five years, and can be downloaded at the Census Bureau's web page (www.census.gov) by clicking on "Economic Census" under the Business and Industry area, and when that page loads, clicking on the "Industry Series" link. Click on the arrowhead on the "Construction" line and scroll down until you find NAICS code 238220 and download the version of the report you want.

The numbers I'll be sharing with you in the *Field Guide* are taken from the 2007 report and adjusted for the consumer price index (which has risen 5% since the data was published).

➢ ***Sales Per Employee (The Productivity Ratio)***

The Productivity Ratio is simple to compute—merely divide the dealer's annual sales by the number of people he had on the payroll for that same period of time. For example, if John Doe's company had sales of $1,500,000 with thirteen people on the payroll, his Productivity Ratio would be $1,500,000 ÷ 13, which is about $115,385.

The average Productivity Ratio shown in the 2007 report on the HVAC trade is **$159,644 per employee**.

In computing a dealer's Productivity Ratio, you must count all employees who were on the payroll, even if only for part of the year. This means, for instance, that you must count *all* the office employees (including the receptionist, bookkeeper, dispatcher, managers, and so on). You should also count partial-year employees as fractions. For instance, an installer who only worked six months would be counted as 0.5 people.

This is an important ratio as it is a good indicator of how well a dealer is using his most important assets (his people) to produce revenue. Although there is no guarantee that a high ratio company will be profitable or that a low one will not, it is generally the case that the higher the ratio, the stronger the company's profits will be. We'll cover what a dealer can do to improve his ratio later, but first we must make sure that the dealer's local ratio is strong for his market.

The national average of $159,644 may be too high for some markets and too low for others. For instance, it may be that the data for a rural area may show a Productivity Ratio well below this number, while the Productivity Ratio for an upscale region like Fairfax County, Virginia may show a ratio much higher than this. In other words, the local Productivity Ratio should be adjusted upwards or downwards for the local economy to get a good idea of whether or not the dealer's ratio is strong or weak.

To get an idea of what the local Productivity Ratio should be, you can run a state comparison and be reasonably close. To do so, open the "State Throughput Data" PDF file on the CD-ROM that came with this book. Look up the state you want to compare and you will find its actual throughput as of 2007.

Increasing the Productivity Ratio can only involve two general strategies, since there are only two parts of the ratio equation: the dealer either needs to increase revenues, or reduce the number of employees (or do both).

Reducing employees is easy enough (although not necessarily easy to do when it comes time to let someone go). It's the "increasing revenues" part that often stymies a dealer.

The following is not meant to be an exhaustive list, but it is enough to keep the average dealer busy for several years!

- ❑ Learn how to sell more effectively (getting the"success rate" up; finding more leads; selling the jobs for higher dollars; and so on
- ❑ Sell systems instead of just replacement components
- ❑ Advertise more efficiently (and intelligently)

- ❑ Go to flat rate pricing for service work
- ❑ Raise prices in general (see Chapter 9 for more)
- ❑ Improve the collections procedure
- ❑ Keep adequate inventories on hand to facilitate greater job installation efficiency
- ❑ Accept major credit cards; offer job financing
- ❑ Redesign paperwork to improve work flow and reduce errors
- ❑ Combine office jobs when possible and reduce office staff where possible
- ❑ Leverage technology to streamline office operations
- ❑ Use part-time employees to help with seasonal work loads

➢ *The Installation Sales Installed per Installer*

This ratio measures how well the dealer uses his or her installers to install the jobs that get sold. It may seem trivial, but this is the one area where most dealers really drop the ball and waste thousands upon thousands of dollars!

To compute it, merely divide the installation sales by the number of installers putting those jobs in.

The average Installation Sales per Installer (ISI for short) turns out to be $283,239 (which we can round to **$283,000**). This is not based on the economic survey from the government, because that document does not break out field employees by installers versus service. This number is derived from surveys of contractors and represents a blending of the good, the bad, and the ugly.

As with the Productivity Ratio, this number should be adjusted using the state's throughput data. Multiply the state's throughput number by 1.774194 to get the approximate installation sales per installer.

If a contractor wants to raise his or her ISI, there are only two general areas to work on: installation sales, and the number of installers (or both). I usually recommend to let installers go as a last resort (since these are the hands that are doing the work for which a company gets paid in the first place— unless, of course, the installer is inefficient, lazy or inept), so we need to focus heavily on the revenue side of the equation again.

Many of the things that we looked at for improving the Productivity Ratio would work here too, of course. In addition to those, a dealer should also consider some of these ideas:

- ❑ Examine the job pricing; cost out several jobs and look for repetitive problems and address the causes
- ❑ Review how jobs are pulled, staged, loaded, and delivered to the job site
- ❑ Review job engineering; is there a simpler, easier way to do the jobs?
- ❑ Count the number of overhead doors (too few doors means crews form log jams in the morning)
- ❑ Map out the work flow in the shop; is it maximally efficient?
- ❑ Review how crews are compensated for their work
- ❑ Review each crew's efficiency; are some better than others? Why?

➢ *Service Sales Per Service Truck (SST)*

The Service Sales per Service Truck (SST ratio) should, like an SST, be a fast, high-flying number! It is computed by dividing the annual service sales by the number of service trucks. The national average right now runs around $130,000, but here is what the SST *should* be:

Residential service truck:	**$160,000 per year**
Commercial service truck:	**$190,000 per year**

If a contractor wants to raise the SST, there are only two areas he can focus on: service revenues, or the number of service trucks (surprised?). Here is a partial laundry list of what a dealer can do to improve his or her SST:

- ❑ Departmentalize the income statement, showing the installation and service departments as separate profit centers; this way, a loss can be spotted quickly and fixed. (We'll cover how to do this in Chapter 9.)
- ❑ Calculate the average gross margin on parts. It should be around 65%. (If a part costs, for example, $30, it should sell for $30 x (1 / 0.35), or about $86.)
- ❑ Review the street rate for labor. As a general rule, the breakeven street rate is three times the highest paid tech's wages plus benefits. It becomes profitable at four times that number!
- ❑ Adopt flat rate pricing for service. (After the previous bullet point, the contractor

will have to.)

- ❑ Get into the service agreement business big time (that means 500 or more new agreements per year with 85% renewal on old agreements)

➢ *The Sales per Comfort Consultant Ratio (SCC)*

If a contractor has a full-time comfort consultant (sales person) on the payroll, he can calculate his or her SCC. Simply divide the sales made by the comfort consultants by the number of comfort consultants.

Surveys of comfort consultants who work for dealers now show us a two-tiered SCC ratio. We find:

Residential Add-on and Replacement SCC:	**$900,000**
Residential New Construction SCC:	**$1,500,000**

The higher number in the new construction SCC indicates that the comfort consultants in most of the firms sampled call on only a few builders, but that these builders are quite large.

To improve the SCC, a dealer can only increase sales made by the comfort consultants, or reduce the number of comfort consultants (or both).

Some of the ideas to boost sales have already been discussed in the other ratios we've looked at so far. Here are a few new ones:

- ❑ Review the job pricing system. Is the comfort consultant using the right markup for the desired margin?
- ❑ Send the comfort consultant(s) to *good* sales training; bad sales training is out there in force, and does more harm than good.
- ❑ Measure the performance of the comfort consultants and review it with them at least monthly.
- ❑ Equip the comfort consultants with powerful sales tools (such as laptop computers, ultrasonic tape measures, presentation binders, and the like).

➤ *The Staffing Ratio (SR)*

The Staffing Ratio, or SR, is simply the ratio of direct labor to office labor.

For the purposes of this ratio, count as direct labor anyone whose time card can be directly billed back to a specific job (or jobs). This includes all installers and service technicians, but it could also include shop people (if their time is charged to specific jobs).

Office labor would include anyone whose pay is not job-specific, such as the receptionist, bookkeeper, managers, comfort consultants, and the like.

When you consider that a company only gets paid when the hands it has on payroll are doing value-adding work to a customer's property, it should come as no surprise that the higher the SR, the better (to a point, at least, as we'll see in a moment). For every pair of hands in the office consuming revenues, you want as many pairs of hands as possible out in the field doing work for which you are going to be paid.

Staffing ratios can vary depending on how much supervision labor requires. Probably the simplest type of work to supervise is the installation of residential new construction jobs. The jobs tend to be repetitive, and the skill level and supervision required are, once a house plan is learned, minimal. Next up in complexity would be supervising add-on and replacement work. Here, each job is different, every customer is different, and skill levels and job prep work must be of a higher caliber. At the high end of the scale would be service work. Here, techs need to be monitored hour by hour so the work schedule can be adjusted on the fly; time cards are complex, and material tickets require frequent entries into the accounting system and extra work for the purchasing agent.

As a result of these considerations, I recommend staff ratios along these lines, based on the dominant type of work done by a contractor:

Residential New Construction: 4.5 to 6.0 (+ / -)

Residential Add-on and Replacement: 2.75 to 4.0 (+ / -)

Residential and Light Commercial Service: 1.5 to 2.5 (+ / -)

Commercial and Industrial work: 5.0 to 7.0 (+ / -)

These are the guidelines. What surveys reveal is that the average residential new construction shop runs 3.57 to 1.00 field laborers to office workers; the average residential add-on and replacement shop runs 2.09 to 1.00 field to office; and the average service shop runs 2.03 to 1.00 field to office. Only the service shops seem, on average, to be about where they should be!

Which is a sad commentary on the state of affairs in the offices of many HVAC contractors! To see why, consider this question: which hands bring in the revenue for a company? (Obviously, the field workers!) So which side of the ledger needs more employees, the revenue generating side (field workers) or the revenue *consuming* side (office workers)? (Again, obviously, field workers!)

I don't like to see SRs above 7.00 for the brutal fact that the office staff is so frenzied trying to keep tabs on everybody that morale in the office is often low and tension high. When a contractor has a crabby office in which everyone is on a hair trigger status, he probably needs to adjust the SR!

If a contractor has a staff ratio (SR) that is outside the guidelines and he or she wants to get it within the guidelines, there are only two places to look — the direct labor or the office labor (or both).

Here are a few ways a contractor can improve his or her SR:

- Try to get by with fewer office workers. (Leverage technology; combine office jobs into one; review procedures—where is there waste and duplication of effort?)
- Try to hire more installers and service techs (assuming you can generate the sales to keep them busy).

- ***The Service Sales to Replacement Sales Ratio (SS to RS)***

For this ratio, a contractor needs to be able to separate from his or her income records the service sales total and replacement sales total. (Count both residential and commercial service, as well as residential and commercial replacement work.) **The ratio should fall between 25% and 50%.**

Why this "magic zone"? Many contractors will argue that they make a better profit on service than installation, so why shouldn't the SS to SR ratio be higher than 50%? Why not 100% or even higher?

For two reasons. First, most contractors make the mistake of thinking of their service profits as percentages, not as real dollars. Percentage wise, it is probably true that the typical contractor makes more profit on service than installation. But this is a percentage figure only.

To illustrate the point, suppose a dealership runs 8% profit on installation jobs and 15% profit on service jobs. Which department is more profitable? We cannot just say, "Service." For one thing, if installation is making 8% profit on $800,000 in revenues, that's $64,000 profit. The service department may be billing out $300,000 in revenues, and making almost twice the profit in percentages—but not in real dollars. The service department profit would be only $45,000. So which department is more profitable?

Unless a contractor has set an outlandishly high price for service (by going to an overstated flat rate), he probably cannot make more profit in service than installation.

The key to the replacement business is the service business. If a contractor wants to play in the replacement market but has a weak service department (or none at all), he will have to advertise heavily (and expensively) to get the phone to ring. (And many of these calls will be price shoppers.) As it turns out, the point at which service work begins to efficiently feed replacement job leads to the installation department is at about 25% service sales to replacement sales. At that level of service work, there are enough service calls being run to generate a pretty strong flow of replacement leads. Service-generated replacement leads tend to be high success leads. A properly trained service technician can either make the sale himself or refer it to a comfort consultant. The result is a steady stream of high dollar, profitable replacement jobs flowing into the company.

But too much service can be a bad thing too. Beyond about 50% service sales to replacement sales, the contractor is dispatching and overseeing too much labor to generate small hourly profits (in service) and not the bigger hourly profits typical of replacement jobs.

So that's why there is a sweet spot range of 25 to 50%. Below 25%, the service department is not generating enough replacement leads to keep the replacement crews busy. The contractor must supplement the installation business by heavy (and often expensive) advertising.

But beyond 50%, more profits could be made per hour doing installations rather than service. The service work may well be profitable beyond this range. But the question is not whether or not service is profitable. The question is: is the dealer doing the type of activity with his direct labor that brings the greatest hourly flow of profit dollars to the company?

If a dealer finds his SS to RS ratio lying below 25%, he will have to boost his service business and use it as radar to detect and root out good replacement jobs. Here are some things a contractor can do to fine tune the SS to RS ratio.

- ❑ Measure the service department's present lead generation rate. (In other words, how many replacement leads do the techs generate per week, on average?) A good replacement lead rate would be 1.5 replacement leads for every tech per week. If the lead generation rate is below that, training can be provided to the service techs to teach them how to either make the sale themselves or set up a comfort consultant call. (We are dealing with a major psychological issue here: most service techs view turning in a replacement lead as a sign of defeat rather than a wise move in the customer's best interest. That attitude must be dealt with carefully in well-designed training.)
- ❑ Add service technicians if the business is there to support it (and the dealer has the capital to make it happen; more on that in Chapter 9).
- ❑ Aggressively market the service department. Forget mass media. Focus instead on direct mail, word of mouth, and other low-profile, low-budget methods. (Consider, for instance, working with the local Welcome Wagon or realtors to provide a new homeowner checkup service.)
- ❑ Find a way to run more calls per day per service technician. But be careful—you don't want to run so many that work becomes careless and callbacks start to increase!

The other side of the SS to RS ratio is the replacement sales. Here are some things that can be done to improve that part of the ratio.

- ❑ Increase the success rate (how many replacement orders you get per 100 replacement sales calls made). This will require high-caliber, high-quality training. Much of the training on the market in this area is weak at best.
- ❑ Review the product mix and start a program to move more high-end product to the right customers.
- ❑ Review how jobs are priced. (It is actually possible for a dealer to use the wrong type of job pricing math and end up losing high productivity ratio jobs because the math results in an inflated price. (See Chapter 15.)
- ❑ Offer a free second opinion on compressor and heat exchanger condemnations. (Most homeowners will buy from the last guy in the door.)

The Overhead Per Installer Per Day (OPID) Ratio

This ratio is a powerful measure of how efficiently a dealer runs his or her installation department, but it is not that easy to calculate.

To compute it, a dealer must have a departmentalized income statement (we'll cover that in Chapter 15), one that shows the overhead as adjusted for each department of the company (in particular, installation and, for the next ratio, service). It is not enough to use the overhead on a combined income statement. (A combined income statement is one in which both the installation and service departments are combined into one set of numbers.)

It is also important to know how many days the installers work per year. For shops that have the enviable position of being able to offer full employment to installers all year long, this is easy to do. Here is some sample math:

Weeks in the year	52
Days in the work week	5
Work days per year (multiply)	260
Less days not at work:	
Vacation (most senior installer)	10
Holidays	7
Sick days	3
Other days	2
Total days not at work	22
Days left for work (260 – 22)	238

It gets a little tougher for shops where the installers don't work all year long, but the math follows the same outline as above.

Once we know how many days the installers are available for work, we multiply that number by the number of installers to get the number of installer days we need to sell each year. To get the OPID, we simply divide the installation overhead by the total number of installer days.

The average OPID runs **$312** per man, per day.

If a dealer has an OPID lower than this, he is more efficient than the average and if over it, less efficient. (He can still make a profit; it's just that a lower OPID makes earning a profit an easier thing than a high OPID.)

To improve the OPID ratio, a dealer needs to lower the installation department overhead and/or increase the number of installers without increasing overhead the same amount (a tricky thing to do, but possible!).

Here are some things a dealer can do to improve the OPID ratio.

- ❑ Viciously attack every overhead expense item and make it justify its existence
- ❑ Install more work with the same number of installers (by better job design, job staging, paying for productive work, and so on)
- ❑ Install the same amount of work with fewer people
- ❑ Use temporary help during peak seasons

➤ ***The Overhead Per Service Technician per Day (OPST)***

This ratio is just like the OPID, except we use the service department overhead and service technician annual days.

The national average is <u>$218</u> per service tech per day.

Like the OPID, this ratio can be improved by doing some (or all) of the following:

- ❑ Viciously attack every overhead expense item and make it justify its existence
- ❑ Run more calls per day with the same number of technicians (but be careful about work overload that can lead to callbacks, mistakes, and customer dissatisfaction)
- ❑ Run the same number of calls per day with fewer techs

➤ ***Productivity Robbers***

Several little things can literally steal a dealer blind if he or she does not keep an eye on them.

One of the most insidious is *unbillable time*. Unbillable time can be defined as any time the dealer must pay an installer or service technician for (because they are on the time clock) but for which he cannot invoice a customer. Examples could include driving back and forth to the shop to get materials for a job (if the dealer did not allow for the drive time in his original estimate), time driving back and forth to suppliers for parts and/or equipment and supplies, or time when an installer or service tech has to wait in a car repair shop while their vehicle is being repaired, among other things.

Unbillable time should be tracked in a special overhead account (it goes in overhead because it cannot be billed to a job; if it could, it would not be unbillable). However, you should know that most dealers do not have an unbillable time account and don't bother to measure it.

Too bad. If they did, they'd probably have high blood pressure. SMACNA, a national organization of quality HVAC contractors, does annual surveys of its membership, and they usually ask a question on the survey about unbillable time. It varies from year to year, but on average, the unbillable time reported by SMACNA members (and these, being better than average contractors, I can only assume that non-SMACNA members would have numbers as bad or worse) runs *a staggering 15% of the day for installers and up to 30% of the day for service technicians!*

For a typical 8 hour day, this means that the typical installer has 8 x 0.15 or 1.2 hours (1 hour and 12 minutes) that cannot be billed to a customer but for which he or she is being paid their wage. For service techs, it is twice that!

Think how much sales could rise if a dealer could find a way to bill out that 1 hour and 12 minutes per installer per day. Why, sales would go up 15%! Service sales could rise 30%!

That's if a contractor could get to absolutely no unbillable time. That is probably not likely (if it is, it may be that management is so inflexible that field workers have a high rate of turnover).

So I like to see unbillable time run between 5% and 10% of the day for the installers and no more than 15% of the day for service technicians.

If unbillable time is not even being tracked by a dealer in the financial statements, they may find upon measurement that it may even exceed the outlandish amounts reported in the SMACNA surveys. So here is how I suggest a dealer get control of unbillable time.

First, *measure time use precisely*. This requires the use of a *daily time ticket*. I don't like to see weekly time cards. They are never filled out accurately. Daily time tickets need to be filled out every day as the workers do the jobs they are assigned to do, and they should log on and off the jobs as they are dispatched or finish. A dealer should not see installers and service techs filling out time cards at the counter back at the office!

Second, use a good form. Good forms are produced by most business forms companies (Wilson, Reynolds and Reynolds, Standard Register, and others). A good form allows ample space for several jobs a day (a must for a service tech) and has a column for a code for the type of activity done during that time.

For example, if John Doe is an installer, he might show on the first line of his Tuesday time card,

8:00 – 8:15 JL 01369

This means that from 8:00 to 8:15 he spent his time loading the job materials on his truck and that he was doing this for job number 01369 (which should tie to a job name somewhere in the system).

John might then show,

8:15 – 8:45 T 01369

This means he spent 30 minutes traveling (T) to the job.

He might then show

8:45 – 4:15 I 01369

Which means he spent from 8:45 a.m. to 4:15 p.m. installing (I) the job.

If on Wednesday he had to come back to the shop and fabricate a plenum (because the comfort consultant supplied the wrong dimensions), he might show an hour of F time (fabrication) as well as another hour of T (travel) time.

However, John could also be taught that the hour of T on Wednesday should be recorded as an hour of U (unbillable).

However, if this is the policy, we must communicate it to John very carefully! Most installers and service techs don't like being burdened with unbillable time. It looks bad on their record.

For this to work, the dealer must convince the installers and service techs that a U is not grounds for discipline. It simply means that somewhere, management messed up and let down the crew or service tech. The U is not a grade on the installer or tech—it is a grade on management, whose job it is to revamp the systems and procedures until unbillable time is at a minimum.

To drive home to a dealer what unbillable time could be costing him or her, you can use a rule of thumb:

Every hour of unbillable time per day costs the company about 2,700 times the wages and benefits of that worker.

Here's an example. If Joe averages an hour of unbillable time per day and Joe makes $25 an hour (counting benefits), it could be costing the company $25 x 2,700 or close to $67,500 a year. That's $67,500 in extra expenses (like payroll and benefits), plus some overhead not being carried by a billed hour, and the fact that a cash-paying customer could not buy that unbilled hour. Adds up pretty quick, doesn't it! And what if the dealer has eight installers? And three service techs? It can make one ill before long…

The third thing a dealer can do to reduce unbillable time is *compensate workers (installers and service techs) for billing out more hours a day than they charge the company.* On the installation side, this means that if a job is sold with 32 man-hours of labor built into it and the crew gets it done in 24 hours, they billed the company 24 man-hours but "sold" 32. They sold 8 hours more than they billed. They should get half of that difference as a bonus.

On the service side, the dealer needs to be on flat rate to do this. Here, a service tech may turn in a time card for 8 hours but bill out an equivalent of 15 hours of flat rate time allowances on the tasks he or she did. That's a difference of 7 hours. Half of that goes to the tech as a bonus. The other half goes to the company to support the growth of the company.

Where such systems have been implemented (and this is a very brief description, not a detailed treatment plan), unbillable time drops to nearly zero as crews see that they can make a lot of money this way.

Some other things a dealer can do to reduce unbillable time include:

- ❑ Let the service techs take the service trucks home at night (in return for which they agree to be at their first service call by 8:00 a.m.). This requires radio dispatching.
- ❑ Don't let the installation crews load their own trucks in the morning. Instead, have a retiree who wants to work only partial days (or a high school student who can come in for a couple of hours in the morning before school starts) pull the material and stack it in labeled positions on the warehouse floor (or better yet, load it onto the installation trucks).
- ❑ Have service techs carry common hand tools on a tool belt or in a small toolbox and make sure they take these tools with them to the unit on every call.
- ❑ Review the service dispatching system. Is it resulting in wasted travel time?

Another thing that reduces productivity is *callbacks*. This is a term that is thrown around a lot in this industry and often with different meanings, so let's be clear for our purposes about what a callback really is:

A *callback* occurs any time a *service technician* must return to a completed job to repair again what should have been fixed correctly or completely on the first call.

Notice that we limit the definition to service technicians. What about installers? If, for example, an installer hangs the ductwork on a job and that ductwork must be re-hung because it was not located properly in the first place, that would be considered an "Errors and Omissions Account" entry, not a callback. Most dealers don't have an "Errors and Omissions Account" in their chart of accounts, but they should, as this is where installation error fix-ups get charged.

Callbacks should be recorded carefully, as most service technicians get very defensive when you say they had a callback. So it helps for the dealer to tightly define the term before he starts measuring callbacks with his techs.

Using the definition I give above, which of the following would qualify as callbacks?

- ❑ A service tech must go back out to a job to replace a fan motor that was running per specs during the last service call (three days ago).

- ❑ A service tech must go back to a job and fix a leak after running a service call five days earlier. The earlier call was to replace a bad start relay.

- ❑ A service tech must go back to a job and rewire the heat pump thermostat he mis-wired on the service call four days earlier.
- ❑ A service tech must go back to a job and replace a burned out condensing fan motor. On the call eight days earlier, he had noted that it was drawing high amps, but did nothing about it at the time.

Only the last two really qualify as callbacks. The first two are totally different (and unrelated) problems from the original calls. True, the dealer might not be able to convince the customer of that and therefore invoice for the work (that is, the dealer may have to "eat" the call), but the first two cases involve whole new situations from the first calls. The last one is a tough call to make, but frankly, if a technician finds *any* component operating at the extreme edge of its performance specs, there is a deeper problem that needs to be addressed. In this case, he needed to advise the customer that a new fan motor was required because the old one was starting to show signs of over-current operation.

Federal labor law allows a contractor to pay an employee *minimum wages* for time spent on a callback, but a contractor may *not* withhold wages entirely for a callback. Often, a contractor will send a technician out to run a callback on the tech's own time. This is a common practice in some areas, and your dealers should be aware that it is not legal.

A contractor should have someone (service manager, dispatcher, a clerk) keep track of all callbacks and sort them according to type of problem. If a pattern emerges, training should be conducted to address the problem if it is one of knowledge.

But another cause of callbacks can be the service policy of the dealership! I knew of one case where a dealer demanded that his service techs average six billed calls a day. They often had to hurry so much that they made errors which often resulted in callbacks—about 30% of all the calls in this case had to be re-run! I advised that they cut back to five calls a day (and run six or more if the day was easy) and advise the techs to take their time to get everything on the first call. The dealer ended up running five fewer calls per week per tech, but watched his callback rate drop to under 5%. This was clearly a smart move for the dealer!

The callback rate is easy to calculate (assuming the dealer tracks the costs in the right accounts). Here is how it is calculated:

$$\text{Callback Rate} = \frac{\text{Labor cost of callbacks}}{\text{Labor cost of all service labor}}$$

For instance, if a dealer has a "Callbacks" account and it shows $4,786 in it compared to service labor of $113,247, his callback rate would be $4,786 / $113,247 or 4.2%.

Callbacks should be under 2% of service labor costs when measured this way.

Here are some ways to help your dealer reduce his or her callback rate:

- ❑ Train the dispatcher how to work with the customer to prevent nuisance callbacks
- ❑ Make callbacks cause pain to those who cause them (for example, pay minimum wage or adopt a policy that no tech with a callback rate greater than 10% will remain employed, etc.)
- ❑ Do a callback analysis to see if patterns emerge (see above)
- ❑ Review the daily dispatched call volume (see above)

<u>General Rules of Thumb</u>

Now we will examine some other more generic rules of thumb that can help you understand your territory and your dealer's business better.

➢ ***Material as a Percent of Sales***

First, you should understand that the average contractor in America spends about **<u>37%</u>** of what he or she bills out **<u>on material</u>**, including equipment, parts and supplies.

For instance, if Jane Doe Heating has annual sales of $2,000,000, Jane is *probably* spending around 37% of this, or $740,000 on equipment, parts, materials, and so on. We cannot say for sure, of course, unless Jane shows us her income statement where we can then see the actual amounts spent for equipment and material. But this is a good estimate.

We can combine this rule of thumb with the productivity ratio we looked at earlier and see that if the average dealer posts sales of $156,082, then the average dealer is probably spending about 37% of this (per employee) with suppliers. In this case, 37% of $156,082 is $57,750. Let's just round it off and say that the average dealer probably buys about ***$58,000 in material from suppliers for every employee on the payroll***.

How can you use this? *If you have a dealer who does not want to show you his or her income statement, you can get a ballpark idea of what he or she is spending with suppliers and figure out how much of the business you are getting* (what I call your "share of wallet").

Here's how. Suppose that Jack buys from you but does not want you to see his income statement. You know that Jack has eleven employees and you sell Jack $135,000 a year in equipment and material. How much of Jack's business are you probably getting?

A quick calculation shows 11 employees x $58,000 per employee for material purchases means Jack is probably buying around $638,000 or so from suppliers. You have $135,000 of that, or about 21%. Clearly, you could sell more to Jack—if you can find out what it takes to earn more of his business!

➢ *Dealer Sales Per Capita for an Area*

Another useful rule of thumb for a TM is to know what the contractor sales are per person in the area served by the contractor. Whereas there are rigorous and detailed ways to derive this number with high accuracy, often a rule of thumb will do for quick analysis or for having a discussion with a dealer about the potential for business in his trade area.

If we use data from the 2007 Economic Survey of the HVAC Trade (cited earlier), and look just at the residential and light commercial business (units 25 tons and smaller), we see that the ***average dealer sales per capita is about $250 per person.***

Suppose a dealer serves an area with a population of 180,000 people. Then the total HVAC sales for residential and light commercial in that area would be about 180,000 x $250 or about $45 million. If your dealer has sales of $1.3 million, his or her share of market would then be about 1.3 / 45 or 2.9%.

But be aware that the $250 figure is the U.S. average, and that any given region in the United States can vary a lot from this! Consult the State Throughput Data file for state by state averages.

Also bear in mind that $250 is the figure to use for residential and light commercial HVAC sales. If you wanted to consider ALL the HVAC sales in the USA (commercial, residential, parts and supplies), you would need to use $520 per person for the aggregate sales of ALL types of HVAC work. State by state averages could be found by taking the state per capita residential and light commercial sales and multiplying that by 520/250 or 2.08.

➤ ***Dealer Saturation Level***

The dealer saturation level is the point at which you have so many dealers selling your brand in an area that your sales peak and can rise no further (or they may even decrease for a while if you have over-saturated the area). The reason is simple: if too many dealers have the same brand, it won't take long for some of them to find something else to offer so they can differentiate themselves from their competitors on sales calls.

To estimate a dealer saturation level for your territory, you need to know how big an ideal dealer would be for your portfolio (list of accounts). This is not necessarily the *biggest* dealer you have, but the size of account you'd like for *all* of your accounts to be if you could have your wish.

Let's suppose for illustrative purposes that you think an account that buys $150,000 a year from you would be an ideal account. Let's also assume that you want to see how many dealers you could sign up in an area to achieve a 20% share of market goal.

An account that buys $150,000 a year from you probably has sales around three times that amount. (I got that by reasoning that if about 1/3 of what a dealer sells he buys from you, and then whatever you sell him must be multiplied by three to get the sales volume.) So your dealer probably sells around $450,000 a year or so.

Let's suppose that you are looking at a trade area with 100,000 people in it. Using the per capita rule of thumb, this means that the total residential and light commercial HVAC sales here should be around $25 million. Since you want 20% share of market, you want 20% of this, or $5 million in dealer sales. Applying our dealer purchases rule again (37% of sales equals purchases), this means purchases of about $1.85 million. Since your ideal account is $150,000 in size, this means you need $1.85 million / $150,000 or about twelve typical dealers in this trade area.

Given the 100,000 population level, this means that for your territory, you want one dealer for every (100,000 ¸ 12) 8,333 people.

Had you selected a larger dealer for your ideal dealer size, you would need fewer dealers and have more people per dealer.

When I was doing territory management, my ratio was 25,000 people per dealer. That got me to the share I wanted with the size of accounts I considered to be ideal.

This makes it very easy to make decisions about adding accounts, doesn't it? For instance, suppose you have a territory where the ratio works out to 20,000 people per dealer (for your ideal dealer size and share goals). You have an area with 120,000 people in it and you have only four dealers covering the area. A dealer contacts you about selling your brand. Should you pursue it?

Since your rule of thumb dictates you need six dealers to cover this area, and you only have four, I would certainly meet with the dealer to see if it might work out or not. (More on that in Chapter 14.)

On the other hand, if you already had seven dealers in this area, adding an eighth would probably cause one or more of your existing accounts to react by changing brands (or at least picking up another line), so your share would not rise appreciably. I would probably hold off on adding this inquisitive dealer. I would certainly meet with him and check the fit and so forth, and if he might do better than one of the dealers I already have in the area, I might go ahead and add him counting on the one I wanted to prune to prune himself—or even be "de-selected" by me later.

So to summarize, here is *how to set up your own dealer saturation level ratio:*

1. Determine your ideal dealer size in terms of purchases per year.

2. Set a goal for your share of market (as a percentage figure).

3. Take the population of the area in question times $250 to get the area's total HVAC sales.

4. Find your share of sales by multiplying step 2 by step 3.

5. Find your ratio by dividing step 4 by step 1.

6. Divide the population by the results of step 5.

EXAMPLE 1— MID-SIZED DEALERS:

1. Ideal dealer size is $240,000 in annual purchases.
2. Share of market goal is 24% of all sales.
3. Area population is 160,000 people. Area sales are $40 million.
4. My share of sales is 24% of $40 million, or $9.6 million.
5. My dealer saturation level is $9.6 million divided by $240,000 or forty dealers.
6. My saturation ratio is 160,000 divided by 40, or about 4,000 people per dealer.

EXAMPLE 2— LARGE DEALERS

1. Ideal dealer is $750,000 in annual purchases.
2. Share goal is 24%.
3. Population is 160,000 people, with $40 million total sales.
4. Share goal is still $9.6 million.
5. Dealer saturation level is $9.6 million divided by $750,000 or 12.8 dealers. Call it thirteen.
6. Saturation ratio is 160,000 divided by 13 or 12,307 per dealer.

EXAMPLE 3— SMALL DEALERS, SMALL SHARE

1. Ideal dealer is $50,000 in purchases.
2. Share goal is 6%.
3. Area population is 160,000, sales of $40 million.
4. Share of sales is 6% of this or $2.4 million.
5. Dealer saturation level is $2.4 million divided by $50,000 or forty-eight dealers.
6. Saturation ratio is 3,333 people per dealer.

Review Questions for Chapter 4

1. You have a dealer named Clyde Bodenhammer. Clyde has sixteen employees and has sales of $2,010,322. He lives and works (mostly) in Yell County, Arkansas. How is his productivity? (Explain your answer)

2. Same dealer, but now Clyde is located in Napa County, California. How is his productivity now? (Explain your answer)

3. Clyde's service trucks average $105,000 in sales each per year. If this is okay, skip to question 4. If it is weak, name two things you could suggest to Clyde to improve his service sales per truck.

4.You currently sell Clyde $340,000 a year in equipment, parts and materials. Clyde won't show you his income statement yet, so you have to estimate your share of wallet.

5.Of Clyde's sixteen employees, six work in the office and ten in the field. Clyde is an add-on and replacement oriented dealer. Is his staff ratio okay? If not, what would you suggest to Clyde to make him more profitable?

Chapter 5: Territory Analysis

History is full of examples of situations where people were engaged in some activity, before which someone did a good (or bad) job of figuring out the lay of the land. In military history, it is easy to find examples of when commanders did a good job of reconnaissance before a battle and were able to maximize the impact of their own forces because of it. (Of course, there are also examples where commanders failed to do this and often they lost grievously.) In business, it is not difficult to find examples of where a company did superb market research and was able to launch a new product with stunning success. (And, again, where companies did not do good market intelligence and introduced a real turkey into the market.)

The same principal holds true for a Territory Manager too. Solid and scientific analysis of a territory can show a TM where he or she is already doing well—and where they need to exert some effort to get better. In this day of high technology, no military officer would think of going into battle without first identifying all the targets and threats and allocating resources (military talk for weapons) to neutralize them.

What Is Your Territory?

Most territory managers have been assigned a geographic territory. This means they have been given a set of counties (or, if you are in Louisiana, parishes; or in Alaska, boroughs) or pieces of such political entities. If you have a territory in a densely-populated area like Los Angeles, Dallas, New York or Chicago, you might only have a part of a county, or even a few ZIP codes assigned to you. Conversely, if your territory is mostly rural, you may have several counties assigned to you. It is not the geographical space that is the question—it is about the number of people and the dollar bills they have in their bank accounts.

A physically large territory poses its own unique problems for the TM who has it—such as travel time (which can consume up to half the week's hours in extreme cases) and with it, travel costs; weather that can make travel difficult or even dangerous, and often a wide range of communities and cultural backgrounds to deal with. While an urban TM may not have the hard travel demands of her rural cousin, she will face her own special problems—such as the overall general tendency for people in large cities to be a little terser in their dealings with others, and ethnic issues that can be more pronounced in densely packed urban areas.

But whatever special challenges your territory gives to you because of the way it is composed, you still have the same job to do—find and develop profitable business for your distributorship.

A Different Way of Slicing It

Some distributors have learned that there are two basic types of dealer in the world, and two basic types of territory manager. These both are natural outflows of the shape of the market discussion in Chapter 1. There are dealers who are price driven, and there are dealers who are value conscious.

Likewise, there are TMs who fall into both camps as well.

A TM who has a geographic area to cover will have both types of dealers in his territory. If the TM happens to be a value-driven TM, he will be most comfortable on calls with value-driven dealers. The price-driven dealers will drive such a TM insane. Conversely, a TM who is adept at selling on price will be about as comfortable with a slate of value-driven dealers as a lion in a den full of Daniels! The more price (or value) driven a TM is, the more dealers at the opposite end of the scale will bother him.

This is not to say that a price TM cannot work effectively with value-driven dealers, but it does suggest that the price TM will have to flex out of his normal element a lot to be successful with the value group, and vice versa.

There is an exercise on the CD titled "The XO Survey." You may want to take it right now to see where you fall in the Price – to – Value spectrum. You can also have your dealers take it and see where they plot out on the spectrum. You may learn why certain dealers give you ulcers!

Distributors who understand this TM to dealer matching often assign territory based on account relationships, not geography. For instance, if a distributor has five TMs, four of whom are value-driven and one who is price-driven, that distributor may assign the price driven accounts to the price TM and the value accounts to the value TMs no matter where the geographical boundaries fall. After all, this is a business based on relationship more than anything else, and usually when a TM and a dealer have similar outlooks, the relationship can flourish better.

Where to Begin

Since your territory will be serviced by your dealers, you start with analyzing your territory by going down to the dealer level—you start with the counties (or parts of counties) where the dealer lives and works and work your way up from there.

Lodestar Consulting has a powerful territory analysis tool titled *The Territory Navigator*. This tool can be obtained by going to Lodestar's web site and ordering the program there.[2]

Even without software tools, there are still a number of things you can do that are pretty easy and very revealing in terms of territory analysis. As you learned in Chapter 4, as of the 2007 Economic Census of the HVAC trade, the average dealer sales for residential and light commercial work average $250 per person in the United States ($520 if you figure *all* HVAC work). That number is very sensitive to the local income, though.

Let's take an example to see how this would work. Suppose you are assigned the following counties in Kentucky for your territory. For Kentucky, we refer to the State Throughput Data file and see that the per capita sales of Residential and Light Commercial equipment is $205.

County	Population	Potential Resid/ Light Comm'l Sales
Fulton	6,949	$1,424,545
Hickman	4,974	$1,019,670
Carlisle	5,317	$1,089,985
Ballard	8,245	$1,690,225
McCracken	64,950	$13,314,750
Graves	37,872	$7,763,760
Calloway	35,421	$7,261,305
Marshall	31,278	$6,411,990
Livingston	9,797	$2,008,385
Lyon	8,273	$1,695,965
Trigg	13,399	$2,746,795
Caldwell	12,916	$2,647,780
Crittenden	9,070	$1,244,350

2 www.lodestarconsultinginc.com

County	Population	Potential Resid/ Light Comm'l Sales
TOTAL	248,461	$50,934,505

We now find each county's purchases (based on the assumption that about 37% of a contractor's sales goes toward equipment and materials) and compute each county's total residential and light commercial HVAC purchase potential:

County	Res/Lt Comm'l	Local Purchases
Fulton	$1,424,545	$527,082
Hickman	$1,019,670	$377,278
Carlisle	$1,089,985	$392,194
Ballard	$1,690,225	$625,383
McCracken	$13,314,750	$4,926,458
Graves	$7,763,760	$2,872,591
Calloway	$7,261,305	$2,686,683
Marshall	$6,411,990	$2,372,436
Livingston	$2,008,385	$743,102
Lyon	$1,695,965	$627,507
Trigg	$2,746,795	$1,016,314
Caldwell	$2,647,780	$979,679
Crittenden	$1,244,350	$460,410
TOTAL		$18,845,767

Several wonderful facts come to light in this simple analysis so far. First, we see that not all counties have the same purchase weight. One—McCracken—clearly outweighs all the other counties by a huge margin, and in fact, five of our thirteen counties make up $14 million in sales, or some 74% of the entire territory! Perhaps the TM should spend her time in this territory along those same lines?

We can also see that each percentage point of share of market is about $18,800 ($18.8 million divided by 100) for equipment and supplies. If the TM was charged with gaining three points of share next year, she would need to increase sales by three times $18,800 or $56,400 over this year's level, not counting inflation or population changes.

Also with this territory data, we can easily calculate any one dealer's share of market. We can take that dealer's purchases and compare it to the county's purchase weight.

For instance, suppose that Sam is a dealer in McCracken County. He works 95% of the time in McCracken County, and he buys all his equipment from the TM. She sold him $100,000 in equipment last year. Sam then has a share of market of $100,000/$4,926,458, or a whopping 2%! (Actually, 2% is a decent share for any one dealer to have in a crowded market; but Sam probably thinks his share is up around 25% or 30%! At last count, there were thirty-one dealers in McCracken County, so an equal share would be 1/31, or 3.2%. Sam is even smaller than the average.)

If this TM had four dealers in McCracken County with a total share of, let's say, 9%, and her goal was 15%, she could show each dealer the county's purchase weight and the dealer's actual share, and then ask how they can (together) get to 15% as a group? At some point, she will probably have to add a dealer or two, and this data gives her some ammunition to support her case. (But more on that conversation later.)

Other Cuts at the Data

It also helps to know something about the makeup of the local HVAC market when doing a territory analysis. For instance, how much of the market is new construction versus add-on and replacement, or service? How much is residential versus commercial? How many units should be replaced each year?

Let's consider the last question first—how many units should be replaced each year in the residential market. We can get pretty good ideas of how many units should be replaced each year if we know the *average life expectancy* of condensing units, heat pumps, and furnaces in an area. This data can be obtained through several sources, including manufacturers (who usually guard it closely, so it may not be easy to obtain from your brand's information department), utility companies, and distributor records. Utility companies can often report the average age because they may at some time in the past (or present) offered conversion rebates, and usually the rebate process required the dealer (or homeowner) to report the age of the unit that was replaced. (Be careful, though. Because a utility company may offer a customer over a thousand dollars to switch out equipment for energy efficiency programs, the customer may change out a unit that is still perfectly functional. This would obviously not be the unit's average lifetime then, but an artificially shortened one, brought on by the lure of the replacement rebate.)

Sometimes, a distributor will track replacement data in a similar way as part of a manufacturer's rebate program, but the same caution about skewing the data due to the rebate applies here too.

You must also be able to make some allowances for harsh environmental conditions. For instance, in Texas, a condensing unit may normally see fourteen or fifteen years of useful life, but if that unit is within three to five miles of the Gulf of Mexico, salt corrosion will shorten its life drastically, sometimes to only three or four years. Likewise, a condensing unit sitting beside a home two miles downwind of an oil refinery in west Texas will be exposed to airborne acids and sulfur compounds, hastening corrosion and decay.

Similarly, a gas furnace in a light commercial application (such as a hair salon or animal hospital) will be exposed to caustic vapors. If the furnace draws its combustion air from inside the space, this will attack the heat exchanger and cause it to age prematurely.

The process for estimating the probable annual replacement numbers for condensing units, heat pumps and furnaces goes something like this. Start by getting a count of the housing units in the area (usually county). To do this, go to www.census.gov and click on the QuickFacts menu to find the state you want.

For instance, suppose we wanted to analyze Bexar County, Texas. We begin by selecting Texas from the QuickFacts menu. Once the Texas page loads, we select Bexar County at the top of the Texas page and when it loads, we consult the county facts to gather two key pieces of information: how many people live in Bexar County, and the average number of persons per household. Using the data as of the date of this writing, we get a population of 1,622,899 people with an average household size of 2.78. Dividing the population by the persons per household tells us how many households (roughly the equivalent of living units) are in Bexar County. In this case, it is 583,777.

Another useful fact we'll need is also shown on the County page, and it is the percentage of home ownership. If we are going to try to estimate the number of homes that need new units per year, we need to focus our search on those homes that are occupied by their owners, since rental units will be handled by the property management association, which probably has its own installers on payroll or will deal with the lowest price company they can find, and most successful replacement dealers will not (and cannot) play successfully in that market.

At the time of this writing, the home ownership rate in Bexar County was 61.2%. This means of the 583,777 homes in Bexar County, about 61.2% of them, or some 357,272 of them, are occupied by their owners. It is these homes that will give us our most viable replacement pool.

The data I have available suggests a thirteen year life expectancy for condensing units in Texas, twelve for heat pumps, and twenty-two years for furnaces. Since Bexar County is not near the ocean nor heavily polluted by industrial wastes, we can use those figures for our survey and be fairly safe.

This means that each year, then, about 1/13th of all the condensing units should go "belly up"; and 1/12th of the heat pumps, and 1/22nd of the furnaces: in percentages, about 7.7% of the condensing units, 8.3% of the heat pumps, and 4.5% of the furnaces.

If we assumed that each home in Bexar County had at least one condensing unit (or heat pump) and one furnace, we may be incorrect, as some homes will not have a central system and others will have two or more. We also don't know the heating fuel saturation for the county—yet.

Every five years, the Census Bureau does detailed counts of housing data for selected cities in the United States. These cities are called "Metropolitan Statistical Areas" or MSAs for short, and there are about thirty of them. Bexar County is one of those MSAs. (I will leave it to you to search the web for the PDF files of these MSA reports; they are available for free from the Census.)

In Bexar County, the Census tells us that 67.8% of the homes have central air conditioning of some kind, and 50.4% use fossil fuel (natural gas, propane or oil) for central heat.

On the Bexar County data page, there is a yellow-shaded link to the upper right of the data table, titled "Browse Data Sets for Bexar County." Click on it and a new page appears, giving you links to lots of new data. One of the links we will check first is titled "Housing Characteristics" and is about ten lines down from the top of the page. Clicking it lets us view statistical data about the houses in Bexar County, including:

- ★ Total housing units (more accurate than the calculation we ran earlier)
- ★ The year the structure was built
- ★ The home heating fuel

… and other data of little interest to us at the moment.

The home heating fuel data is important as it tells us the number (and percent) of homes with natural gas fuel, propane, oil, and so on. The data I see today shows 48.3% use natural gas, 2.1% use propane, and none use oil. A whopping 48.9% use electric heat (this can be heat pumps, but it can also be straight resistance heating too, so don't assume it is all heat pumps). Other fuel types bring the total to 100%.

So applying what we now know, we can say that of the 357,272 owner-occupied homes, about 50.4% of these use some form of fossil fuel heat —some 180,065 homes. Most of these will be using a gas furnace of some type (there are few boilers in Bexar County, the MSA report tells us). So we can conclude that there are about 180,000 homes with gas furnaces that are replacement candidates at some point in their lives.

If 1/22nd (or 4.5%) of these units are up for replacement every year, then about 8,100 gas furnaces should go into Bexar County each year just to replace old, worn-out furnaces in owner-occupied housing.

The MSA report I mentioned earlier said that 67.8% of the homes in Bexar County had central air, so for our owner-occupied homes, this means 67.8% of 357,272 homes, or 242,230 homes, would have central air.

If each year, we can expect about 7.7% of the central units to go "belly up" in this market, we should see, on average, about 18,650 condensing units and heat pumps going into owner-occupied homes as replacement equipment.

To get a handle on the number of units going into new housing unit construction, we need just a little more information, and some of it must come from outside the U.S. Census. The National Association of Homebuilders makes available reports (there may be a fee for them) that describe the typical new home traits for each state of the United States for recent years. In the case of Texas, I found that the average new home gets 1.69 condensing units and 1.13 gas furnaces (the difference is probably due to some of the condensing units being heat pumps with air handlers).

Since we already know the current population and the last census population, we can get a change in populations. In the case of Bexar County as of the time of this writing, we get 1,392,931 in the 2000 Census and 1,622,899 for the current estimate, dated 2008. That's a change of 273,968 people in eight years, or about 34,246 per year. These people need a place to live, and if the average household size is 2.78, we can divide the people per year by 2.78 to see how many housing units must be built to provide shelter for these people. The answer is

12,318 housing units (some of which will be single-family, some multi-family).

Single-family units comprise about 70% of the housing in Bexar County, and we could expect new housing to follow that trend more or less. So of the 12,318 housing units that are built each year, about 70%, or 8,622, should be single-family units.

For new construction, it does not matter whether or not the unit will be owner-occupied or a rental, as it is a new building coming out of the ground and must be installed by a contractor. Thus, our 8,622 new units should, on average, have about 1.13 gas furnaces and 1.69 condensing units and/or heat pumps. This means the new construction market in Bexar County should produce about 8,622 x 1.13 = 9,750 gas furnaces and 8,622 x 1.69 = 14,570 condensing units and heat pumps.

So here's a recap of what we have so far:

Unit Type	Replacement*	New Const.	Total
Condensing Units/Heat Pumps	18,650	14,750	33,400
Gas Furnaces	8,100	9,750	17,850
TOTALS	26,750	24,500	51,250
Percent of Market	52%	48%	100%

The Commercial Piece: Largely Unknowable

I have yet to find truly accurate data on the commercial equipment market in the United States. Data is published by AHRI, but it has always been of a suspicious nature to me due to the way AHRI collects and disseminates the data. (To see what I mean, compare the back of the envelope calculations we just did for Bexar County to an AHRI report on shipments of residential equipment, and you'll see some large differences. Our calculations show what should happen *in* Bexar County, whereas AHRI reports what also goes *through* it.)

I can offer you no good advice on how to estimate the light commercial segment of the market in Bexar County, except to say that on average in the United States, light commercial work is equal to about half of the residential HVAC sales market. If your distributor is active in the light commercial market, you might be able to ball park the light commercial potential by applying your company's percentage of light commercial to residential sales to the results you calculate.

Dealer Estimates

You can obtain excellent data about contractors in an area by purchasing databases from sources like InfoUSA. You may buy data for the entire United States (some of my consulting clients do this every year or two for their sales forces to do local sales planning). Or you can purchase a smaller area, such as a state, or even just a few counties. The smaller the pile of data you buy, the higher the cost per record, but with fewer records, the cost drops off overall. (For instance, I know of at least two territory managers who buy the contractor database for their own sales territory every year, for a cost of under $250.)

For example, this database shows that in Bexar County, there are 346 contractors. They employ a total of 4,245 people. (You can surely use what you learned in Chapter 4 now to do some quick math?)

What is the average dealer's size in Bexar County? Quick! 12.3 people.

What should the average dealer be doing in sales, then? Referring to the State Throughput Data file, we see that in Texas, the average dealership purchases $52,124 per employee. With 12.3 employees, this means the average Bexar county dealer purchases about $641,125. Since his purchases are about 37% of his sales, the average dealer in Bexar County then sells about $1,733,000 a year.

Quick, now, for ALL the dealers in Bexar County, what are the total sales? 346 dealers x $1,733,000 average sales = $599,618,000.

Review Questions for Chapter 5

1. My territory is

A) a set of counties I am responsible for

B) a list of dealers I call on

C) something I should treat as my own business and do all in my power to make it profitable

D) none of the above

Answer: ___________

2. Suppose you are a value-adding territory manager and that your dealer list has a dozen or so dealers on it who are price grubbers. What can you do?

A) fire them (turn them over to another TM or drop them entirely)

B) convert them to value-add dealers

C) just grin and bear it

D) flex my style to make them as comfortable as possible and sell them as much as I can

E) none of the above

Answer: __________

3. The US average dealer purchases per employee is $57,828. What would it be for Deaf Smith County in Texas (yes, there really is such a county!)?

A) $31,454

B) $52,124

C) $71,309

D) $63,409

E) none of the above

Answer: __________

4. For Deaf Smith County, Texas, a particular dealer has sales of $746,335 with five employees in the field and two in the office. What is his Production Rate?

A) $149,267

B) $106,619

C) $156,082

D) $132,461

E) none of the above

Answer: __________

5. Is that dealer in Deaf Smith County, Texas above or below the national average for Production Rate? Explain your answer. Be sure to tell what the Production Rate should be for Deaf Smith County.

6. Assume that 60% of the homes in Deaf Smith County, Texas have central cooling systems and 81% have gas or oil heat. Further assume that the average life expectancy of a condensing unit is thirteen years and twenty-two years for a furnace. Also assume that the average new home has 1.40 condensing units and 1.20 furnaces. How many condensing units and furnaces should go into Deaf Smith County each year? Be sure to break out your answer by RNC (residential new construction) and AOR (add-on and replacement) sub-totals.

Chapter 6: Territory Forecasting and Planning

Once you have done an excellent territory analysis, you are ready to start preparing a powerful and comprehensive forecast and plan for your territory. While such plans should never be rigidly cast in concrete, they can be helpful tools to enable you to maximize your impact in any given market in almost any possible condition.

Life Is Simple: You Have Two Options

Suppose that for next year, your sales manager gives you a quota that is $800,000 over this year's numbers, which (at $3,200,000) was already one of the best years you've ever had. What are you going to do?

Would you panic? Would you take it in stride? Would you not have a clue of what is going on and grin and say, "No problem!" Or would you think to yourself, "Okay, what do I have to do to get there?"

Hint: probably something different from what you are (or have been) doing up to now.

I am a big proponent of giving sales people what I would call stretch goals—goals that are high and difficult to hit (but not impossible), although hitting them may require a different set of behaviors than what the TM is used to.

As one of my mentors, Zig Ziglar so often says, "People don't plan to fail; they just fail to plan!" I believe that is true of many TMs too! Many TMs are washouts, mere order takers at best, milk-route runners, because they don't plan. They did not plan on being duds, but they did not plan on being successes either. As another mentor used to say, "People tend to hit what they aim at; aim at nothing and you'll hit that too!"

And if that is not enough to prime your thinking pump, consider the sage advice of a great philosopher of the ages, the Cheshire cat in the story *Alice in Wonderland.* Alice was walking through a forest, trying desperately to escape Wonderland, when she came upon a tree with arrows pointing every which way with names on them (like those old road signs you may have seen in old photographs). She stopped to ponder the confusing array of arrows when she heard a nonsense song being sung from overhead. (Actually, it's not a nonsense song, as Lewis Carroll had a hidden message in it, but that is for another book.) It turns out that the singer was the Cheshire cat, who slowly brightened into view. Alice explained that she was lost and wanted to get home. The cat said, "Well, where do you wish to go?" Alice replied, "Oh it doesn't really matter. I just want to get out of here." The cat then replied, "If you don't know where you are going, it really doesn't matter which road you take." And then he faded back to invisibility.

If you have no idea where you want to go next year in your territory, it does not matter what you do. You won't make matters any worse, and you probably won't make them any better. You may, however, end up ATI (available to the industry).

I assume you want to avoid the ATI option, so that means you'll have to develop a plan to make your territory work next year. I have met many TMs over the years, and one thing I find that is consistent among the best of the best is they always have a plan they are working. It may not be committed to paper (I think it is better if it is), but they have thought about what they want to achieve in this fiscal year and they are taking positive steps to make it happen. Conversely, those TMs I meet who are better off making donuts at the local donut heaven don't have a plan at all.

If you have been given a substantial increase for your territory numbers next year (either in sales, gross margin, net margin, number of dealers, or any combination of these, plus others not named), there are really only two ways you can do it: ***sell more to your existing accounts, and set up new accounts.***

That's it. There are no other ways.

Later (Chapters 10 and 11), we'll cover detailed steps in doing both of these tasks. For now, we just want to focus on how to create a forecast for the next fiscal year.

Selling More to Existing Accounts

Most TMs have no idea how little of their present customers' business they actually have. This is because they have no idea what share of wallet they have of their dealers' business.

Share of wallet is a simple measurement. It is found by taking the total dollars of stuff you sold the dealer last fiscal year and dividing it by his total Cost of Goods sold (equipment and materials that *you* sell). The result, expressed as a percent, is your share of wallet.

Example: Last year, you sold Billy Bob's Heatin' and Air $100,000 in equipment, parts and supplies. Billy Bob shows on his profit and loss statement total purchases for equipment, parts and supplies of $200,000. Your share of wallet is 100,000/200,000 = 50%.

Most TMs believe that they have a stronger share of wallet than they actually do. In the 1990s, I surveyed hundreds of a major brand's territory managers and asked them what they thought their average share of wallet was. I then contacted about 100 dealers these TMs covered and talked to them and got them to agree to divulge to me, in confidence, how much they actually spent for equipment, parts and supplies with suppliers. I compared this to what the TMs reported to me they actually sold. The TMs, on average, thought they had at least 80% of their dealers' business. In reality, it was closer to 54%!

There is one problem with this metric: whereas you will know precisely how much you sold your dealers (because you get monthly sales reports that are accurate), you won't know how much he spent on equipment, parts and supplies unless he shows you his P&L. Some dealers will gladly do this. Others won't. What do you do when the dealer won't reveal his P&L to you?

You use a reliable estimate. In Chapter 4 (Rules of Thumb), we developed a simple rule, the dealer purchases per employee. In case you don't have that number memorized yet, it came to $58,000 per employee, per year. (More accurate state-by-state figures are in the State Throughput Data file on the CD.)

Example: Chester Bestertester's Cooling Company is located in Frumpy Rock, Arkansas, in Yell County. What should we adjust the purchases per employee number to for Chester's case?

The State Throughput Data file shows that for Arkansas, the typical dealer spends $45,082 per employee for equipment and materials.

If Chester has six employees, and you sell him $90,000 a year in equipment, parts and supplies, what would be your *likely* share of wallet?

6 employees x $45,082 per employee purchased = $270,492

Your sales of $90,000 works out to:

90,000 / 270,492 = **33%**

I am always mildly amused by the pushback I get in *Territory Navigator* classes when the TMs enter their dealer data and the spreadsheet crunches the numbers and they discover that in many cases, their share of wallet is lower than they thought it was. Some have argued strongly (and with great emotion) that I was wrong. I always ask the same question in defense of my estimate: "Has the dealer shown you his P&L?" And 99% of the time, the TMs reply, "No." "Then," I say, "you really have *no idea* how much he spends on equipment and material, do you? So how do you *know* you have 90% of his wallet?"

Why Share of Wallet is So Important

It may take some time to compute your share of wallet for each dealer. (You'll need to know their employee counts and work out the purchases per employee factor for their state using the State Throughput Data file), but until you do this first step, you may end up wasting a lot of time doing a lot of stupid stuff with the wrong people!

Here is why I say that: If you want to sell more to an existing account, your options are pretty limited! If the account is already very loyal to you (meaning you have a very high share of wallet), the only way he can buy more from you is to either sell more high-end product (which will involve a culture shift for the dealer), or grow his business physically (by adding employees, and possibly bricks and mortar, trucks, tools, etc.). Neither road is going to be easy, and most dealers don't want to get much bigger (physically) than they already are. I am not saying that you cannot teach an old dealer how to sell new families of equipment, but it just takes a lot longer when he is already oriented to doing business that way from the start.

The other way to sell more to an existing account is to earn more share of his wallet.

And that's it.

So what would I consider a strong share of wallet, a number at which you are probably looking at growing a dealer's size or changing his selling habits? I would say that a 75% share of wallet is pretty strong. Anything above that would be wonderful. But you'll probably *never* hit 100%. And that is because dealers sometimes need items for a job that you simply don't sell. They have to buy it somewhere, and they will. It may be something as small as a bathroom exhaust fan, or as large and complex as a centrifugal chiller that a commercial spec demands. But you will probably never have 100% share of his wallet.

So if your share of wallet is under 75%, you can make headway by capturing more of the dealer's wallet.

Great! How do you do that? You have a frank discussion with the dealer. You show him your estimate of the share of wallet you are getting and ask him to verify if you are close or not. Then, if your share is low, you ask, "Mr. Dealer, I would really like to **earn** more of your business. Tell me—what would you need for me to do in order for it to be comfortable for you to let me have more of your business?"

Be ready for the replies you might hear! The dealer might say, "Well, how about dropping your prices 12% to match what I pay for my other line?" If I were you, I'd smile at this point and say, "Other than that, what can I do?" If he stays on the price point (and if you are a value-adding territory manager), maybe it's time to de-select an account?

Sometimes (most of the time) a dealer has a second line. Why do you suppose this happens? Is it to keep you honest? Actually, most of the time it is because of issues with his line of credit at his suppliers. For instance, he may have started with Brand A ten years ago, and being a small and growing dealer, Brand A's distributor may have given him a line of credit (an open account limit) of $20,000. This is fine for the one-man shop just getting started. But the dealer begins to grow, and the $20,000 open account limit soon gets used up in less than a month. Eventually, the account balance begins to grow and starts to slip into the 31-60 day column, and may eventually even cross that fatal 61 day line (at which point any decent credit manager will put the account on COD status). The fact is, the dealer has grown so much over the last eight years that he really needs a $50,000 open account limit now, but no one (including the TM or the credit manager) has taken the time to look at that! So he finds another supplier, gets a new line of credit, buys Brand B, uses some of the sales of Brand B to pay off Brand A and starts robbing Peter to pay Paul. Maybe something as simple as an account review with your credit manager to adjust the open account limit can close the door on a competitor's brand getting floor space in your dealer's shop!

Sometimes the dealer will say, "Gee, I never thought of it." Then ask him to think about it. Once in a while, it can be something as simple as, "Well, Brand B has a neat golf outing every year I really enjoy. But you guys don't do golf." There were cases where I made a special deal with a dealer to send him off on a weekend golf or fishing trip at my expense in exchange for more wallet.

Other times, he may ask for your help to grow his business beyond his present barriers. (Frankly, this should have been discovered by you much earlier by careful observation and high-gain SPIN question—see Chapter 21.) If that is the case, have a discussion about what he would like help with, and then make a hand-shake deal that in return for providing the help he needs, he'll buy more of your goods.

But perhaps the most powerful thing you can do is a thorough and penetrating *needs analysis*. A needs analysis is where you and the dealer together discuss what things are important to him and how he feels he is doing with those things. You then build an action plan (together) that will help the dealer get better at what he wants to get better at. In return, he should be willing to give you more of his business.

But at any rate, never <u>demand</u> more of a dealer's business. Always ask for it!

How Much Can Be Gained Through Share of Wallet?

Frankly, that depends on what your average share is now, and how many of your dealers are willing to work with you, leveraging share of wallet for business growth advice and service, and how much your quota was raised.

For instance, if your quota was raised $600,000 in sales and $120,000 in gross margin for next year, how much of the $600,000/$120,000 can you get by share of wallet gains?

Suppose you do a share of wallet analysis for your entire dealer list (*The Territory Navigator* does this automatically.) and find that with a volume of $4,000,000, your average share of wallet was 46%. This means that if you got 100% share of wallet (an impossibility, but we are trying to set the boundaries of the playing field here), you would be selling $4,000,000/ 0.46 or about $8.7 million to those same accounts. Now some of them are not going to give you one thermocouple more on their orders this year—they are set with their habits and won't change no matter what you do. But others will.

In fact, we can calculate how much your average share of wallet would need to rise in order to produce your $600,000 sales quota increase. Here is how:

$4,000,000 is to 46% as $4,600,000 is to X

This is a simple ratio. X is found by multiplying $4,600,000 by 0.46 and dividing that by $4,000,000. The answer is 53%.

A rise of only seven points in overall share of wallet (46% to 53%) closes your sales quota increase!

Do you think that would be manageable? It depends on your dealer list and how willing some of them would be to increase your share of wallet.

Start by going down your dealer list and asking yourself, "Would this low share-of-wallet dealer be willing to grow his business with me?" The ones you know would not, check off. What's left is your investment pool. What would you have to do with those dealers to generate more sales?

(**Caution**: Sometimes, we write off a dealer when he would in fact be willing to grow with us. You should, at least once a year, ask each dealer during a sales call if he'd be interested in growing his business with you and your distributor if you could help him achieve what he wants. As Zig Ziglar so beautifully phrases it, "You can have anything you want in life if you help enough other people get what they want in life.")

But let me give you a caution (and we'll go into this more in Chapter 11): don't try to grow share of wallet with more than ten dealers in a given year. More than that and you will be too busy to have a personal life. That's not good.

Adding New Dealers

In many cases, a sales quota increase can be met by share of wallet increases with existing accounts if the approach the TM takes is sound and perceived by the dealer to be in the dealer's best interest.

Even in such perfect conditions, you should still recruit new dealers. Each year, about 1/3 of the businesses in this trade go belly up. (Most of these are one and two-man shops.) If your dealer list is composed of typical dealers, it will have a shocking amount of turnover. If, on the other hand, you were picky in whom you set up to begin with, your account turnover should be much less than 1/3. It may be as low as 10%. That still means about four losses a year for the typical TM. (We'll discuss the ideal account load data in Chapter 14).

That means one dealer a quarter, on average, and since summer is a horrible time to convert a new dealer, it really means picking up four new accounts in three quarters.

That's a Bunch of Bull!

At this point, a lot of TMs argue with me. "Yes," they say, "but you never know when this guy will grow and become a mega-dealer. If he does, I want to be there to sell to him then, and if I ignore him now, he won't give me the time of day then."

I don't buy that argument for one second. First, the odds of a dealer successfully growing (and by successfully I mean staying in business and making a profit) are terribly low. Only 40% can grow beyond four employees, and only 20% can make it beyond nine employees. Second, I can administer some entrepreneurial profiles (see Chapter 10) and see if the dealer has any chance of making it upstream to spawn. Third, dealer loyalty is not as strong as most lower tier TMs think it is. I can assure you that if you ignore a small account today that in six years has become a mega-dealer, and you have the right offering for him, he'll go with you.)

We'll cover in Chapter 10 how to pick prospects and convert them. For now, we simply want to look at what impact on our sales plan new dealers might have.

How much a new dealer can bring to you in volume is a function of two things: his size, and how much of his wallet he is willing to let you capture. A large share of wallet from a small dealer may not be as many dollars as a low share of wallet from a mega-dealer. And it may take more than four small dealers a year to give you the type of sales volume you'll need to sustain your territory (and employment).

But there is a catch to all of this. Most TMs find it easier to convert a small dealer than a large one. There are many reasons for this. One is the fact that you are paying attention to a small dealer which is gratifying to his ego. It can be like giving a dog treat to a lost puppy. Suddenly, you have a friend for life. Small dealers who want to grow are hungry and dry as sponges; in some cases, they will treat every word you say as if you were Moses just off Mount Sinai! This feels good to a TM, and so it is easy to see why many TMs are comfortable with recruiting small dealers to their causes. But it doesn't put many dollars in the till!

The other side of the tennis court is the fact that big dealers have higher demands than smaller ones. Some may demand lower pricing (because their size lets them legitimately earn volume discounts). Others will demand levels of business and engineering expertise that many TMs just don't have.

Here is the awful truth about dealers as they grow: when a dealer is small, he needs everything you can bring him. He'll lick your hands for this and follow you wherever you go. You won't make much money off him, but you'll have a loyal friend. But as he grows, his needs evolve. Eventually he can start hiring the brains he used to get from you, and now you had better have a different and more relevant value-add package, or you'll lose his business to the TM who can come along and provide what he needs. In short, as dealers grow in size, they grow in sophistication and you must be able to match their sophistication. Can you cut it?

So in a new dealer addition plan as part of a territory sales plan, you need to list how many prospects you expect to convert, how much they probably buy from suppliers now, and how much you expect to earn from them the first year out. Add it all up. Is it enough to meet your quota? If not, adjust your plan, NOW, before too much of the year elapses and you don't have time to close the gaps.

Combining Share of Wallet With Conversions

So you've done your share of wallet planning (more on how to flesh that out in Chapter 11), and you have your recruiting plan. You now need to add the numbers that both plans contribute and see if you make your quota.

And you need to factor in attrition.

That's a nasty little surprise I saved until now.

I can promise you this: if you target Brand A's dealer(s) for conversion, Brand A will counterattack you—**viciously**. You had better be ready for it, and expect to take a few casualties along the way.

I always planned on 10% attrition per year when I was a TM. Some years, this was way more than I experienced; other years, it was a little light.

Here is how this all comes together.

Suppose your quota is $4,600,000 next year (it was $4,000,000 last year). A careful review of your account list shows you can probably work with eight key accounts and increase share of wallet by $400,000. This leaves $200,000 to pick up through new dealers.

Suppose now your sales plan shows you picking up five new dealers at an average of $100,000 each. How does the plan look now?

Required gain:	$600,000
Share of wallet gains:	$400,000
New dealer gains:	$500,000
Total gains:	$900,000
Variance to plan:	+ $300,000
Less attrition:	- $400,000
Final variance to plan:	- $100,000

Hmmm. Better rework the plan!

Other Factors to Weigh: Things That Go Bump In the Night

As part of your territory plan and forecast, you should also do a SWOT analysis. (SWOT stands for "strengths, weaknesses, opportunities and threats.")

What are your personal **strengths**? Those of your distributor? Your brand? What strengths do you see in your territory? How about the strengths of each of your dealers? What is the economic strength of your territory? What is forecast for the coming year? (You can often get help on this from your state University's local extension offices. Most Universities have an economic forecasting function to help the state's businesses plan for the future.) If you have an agricultural territory, what are the forecasts for weather long-term? What about crop forecasts? If the territory is industrial or retail in nature, what are you hearing about the plans of manufacturers in the area? Retail estimates?

What **weaknesses** do you need to be aware of personally? How will you cope with them? What can you do to make up for them? How about for your distributorship? Does it have any weaknesses, like inventory problems or delivery issues? If so, how will you work around them? What about your manufacturer? Any problems there? With availability? Reliability? Quality? What weaknesses do your dealers show? What can you do to help them work around them? What about the economic weaknesses of your territory? Is there one huge employer that, if it left the area or downsized, could kill your sales next year?

What **opportunities** do you face this year? What about your personal growth? What classes will you attend to get better as a TM? What will you read? How about your distributorship? Is there going to be a new branch store built in your territory next year? Is the home warehouse going to expand and carry more inventory? What opportunities do you see with your manufacturer? New product lines? Does a change in the territory's economic health bode for an opportunity for you and your dealers?

Finally, what **threats** do you see on the horizon? What threats might affect you personally? (Spending too many hours on the job? Not having enough skills and knowledge to work well with sophisticated dealers?) What threats does your distributor face? Any other distributors coming into your territory, or expanding? What threats does your manufacturer face? (New union contract negotiations? Supplier negotiations? Freight issues?) What threats do your dealers face? Consolidation? Retirement of some dealers? The economic health of some dealers (or its lack)? What about the territory? (Is a major employer going to close an operation? Will a military base in the area be mothballed? Is the threat of severe weather higher this year than normal?)

Writing it Down

A plan not written down on paper is a wish list.

As Zig Ziglar likes to say, "You'll never make it in life as a wandering generality; you must become a meaningful specific."

The plan does not have to be long or complex, but it does need to be written down, and it does need to be measurable. You have probably already run into the little acrostic **SMART** for plans. Plans must be

Specific
Measurable
Action-oriented
Realistic
Time-defined

Here is a brief but adequate plan for our $4 to $4.6 million quota:

1. Increase existing business

I will work with the following nine accounts to increase my share of wallet: A1, A2, A3, A4, A5, A6, A7, A8 and A9. These accounts are expected to bring in $600,000 in additional revenues.

2. Obtain new business

I will convert five accounts to our brand this year. These accounts (and their locations) are: P1, P2, P3, P4, and P5. I expect to sign $450,000 in new business with these accounts. (Also give details about each prospect.)

3. Attrition

I expect a loss of $400,000 in sales due to attrition this year.

4. Net gain/loss compared to Quota

Sales gains from increased share of wallet and recruiting come to $1,050,000. Losses from attrition come to $400,000. Net gain is $650,000 or $50,000 over quota.

5. Strengths

Me: superb service orientation; excellent value-add resource to my dealers; good communication skills; good problem-solver; good at resolving conflict.

My company: recognized leader in quality service and dealer development in the area; superb and deep talent among the staff; well-capitalized.

My brand: perceived leader among contractors; high unaided awareness rating; innovative products.

My dealers: list each dealer and describe his strengths.

My territory: high MHI; large percentage college-educated; good jobs base; growing area with strong economy; several respected universities; four tremendous regional hospitals.

6. Weaknesses

Me: not good all the time on follow-up; tend to promise more than I can deliver; not as strong as I'd like to be on psychrometrics.

My company: we are not low-priced and many competitors use that against us.

My brand: lack of a branded integrated controls line costs us some good commercial business.

My dealers: list each one with their weaknesses.

My territory: heavily service-oriented economy could suffer if infrastructure economies, like manufacturing, were to take a downturn.

7. Opportunities

Me: I qualify for my brand's special advanced TM training this year; I will go to this no matter what happens.

My company: with the recent stumble of Brand X, we could pick up some hefty business in D County if we had a branch in that area to pick off Brand X's disaffected dealers.

My brand: the launch of the new cooling platform this spring could send shock waves through the industry.

My dealers: list each one and the opportunities available to each.

My territory: F County is one of three finalists for the new Honda plant; if this becomes a reality, expect a tremendous building and job boom in the next five years.

8. Threats

Me: I know I will be counterattacked by Brand X for going after their dealers in D County; my planned response is [details].

My company: there has been talk on the street the last two months that Brand C may hit the street with a new builder rebate program that takes the builder's cost about $800 a system under OUR costs.

My brand: new union contract due this summer with the air conditioning plant.

My dealers: list each and describe the threats they face.

My territory: depending on the elections next fall, the government could act to either close down the Air Force Base in E County, or expand it. Closure would be catastrophic to E County.

That's an adequate plan. It might take ten pages to print out, once you flesh out the individual dealer details, but not too difficult a project.

The Plan is Done; What About the Forecast?

This chapter is about planning *and* forecasting. So far, we have not said a word about a forecast. Now we can and must.

Forecasting is not an exact science. But that does not mean you can use that fact as an excuse not to do it! It is better to forecast a plan and hit 90% of it than forecast nothing and hit 100% of that!

There are many mathematical models and methods that can be used for forecasting. Some are quite elaborate and require the help of a computer to do. They tend to be highly accurate, but beyond the skills of most TMs to work. Others are simple and easy to work, but the accuracy may be a little low because of the assumptions made. No forecast is perfect.

I generally advise a simple but relatively accurate method called the *weighted average* method. In the weighted average method, you average data over the past few years, giving extra weight to recent years, to see if you can spot trends in business and capitalize on them.

There are several steps in doing a sales forecast and I will cover them in order for you.

Step 1: Know your distributor's historical sales percentages month by month.

In other words, what percentage of your distributor's total annual sales occurs in January, February, March, and so on?[3]

This data will normally come from your sales manager or your information technology department. To be as accurate as possible, your manager or IT department should use a weighted average.

Here is how a weighted average is calculated. Suppose that in January of 2009, your distributor's sales were $4,800,000; that they were $4,200,000 in 2008; and $3,900,000 in 2007. What would be the weighted average using the most recent history as the trend base?

We would take the 2009 sales times three (3 x $4,800,000 = $14,400,000), the 2008 sales times two (2 x $4,200,000 = $8,400,000) and the 2007 sales times one ($3,900,000), then add

3 The monthly data for your territory should closely mirror your distributor data. If it does not, use YOUR data for your forecast.

these three numbers to get $26,700,000. Notice that we have a total of six weight factors (3 + 2 + 1 = 6), so we divide $26,700,000 by 6 to get a weighted average of $4,450,000. This gives more power to the recent years, which is probably more reflective of where the business is going than a straight three-year average.

The sales manager (or IT department) should then do the same thing for each month of the year. Then all the weighted averages should be added to get a total of weighted averages, which we can call the weighted year. Finally, each month's weighted average is divided by the weighted year to get a month by month percentage. You will then apply that monthly percentage to your sales plan's total sales to get a month by month forecast of sales dollars.

For example, let's suppose your sales manager gives you the following sales percentages for the year:

Month	Percentage
January	4.5%
February	3.6%
March	4.6%
April	8.7%
May	11.6%
June	14.8%

Month	Percentage
July	16.9%
August	9.3%
September	6.1%
October	7.8%
November	8.4%
December	3.7%

Step 2: Calculate your expected sales month by month.

For a $4,650,000 sales plan like we sketched out a few pages ago, here is what you should expect to see for monthly sales:

Month	Sales
January	$209,250
February	$167,400
March	$213,900
April	$404,550
May	$539,400
June	$688,200

Month	Sales
July	$785,850
August	$432,450
September	$283,650
October	$362,700
November	$390,600
December	$172,050

You could also, of course, do the same math for the monthly gross margin production forecast.

Step 3 (Optional): Calculate your monthly expenses

For those who want to forecast down to the gnat's eyelash (and whose managers don't mind them doing this), you can also get from your sales manager or IT department the annual costs charged to your territory. This would include you salary and commissions, co-op advertising expense, incentive trip expenses, expense reports, freight, and the myriads of other costs that go into supporting a territory every year. Since these costs are largely fixed for a distributorship, you could divide the total by twelve and charge that amount to each month to see how your imputed gross margin compares to the forecast one. Doing so will show you that in some months, your territory will operate at a loss, while in others it will make tons of profit (commissions, of course, will vary month to month).

Technically, some of these expenses are variable—they fluctuate with the sales volume. But the work required to manually break them out and track them separately is not worth the small gains in accuracy. (It's quite another thing for a spreadsheet to track such expenses.)

Consult the Forecasting Worksheet on the book CD to find an electronic version that will be easier than doing a forecast by hand.

Step 4: Track Your Actual Results Against the Forecast

Now that you have a forecast, you need to track your monthly sales results against the forecast to see how your year is going. (Check the Territory Forecast worksheet on the book CD for a good template.)

Once you know your distributor's monthly sales percentages, you can calculate the going rate of sales for the whole year at any point in the year. Doing a going rate calculation is easy, and critical to the success of executing a well-articulated sales plan.

To compute the going rate for a sales chart, take the sales year to date and divide them by the total monthly sales percentages year to date. The result is what the annual sales should come in at with the current rate. The more the number of months in the year to date figure, the more accurate the forecast will be.

Here's an example. By the end of April, the monthly percentages we used in our example on page 93 totaled 21.4%. Suppose that your sales for April YTD are $846,800. What can you expect the year-end sales to be?

Dividing $846,800 by 0.214 gives us 3,957,009. This is $693,000 or so short of the sales goal we had set for the year. This should be a wake-up call that you have eight months left to get your numbers back on track. The job will be difficult, but not impossible. You can normally tell after four or five months how the year will probably end up by doing a going rate calculation. If you are under plan, either up your call rate or change what you are doing on sales calls, because what you are doing so far is not working.

Step 5: Adjust Your Activity to Keep the Plan on Track

In the plan we wrote for our territory, we decided to work with nine dealers to increase our share of wallet. We should be able to tell with each of those nine dealers (by using going rate calculations) if our efforts are moving us in the right direction within four months.

If any of the lucky nine are not showing increases in sales as we expected, we may end up falling short of our plan. That's a risk you should not be willing to accept. So when you find some of your targeted-for-development dealers falling off the pace you thought they'd set, you need to ask yourself (and perhaps them) some hard questions, like:

★ Have I chosen the right dealer development strategies to excite this dealer and get him gung-ho about growing?

★ Was this dealer really serious about growing his business with me when we had our conversation at the end of last fiscal year?

★ Is this dealer really capable of making the changes our development plan calls for?

★ Is this dealer just using me to further his own ends?

If the answer to any of these questions is "No" (or "Yes" to the last one) you may want to have a heart to heart chat with the dealer and see if you can get things off the ground. If not, you had better shelve any development plans you made for this dealer for this year and find another dealer to work with for share of wallet increases. Remember, you are leveraging knowledge and expertise the dealer says he wants for share of wallet, and if that does not happen, you are being used. *The earlier in the year you can spot the lame ducks and make changes to your targeted dealer list, the more likely you are to maintain the integrity of your plan.*

You also need to keep a close eye on the new dealer business you convert and track it to see if it is coming in at the pace you expected it to. If it is, you are doing things right and don't need to worry. But if it is not, you need to make sure you are really converting a dealer and not just getting him to use you as a second leverage line. (By a leverage line, I mean using your stuff to keep his main supplier in line—by threatening to shift more of his business to you if the old supplier does not offer better training, or better dealer programs, or better pricing, etc.) If you are happy to be a second fiddle brand with a dealer, you are not Tier One material.

When I speak of really converting a dealer, I mean you are truly getting him excited and on-board with your brand. If he stocks equipment, he should be willing to put in a *hefty* start-up order—six or eight systems (or more), not one or two units. A dealer who only wants to dip his toe in the water is not likely to make a big splash later. If he is really turned on by your brand, your distributorship, and you, he should place a sizable first order. He should also be willing to put up a sign on his building, put logos on his trucks and his uniforms. He should be willing to put up a literature rack with current literature in his show room (if he has one), and do all the other things a bona fide dealer will do.

Granted, a new convert may not give you the lion's share of his business at first, but your attitude must be (and it should be communicated to the dealer early on), "I am going to EARN your business, and when I do, I will guard it as a jealous lover!" If you out serve his old supplier by leaps and bounds, he should have no problems giving you the lion's share of his business. If he doesn't give you the business, you have not done a credible job, in my opinion, of finding his real hot buttons and addressing them in your business proposition.

Step 6: Always Be On the Alert for the Unexpected Opportunity

---

Finally, never be content to just sit on your plan if it is going well. Be on the lookout for the unexpected opportunity, that unplanned surprise that can make the difference between a great year and a record year.

You should know the competitors in your territory well—and that means not only the brands you compete with, but the *people* you compete with too. Do you know your rival territory managers? Have you ever met with any of them for breakfast or lunch? Do you know their strengths (and weaknesses)?

Suppose, for example, that a rival territory manager gets fired by his employer. This would be a perfect time to start calling on his accounts to convert them while there is a gap in the coverage. The same holds for a rival TM who is promoted and removed from his territory.

What about the case where a rival TM experiences a setback, such as finding out she has cancer and spends several months fighting the disease? What should you do in a case like that?

How would *you* want to be treated in a case like that? Suppose *you* had the cancer. Would you want her calling on your dealers while you were fighting the disease? It's a tough call, with no absolute and clear answers. Personally, I would probably leave her accounts alone until her status clarified. If she got over the cancer and came back to work, she will come back grateful I did not try to bury her while she was still alive. I always maintained the philosophy as a TM that when it came to my rivals, we should eat and drink as friends, and compete as foes, but only when the playing field was level. To me, it is a little hard to hit a TM's accounts when she is undergoing chemotherapy. If, however, her diagnosis was not good and she did not beat the cancer, then when I sensed the time was right, I would start calling on some of her accounts. But not until she was clearly out of the territory and not coming back.

Be on the alert too for a dealer who suddenly has a bad experience with his supplier—a bad enough experience to motivate him to look for an alternative. (I picked up a great account this way once when a rival brand set up their *third* dealer in a town of 12,000 people!)

Stay on top of competitor news, such as model recalls, warranty problems, supply problems, strikes at their plants, transportation problems, and all the other little things that can impede the flow of product from a factory to a dealer.

If a competitor suffers a disaster such as a fire or flood, they may be out of action only a short time. It really depends on their disaster plan and how well they execute it. But if they are showing signs of confusion and distress that would be a good time to call on their dealers.

Don't overlook highway repair and construction in your area. If a major dealer finds he must now have his shipments rerouted or shipped from a different warehouse because of road work between him and his normal supplier, this may become an opportunity to convert some business.

Get to know the local utility marketing reps well. I used to take such people to lunch once a quarter and just chat about what they saw coming up in the residential and light commercial development side. (Remember, a utility company will see plats for sub-divisions and shopping centers months, if not years, before the information is general knowledge.) You can also find out about any plans they have for a rebate program or other marketing plans they may have that you can align with ahead of time to jump the competition when the plan becomes general knowledge.

Maintain strong ties to local governments. When I was a territory manager, my area included our state's capital. I got to know several key people in the engineering and specifying offices of the state government and often, as a result, had an inside track on specs and sales opportunities.

I also covered several universities and colleges in my territory (one of them a major one). I got to know the staff engineers at these schools and as a result, also had inside tracks on replacement equipment and remodel work that did not normally go the full plan and spec route.

In one case, I worked closely with a contractor to help a small hospital add an HVAC system to a new X-Ray lab. We had to use a commercial lease program since the bids came in over budget, and the lease saved the job for the hospital. As a result, the hospital's maintenance chief used my dealer from then on to do HVAC work at the hospital.

In short, keep your eyes and ears open. You never know what will pop up suddenly or from what quarter it will arise. Sometimes, you can get a shot at some great business (and future business) by staying alert.

Review Questions for Chapter 6

1. What are the only two methods for increasing sales in your territory?

A) raise your prices and add more dealers

B) sell more to existing accounts and sell more to new accounts

C) sell more upscale products

D) work closely with the top 20% of your accounts

E) none of the above

Answer: ____________

2. In a county where the per capita equipment and material purchases of dealers average $49,732, you are selling to a dealer with fourteen employees. She buys $364,000 a year from you in equipment. What is your probable share of wallet with regards to equipment?

A) 52%

B) 39%

C) 19%

D) 70%

E) none of the above

Answer: ____________

3. With a particular dealer in a certain city, you have a share of wallet (for equipment and materials) of 72%. This is a ________ strong share of wallet.

A) strong

B) moderate

C) weak

Answer: ____________

4. Which account makes the most sense to create a development plan that leverages expertise against share of wallet?

A) dealer shows 84% share of wallet and wants to get into service agreements

B) dealer shows 19% share of wallet but does not want to make any changes in her business right now

C) dealer shows 35% share of wallet and has asked you to help him grow to the next level

D) dealer is a hot prospect who wants most of the programs and dealer services your distributorship offers

E) none of the above

Answer: ____________

5. Your territory posted $5,180,000 in sales last year. You estimate your overall share of wallet to be 48%. What share of wallet would you need to hit $6,000,000 in sales?

A) 56%

B) 41%

C) 48%

D) 65%

E) none of the above

Answer: ____________

6. To convert a large dealer (annual purchases over $1 million), you probably need to

A) offer a great price (not necessarily low, but competitive)

B) offer a level of service that outstrips his current supplier

C) have the business expertise he needs to grow and manage his business

D) all of the above

E) only some of the above

Answer: ____________

7. How much attrition should you figure per year in your annual territory sales plan?

   A) 10%

   B) 20%

   C) 34%

   D) 50%

   E) 62.5%

   Answer: ____________

8. List the six steps in writing and monitoring a territory plan:

   1)

   2)

   3)

   4)

   5)

   6)

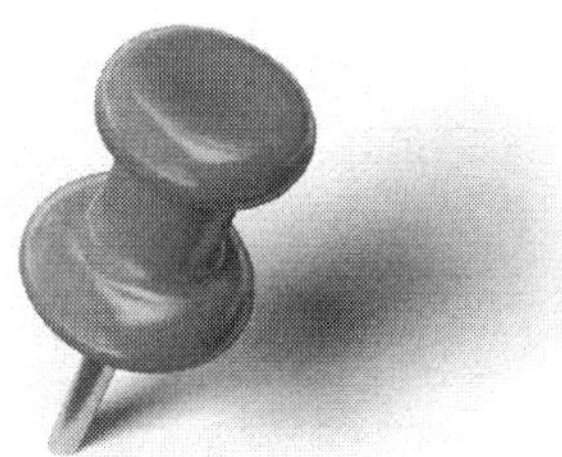

Chapter 7: The Types of Contractor

HVAC contractors come in all sorts of shapes and sizes. And we are not referring to their physical appearance. We are referring to how their companies are set up. As it turns out, HVAC firms can specialize in different types of HVAC work, and this in turn can dictate how a company should best be organized to be maximally effective for that type of work. Many contractors stumble into a good organization gradually and with much pain and many errors; if you can show them some tips and techniques that can help them be effective quicker with less pain, you will probably have good business associates for as long as you care to be a territory manager.

Specialty By Market Segment

The most common way HVAC dealerships are classified is by the type of market segment they serve. There are only a few major segments (and many sub-segments). They include:

- ★ Commercial Market
  - o Plan and Spec
  - o Negotiated
  - o Design-Build
  - o Service
- ★ Residential Market
  - o New Construction—Single Family (Tract)
  - o New Construction—Multi-Family
  - o New Construction—Custom Home
  - o Add-on and Replacement
  - o Service
- ★ Refrigeration
  - o Low-Temperature (Walk-ins, meat cases, etc.)
  - o Ice machines

★ Service

To briefly define each type:

Commercial Plan and Spec—the new construction segment of the commercial market in which plans and specifications are drawn up by architects and engineers and the plans and specs are advertised publicly for bids by general and specialty contractors. This market is usually driven by price (lowest bid wins), but a tight favorable spec (one that means about the only units that can meet the engineer's design requirements is your stuff) can help elevate the price a little.

Commercial Negotiated—work in which the mechanical contractor works directly with the owner of an existing property to make changes or replace older equipment; does not go out for general bid, and hence tends to be more profitable than the plan and spec segment.

Commercial Design-Build—a process in which the expense and time of using a consulting engineer to design a new building is supplied by the mechanical contractor (who either has such an engineer on staff, or who can get their plans stamped [approved] by a mechanical engineer). The result is a much faster construction cycle at a lower overall cost, even though the design-build contractor can own a tight favorable spec on the job and make a very good margin on it.

Commercial Service—repairing of existing commercial equipment and the promotion of commercial service agreements as well as air treatment services. Because commercial accounts can often amortize agreement expenses or treat them in novel and favorable ways in their accounting systems, commercial service agreements can often be very lucrative for the contractor and at prices that would often stun a residential contractor.

Residential New Construction, Single Family (Tract)—installation of equipment and associated ductwork and peripherals on brand new homes that are usually built in close proximity to each other in sub-divisions and developments. Historically low margin work, it can be very profitable if done right due to its assembly line nature.

Residential New Construction, Multi-Family—apartment and condominium work, normally involving traditional single-family types of equipment (although more and more multi-family jobs are going the way of ductless-splits).

Residential New Construction Custom Home—work on single-family homes but for a known buyer. Normally, the emphasis is on quality and premium equipment while price is a lower-ranking concern.

Residential Add-on and Replacement—work involving the change-out of old (and failed or failing) residential equipment for new units. In some cases, the homeowner is adding central air where he did not have it before (the Add-on part of the market description).

Residential Service—repairing failed or failing residential equipment and providing air quality treatment services and equipment. This segment is a vital key in the successful exploitation of the Residential Replacement Market. It can also include service agreements (usually just inspection agreements, as few dealers can successfully market full coverage [parts and labor] agreements). May also include specialty services such as duct cleaning and indoor air quality.

Refrigeration, Low Temperature—installation and servicing of low temperature refrigeration systems, such as used in grocery stores, dairies, restaurants, ice skating rinks, and so forth. Some of these systems can get very large (over 5,000 tons) and some use exotic refrigerants.

Refrigeration, Ice Machines—sale, installation and service of ice machines, primarily for restaurants, but can also be for larger systems (such as bulk ice plants). Units can range from small units (under a wet bar, for example), up to over 10 thousand tons of ice per day.

Special Skills Needed

As can be seen by the description of each market segment, there are special skills required to succeed in each segment, and usually those skills make it difficult for a contractor to be successful in more than one segment at a time with the same employees. It is quite possible, on the other hand, for a contractor to be successful in many markets simultaneously if the contractor uses different personnel for each segment (assuming, of course, the personnel have the skills needed for that segment).

For this reason, many contractors underestimate the effort it will take to branch out into new markets, especially when their normal market goes soft. For instance, many commercial contractors have a hard time in the residential business when the commercial market slows down because the skill sets (especially the selling skills) are so different from what they are used to. Similarly, a residential new construction contractor who wants to get into add-on and replacement when the housing market gets soft often makes huge selling and pricing errors, and finds that his installers (who can afford to be sloppy in a new home since their errors will be covered by dry wall installers, painters and trim carpenters) often botch a finished home job.

Special Fiscal Constraints

There are also special fiscal constraints at work in each type of market segment. As you will learn in Chapter 15, to stay healthy, a contractor needs to have about 10% of next year's sales in the form of working capital. Working capital is defined as a firm's current assets (essentially cash, accounts receivable and inventory, plus a few other little items) less its current liabilities (essentially its accounts payable, taxes payable, and other little accounts). Thus a contractor who plans on doing $2 million in sales next year should have $200,000 or more in working capital.

The problem is that most contractors today don't have 10% working capital in the business. What this means is that there is not enough cash or accounts receivable (cash that will eventually come in) to pay the bills on time. As a result, a contractor either has to ride his suppliers or slip into 31-60 and even 61-90 day accounts aging status. (Usually the contractor becomes a COD account once it hits 61 or more days.)

Here's the rub. Suppose that a residential new construction dealer (a group that is, as a whole, notoriously under-capitalized) decides to burst into the commercial market when the housing market dries up? What might happen? Since the dealer is not used to the commercial market's financial conventions, he may be in for a horrible surprise. For instance, he may not be aware that most commercial jobs escrow 10% of the contract price into what is called retainage. Retainage is basically hostage money to make sure the contractor honors his first-year warranty service obligations and makes the job meet the owner's satisfaction. Since most dealers don't even plan on 10% net profit on commercial jobs to begin with, this means that a dealer won't see his profit (and possibly some of his overhead money) until a year after the job is done, and then only if he does a great job of keeping the customer happy!

Meanwhile, bills come in and must be paid. Those two 60-ton rooftop units he installed must be paid for within a month or so; and the payroll for the workers has to be met weekly. Then there are the payroll taxes that are due each month… and so on. The result is that an undercapitalized dealer diving into the commercial market usually does not have the cash reserves needed to pay the bills as they come due, so they end up on COD with suppliers, or worse yet, go out of business.

There is also the issue of the costs of doing business in different market segments—they are different (that should come as no surprise!). A residential new construction contractor entering the replacement market may not realize that the replacement contractor's overhead is higher as a percentage of sales than a new construction dealer's. As a result, the new construction dealer will tend to price replacement jobs way to low for the market (making the legitimate replacement dealers in that market upset) and pricing himself out of existence. It happens.

Multi-Market Success Requires Diversity

A contractor can successfully work in more than one market if she is aware of these special constraints and chooses to run the various operations under different management and fiscal rules. This usually means that the operation must be diversified on purpose. A successful mechanical contractor may find success in the custom new home market if the owner sets up a second company (with a similar or different name) operating with different people out of a different part of the parent company's building (or a whole new physical plant altogether). Certain functions may be shared— for example, the back room is used for accounting and purchasing), but the special functions, such as installation, sales and scheduling, need to be run as separate stand-alone divisions (or companies). Otherwise, the temptation will be too great at times to lump everyone together again and slide back into the muddy waters of monolithic marketing.

A Successful Portfolio Should Be Balanced

A Tier One TM will have strong accounts in each market segment that is significant in his or her territory. This does not necessarily mean you need to have some of each type in your portfolio, because some of the segments may not be major contributors to your territory. But it does mean that if a market segment is a major contributor, you need to have strong players working with you in it.

Historically in the HVAC business, when one market segment hits a slump, the other segments may not hit a slump until many months later, by which time the original segment may be coming back. Rarely do *all* the segments hit a low at the same time. By having a balanced sales portfolio, you can help protect your sales plan from a disaster if one major market segment takes a tumble this year.

The Legal Setup of Businesses

Not only do contractors segregate by type of market; they can also be sifted by their legal status as well.

The Sole Proprietorship

This is probably the most common type of organization for a **small** HVAC business as it is the simplest to set up and operate. In most states and legal jurisdictions, the setup of a sole proprietorship is a simple process, usually only requiring that the entity file its name with the State. It simply means that John Doe (the principal's name) is the sole proprietor and owner of said business. All benefits of the business accrue to him as well as all liabilities.

> **Advantages:** Ease of organization and operation (the owner can do as he pleases, within the bounds of law); few legal forms, hence little or no legal fees to create the company; simple structure and hence ability to respond quickly to external forces.

> **Disadvantages:** The owner has unlimited liability (in other words, if a customer sues the company, he can go for the owner as well, and there is no limit to the damages that may be requested). It can be difficult to obtain outside capital. Under certain conditions, there are also tax disadvantages for being a sole proprietorship.

The Partnership

The next step up in organizational complexity is a **partnership**, where two or more people come together to form a business enterprise. Setup requirements with state authorities are the same as for sole proprietorships, so an attorney is not needed, thus saving on startup fees.

> **Advantages:** Low startup fees due to no need for attorneys; authority is at a low level, making for a company that can respond quickly to external forces and internal developments; two or more people can pool their talents and capital to create something bigger than either one alone could create. Each partner has equal rights to participation in management (but this *can* be a disadvantage), examine the books and share in the profits. A partner *may* receive compensation for services if the other partners vote the approval of such.

> **Disadvantages:** Unlimited liability for all partners; mutual liability of all partners (e.g., a legal offense by one partner also exposes the other partner(s) to personal liability too); any change in the partners (death, resignation, addition, etc.) automatically ends the legality of the company (it must re-organize); disagreements between partners can become serious; it is often difficult to obtain outside capital; the interplay of relationships between partners can create hazardous seas for the company to navigate; withdrawal of capital requires the authorization of **all** the partners. Inasmuch as each partner has a legal right to a share of the profits, each partner also has a legal responsibility to share in the losses, liability and exposure.

Upon dissolution, the payment of debt must follow this order: *creditors* (other than the partners), *partners* (for loans and advances), *partners* (for general capital), and *partners* (for divvying up of the remaining assets, if any).

In a partnership, the **firm** is **not** responsible for taxes—the **partners** are.

Limited Partnerships

Limited Partnerships are a special form of partnership in which the company is chartered to exist for a specified period of time and for a specified purpose. When that time and/or purpose is met, the company no longer exists legally.

Because the firm is bound by its charter, legal expenses for setup are higher since the partners must file with the Secretary of State. This charter will identify two types of partner: *general* and *limited.* A **general partner** has the full rights and responsibilities of the partner in a standard partnership, while a **limited partner** is merely an investor and has no other rights other than to share in the profits or losses of the firm.

> **Advantages:** The liability of one or more partners is limited to the amount of capital contributed at startup. The investors also have limited liability. A limited partnership is usually eligible for accelerated depreciation and investment tax credits (since they often don't exist long enough to get the standard depreciation and write-offs).

> **Disadvantages:** They cannot be dissolved voluntarily before the time stated in the charter unless there is a filing and publication of a notice of dissolution in local newspapers.

Limited Liability Partnerships

A relatively new business entity, recognized in most (but not all) states is the **limited liability partnership**. LLPs (as they are sometimes called) offer the advantages of partnership ownership with the protection inherent in corporations.

> **Advantages:** An LLP provides the flexibility and tax advantages of a partnership, and offers the limited-liability features of corporations. While doing this, it also eliminates restrictions on ownership. LLPs offer their owners the same protection from business obligations that shareholders of corporations enjoy—personal exposure is limited to the amount of investment by the owners. Unlike standard partnerships (where a lawsuit could make all the owners' personal assets at risk), the LLP protects the owners'

personal assets. As long as the firm has no more than two of the IRS's four corporate characteristics, they are taxed as partnerships. (These four characteristics are: limited liability, centralized management, free transferability of ownership interests, and continuity of life.) Transfer of an owner's assets to a trust would probably not affect the legal status of the business or its single tax-level status. (This is not always true in other types of businesses.) General and limited partnerships can be converted to LLPs tax free. Corporations can be converted provided they are first liquidated, followed by a contribution to the assets to form an LLP.

Disadvantages: LLPs are a new type of business, so there is not much legal precedent in case law to predict exactly how the law will be applied. Other than the liability issues raised above for general and limited partnerships, the disadvantages of those forms of business apply here too.

Corporations

The next step up in legal complexity is the **corporation**, formed when an investor or investors band together in covenant to form a business venture.

The legal process of setup is rather complex and can therefore be expensive. This process includes the creation and filing of "articles of confederation" (the firm's charter), and rigid definitions of entities and legal responsibilities.

Corporations are *fully legal entities*, are *perpetual*, and have ownership that is separate from control (that is, investors own the firm, but managers run it).

When a corporation's stock is not traded publicly, it is said to be a "closely held" or "closed" corporation. A closed corporation is normally owned and managed by a small number of people.

Advantages: There are several, including **limited liability** of the owners. In other words, the share holders are not responsible for the firm's debts, other than the loss of their investment.

There are numerous **tax advantages** that a corporation enjoys. Among these are: profit sharing and pensions plans (they may exempt up to 25% of the payroll total from taxation this way), deductibility (from earnings) of the cost of insurance (life and health) and medical plans (no limitation), the ability to create and administer deferred compensation plans, and the deduction of reasonable salaries from earnings prior to taxes.

In addition, earnings are taxed on a graduating scale: the more earnings there are, the higher the tax rate. Also, accumulated income (retained earnings) can be withdrawn as a capital gain upon dissolution.

Corporations can usually raise larger sums of capital with less trouble than partnerships or proprietorships. And normal usury laws do not apply to funds used by the corporation for business purposes (as when a customer's purchase is financed by the firm).

Corporations often enjoy greater management flexibility as the talent pool from which they can draw is virtually limitless.

Corporations do not cease to exist when the proprietors or partners do. In fact, the ownership can be transferred simply by the sale of stock from the present owner(s) to a new owner or owners.

Disadvantages: Among the biggest setbacks is the **cost of setup**, as legal fees can run into the tens of thousands of dollars. There are also licensing fees and, in some cases, franchise taxes to pay too.

Income is **taxed at a higher level** than in proprietorships and partnerships.

If the firm does business in more than one state, the legal setup must be done in those other states as well.

Because they are legal entities on file with the state's Secretary of State, corporations are more **closely regulated** than non-legal businesses.

Since the ownership of the firm lies with the investors, voting blocs of owners can seize control of the firm (sometimes without the expertise or skills needed to exercise wise oversight).

And litigation, should it arise, will demand the services of an **attorney** to protect the investors.

Sub-Chapter "S" Corporations

Sub-chapter "S" Corporations get their name from Sub-chapter "S" of the Internal Revenue Service Code. "S" corporations, or "S" corps as they are often called, are just like standard corporations except for some minor changes.

In one sense, an "S" corp is a hybrid between a partnership and a corporation. An "S" corp is chartered with ten or fewer shareholders at startup and, after five years, may increase the number of shareholders to fifteen. These shareholders can elect to be *paid (and thus taxed) as partners* rather than as a corporation. In such a case, the corporation files earnings information with the IRS and the *shareholders* pay the tax regardless of dividend distributions.

However, corporations which receive 20% or more of their *income* from rents, royalties, interest or dividends do not qualify to become "S" corps. Also, "S" corps are not legal in all states.

The tax advantages of an "S" corp should be apparent, and are especially important during times of loss (the shareholders can file the losses as personal losses regardless of their salaries for the year) and/or when net profits are paid out and not retained (due to capital gains tax rates).

An Illustrative Example

Let's compare two contractors, Billy Bob Burgelson, and Michael Martingale. Billy is a proprietorship while Michael is a sub-chapter S corporation.

Both businesses have good years, and in both cases, the principals decide to pay themselves year-end dividends of $25,000.

Because Billy Bob is a proprietorship, *all* of his $25,000 dividend is treated as personal income and is subject to federal withholding tax, as well as FICA ("Social Security") and Medicare. Currently, FICA withholdings run 15.72% of wages while Medicare is 2.90%. When a person is self-employed (like Billy Bob and Michael are), all of these taxes must come out of the paycheck. (If you work for a distributor, by law, *half* of these taxes are paid by your employer and the other half by you. But of course, if your employer did not have to pay his half, he could afford to pay you more in salary and commissions, so you really do end up paying all of it yourself, don't you?)

So Billy Bob pays his federal withholdings (let's say they are 40%), plus a check for 15.72% for FICA and 2.90% for Medicare, or 18.62% total. So for his $25,000 dividend check, Billy Bob must write checks to the government entities for 40% + 18.62%, or 58.62% of the dividend, or $14,655.

Michael is also liable for the 40% withholdings tax, but in a corporation, dividends are treated differently from regular income *and are not subject to FICA and Medicare withholdings.* So Michael saves 18.62% of the dividend, or $4,655 in taxes.

Tax law also allows a corporation to deduct most of the expenses of an annual board meeting from their profits before paying taxes. This also applies to S corporations (with some restrictions). Tax law also requires that the board meeting be held in the United States.

Billy Bob cannot have a board meeting as a proprietorship does not have a board. But Michael may, and since his wife is a shareholder, and his daughter and son are both shareholders, his company has its annual board meeting in Hawaii, much of the expense being tax deductible for Michael's company. Nice little perk for becoming incorporated, wouldn't you say?

And lest we forget, in the fourth quarter of this year, Billy Bob and Michael both install gas furnaces in customer homes. Both homes have a fire that week and do $100,000 in damages to the homes. In Billy Bob's case, the plaintiff can sue him for damages and punitive amounts and everything Billy Bob owns can be touched by the court in awarding the settlement. But Michael is only exposed by the worth of the corporation. His home, his vehicles, his boat, his golf cart—all these assets are protected from confiscation by the court and business law. Michael can recover from losing his case with some damage, but not enough to kill his business. Billy Bob, on the other hand, may not be able to go on.

Summary Table of Business Setups

	Corporations		Proprietorships	Partnerships		
	"C"	"S"	General	General	L P	L L P
	Legal	Legal	Not legal	Not legal	Not legal	Legal
Creation	State charter	State charter and IRS	Proprietor	Partners	Partners and State	Partners and State and IRS
Purposes and Powers	Limited by the charter	Limited by the charter	Self-determined	Agreement among partners	Agreement among partners	Agreement among partners
Liability	Shareholders (limited)	Shareholders (limited)	Unlimited	Unlimited	Gen Partners: unlimited Lim Partners: Limited	All Partners: limited
Duration	Perpetual	Perpetual	Ends on change of ownership	Ends on change in partners	Limited by certificate	Limited by certificate
Taxes	Corporate earnings and shareholders' dividends	Shareholders as if they were partners	Owner pays as personal income	Partners pay as personal income	Partners pay as personal income	Partners pay as personal income
Transfer of Interest	Freely by sale of shareholders	Freely by sale of shareholders	Not transferable	Not transferable	Gen Partners: no Lim Partners: yes	Free by partners
Management	Elected directors	Elected directors	Owner	All partners	Gen Partners: all as equals Lim Partners: none	All partners
Org fee, annual licenses, annual reports	All required	All required	No	No	No	No

Review Questions for Chapter 7

1. What are the key market segments in your territory? Can you estimate the total business potential of each segment?

Segment	Importance[1]	Estimated Potential Sales	My Sales to that Segment	Your SOW[2] in Segment
Comm P&S		$	$	%
Comm Negot.		$	$	%
Comm D-B		$	$	%
Comm Service		$	$	%
Res SF Tract		$	$	%
Res Mult Fam		$	$	%
Res Custom Home		$	$	%
Res AO&R		$	$	%
Res Service		$	$	%
Refrig Lo Temp		$	$	%
Refrig Ice		$	$	%
Service		$	$	%

1 Use a scale of 1 to 5, 1 = not important, 5 = very important

2 SOW = share of wallet

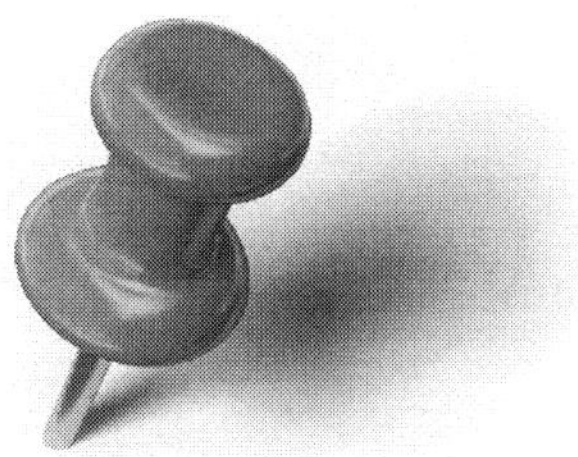

Chapter 8: The Life Cycles of Contractors

Most companies must change their shape as they grow, and many HVAC contractors don't have a good idea of how to do this. With your help and steady guidance, you can usually help a smaller contractor grow successfully into a bigger one. (And by successfully, I mean that the growth results in the contractor buying more and more from you and staying current with your credit department!)

The Lay of the Contractor Landscape

Every five years, the United States government issues a report on various sectors of the economy. The construction trade (of which HVAC is a part) is issued in years ending in x2 and x7. The last report (as of this writing) was collected in 2007 and was posted on the internet in 2009.

The report is titled *Plumbing, Heating, and Air Conditioning Contractor: 2007 Economic Census*. In this release, the Census Bureau changed the report format. In prior years, a nice PDF file was issued that was easy to read and digest; in 2009, they released the raw data and you need to have some finesse with databases to build an accurate picture, so I don't recommend the average territory manager bother with downloading the new data.

Here is a 40,000 foot view of the information it contains:

★ Plumbing is about 28% of the reported business

★ HVAC is about 57% of the business

★ "Other" accounts for the balance (15%) and includes things like controls contractors, sprinklers, irrigation systems, etc.

★ There were a total of 100,469 plumbing and HVAC firms in the 2007 release. If their sales were roughly equal across the board (a rough assumption), then about 50,000 of them are HVAC shops. (Some plumbing shops also do HVAC of course, so the total count of HVAC contractors would reach about 70,000 counting plumbers who also do HVAC.)

- About 40,600 of these shops employ 1 to 4 people
- Another 19,300 employ 5 to 9 people
- Some 8,600 employ 10 to 19 people
- About 5,300 employ 20 to 49 people
- 1,500 employ 50 to 99 people
- And some 790 employ over 100 people

★ Total HVAC sales were $78 billion (in 2007 dollars; about $80 billion in 2009 dollars)

★ The 1-4 man shops contribute about 8% of the sales

★ The 5-9 man shops make up about 10% of the sales

★ The 10-19 man shops comprise 14% in sales

★ The 20-49 man shops chalked up 21% in sales

★ The 50-99 man shops racked up 16% in sales

★ And the large houses totaled about 30% of the sales

I will ignore the mega-house accounts at the end of this list since most of these firms deal with suppliers at a level much higher than a territory manager. Look at the first five size tiers. If we graphed this data, we'd find a very pronounced hump in the middle. Where would the peak of the curve be? In the 20-49 man shops, what most TMs would consider to be large dealers.

Let's now do an interesting thing: let's overlay the number of businesses by size against their sales by size and find a stunning relationship:

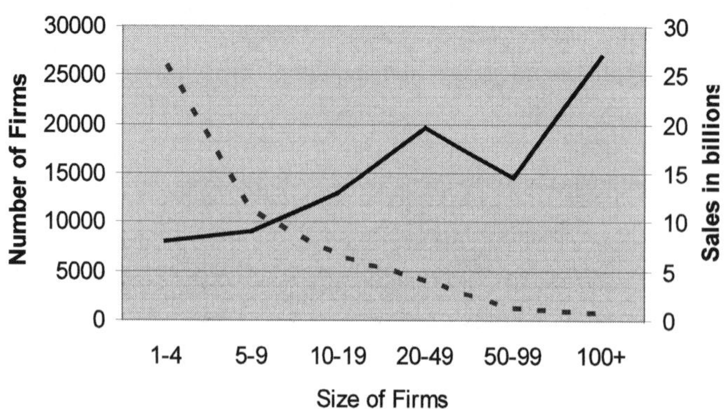

The most productive part of the sales graph occurs in a thinly populated part of the number of firms data! Conversely, the heaviest part of the data shows the lightest number of dollars generated.

This poses a dilemma for the average TM (especially those in Tiers Three and Four: the dealers who are the most fun to call on are the smaller ones. They will display great loyalty and enthusiasm when a TM shows them any significant attention, and that in turn gives the TM a good feeling. But the dollars of sales production just are not there! The best fishing hole in this data looks to be in the 16 or so to 50 man shop size, a size of shop that intimidates many Tier Three and Four TMs. These shops are usually a little more sophisticated than the starter uppers and a lot of inexperienced TMs don't feel they can deliver what these dealers demand. (Indeed, a lot of them cannot, which is why they like to feed in the 1-10 man shop pool.)

Let's look at one more correlation in the data to find some information that will be helpful in designing a territory plan. Let's look at the average *purchases* by each firm:

Size of Firm (headcount)	Annual Purchases (E&M)
1-4	$58,325
5-9	$153,368
10-19	$481,861
20-49	$1,172,830
50-99	$3,157,333
100+	$11,610,510

Let's put some rubber on the road. Suppose your quota for next year is $5,000,000. If you are a TM who feels that the small shops really need you, how many of them will you need to make your quota?

$5,000,000 divided by $58,325 = 86 customers

If you saw each customer every three weeks, you'd need to see twenty-nine a week or about six a day. That means at least six hours a day in front of the customers, plus drive time, plus your other activities. It is just not doable!

If you focused on the 10-19 man shops, you'd only need ten of them to produce your quota, meaning you could see them more often and spend more time with them when you do. You'd travel less, be home with your family more, and make good money. Sounds great, except you'd better have some TM smarts at this level to pull it off.

Of course, if you were really good, you'd probably just work with four bigger shops (20-49 people) and spend half a day at each shop each week.

Did you ever go fishing when you were a youngster? You may have had a time when your dad or an uncle or some other adult took you to a spot where the fish would almost jump onto your hook as soon as you put it in the water. If so, you were probably in a blue gill hole—a spot in a lake or pond where small fish called blue gill congregate. They are feisty little fish and put up a good fight for a kid, but they don't have much meat on them.

However, most adults who fish in competitions will tell you that you can never win a tournament fishing the blue gill holes. You have to find the deep water where the really big fish live, and catch them.

The point is, while the fishing is easy (and fun) at the blue gill pond, it takes the lunker heaven to make a good living in the professional fishing trade. As I coach TMs around the country, I find that many of them are afraid to launch out into the deeper waters of lunker heaven. For a Tier Four or Tier Three TM, that is probably a good fear to have. Those TMs usually don't have the skills to fish in water that deep and if they did catch a lunker, it would probably get away!

Like Salmon Trying to Spawn

I am always intrigued by nature programs on TV that depict things like salmon swimming upstream to spawn, or crabs migrating across beaches to reproduce. The urge to reproduce and insure the survival of the species has always left me spellbound! I am also staggered by the sheer attrition such mating rituals extract from the species. Only the strongest make it, only the strongest survive and pass on their genes—which is nature's grand way to slowly but constantly ratchet up the survival rate of a species.

Like salmon swimming upstream to reproduce, dealers too often try to grow and reproduce (by adding employees, spinning off satellite offices or acquiring other shops in key areas). Yet, like salmon, many dealers don't make the trip and survive. Many are eaten along the way by bears, eagles, and other predators, while some just tucker out and call it quits.

If you look at the data on the number of firms by size on the second page of this chapter, you may have seen a shocking and rapid drop-off in the number of dealers in each size bracket. In fact, the attrition rate from 1-4 to 5-9 man shops is high—with 40,600 dealers in the 1-4 man group and about 30,000 in all the other size groups, the attrition rate from 1-4 man to the next larger size is a staggering 44%!

Now imagine what this means for the Tier Four or Tier Three TM who thinks that he can build a powerful territory by catering to the 1-4 man shops. Some of them, he knows, will grow and go on to become big shops some day, and he'll be right there with them selling them his stuff at every step along the way. Yet, almost half of the dealers on his list won't make the transition successfully. Only half are qualified to move on up the evolutionary ladder!

So I need to ask the Tier Four or Tier Three TM a crucial question: Do you know which half of your dealers will make it? You don't! Then how do you know where to spend your time helping them grow? Won't you waste an awful lot of effort on dealers who are destined to become auction fodder?

It is not much better in migrating from a 5-9 man shop to the 10-19 man class. Here the extinction rate is 19,300 down to 8,600 shops, or some 10,700 shops, a loss rate of 55%. Attrition from the 10-19 man shop to the 20-49 man class is 38%. (It gets better as you move up the evolutionary tree; dealers who can grow some, usually can keep on growing and not go bust in the process.)

The odds of a Tier Four or Tier Three TM taking a dealer from the 1-4 man size to the 10-19 man size are therefore 48% successful at the first stage times 62% successful at the second stage, or only 30%. Only one dealer in three will make it to the 10-19 man size shop.

And his odds of producing a 20-49 man shop mega dealer are only 18%.

Not really good odds, are they?

Can We Predict Entrepreneurial Success?

If the odds are high that a dealer on my account list cannot successfully grow his or her business, wouldn't I want to know, as a TM with limited time resources, which ones might make it and spend more of my time with *them* to help them grow? And wouldn't it be great if there were ways to tell whether or not a company owner has what it takes to grow before I spend my time with them on what may end up as a lost cause?

Actually, it is possible to predict entrepreneurial aptitude to a fairly reliable degree. It involves a simple assessment that was originally developed by the Department of Human Resources and Skills Development of the Canadian government. A copy of that assessment appears here:

The Entrepreneurial Aptitude Pre-Test

Question	Yes	No
1. Do I have a burning desire to be on my own?	☐	☐
2. Am I confident that I can succeed?	☐	☐
3. Am I willing to take calculated and moderate risks?	☐	☐
4. Am I a self-starter?	☐	☐
5. Am I able to set long-term goals? Can I stick with them? Even if I am faced with a difficult problem or situation?	☐	☐
6. Do I believe that money is not the only measure of success?	☐	☐
7. Am I creative? Am I always looking for new approaches and ideas? Am I innovative?	☐	☐
8. Am I good at making decisions? Are my decisions generally sound?	☐	☐
9. Am I willing to market my product or service?	☐	☐
10. Am I a good organizer? Do I pay attention to details?	☐	☐
11. Am I flexible? Do I adapt to change? Can I handle surprises?	☐	☐
Count the boxes you checked for "Yes"		

A score of six or more suggests the dealer may have (repeat, *may* have) what it takes to grow his or her business successfully. The higher the score, the more likely a dealer can grow successfully. There are no guarantees as this is not *that* sophisticated of an assessment, but it does show the level of intensity entrepreneurial success factors the dealer may possess. (For a more thorough analysis tool, contact Lodestar Consulting about the Entrepreneurial Assessments that are part of Lodestar's *Stages* program.)

You may want to copy the form above and give it to your key dealers and ask them if they would mind filling it out and giving it back to you. Don't tell them the minimum score requirement. If a dealer scores six or more, it will probably pay off to work with that dealer in growing his or her business. If the score is five or less, you can always say on your next sales call, "That was kind of neat, wasn't it?" and go on.

Drive Is Important, But so is Money

If drive was all a person needed in order to be a successful business person, America would probably have three times as many businesses in it as it does. But drive is not all a dealer needs to grow.

He or she also needs money. And a considerable amount of it.

How much? About 15% of sales!

This 15% number is not carved in stone, but it is the distillation of what thousands of successful HVAC firms show in terms of their capitalization. It is composed of two major elements: working capital and fixed assets.

Recall from the last chapter that working capital is defined as the difference between the *current assets* and the *current liabilities*, both of which are recorded on a firm's *balance sheet.* Current assets consist mainly of cash, accounts receivable, and inventory. Current liabilities consist of accounts payable, taxes payable, and a few other minor items, such as current portion of notes payable. (I will explain all of these terms in more detail in Chapter 15.) If a firm has current assets of $400,000 and current liabilities of $150,000, it has working capital of $250,000 (the difference in the two current amounts).

Fixed assets are defined as assets a business uses to support its normal activity and excludes, for this purpose, real estate.[4] Fixed assets could include sheet metal tools (like shears and brakes), vacuum pumps, vehicles, fork lift trucks, office furniture, computers, radios, and so on.

Over the years, we find that successful HVAC firms seem to cluster around 10% of sales in working capital and 5% of sales in fixed assets. This is a total of *15% of sales*.

If a dealer plans on doing $1,000,000 in sales next year, she needs to have $150,000 in investment ahead of time ($100,000 in working capital, $50,000 in fixed assets, not counting real estate).

If you have a dealer you would like to grow, you might start by having her do the entrepreneurial self-assessment and, if she scores six or higher, have a conversation with her about growth. Does she want to grow? If so, how much? How large would she have to become before

4 The reason is that real estate does not wear out with use and its value appreciates over time, whereas other fixed assets depreciate over time and wear out.

she began to feel uncomfortable with running such a large company? If she wants to grow, you must, at some point, bring up the money issue. Ask her if she has the investment she'll need to fund this growth, or if she can get it by time it will be needed? Do the numbers, crunch the math. It's better to find out now that she hasn't got the fiscal means to do it than to try it and destroy the company in the effort.

Let's suppose that your dealer, Sara Steele, is presently a three-person business and is doing $400,000 a year in sales. Sara scores eight out of eleven on the entrepreneurial pre-quiz and says that she'd like to be at $2,000,000 in sales in six years. She agrees to share her books with you and together you figure out that she has working capital of $32,000 and fixed assets of $18,000. Is her plan doable?

> Let's begin with where she is. Her working capital is 32/400 of sales, or 8%. She is a little light in this department, but her fixed assets are 18/400 or 4.5% of sales, about where they should be. So out of the gate, she is a bit light on capital. She may need to build up a war chest the first year to get her working capital up to 10% (which means another $8,000 in cash, receivables and inventory). I would counsel her to put the $8,000 capital into cash and receivables.
>
> That leaves five years to grow $1.6 million in sales. This is an increase in size of 500% from her present level. That's a compounded annual growth rate of about 38%. If she maintains her present productivity rate, she would grow from three employees to fifteen people. That's twelve new people over five years, or better than two a year. (In reality, she will probably grow slower at first and faster than this at the end of the five years, with 2.4 people a year being the average.)
>
> Her total investment must rise from $60,000 ($40,000 in working capital, $20,000 in fixed assets) to $300,000 ($200,000 in working capital and $100,000 in fixed assets).
>
> It is easy to see where the fixed assets need to go—furniture and vehicles for the people she will add over the next five years.
>
> But increasing working capital from $40,000 now to $200,000 over five years will be a daunting task! On a straight-line growth curve (not realistic, but simpler to calculate), she needs to raise working capital by $32,000 a year.
>
> There are only two places she can get this much capital: she can borrow it or grow it. If she borrows it, her leverage ratios will go to the dogs, and she may not be able to generate enough cash flow to service the debt when it comes due. But to grow this much capital will require Herculean effort too. She would have to, on average, make about 5% net profit after taxes (roughly double this before taxes, if she is a corporation after taxes) to build up her war chest from company profits, not bank loans. This is certainly doable, but when you consider that the average dealer in the United States usually makes under 3% pre-tax net (and about 2% or less after-tax net), she had better be awfully good!

So yes, on paper, Sara could do it. But it won't be easy and it could end up wrecking her life. It's an awfully aggressive growth plan. I usually advise dealers to grow at a more conservative and controllable rate instead of 38% a year, 20-25% is more doable, and 15% to 20% should certainly be within the reach of any dealer of average or better intelligence and competence.

Barriers to Growth: Overhead or People?

As a dealership grows, it reaches certain points where continued growth becomes very difficult and the dealer tends to stall for a time until either a way is found around the barrier, or the dealer decides to give up the growth game and stay where he is or even downsize.

Most consultants teach that these barriers are points of significant overhead increase and that the dealer has a hard time adjusting his pricing policy to absorb it as he learns how to cope with a larger company. Although this is true to some extent, I don't think it is the ultimate reason why dealers face growth hurdles.

I think that growth hurdles are more an issue of people management and control of the dream than they are issues of carrying more overhead. To be sure, adding people adds overhead, but most overhead scenarios can be handled with simple and accurate forecasting.

Dealers fail to grow (or stay at a larger size once they get that big) because of only a few factors. First, there are financial issues (lack of capital). Second, there are process issues. A dealer grows, but the way jobs were done before is not changed, and so with more people, the old way becomes inefficient. Even though there may be more heads on the payroll, the productivity does not rise very much, so the extra hands end up being drains on the company's profitability. Third, marketing can be poor, meaning not enough leads come in, so sales become anemic, and with poor sales, overhead soars to disastrous levels. Fourth, because marketing is wimpy, sales will be weak and weak sales can never make up enough profit to save a company. Fifth, leadership may not be up to the task (part of the reason we do the pre-assessment). And finally, there is the great unknown, motivation. Does the dealer *want* to grow? This is also addressed in the pre-assessment.

But ultimately, I think all of a dealer's growth problems tie back to people issues and control of the dream.

A dealer can add production personnel without too much impact on overhead and as long as the sales rise with the head count, the company will continue to grow successfully. There are not too many serious overhead barriers in the way. But that is the key—adding *production* personnel. This means installers and service techs. Not office people or managers.

What happens as a small firm grows? Suppose Sara Steele has her three employees (herself, her brother the installer, and her cousin who runs service and helps her brother install jobs) and she starts to grow. Sara will probably start by adding an installer to help her brother install all the jobs she sells, because she quickly learns she can sell jobs a whole lot faster than her people can install them. She may later add a third installer and even a fourth, because at about this point, her cousin must go full-time on service to support the warranty calls and to start locating replacement prospects for Sara to sell. Eventually, she will hire another service tech and perhaps two more installers, but now she is up to eight people and she finds that the phone rings so much and her administrative tasks consume so much time she has less and less time for sales, and for her family. So she has to make a major decision—does she bring in someone for the office (and watch the overhead suddenly swell up like a pig in a python[5]) and keep growing, or does she put the brakes on this thing and leave it where it is? If she lacks the entrepreneurial fire, she will probably halt the growth at this point and continue as an eight person firm for as long as she cares to do it. But if she is really entrepreneurially-minded, she will add the office person, and adjust her pricing on sales calls to cover the extra overhead. She finds her sales success rate dropping a little, so she has to work harder at making sales and getting good leads. She attends sales courses (some good, most awful).

You see, her first barrier was not so much an overhead hiccup (it was there), but more of an emotional issue she had to settle in her heart. Does she continue to grow and let someone else be the nanny to part of her dream, or does she keep control and stop the growth?

Sometime at around ten to twelve employees, a major barrier arises. Sara is now stretched so thin running the crews and two service techs and doing the sales calls that she is putting in eighteen hour days. With an emotional disaster on the horizon, she bites the bullet and looks for a good job foreman to help her run the installers and prepare the jobs. This is a purely overhead position, and it won't be filled cheaply. Good job foremen can command substantially more money than good installers, plus he'll need a truck, a cell phone or radio, a desk, a computer terminal, a desk phone, and benefits... Sara's overhead, which may have been running at around $400,000 a year, now suddenly takes a $120,000 annual hit just to add the job foreman—with no extra hands turning wrenches on the jobs. Yes, there is an overhead barrier here, and a sizeable one. But it is brought about by the psychological pressure Sara is under to take some of the daily grind duties of running this monster and transfer them to a competent other person (and boy does she hope the man she hires for the job works out!). In the process, she will learn that the new man has a different way of doing things than she did, a different way of handling the installers, and it may not set well with her at first. She may have to either just bite the bullet, let the new man do his job as best he sees fit, or make him ATI (available to the

5 Up to now, adding installers and service techs may add vehicles and their expenses to the overhead, but job pricing factors do not have to be adjusted unless the ratios of wages to vehicle and overhead expenses for the new hires is significantly different from the present staff. This will rarely be the case, so Sara's job pricing does not have to add any money to cover new installers or service techs and things continue business as usual.

industry) again. Neither option will be comfortable for Sara in the months ahead.

Supposing Sara works out her feelings and fears about the loss of some control to the job foreman, she continues to grow the business, adding service techs and installers until she now needs to add a dispatcher (another pure-overhead position), and soon thereafter, a service manager. These are not so much overhead hits (they are) as much as they are psychological barriers—ceding more control to others so she can continue to concentrate on sales and company development.[6]

There have been volumes and volumes written about dealer growth stages and how to get them through their growth barriers, and most of that training material is based on overhead barriers. I think those barriers are really psychological in nature.

You will find jargon like "the dealer hits a wall" and then you will be told what you must do to help the dealer get past his wall. I don't take issue with the walls, just their source. They are not overhead walls as such (that is what a superficial analysis shows). They are really control issues that show up as management and office help, positions which quickly bloat the overhead, but because the owner could not cope with the psychological pressures and demands of overseeing (directly) fifteen or twenty people. The owner must make a tradeoff between direct control (and to some extent control of the vision for the company) and hiring help to run the production teams and office. The financial barriers are, as it turns out, ridiculously easy to work around. The emotional ones may take longer, much longer, and may even end up causing the owner to implode.

Tricky business, isn't it?

With Growth Comes New Needs

Most material on dealer growth barriers starts with the one-man shop (called in various sources the lone wolf, the one-man wonder, the one-man blunder, the lone ranger, and so on). Whatever you want to call the one- man shop, he has made a clean break from his prior employment (probably as a service tech or installer for someone else) and has become a full-time HVAC professional on his or her own.

6 In the military, there is a concept called "span of control". It is the idea that in combat, an officer can effectively coordinate the combat activities of only twelve to sixteen people effectively. This size unit is a "squad", and a platoon consists of two squads. The platoon leader (a lieutenant) oversees two squad leaders (usually sergeants). Several platoons in turn make up a company, overseen by a captain; several companies form a battalion, overseen by a major. And several battalions form a regiment, overseen by a colonel, and so on up the chain of command. Each command position is directly responsible for sixteen or fewer people in combat situations. And the greatest Leader I know of only worked with twelve men (one of whom became a failure). Who am I to suggest a business owner can work with more than this effectively?

Almost every dealer in this trade got into it by means of what Michael Gerber, author of *The E-Myth* series of business books, calls an entrepreneurial seizure. Typically, a man or woman is working for another HVAC company, either running service calls or doing installs. One day, while driving back to the office after the day's assignments, the inspiration comes: "I could do this for myself and make a *lot* more money than my boss is paying me!" Then the seizure strikes. The employee goes into the boss's office and says they are resigning. The boss knows what's coming next, but asks anyway: "And what are you going to do?" Then comes the confident and triumphant reply, "I'm going into business for myself!"

An old familiar knot forms in the boss' stomach because the boss knows that this clown's first few customers are going to be *his* customers that this worker, blinded by the light of revelation, will steal by offering much lower prices for everything.

At first, being on one's own is great! The new "entrepreneur" (and I put that word in quotes because most of these folks are not really entrepreneurs) enjoys his or her new freedom and sense of pride and autonomy. But eventually the e-myth comes home to roost, and as Gerber puts it, the e-myth is the fallacious theory that small businesses are run by entrepreneurs. This is true in *some* cases, but the hefty majority of them are not. Most small businesses are run by excellent *craftsmen*, skilled tradesmen, who don't know beans about running a business. They can size any job, design any layout, install any kind of equipment and service things that would even confuse engineers, but they don't know squat about running a business. How much, for example, should they charge for that furnace? They don't know. They have a gut feel and go with it. Trouble is the gut is wrong over half the time.

So this one-man (or one-woman) wonder starts experiencing growing pains. As business grows (usually in the 24% price-oriented part of the market), demand for his or her services grows faster than they can keep up with it. (Price shoppers are quick to pass on the word about a steal when they see one!) Soon, the one-man wonder has to start thinking about getting some help. But who? Another installer? A service tech? Someone to answer the phones and do all the paper work? And before you know it, they have outgrown their garage. They need more space (partly because the old equipment they have taken out on their installations is piling up because they don't have time to haul it to the dump). In fact, there are at least six major issues a one-man wonder has to face if he or she wants to grow the business:

1. Need for an office or building apart from the basement or garage
2. Hiring a staff person to handle calls, paperwork
3. Need to find enough work to support two or more people (self, staff person, plus any others that are added as the business grows)
4. Need to buy and equip a truck
5. Need to become legitimate

6. Eventual need to hire a service technician to take care of the problems while he keeps on selling and installing (because there isn't enough time in the day to do both)

Perhaps the biggest ogre in this list is number 3, and it can cause a one-man wonder to lose a lot of sleep. But not far behind that is the fact that as people are added, the owner quickly learns that they don't always do things the way he does them (or wants them done), and so he has his first run-in with the "people factor." If a condensing unit or furnace is not working right, he can put a meter on it or run some tests and find out what's wrong and fix it. But if an employee comes to work that morning with an attitude (because maybe she had a fight with her significant other at the breakfast table), how does one fix *that*? With growth comes some loss of control and the addition of sticky variables that cannot be predicted or easily fixed.

So a one-man wonder usually solves his growth issues by doing something like the following:

- Lots of talking with wife, friends, supply house personnel
- Hires a service tech he knows personally (a friend)
- Staff person is normally his wife or girl friend (who usually works at little or no pay)
- Buys and rudely equips a truck (often used), resulting in a slight rise in overhead[7]
- Rents an office with a little storage space out back, maybe even enough for a small shop, with a slight rise in overhead
- Buys space in the local Yellow Pages, adding to overhead

All of these help, but he eventually learns that he must do more. But what?

If you have some of these one-man wonders in your portfolio, what can you do to help them grow successfully?

For starters, consider the entrepreneurial profiles we have discussed. Also, ask good high-gain questions to find out where your one-man wonder wants to go and why, then help him find the programs, resources, learning, and tools to get there. It often helps to arrange for him to talk to other dealers in your portfolio who have grown successfully from the one-man wonder stage. (Make sure the other dealer is not a local competitor!)

7 One of the biggest surprises to most dealers (and TMs) is the revelation that the overhead of a small shop, like a one-man wonder, usually runs *more* than the overhead for a larger shop, at least as a percentage of sales. (The dollars will be smaller, but because the sales are so much smaller too, the overhead as a percentage of sales is often quite a lot higher than that of a larger shop.) As you'll learn in Chapter 15, overhead drives everything!

Share advice on simple procedures and business processes to help him accomplish more in a day.

Help him find a good service technician.

And make it easy for him to buy from you.

From One-Man Wonder to a House of Blunders

Suppose that by a combination of good genes (your one-man wonder has the entrepreneurial aptitude to run a growing business) and the skills of a good TM, the one-man wonder is one of the 48% who can successfully make it to the next stage, what I call the House of Blunders. (It is called the House of Blunders because at this stage, the company starts picking up employees, and with every employee added, the lines of communication —and hence the chance for mistakes and misunderstandings—rises with the factorial[8].) With all the flow of information that *can* happen, and all the ways it can be garbled, errors begin to crop up faster than dandelions after a May rain. And because the one-man wonder has never taken the time (yet) to codify how procedures should flow, the result is mass chaos and confusion.

Statistically, most contractors get burned out at this stage and decide that further growth is not for them. Many of them run successful shops at this level, but that's not the issue. The issue is that most will decide at this point that this is as large as they want to get and won't go on. You will not be able to grow your sales very much with this type of dealer. He may be loyal to you, and he may buy $200,000 or so a year from you—certainly solid, good business that should not be thrown away! But he is not the kind of dealer who can take you to new heights of sales.

At this stage, the owner must think about a number of scary issues as he contemplates growing some more:

1. Fear of losing all that has been accomplished so far
2. Fear that nobody else can do it quite the way he can ("nobody does it better...")
3. Must hire a good service manager or installation manager, neither of which are easy to find these days
4. He must stop running service or installation himself (which he enjoys) and focus on

8 A factorial is a number times itself, times itself less one, times itself less two, and so on down to one. For instance, 6 factorial is equal to 6 x 5 x 4 x 3 x 2 x 1 or 720. For a five person company, the number of lines of communication are four factorial (24); for a six person company, they rise to 120; for a seven person company, they become 720, as you just saw. For a twelve person company, there are a dizzying 479 million ways people can communicate!

the part of the business he decides to keep direct control of

5. He finds himself spending more and more time hiring, training, and supervising people than he did installing and fixing things; he is usually not comfortable doing this and often resents it

Notice how much of this list is purely psychological.

To circumnavigate these issues, he may try these approaches:

- Talk a lot to wife, friends, suppliers, accountant, bookkeeper, and maybe even the TM
- Promote lead service tech to service manager (often a mistake!)
- May offer new manager(s) a chance to buy into business (few have heard of "phantom stock"—see page 141
- Departmentalizes the company into "installation" and "service"
- Owner shifts more effort toward selling than installing and servicing

What can you as a TM do to help the House of Blunders become stable and grow to the next level?

Perhaps the most important thing you can do is *help this dealer install systems* in the business—routines for doing repetitive tasks that make things go smoother with fewer errors and less time.

Provide advice, information, guidance and resources on business management, including human resource issues and financial acumen. Find good schools and bring them to your distributor, then get your dealer to attend them (and go with him!).

Show him how to bid jobs intelligently and how to set a profitable labor rate.

Help him find an accounting software package and, later, a service dispatching system.

Be a silent partner; be there for him, an available ear, a sounding board.

Granted, some of the barriers to growth at this point become financial—the increase in overhead due to adding management and their supporting assets is substantial. But it is not the addition of overhead that usually chokes the dealer at this point—it is the psychological soup that is about to boil over on his stove.

The Thunder Machine

If the dealer successfully resolves his growth issues in the House of Blunders, he can move on to become a Thunder Machine—a power house business with huge sales and (for you) massive purchases. This dealer is the 1200 pound gorilla. The king of the hill.

Up to this point, the focus of the owner was more or less technical—how to sell jobs and get them installed and serviced; finding good installers and good service techs; getting a good dispatching system worked out, and so on.

At this point, however, the emphasis begins to shift toward marketing—making the phone ring. Because this is such a radical sea change for so many technocrat dealers, it is a change few successfully make. But those who do—they can dominate their markets in unbelievable ways!

It is also important to realize that up to this point, the dealer may have looked to you as a source of wisdom and advice for growing his business. At this level, he can now afford to hire any brains he needs to solve those sticky issues. What he needs now, more than ever, is a person he can confide in and lean on for difficult emotional issues that running a business of this size can create. He needs less of your laptop computer and engineering skill and more of your heart and ears.

So what can you do to help him?

Strengthen the relationship. At this level more than any other, it is not about boxes and BTUs as much as it is about feelings and how to cope with them and still grow a successful business. You still need to be able to handle the hard technical issues, but you also need to be adept at working with your dealer on a relational level. This does not necessarily mean you have to play golf every weekend (although it might!), but it does mean that you spend a significant amount of time talking about non-technical issues too.

***Earn** your right to be a sound and sage advisor.* Do this by providing solid and practical advice and solutions, and by keeping confidential information confidential. The first time you blab a secret a dealer entrusts to you is the last time you will have a significant conversation with that dealer.

Become a more active and visible partner. Offer to get involved with such things as manager training, or helping do interviews for key employee positions. If the dealer asks you to get involved in mediating a dispute, weigh your decision carefully. Sometimes this can be a great way to build a partner mentality, but if done the wrong way, you can also disembowel yourself before your dealer's eyes. Generally, you will need to come in on the dealer's side if you expect to develop trust and an alliance, and if you cannot accept the dealer's position, graciously ask that he not bring you in as an arbitrator.

Bring marketing savvy and programs to the party. At some point in their development, every Tier One TM spends effort and time to learn some of the finer points of marketing and advertising. Get to know some good marketing firms in the area (perhaps your distributorship works with a good marketing house; if so, try to connect your dealer and that firm directly). Strive to bring marketing programs to the Thunder Machine that are not the cut-and-dried one-size-fits-all programs most factories and distributors push out the door. A factory program for a spring or fall promotion may be good and solid for the typical dealer, but it won't do enough for the Thunder Machine. If your distributorship has a marketing person (or even a department) consider bringing that person (or department) out to the Thunder Machine's office to help plan marketing programs, and be willing as a TM to leverage such service and perhaps a more-than-normal co-op allowance for changes in sales mix, development of new business segments, or other areas where you think the Thunder Machine could grow effectively. (I know of some TMs who actually enter into contracts with their best dealers. These contracts spell out that when the dealer advertises the top tier products, he gets 75% co-op funds from the distributor, not the normal 50%. He also can earn two or three times the fund accrual rate on top tier purchases. For example, if the standard dealer earns 1.5% of the purchase price of top tier products towards a 50-50 co-op advertising bank, the Thunder Machine might earn 5% to 7% funds on a 75-25 bank. You will be amazed how fast a dealer will shift his mix when this sort of carrot is dangled in front of him, especially if that marketing fund can be applied to non-standard venues like direct mail or telemarketing.)

One final word of advice: this is your most important account. Protect it at all costs. Guard it from incursions by competitors. Every brand in the area will be drooling over this kind of dealer and will be mounting serious and ongoing efforts to convert it. A solid relationship is as valuable here as three feet of solid armor plate!

The Sunset Years: The Plunder of the Village

At some point, the dealer will decide to exit the trade and retire. When he does this depends on his personal ambitions and how much he has amassed over the years in savings. Every dealer eventually will leave the trade, either by retirement, or death.

When a Thunder Machine leaves, it can be a time of Plunder of the Village. The owner has built an empire (it might be a small empire, but it is still an empire) and rightfully feels he has a right to a good deal when he exits. This deal may take on the form of Plunder to an outsider, but I normally don't have a quarrel with a dealer who wants to cash out well (unless his price is just totally unreasonable, but that rarely happens).

A dealer needs to plan his exit strategy at least five years before he walks off into the sunset. That is because this is about how long it takes to formally (and safely) prepare the financial transition of ownership and build a funding method for the new owners (usually the current employees or its present key managers), as well as prepare the company and its customer base for the changes that will occur. The process that a dealer must go through is too complex to go into here. I always suggest that when a Thunder Machine is ready to plan the retirement strategy that they hire a certified transition specialist. This may cost $50,000 or more, but usually a good transition specialist can more than recoup their fees by the tax savings and selling price they help the owner realize. Some good sources to help you find such specialists would include the following:

The Institute of Business Appraisers
P.O. Box 17410
Plantation, FL 33318
Phone: 954-584-1144
Internet: www.go-iba.org

The American Society of Appraisers
555 Herndon Parkway, Suite 125
Herndon, VA 20170
Phone: 703-478-2228
Internet: www.apo.com

The Appraisal Foundation
1155 15th Street NW
Suite 111
Washington, DC 20005
Phone: 202-347-7722
Internet: www.appraisalfoundation.org

All of the above are professional organizations that can refer you or your dealer to competent transition specialists in the area.

There are basically two paths before you when a dealer chooses to leave the trade and retire. Either the business will close when he leaves, or it will continue under new ownership. If it closes, you have no choice but to find new businesses to replace the business you are going to lose. But if the business will continue, you should try to work with the new owners as closely as you did with the original one.

Sometimes, they won't want that relationship and will, in fact, seek new relationships after the boss retires. They may change brands or pick up a second (or third, or fourth) line. Work with it as best you can and if you find your share of wallet falling off and the new owners don't want to change that trend, find some new dealers in the area to pick up the slack.

This chart summarizes some of the issues a dealer will face as it grows.

Growth Curve Summary Matrix

Category	The One-Man Wonder	House of Blunder	Thunder Machine
Challenges	Sell enough to go it full time; time management	Sell enough to keep several folks employed; offset new overhead; division of labor; control of labor; HR problems	Finding competent managers; learning how to lead; develop systems/procedures; control/monitoring systems, maintain company culture
Time use	Servicing; pickup up stuff; bidding jobs	Servicing; supervision; selling/bidding; HR issues	Supervision; selling; meetings with professional services (acct, legal, etc); vision
Assets/ Expenses	Hand tools; some parts; personal vehicle; answering machine	One or more new vehicles; rent; parts for service trucks; support salaries; office equip; radios/cell phones/pagers	Ten or more vehicles; $100K or more inventory; office furniture/equipment; good benefits; computer; satellite offices?
Sales	Friends, referrals; based on price, price, price	May still be based on price; Yellow Pages; owner does all selling.	Owner and full-time sales staff; sales rep sells replacements; advertising program; no longer price-based; lead generation vital
Service	Owner does, cash basis	Handled by another person; owner handles toughies; service is still major piece of business	Service agreements; sharp price increase; specializing in res/comm; service techs internally grown
Installation	Mostly AO&R; avoid sheet metal; low prices; 10-30 units a year	20-50 units a year and up; mostly AO&R; sheet metal still avoided	50-100+ units a year; full-time installers and foreman; sheet metal shop; next-day installation capability
Administration	Business checking acct; quarterly income tax; licensed; open account; family employees	Payroll + withholdings; time cards; invoices; A/P, A/R	Job costing; inventory control; insurance; employee handbooks; business plan; one brand tends to be favored; customer files

What a Dealer Expects From His or Her Territory Manager

While what I am about to say may not be true of every dealer out there, it is true of enough of them to warrant your consideration.

Dealers usually have expectations of their territory managers, and if you don't meet them, you will let them down and they will not value their relationship with you as much as you may want them to. But when you meet or exceed their expectations, you are in a good position to earn their respect and trust, and with that, the lion's share of their business!

So what does a typical good dealer expect from his or her territory manager?

- *They expect you to build a long-term relationship*. They expect (and request) of you consistent face-to-face time and regularly-scheduled visits (even though they may ask you to back off during the busy summer season). They expect you to be a part of *their* team (and are often willing, when they sense this in you, to be a part of yours as well). (In fact, one of the highest honors a Tier One TM can earn is to hear one of his dealers tell his manager, "Who does Tom work for, anyway? You or me? He's always in my corner, fighting like a trooper for me!")

  They expect you to give them your undivided attention and to respond quickly to them when they need you. (So leave your cell phone in the car.)

  They expect you to bear a positive attitude and be a contagious carrier of courage and confidence. (Like it or not, you are the thermostat for your entire territory. If you get down, your dealers will follow you into that pit and wallow with you in it. But if you are up and energized, they'll probably catch what you've got! Dealers reflect what you are, not what you say. If you have the flu when you visit a dealer but talk about chicken pox, the dealer will catch the flu from you, not the chicken pox! Remember: you are a leader of leaders, and your attitude can make or break your territory.)

- *They expect you to assist them in business planning*. Not all of them will do this, of course, but many of them will. And they will expect you to assist them not only with sales forecasts and budgets, but also with marketing and advertising planning and general business growth and development. When a dealer asks for your assistance in developing a plan for his business, he is telling you that he sees professionalism in you.

- *They expect you to have your goods in stock and in their hands in short time frames*. They may not necessarily stock inventory, but they do expect your company to and to make it available to them on short notice.

- *They look to you for training and skills development*. This not only includes product training (for sales, installation and service), but also general sales skills, management skills, and financial acumen. You do not have to necessarily provide all this training to them personally, but you do need to make it available to them, and they usually expect you to be present with them when they go through it.

- *They expect your full and total support, twenty-four hours a day, seven days a week*. Whether it is in the area of product application, engineering support and analysis, or business coaching, they will often need knowledge they do not themselves possess, and if you can bring it to them (either yourself or through a resource you engage for their use), they will give you more of their heart (and wallet). And they also expect you to be up-to-date on technology and your brand's products and programs.

A territory manager who can provide that level of support usually enjoys a huge share of the dealer's wallet and long-lasting and powerful friendships besides! (To this day, I still number among my dearest friends dealers I called upon thirty years ago! And many of them feel the same way toward me.)

Review Questions for Chapter 8

1. The total number of HVAC shops (and plumbing shops who do HVAC work) is estimated to currently be about

A) 87,500

B) 50,000

C) 61,000

D) 71,000

E) none of the above

Answer: _______

2. The biggest production of sales in the HVAC trade comes from the companies that employ

A) 1-4 people

B) 5-9 people

C) 10-19 people

D) 20-49 people

E) 50-99 people

Answer: _______

3. The largest number of HVAC shops can be found in which size class?

A) 1-4 people

B) 5-9 people

C) 10-19 people

D) 20-49 people

E) 50-99 people

Answer: _______

4. Carolyn is a TM with several accounts in her portfolio. Of them, eight are in the 1-4 man size class. She has identified three of them who want to grow and probably have the ability to grow, based on assessments and an analysis of each company's capital. If these three dealers can grow to the 10-19 man shop size class over the next three years, how much in extra sales per year could Carolyn figure would come her way?

A) about $1.2 million more

B) about $670,000 more

C) about $104,600 more

D) about $565,000 more

E) none of these

Answer: _______

5. Not all 1-4 man shops can successfully grow to the 5-9 man size class (nor do all want to grow). What is the approximate rate of attrition among dealers who migrate from the 1-4 man class to the 5-9 man class?

A) 44%

B) 34%

C) 58%

D) 77%

E) none of the above

Answer: _______

6. Melvin is a dealer doing about $500,000 a year in sales (buying $200,000 a year from his TM). Melvin's TM gave him the entrepreneurial aptitude survey and Melvin scored nine out of eleven on it. The TM then reviewed with Melvin the firm's capitalization and found out that Melvin's working capital is $36,000 and his fixed assets are $18,500. Based on this, is Melvin a good candidate to grow his business over the next two years?

A) Yes

B) No

Answer: _______

Now, explain your answer:

7. Most barriers to growth show up as overhead chunks that suddenly appear on the income statement. The real cause, however, for most dealer growth problems is

A) finding the right people

B) psychological issues—fear, anxiety, loss of control, ability to work with people

C) job pricing

D) all of the above

E) none of the above

Answer: _______

Note on "Phantom Stock"

(Third bullet point on page 131)

The "phantom stock" of the third bullet point is an interesting way a corporation can keep a good employee hooked to the business. Rather than actually sell or give stock to a key employee (and thus dilute ownership and create possible problems when it comes time for the owner to sell the company to successors), the owner draws up a contract with the key employee stating that as the value of the company increases (based on a clearly defined valuation method, conducted by an outside firm on an annual basis), a special account will be established for the key person and funded on the basis of some percentage of company value increase. Usually a vesting schedule is spelled out and a payout provision is also included. As an example, if Joe Smart wanted to keep Bill Technowiz as his service manager (and future owner?), Joe could offer Bill phantom stock. He does not actually sell Bill any stock (so Bill cannot in turn sell it or deed it to someone else later), but he tells Bill that an account will be established for him that will put 10% of the increase in the company value every year. Bill will be vested in the account at the rate of 1/7 per year and be fully vested in seven years (meaning all the money in the account from that time forward is his). Upon retirement or voluntary termination, Bill can have his money as ten equal annual checks, based on the value of the account at the time of termination of employment. Joe can also stipulate that should Bill decease before retirement or before all his funds have been paid that all or part of the balance will be paid to his beneficiary on some sort of payout schedule. Phantom stock is a great way to keep a good person on the payroll, and since the size of the account grows with company value, the key person will be motivated to make decisions that add to the company value, not that are just convenient for him. I have heard of cases where a service manager with a phantom stock plan elected to drive his pickup truck another year or two rather than get a brand new one, since he saw the impact it could have on his phantom stock plan. As long as the present truck is in good condition and safe to drive, there is nothing wrong with such frugality!

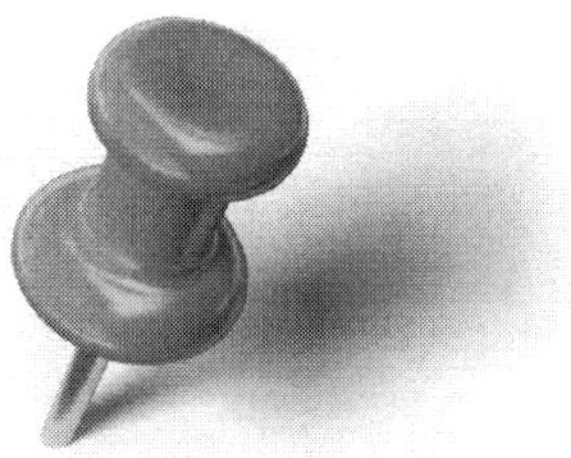

Chapter 9: Hey, It's a Business! (Or, Walk a Mile in Their Boots)

The most successful territory managers I know of are also good students of the HVAC business. And what I mean is that they understand the **business** of HVAC contracting, not just the product lines or how to do a load calculation or design a duct system.

They Stumbled Into It

As described in Chapter 8, most contractors don't start out going to a special school for contractors, getting a degree, and then starting a business. They stumble into it much like Michael Gerber describes in his classic, *The E Myth*. As a result, they tend to be practical geniuses when it comes to sizing a system, designing ductwork, or fixing broken equipment. But they have no idea how to charge properly for these services or how to run a business that provides them. That's where they usually turn to their supplier (and particularly their territory manager) for the help in getting the business savvy they need.

I have known TMs who look down on their dealers for their lack of business skills. That's a big mistake! If that is true of you, change that attitude fast or find another line of work, because you'll never be a Tier One TM if you feel that way about your dealers (even *some* of your dealers). These men and women have taken a risk you are not willing to take yourself, and are putting everything on the line—their fortunes (what they have of them), their names, and their sacred honor to provide a good service to their community and provide food and shelter for the dependants of the people who work there. They deserve our respect and admiration for that!

A research poll conducted in 2007 by Clear Seas Research[9] revealed some surprising things about what a contractor looks for when he decides what brand(s) he wants to represent. Number one on the list (based on 324 responses) was product **reliability**. That is good news if you represent a brand with a strong reputation for reliability. Second on the list was product **qual-**

9 See www.clearseasresearch.com June, 2007.

ity. Next came product **availability**. These three were the overall winners by a large margin. Competitive (not necessarily low) **pricing** came in fourth. Only slightly behind pricing was the **relationship** with the TM. Manufacturer and distributor training came in surprisingly low on the survey. (However, these issues tend to assume more importance as a dealership grows.)

The Basics of This Business

Over the years, I have heard many experts in this field talk about what is needed to be successful in this trade, and all of them say essentially the same things, just in different ways. So I will add my ideas to the hopper and see what drops out!

There are three basic pillars that must support any successful HVAC business. As any eighth grade geometry student can tell you, three points define a plane. (Think of a plane as a surface, like the ground). If the three points are on the same level, the plane will be level. If we are talking about ground, the ground will be level. It will be easier to build on such ground than if it sloped steeply, such as a mountain side.

If a dealer has these three pillars in roughly equal strength, he is fortunate, and if they are large enough pillars, he is a rare specimen. Most dealers don't have all three pillars in the same strength, or in enough quantity to grow successfully (which is why most dealers don't grow and why turnover is so staggeringly high in this trade).

Here are the three pillars every HVAC business is built on:

- ★ The **psychological makeup** of the owner
- ★ The **capital** base for the operation
- ★ Efficient **systems** to bring the first two together

We will spend the rest of this chapter seeing what goes into each of these pillars so you can give wise counsel to your dealers as they grow.

The Psychological Makeup of the Dealer

This is the pillar where a great business is made or broken. The dealer must have the right psychological chemistry to make it possible to create a growing, thriving, successful business. There is not a whole lot you can do about this because most adults are more or less set in their psychological cement by the time you come along. People (especially adults) don't usually change much, if at all, unless there are powerful reasons to do so. So lesson 1: *If your dealer lacks a full bag of psychological marbles, don't expect him to build an HVAC empire to rival Microsoft.*

You'll have to live with it, the best you can.

So what do you look for in a dealer to find evidence of this pillar?

We have already talked about what is probably the most important element overall—the **entrepreneurial drive** of the dealer. (See Chapter 8.) If a dealer does not have the fire in his belly to build a powerful and successful company, odds are he won't be able to do it. Building a successful company is hard work; a lot harder than those who have never done it before realize. And if the fire in the belly is only a smoldering ember or a glowing coal from a moment of euphoric inspiration, it won't go far toward making enough steam to turn the turbines.

Another basic ingredient is the **basic intelligence** of the dealer. How smart is she? Does she have a good mind and can she make good decisions with the facts in a short time? Can she solve problems? Can she bring unlinked things together in new ways to create new solutions and new products or services? Does she communicate well, verbally and in writing? Does she have a strong presence in front of other people, or does she come across as weak, confused, or withdrawn? Again, this is more or less set by the time you get the dealer, so you get what you get. You can't do much to change it. If the dealer is already reasonably intelligent and has the ability to learn, seminars and workshops will help them grow even more. If they don't, they may attend, but probably won't get much out of the experience, and certainly will make few (if any) changes based on the things they learn.

People skills is another key trait to look for. How good are they with people? How do their employees feel about them? How do *you* feel around them? Are you comfortable? Fearful? Apprehensive? Do you feel you can trust them? Do they center everything around themselves? Or do they make *you* feel like the most important person on earth? A successful business is the way it is in part because the people who work there (especially the top dog) have good people skills. Business is more relationship-oriented than most people realize, and those who are good at forming and maintaining good relationships have an edge!

Perhaps you've seen this statistic about customers somewhere:

3% move away giving no reasons

5% develop other supplier relationships

9% leave for competitive reasons

14% are dissatisfied with the product

68% quit because of an attitude of indifference toward the customer by the owner, manager, or some employee

I do not know the source of this statistic, but I have seen it for years and believe it is probably reasonably accurate. Even if it is off a little, it is still a stunning thought, isn't it? To think that over 2/3 of the customers in America switch suppliers because they don't feel they were treated right, right should grab our attention! A boss with good people skills will tend to build a company made of other people with good people skills too and thereby avoid this awful fate.

We'll have more to say about the psychological element in Chapter 23. But this gives us enough for the present to strengthen your skills as a territory manager.

The Capital Base of Operations

We covered this briefly in Chapter 8, where we concluded that most successful HVAC firms have working capital equal to about 10% of next year's sales and fixed assets of about 5% of next year's sales.

Let's dig deeper into this rule of thumb to see what else might be implied.

Not only does the capital base include the 15% of sales rule of thumb just quoted—it also includes adequate lines of credit with banks and suppliers. A line of credit can be defined as "an arrangement in which a bankor vendorextends a specified amount of unsecured creditto a specified borrower for a specified time period. (Also called credit line.)[10]" The key here is the use of the term "unsecured." Traditional loans a business might obtain are secured—the business must pledge some type of asset (a house, cars, investments, accounts receivable, inventory, sons or daughters) to the creditor to obtain the loan. If the business defaults, the creditor assumes title to the pledged collateral and may liquidate it to recover some of the defaulted loan.

A line of credit is different. It is more of a trust arrangement between a creditor and the business. Security for the line of credit is not required; a good relationship with the creditor ***is***. When a dealer is first starting up his business, he may not be known well by any bank in the

10 Source: www.investorwords.com/2830/line_of_credit.html, July 9, 2007.

area, so obtaining a bank line of credit may be difficult (unless the principal is already well-known). Usually, a fledgling HVAC firm must rely on suppliers for an initial line of credit. Then, as the business grows and the owner establishes a solid payment history, banks will be more likely to look favorably on the business when the owner comes in to establish a line of credit.

How big a line of credit does an HVAC business need? When it first gets started and relies on suppliers for the line, it may be based purely on what the territory manager projects the dealer will buy, tempered by the conservative judgment (in most cases) of the distributor's credit manager. The result is that usually, the line of credit is not adequate, or if it is, the dealer soon outgrows it.

Suppose, for instance, that as a TM, you want to set up a new account, Jones Heating. You bring your paperwork to the credit manager and say that Jones buys $100,000 a year from suppliers and will probably give you about $60,000 first year out. Your credit manager may then decide to allow Jones up to 60 days in the line of credit. Since 60 days is 1/6 of a year (in banking terms), the credit manager may extend to Jones 1/6 of the $60,000, or a line of credit for $10,000.

So Jones starts buying your stuff and it starts off well. But then Jones grows, or he likes your stuff so he buys more and more of it, soon buying all of his $100,000 from you. Now his $10,000 line of credit is only 1/10 of the year, not 1/6, and so he finds he must pay his bills faster and faster or his account starts getting into the 31-60 day accounts payable column (always a sign that makes credit managers fidgety), and maybe someday even hitting the 61+ day column (at which point klaxons sound, red strobe lights flash throughout the building, and the credit manager can be heard screaming over the loudspeaker, "COD, COD! Prepare account for COD!")

My advice to dealers is to *secure lines of credit that can get them through their slowest three months of cash flow*. Notice how I worded that—their **three slowest months of cash flow**, not sales. Why cash flow and not sales? Because between the sale and the collection of cash is usually a gap of time. Even for shops who do almost all their work on a COD basis (for instance, service, or add-on and replacement work), there will be times when a customer will request and receive terms or just not pay the bill on time. And it is cash that is used to pay bills as they come due, not sales. (If you don't think so, see if you can deposit your sales report into your checking account next month…)

So what are a dealer's slowest three months of cash flow? It will vary from dealer to dealer, but for most dealers who have a heavy summer spike in business, it will be—ready for this?

July, August and September! The three biggest months of the year in sales, and the three slowest for cash flow! (Some dealers who live in a warmer climate may see June, July and August.)

For instance, Jones (from above) may have 60% of his business in June, July and August—some $60,000 in purchases, resulting in sales of at least $180,000. At Jones' shop, it is elbows and buttocks as crews race frantically from job to job and often work overtime. Yet Jones' line of credit is only $10,000—enough to fund only 1/6 of this work, or about two plus weeks! Some of the cash comes in the day the service call is run, or the day the installers finish the job (because Jones uses "due upon completion" contracts), but some folks either won't pay when the job is done, or a commercial service account must have the bill sent to the home office (always nine states away), and so on. It's not an easy exercise to do, but the cash coming in versus the cash going out for the crunch season can be computed with a fairly high degree of accuracy, but it takes a complex spreadsheet to do it. Basically, the line of credit should cover the worst case net cash flow gaps for the crunch season.

Getting back to Jones, if Jones buys $60,000 of equipment and material during the crunch, he is probably also spending about $30,000 to $40,000 on labor. He also has ongoing expenses, such as rent, advertising, Yellow Pages, fuel, etc. Jones' total cash outgo for the crunch may amount to something like $120,000 or more. Cash coming in during that same time may come to only $80,000. So Jones needs lines of credit totaling at least $40,000 (the difference between income and outgo) to stay current with suppliers and avoid COD conditions, and still have enough cash on hand to run the business day to day, and then pay off the short term debt with creditors after the crunch is over and the cash comes in faster than Jones can spend it.

A contractor also needs a source of **inventory financing**. This is one thing that has changed a lot since my days as a TM, and I find current practice to not necessarily be in the best interests of the dealer. Today's distributors have gotten pretty good at maintaining deep stocking levels of key products, and most now have their own delivery fleet (or pay for freight on certain minimum size orders), so dealer stocking requirements are not as critical today as they were in the past. Maintaining a local stock of key inventory in-house is good practice for a dealer even when he is in the same city as a well-stocked distributor. And if you can't prove that to a dealer, you need to be able to.

Is stocking good for a dealer?

That depends. The first step to see if the dealer has adequate inventory levels is to compute two simple ratios and then compute a ratio of these two ratios.

Begin by computing the dealer's ***current ratio***. Go to his last three year-end balance sheets and find the total *current assets* on each one. Then find the total *current liabilities*. Divide each current asset figure by its corresponding current liability figure. Average the three results. This is his *current ratio*.

As a rule, it should be at least 1.50, and strong firms run 2.0 and higher.

The next step is to find the total *inventory* on each of those three balance sheets. Subtract it from each corresponding *current asset* figure, and then divide those results by their corresponding *current liabilities*. Average the six results. This is the dealer's ***quick ratio***.

It should be at least 0.67, and strong firms run 1.50 and up.

The third step is to divide the average current ratio by the average quick ratio. The result should lie *between 1.50 and 2.00*—no higher, no lower.[11] If the ratio is above 2.00, it is probably because the dealer has too *much* inventory. If it is below 1.50, it is probably because he doesn't have *enough* inventory.

If a dealer's ratio of ratios is below 1.50, he should check with his sales staff to see if they are losing a significant number of sales (significant being 10% or more of his leads) due to stock-outs. If they do, he could stand to bring in more inventory (based, of course, on the season and his market's usual product mix).

If his ratio is below 1.50 and he is *not* losing a significant amount of sales, he may be safe provided his distributor is well-stocked and close enough to get his orders to him within twenty-four hours.

EXAMPLE: *Bill's last three fiscal year-end balance sheets show current assets, current liabilities, and inventory as follow:*

Category	200z	200y	200x
Current Assets	$325,700	$298,500	$260,100
Current Liabilities	$164,500	$158,700	$148,200
Inventory	$74,200	$66,300	$89,200

11 For the typical contractor, this represents between six and eight inventory turns per year, a target most experts believe is healthy.

Bill finds that his ratios are as follow:

Ratio	200z	200y	200x
Current	1.98	1.88	1.76
Quick	1.53	1.46	1.15
Cur to Quick	1.29	1.29	1.53

From this, we see that Bill is getting financially stronger (200z being the latest year) and that his ratios, which have always been in a decent range, are getting stronger.

But in my opinion, nothing beats having a badly needed unit in stock the day the customer needs it. If a customer has to wait a day or two while the dealer brings the unit in from the supplier, the customer has time to shop and get other bids and, maybe, buy from someone else—who *does* have the unit in stock!

A Common Misconception

A dealer's ratios will float around if he does stock orders (either pre-season or monthly) with a bank or a manufacturer's financing services. Many contractors are under the mistaken notion that a financed order does not go on their balance sheets. "After all," they say, "it's not mine until I pay the auditor for it." Not so! The financial house only owns the paper instrument on the inventory. *The dealer* owns the title to the inventory. Most stock orders are shipped "FOB Shipping Point." This indicates the point at which the title to the merchandise changes hands (in this case, the shipping point, or the distributor's dock). It has nothing to do with free freight.

The invoice value of the shipment goes on the dealer's balance sheet under inventory, with the offsetting liability being Floor Plan Payable. (This is under current liabilities.) Even though these entries don't change the balance of the balance sheet, they do change the ratios! Consider this example of a balance sheet with and without a floor plan on it:

Without Inventory On The Books

Cash	$30,000	Accounts Payable	$20,000
Accts Receivable	$80,000	Notes Payable	$10,000
Inventory	$30,000	Current Liabilities	$30,000
Current Assets	$140,000	Long Term Liabilities	$30,000
Fixed Assets	$30,000	Equity	$110,000
Total Assets	$170,000	Total Liab. and Equity	$170,000

With Inventory On The Book ($50,000 Stock Order)

Cash	$30,000	Accts Payable	$20,000
Accts Receivable	$80,000	Accts Payable–Inventory	$50,000
Inventory	$80,000	Notes Payable	$10,000
Current Assets	$190,000	Current Liabilities	$80,000
Fixed Assets	$30,000	Long Term Liabilities	$30,000
		Equity	$110,000
Total Assets	$220,000	Total Liab. and Equity	$220,000

The Ratios

	Current	Quick	Current to Quick
Without Floor Plan	4.67	3.67	1.27
With Floor Plan	2.38	1.38	1.72

As you can see, the balance sheet still balances (and we did not touch equity) but the ratios are much different!

How Much to Order?

If floor planning can save a dealer money, how does he know how much to order and when?

The accounting programs used by most distributors allow them to generate reports that show exactly *what* equipment a dealer purchased last year, *how much* of it he bought, and exactly *when* he bought it. You can review this report with your dealer and help him set realistic order quantities and trigger dates.

When the dealer adds the other benefits your company may provide for large pre-season orders (things like free freight, bonus incentive trip points, bonus advertising co-op, free or deeply discounted electronic air cleaners and humidifiers, and credit on unsold floor-plan *current* inventory that was returned if an equal value of product for the upcoming season was purchased on floor plan and so on), using financing for pre-season orders becomes a no-brainer.

The Confusion of the UCC-1

Some distributors (but surprisingly not all) require dealers who buy monthly stocking plans to fill out a UCC-1 form. *Those who don't use this form may be at risk.* And dealers often do not understand what it is for and are reluctant to sign one if it is required.

UCC-1 stands for Uniform Commercial Code Form 1. It is a security agreement used to place liens against specified business property. Many dealers think it gives the distributor rights to seize a dealer's personal property if an obligation is not met. That is *not* the case.

"The Uniform Commercial Code is one of the greatest works of jurisprudence of the century.[12]"

The full UCC is very complex and too technical to discuss here. Suffice it to say that the main purpose of the UCC-1 is to protect *creditors* for specified assets for a specified period. For instance, when I had my dealers sign UCC-1 forms, I had to help them get around the misconception that the form gave our company rights to their homes, boats, cars, moonshine stills and any other assets they owned. The form specifically spells out what the dealer is responsible for ("monthly stock orders of HVAC equipment" or "pre-season order of HVAC equipment"), and for what period of time. Once signed, the credit manager files a copy with the county court which is in the dealer's county of residence.

All the UCC-1 form does that is important to know for now is that in the event a dealer goes bankrupt, the distributor is one of the protected creditors in the settlement. You may have heard of cases in the news where a large corporation filed for bankruptcy and the article mentions how protected creditors had to approve the plan filed with the court. A protected creditor is one who has legal protection, like a UCC-1 on file with the local court. In the case of a bankruptcy,

12 Source: www.supremelaw.org/ref/ucc/ucc1.htm, July 9, 2007.

if it comes to liquidation, the court will assign proceeds from the liquidation to the protected creditors first. Any money that is left over after paying them off goes into the unprotected creditors pot and gets distributed to creditors who file for a piece of the decimated pie. (But recent court rulings involving the Federal Government's bailout of large manufacturers have cast a shadow on the validity of secured creditor law.) However, the 2008-2009 down-turn in the U.S. economy had many credit sources becoming very reluctant to make loans, even to people who before the down-turn would have been considered safe credit risks.

The Final Component of Capital

The final component of the dealer's capital pillar is that he must have a **source of retail sales financing**. Whether it is to help a homeowner buy a new system, or a commercial client install a new rooftop unit, a successful contractor will have sources of financing for all markets he works in. Most manufacturers today offer consumer financing plans of various kinds, and some of the larger ones offer commercial programs as well.

It doesn't matter what your dealer personally thinks of financing plans. (He may have been stung by one in the past, or thinks that their interest rates are too high.) The fact is, consumers use them all the time, and most don't care a nickel about the rate, as long as they can swing the monthly payments.[13] Most consumers don't have $10,000 to $20,000 sitting in a bank doing nothing, money they can apply to a new deluxe system when theirs goes caput! (They may have that much in savings, but it may be tied up in a CD that has stiff penalties for early withdrawal, and so on.) Dealers who don't offer their customers financing on every sale, and mention it *early* in the sales call, are depriving their customers of a vital service!

The Systems Pillar

This is the broadest-based pillar of all, and has the most components in it. But don't think it is the most important. All three of the base pillars are *equally* important, regardless of the number of their components.

The first thing to consider in a solid systems pillar is not really a system at all, but rather how it supports all the other systems—this would be **the physical plant** of the dealership.

Where is her shop located? Is it visible to passers-by? Is it close to her main theaters of work? Is it close to shipping routes? Does it have a show room with working equipment in it?

13 This, too, is changing with the new realities of the damaged American Economy. More and more consumers *are* looking at interest rates and finance charges, and fewer are qualifying for finance now.

Is there ample parking? Is the building well-identified, with lighted signage at night? Is it neat and clean? Is there room for expansion?

One of the most important things to look for is a physical trait that will feed directly into the first systems component we will look at in a moment. I advise you to count the **number of overhead doors and loading docks** the dealer has.

Why? Because if she has only one loading dock and overhead door, she will bottleneck her crews every day as they wait for their turn to load up and head out. Which leads us to our first true system component:

This business is all about the successful use of labor.

I have taught contractor financial and management courses for over twenty-five years and I have developed a little slogan over that time to drive this point home. Here it is:

Labor brings in the DOUGH
but Management makes it GO.

The *only time* an HVAC shop can make any money is when it has mechanics on someone's property doing work that adds value to that property. This could be in the form of installing new equipment and/or accessories, or doing a service call. In either case, the customer is exchanging an agreed upon amount of money for a specified product or service.

If a dealer's installers or service techs cannot work that day—say, due to inclement weather, or a broken vehicle, the dealer cannot bill out any time or services for that employee for that time. Also, customers don't pay for time the mechanics are not doing work on their property, so often things like a trip to the supply house have to be eaten by the dealer.

So it is to a dealer's best interests (and profit) to keep her crews as busy as possible *on customer property* doing value-adding work. Anything that gets in the way of that—*anything*—robs the dealer of sales and profits.

But management makes it GO. If a dealer does not make a profit (or enough profit) from her sales, who is to blame? She can't blame the weather. Every dealer in that area had the same weather she did, and some of them made fairly good (maybe outstanding) profits that year. She can't blame the competition—everyone in her area has the same competition, and some did well that year. And she sure can't blame her help (because she hired them and oversees them). She can only blame herself and her inefficient systems.

So do you see now why a lack of overhead doors can drain some life out of a dealership? Suppose Sally has four installation crews (two men each), with an average hourly wage of $22 per man. Each day, each crew must load its own trucks for the day's work. Since she only has one overhead door and bay, only one crew at a time can load the trucks. Suppose the average crew takes 20 minutes to pull all its material and load it on the truck. That's 4 x 20 minutes = 80 minutes of time shot due to loading alone. At two men per crew, that's 80 x 2 = 160 minutes of time lost a day, or 2.67 hours a day, at $22 per hour. Sally is throwing away almost $60 per day on wasted time. If we add benefits, it's closer to $80 per day. And if we take into account that she could have *sold* that time to a cash customer, it could come to around $200 a day she is pouring down the drain. At 260 working days a year, that only amounts to $52,000!

How much would a second overhead door cost to install? Probably not $26,000 (which would cut her losses in half).

Better yet, what if she paid some part-time worker (say, a retiree or a young apprentice) to pull the material and load it onto the trucks before 7:00 a.m.? She pays the part-timer maybe $15 an hour. She saves at least $40 a day, plus she can sell the extra crew time now, so she might save around $160 a day—times 260 days, some $41,000 in savings.

You see, it's just one little idea. Another overhead door. Or a part-time loader. Not much.

Other systems could include how jobs are processed (from initial customer call through to sales call form, to sales report, to contract, to warehouse release forms, to job costing and close-out); how people are dispatched to their work; how the shop is laid out; even how jobs are designed to maximize output and minimize input.

The problem is that most dealers don't sit down and consciously design systems as they grow. They just start off on Day One doing work and then repeat it on Day Two, and so on, so the work process becomes a habit. Maybe a bad habit. As the business grows, no one stops to design a process ahead of time. The job is just somehow done and how it got done gets ingrained in the company's DNA and is transmitted to the genes of the next job, and so on, becoming another habit of routine. As a result, most company processes are messy, inefficient, and costly.

More than once, on consulting visits to dealerships, I have had the owner, office staff and service manager/dispatcher sit down together and map out step by step how a service call takes place. (I use 3x5 Post-It Notes and the exercise usually covers most of an 8x10 foot wall when done!) The results are always the same—the people look at the finished product in disbelief, shake their heads, and mutter something unprintable.

We then attack the mess of lines and back-tracking arrows and clean up the process to fit into a space no larger than four feet square (using the same 3x5 Post-It Notes) and the results are always the same—smiles, hope, and optimism.

Dealers don't design processes that lead to failure. They just fail to design good processes up front.

That's where a Tier One TM shines! He or she can bring the best processes they have seen to bear and help their dealer build a cleaner, tighter ship.

The Service Element

Part of a good systems approach is to run an efficient service department, especially if the dealer is going to have a strong presence in the add-on and replacement market. Implied in that sentence is a combination of good people, good (well-stocked, efficient, reliable) vehicles, good dispatching, top shelf computerized tracking system (including GPS capability), and much more.

Service labor is not like a relay or a fan motor. If you don't use it today, you can't leave it in the parts room for later. Time does not do too well on a shelf! So first and foremost, a successful and growing company knows how to use its service labor efficiently.

Consider this: according to annual surveys by such trade associations as ACCA, SMACNA and others, members typically report *average unbillable time of up to 30% of the service tech's day*! And these tend to be the better companies in the country! Think what that means—for a typical eight hour day, the typical company is unable to bill out 2.4 hours of time. Over a year of 250 days (50 weeks, allowing for tech vacations), that amounts to 600 hours. If an average hour of service brings in $200 (in parts and labor), this means the typical shop is blowing off $120,000 in service sales *per service tech* just because they have poor control of service labor! Now if that company had five techs…

Usually poor control of service labor can be traced back to *poor dispatching practices and / or poor time ticket practices.* This is why I am an advocate of a company having a full-time service dispatcher when they hit four or more service techs. The savings in unbilled time alone will more than pay the salary of a good dispatcher, and if he or she is not busy full time with service dispatching, they can help with warranty paperwork, materials handling and other related chores.

I also strongly urge that dealers use ***daily time tickets*** for their service techs (as well as their installers, but especially the service techs). The time cards should allow service management to analyze labor use by including such labor codes as "T" for travel, "CC" for cash service call, "SA" for service agreement call, "U" for unbillable and so on. It is also very important that the techs understand that the U is not a mark against them, but against management. The dealer must explain to his or her techs that accurate reporting of time use is vital so that management can do a better job of billing out their time, so *everyone* makes more money and can look forward to a more secure future.

Better yet is a computerized dispatching system that can automatically time stamp each task as the tech radios in about his progress. When he finishes a service call, for instance, he radios that he is done. The dispatcher opens his work order on the computer and clicks the "Finished" button (or whatever the software vendor calls it) and the present ticket is closed out. The next ticket starts as soon as the dispatcher opens its work order and assigns it to the tech (usually with a mouse click). At that time, the travel clock starts automatically, and as soon as the tech gets to the next job, he radios in so the dispatcher can update the job log and so on. If the service trucks are also equipped with GPS receivers and transponders, the dispatcher can tell where the truck is and help the tech find a difficult address. (Of course, such transponders also let the owner see how fast the truck was going and where it went. This has opened a messy legal issue with worker privacy, but so far, the courts have wisely upheld the rights of a company to know what its employees are doing with its assets.)

An effective service department must also be **promoted**. The worst way to promote service is by mass media, such as newspapers, television, and radio. Many dealers use these media outlets heavily to promote service and swear by it, but I have always found that most dealers find better results with direct mail and a good referral rewards program. If service is advertised in the mass media, it would be best to promote a seasonal special (such as a pre-season tune up) or free second opinions.

Along with solid promotion, a good service department will be heavily involved in service agreements. I am often asked at what level a dealership can be considered heavily involved? I reply at about 500 agreements. Anything less than 500 means the company can handle the service agreement program without too many internal changes. At about the 500 level, internal changes must occur to handle the business; someone must oversee it closely (including renewals and billings, and scheduling). The 500 agreement point is what separates being involved from being committed. (It's like the old story about the breakfast of ham and eggs. The chicken is involved; the pig is committed.)

I recommend that a dealer not commit to service agreements that specify "pre-season inspections" but rather just say one or two annual inspections. I learned this from a dealer who learned the hard way, when he used to promote a two-inspection agreement with inspections specified for the pre-season. One year, he had an early summer and could not get to all the agreement customers before the cooling season was in full swing. Many were upset that he did not get to them before the summer got hot. After that, he changed to a two-inspections-per-year agreement, with inspections being run at his choosing. Naturally, he would try to run them as close to the season as possible (so his techs could operate the units and check them out under operating conditions), but since his agreement covered his customers for a full twelve months regardless of when the inspections were run, he had a much easier time with the new format and customers had no problem with it either.

I also suggest to dealers that on sales contracts, they include a service agreement on their top tier offerings as a standard part of the package—not as an add-in but as a built-in. With every top tier job sold, a service agreement goes with it. Then, eleven months later, the company sends out a birthday card to the unit and a renewal letter. Studies show that 85% of the customers will renew when they get a renewal letter (sometimes with a phone call too).

And if you really want to lock a customer in for life, why not combine a manufacturer five or ten-year extended warranty with ten or twenty inspections? Think of the promotional possibilities—buy our top tier unit and all you have to pay for the first ten years is electricity (or gas)!

Service agreements are also easy to promote on service calls when the firm uses a flat rate system. Flat rate systems use a standard repair price book from which the tech quotes the customer an exact price to fix the system. The customer then approves the repairs and pays for the repairs quoted plus a modest diagnostic fee (which usually includes travel charges). The better flat rate systems on the market today have a two column format. In one column is the standard repair price. The second column is the price for a service agreement customer, and it is often a substantial discount. The service tech can then show the homeowner the repairs that are needed and point to the standard price column. He can then point to the service agreement column and say that if the customer had a service agreement, they could save this much money on their repairs today. In fact, if they wanted to purchase the agreement today, the tech is authorized to use the service agreement column for the repairs. When you consider that in many cases, the discount is almost as much as the price of an agreement, it's a no brainer! Techs who get good at this method can sell up to one agreement per day (or more).

Another key for a successful service department is the *correct pricing for parts and labor.* Flat rate systems have done wonders in fixing this for most dealers, but it is still a good idea to cover the basics here so your dealers will understand why going to flat rate is good for them.

Parts pricing is a little more complex than it may at first appear. This is because the handling costs to buy a small part, like an igniter, are just as high as those to acquire a large part, like a compressor. (Handling costs are the costs of someone's wage to take the time to order the right part; the order transmission process; the receiving of the part, and placing the part in inventory.) If, let's say, the handling costs for a typical parts transaction for a dealer are $10, then the handling costs could be 50% or more of the cost of the igniter, but only 2% or so of the cost of a compressor.

Because of this, lower-cost parts should be marked up more than higher-cost parts. *As a general rule, a dealer should try to average about 65% gross margin on his parts sales.* (This means that for every dollar of sales, 65 cents is what's left after the cost of the part is taken out.) This is because service department overheads run much higher (as a percentage of sales) than installation overheads (which you'll see in Chapter 15). Even at 65% gross margin, a typical service department may only be making 10% net profit on its parts sales. (This means that of the 65 cents out of every dollar sold that is left for the company, another 55 cents comes out to pay for the service department tech wages and overhead, leaving 10 cents on the dollar for net profit on parts sales.)

All flat rate systems currently on the market understand this and mark up parts prices to allow for this. Those who price their parts on their own need to be aware of it and should use some form of graduated markup schedule.

Here are two typical markup schedules a dealer could use:

Step	Suggested Cost Range	Suggested Multiplier
1	$0.01 to $60.00	3.00
2	$60.01 to $100.00	2.80
3	over $100.01	2.60

Step	Suggested Cost Range	Suggested Multiplier
1	$0.01 to $10.00	4.00
2	$10.01 to $25.00	3.50
3	$25.01 to $50.00	3.00
4	$50.01 to $100.00	2.80
5	over $100.01	2.60

There are other schedules that could be used (I've seen as many as seven steps in the schedule), but all of them have the same general goal: mark up lower-cost parts more than higher-cost parts so the handling costs are recovered correctly across the board.

For instance, using the three-step model above, if a dealer's service department acquired a relay from a supplier that costs $13.77, the multiplier would be three, meaning the part should be set at 3 x $13.77 or $41.31. Under the five-step model, that same relay would sell for $13.77 x 2.60 or $35.80.

On the other end of the spectrum, if the dealer bought a circuit board for $396.00 from a supplier, the three-step model would mark it up to $1,029.60 and the five-step model would take it to the same figure.

The labor rate is a little more difficult to compute! Most dealers have their receptionist or service dispatcher get on the phone and call the competitors and ask what a service call would run. They then take the average and try to set a rate on the high side of the average. So who runs their service business for them?

As a general rule of thumb, *a dealer's service rate should be at least three times his highest-paid service tech's wage (counting benefits).* To be profitable, it would be better to multiply that wage by four.

In reality, a labor rate must not only cover the wages and benefits, but also the overhead and net profit assigned to that labor. A truly accurate computation requires a spreadsheet and extremely accurate financial statements (something most dealers do not have). Without good financial statements, we can ballpark what a labor rate should be. Here is what a dealer has to consider in setting a profitable street rate:

1. How many *gross hours a year* (on average) are available to the dealer's service department?
   a. (Example: 4 techs x 52 weeks x 5 days a week x 8 hours a day = 8,320 gross hours.)
2. How many hours are deducted from the gross hours for such things as vacations, holidays, sick leave, travel time, and other unbillable items? We will figure a labor rate that has travel time built into it.
   a. (Example: for our 4 techs, the worst case is 10 days of vacation, 6 holidays, 3 sick days, 2 personal days, and 2 hours a day of travel time. Calculation is (10 + 6 + 3 + 2 days = 21 days x 8 hours x 4 techs) 672 hours. Gross hours go from 8,320 down to 7,648. For travel time, 7,648 hours divided by 8, then divided by 4, is 239 days per tech, at 2 hours a day travel, is 478 hours a year per tech for travel; x 4 techs, is 1,912 travel hours, taking the gross pool down further to 5,736 hours. These are the *billable hours*!)
3. The highest tech's *wage*.
   a. (Example: $30 per hour.)
4. The service department *overhead* (from a departmental P&L; see Chapter 15).
   a. (Example: $204,000.)
5. The annual *amortization* of any assets that will be acquired by the service department this year.
   a. (Example: 2 new trucks; this year's principal payments would amount to $10,000.)
6. The *net profit* desired on labor sales.
   a. (Example: 20%.)
7. Street rate calculation is as follows: $204,000 overhead plus $10,000 for the new assets, then divided by 5,736 billable hours is $37.31 per hour for overhead and asset acquisition. Add highest wage of $30 to get $67.31 per hour for costs. For 20% net profit, divide this by 0.80 to get $84.14. The dealer should round this off to $88.00 (a number easily divisible by 4 if he uses time and material for service; if he uses flat rate, he could set his rate at $90 or even higher).

Notice how this back of the envelope method gave a result close to the 3x wage rule of thumb we mentioned earlier.

Another essential ingredient for a profitable service department is adequate *parts inventory* on the trucks and control thereof. Most progressive distributor service advisors can supply their dealers with a recommended service truck parts stock list, one for residential service, and another for commercial. Since parts requirements vary from one part of the country to another and from one dealer's installed product mix to another, I cannot give you a one-size-fits-all parts stock list. But you can check with your distributor's service advisor to see if he or she has one they can give you to give to your dealers.

One area where many dealers see profits literally evaporate before their eyes is in *parts inventory control*. Too many dealers have $30,000 or more worth of parts in a locker that is not secured. Any tech who wants to can pick up parts and put them in his or her truck without a paper trail. This is especially handy for a service tech who likes to moonlight using the boss's parts!

I always suggest to dealers that they secure their parts areas with a *locked* door and that only *one person* has access to it. To replenish service stock, each tech must turn in daily service tickets that clearly show what parts were used so the parts can be replenished from inventory. Then, once a month, I like to see dealers do a spot check on inventory. For instance, on the morning of payday (when every tech will be in the office!), hand each tech a sheet of paper with ten or twelve parts selected at random and have them count those parts on their trucks. If the count agrees with what the office records show (hopefully computerized records), no further action is needed. If the counts disagree, someone has to explain why.

Then, once a year, each truck gets a complete inventory count. These counts should *not* be done by the tech who drives the truck, but by someone else. (I am not even comfortable, in some cases, with techs counting each other's trucks; personal grudges can surface this way and untangling the knot can be more trouble than it's worth.)

Every Dealer Needs a Strong and Ongoing Selling Effort

An old adage in business goes, "Nothing happens until something gets sold." That's true, but it is shocking to see how many dealers do not wisely plan to get the leads to make this possible.

A strong sales effort must include consistent (year-round) advertising. This advertising must be in the right places to reach the dealer's target audience.

And therein lies the first problem most dealers have in maintaining an ongoing sales effort. They don't know who their target audience is. They think that everyone out there can use their products and services (they can't).

At some point in its lifetime, an air conditioning business' managers must sit down together and think through a very crucial question: "What kind of customers do we want to attract to our business?" Until that is done, the business is groping about in the dark, hoping to find juicy steaks and not rattlesnakes!

The answer to that question will involve a number of things: typical age range, income bracket, home ownership status, educational level, lifestyle, and a host of others. (My advice is to have your dealers work closely with good local marketing firms to figure this one out. See Chapter 20 for other ideas.)

Once that target has been defined—what the marketing people call the demographic—the dealership is in a position to advertise intelligently. With the help of a good marketing firm (because most dealers don't have the smarts in-house to do this very well themselves), the right forms of media can be selected and the right times of day or placement of media can be made, so that the greatest number of potential customers are reached with the fewest possible dollars, creating a maximum number of impressions per dollar.

What forms of media advertising your dealers use should depend on the market and their targeted demographic. Some demographics are best reached by radio; others by television; still others by direct mail or newspapers, and so on. It will also depend on how much advertising clutter is in the dealer's market.

As a general rule of thumb, new construction dealers probably don't need to spend any more than 1% (or less) of sales on promotion, and most of this would take the form of entertaining key builders. Commercial dealers will spend most of their promotion dollars on direct mail, brochures, and key client entertainment. But residential add-on and replacement dealers may need to spend up to 8% (sometimes even more) of sales on promotion (and that's *before* co-op dollars from the distributor).

The dealer needs a good way to track what media is working for him. His sales desk needs to be able to figure out, by a simple question, what lead the prospect to call the dealer. (That question is, "And may I ask you what lead you to call XYZ Heating today?" Never ask, "And may I ask you where you got our number?" They will say from the Yellow Pages or an internet search, which may be true, but that's not WHY they called you—at least 94% of the time.)

The sales desk also needs a good lead referral system (which sales rep, if more than one, gets the lead). The sales desk should also do all it can to pre-qualify the prospect before a sales rep makes the call. Then the sales desk needs to be able to track results. Did the rep make the sale? If so, when and for how much of a contract? If not, do they know why? (Few dealers bother to keep a Lost Jobs File, yet such a file can eventually produce real gold for the sales team!)

And finally, from all this data, the dealer should be able to generate monthly (better is weekly) sales reports showing each sales rep how well he or she is doing and where they stack up compared to the rest of the team.

The sales force itself needs to be *strongly trained* and well equipped (see Chapter 22). Sadly, there is a great deal of sales training available today in this trade, and much of it is very, very bad. There are, in my estimation, maybe six really good sales training programs available today. A good sales training program should give a sales consultant some good tools to use on sales calls (like presentation skills, how to use physical props, how to bring up the investment issue, how to handle financing, and how to understand the deep and sometimes baffling psychology of the sales process). Bad sales training focuses on scripts, closes, and gimmicks. That sales model may have worked fifty years ago, but folks have wised up to it and most don't trust it any more. (Which is why you probably recoil from a clerk when you go into a store and they run up to you and say, "Hi, may I help you?" "Naw, just lookin'." Yeah, right.)

Comfort consultants should have all the *tools* they need to do their jobs efficiently. They should have access to the best literature from the manufacturer and they should use it on sales calls. (Those who leave literature with the customer have dramatically higher success rates than those who don't! In fact, one study showed that sales consultants who left brochures with the customers and used a retail pricing system [see below] averaged $700 more per sale than those who did not.) They should have product samples for those customers who like to touch and feel things. They should have DVDs and CDs to play audio and video clips for the customer's education. They need modern tools such as sonic or laser tape measures (to quickly and accurately measure rooms for load calculations) and LED flashlights. They may even need a laptop computer! (Dealers need to understand that sales consultants who use laptops sell at a significantly higher success rate and at much higher dollars per job than those who don't. The extra profit a laptop-equipped sales consultant can generate can pay for the laptop in less than a month.)

Comfort consultants who use some form of pre-printed retail pricing guide book also enjoy higher success rates at higher dollars per sale. Do all of your dealers have such pricing cookbooks for their sales forces?

If a comfort consultant has been trained how to use a retail price guide, the final issue on the selling effort is addressed. But if the dealer does not use such a guide, he must be sure that whoever is doing the selling has been trained in how to properly put together a job estimate and *price it correctly*. The dismal profit performance in this trade (usually less than 3% each year) is powerful testimony to the fact that most dealers don't have a clue how to properly price jobs to begin with. (More on that in Chapter 15.)

Making *accurate job estimates* will require the use of a job take-off and planning form of some kind. These can be purchased from office form vendors, but I have yet to find one I really like and that fits the bill for the wide variety of jobs most dealers get into. Better are the forms usually provided by the finer sales training organizations in the trade. Also, a good form should be able to easily generate a warehouse pick and release form for the operations side when it comes time to install the job.

The job estimate needs to be able to apply overhead correctly. (We'll cover this in detail in Chapter 15.) It should come as no surprise that most job pricing methods dealers have learned do not do this.

Finally, to insure that the sales effort comes full circle and is accountable for success, I urge dealers to *job cost at least every third job* (and every tenth service call). Job costing is a process in which an office clerk compares the job labor and material used (as turned in on time cards and warehouse release forms) to the job as estimated. Discrepancies are noted, and if they are large enough, the boss should inquire about what happened.

For instance, Sid is a comfort consultant for Roscoe P. Bogenmeyer Plumbing and Heating. He sold a job last Tuesday that was installed this Thursday. The office clerk who is responsible for job costing notes that Sid pretty much nailed the job as it came in, except he was eight hours light on his labor estimate. (If Sid had been using a retail price guide, this probably would not have happened.) This is serious, but not enough to wreck a company.

But then, the job he sold on Friday—which was done on the following Tuesday—had the same problem. He was twelve hours light on his labor estimate. And a third job comes in just like this. Sid always gets material pretty much right on, but is always light on labor. Shouldn't the sales manager be asking Sid why he always estimates labor so light? (If there is more than one comfort consultant and they use the same crews that do Sid's jobs, but never come out short on labor, it is obviously Sid's problem. But if the crews come out over on *everyone's* job takeoffs, maybe there is a crew problem?) At any rate, once the reason for the errors has been found, it can be fixed.

Good Accounting Procedures Can Make or Break A Dealership

Unless you have a degree in accounting, I suggest you not get too deeply involved with your dealers' bookkeeping. You need to know enough about it to help them (you'll learn what you need to know in Chapter 15), but if you don't know all the ins and outs of accounting and start giving detailed advice, you could actually harm your dealers more than you help them.

Now that I have satisfied my legal department, let me say that any dealer you work with needs to get *financial statements* (and there are three[14] of them) *every month.* I don't have exact counts but my straw poll surveys in dealer financial classes I conduct leads me to believe that fewer than 35% of the dealers in this trade get monthly statements. Perhaps about 20% get them quarterly, and the rest (about 50%) get one a year (at tax time). Surprisingly, some get no statements at all, relying on their accountant to do their tax work and that's all.

Let me give you an analogy. I'll be the coach of a football team and you be the coach of the other team. In the game, I will have offensive and defensive coaches in the press box phoning to me vital data after every play. I have a special TV crew working for me, letting me see an instant replay on any play my team runs. In addition, I have a real-time feed to the official scorekeeper, showing me exactly what the score is, where the ball is, how much time is left, and so on. You, on the other hand, will rely on a 16-mm film crew to send you the game films two months after the game is over (since you have no live-time coaches to help you). You have no live TV replay capability and you have no link to the scorekeeper. In fact, the official scoreboard on the field is broken and does not even work, so you have no way of knowing how much time is left, what the score is, or anything else.

Who would you bet on in that game? (If you bet on yourself, I have a cure for cancer I'd like to get you to invest in too.)

When I say it that way, most dealers start to think that maybe they should be getting monthly statements! But only if they really *use them.* If a dealer just looks at the bottom line and then either smiles or grunts, then files the reports in his file cabinet, he has wasted his money on the

14 These are the Income Statement (sometimes called the Statement of Income and Expenses, or the Profit and Loss Statement, or simply P&L), the Balance Sheet; and the Cash Flow Statement.

reports. If he studies them, though, looking for problems, he will be wiser and wealthier for it!

A dealer needs to have his financial statements in his hands no later than the tenth of the month after the month ends. In other words, a dealer's statements for July should be on his desk by August 10. Any later, and too much water has flowed under the bridge to do much about it.

A good accounting system these days needs to be computerized. No way around it. The question is, does the dealer do his own accounting in-house or rely on a professional outside the house with a powerful program that can generate the reports the dealer needs? I lean toward a combination of the two. The professional should be able to speak plain language to the dealer and be able to explain to him what his numbers mean and to point out growing signs of danger as well as strengthening signs of success.

If a dealer uses an in-house computerized system, the question I usually get is, "Which one?" That depends on how much a dealer wants to spend and how much he wants to rely on internal data to run the business. If all he needs is a good checking account and invoice tracking system, most of off the shelf packages, like Quick Books or Peachtree, should do fine. Most of these programs have setup wizards that help insure that a chart of accounts that is compatible with the construction trades is set up, but be warned—these generic charts of accounts are moderately strong at best. A smart dealer will still pay to have a professional accountant come in and fine tweak the setup.

Programs like Quick Books and Peachtree run around $400 to $600, depending on what version the dealer gets. These packages are low-cost because they are, in the language of software developers, horizontal packages. This means that the development costs are spread out over a large market of users (from flower shops to beauty parlors to roofing contractors).

Vertical packages, on the other hand, must recoup their development costs in a much smaller market. Thus, they tend to be much more expensive ($5,000 up to $50,000). But they are designed by people with good contracting experience and programmed by expert accountants, so they do a tremendous job in providing a dealer with the type of real-time data he needs to maximize his success day to day. Several such vertical packages are on the market, and most are outstanding. In making a selection, I always tell contractors to contact three or four vertical vendors and have them send information kits and sample CDs. See what looks and feels best on the screen, and then call them and see how their phone support works. Look for a good feel. If the fit seems right, it probably is.

The Overlooked Detail: Credit Terms

When is a sale a sale?

When the money is *in the bank*. Until then, it is charity.

Luckily, most people are honest and will pay their bills (not always on time, but at least they eventually pay them). But some (on average, about 3%) won't.

Suppose a dealer did a job for Bob Puckingpatz for $9,700. Suppose that three months later, Puckingpatz still has not paid and refuses to commit to a payment date. Finally, in the fifth month, the dealer's collection agency tries to contact Puckingpatz only to learn he has moved away to some other state and cannot be located.

If the dealer makes 5% net profit on his jobs, how many sales did Puckinpatz just demolish with his no-pay? Divide $9,700 by 5% and you'll get a staggering $194,000!

But so many dealers tell me that they don't have time to check credit or to enforce their credit terms. It always struck me as strange that these same dealers will take their families to a restaurant and use a credit card to pay. Do you know what the server does with the card when the diner hands it to him or her? They run it through a card reader and the credit card company determines if the account is good for the charge being issued against it. In other words, a *credit check* is being run—for a $75 meal! But that same dealer is opposed to running credit checks on all his customers when the tabs are 100 times as great.

A dealer's *credit procedure and policy* should be written down on paper and rigorously followed by all who are involved with offering credit to customers. Individual states may have specific laws that the dealer must obey in creating and enforcing a credit policy, so I always advise dealers to check with their local state attorney general and their own lawyer to be sure their policy is legal within that state. The dealer should also be able to get advice from your distributor's credit manager (who should know your state's credit laws as well as any other professional).

Part of the credit policy should detail when and how credit is approved for a customer. (This may entail the dealer belonging to a credit reporting agency. There is an annual fee for this and a per-inquiry fee as well, but overall in the $15 per use range or less—a small price to pay to be sure a customer is good for a $20,000 HVAC makeover!)

Dealers should invoice for their jobs every day and not wait until some particular day of the month or week and do a batch job. For instance, if the Jones job is completed on Thursday, the invoice to the Jones family should be in the mail by Friday afternoon.

Special care should be devoted to *collecting accounts*. Most people pay on time, but some don't, and those who don't need to be monitored closely. Every dealer needs a written collection procedure and it should be followed exactly every month. If it is, the dealer can reduce his chances of a bad debt write-off.

The Commercial Law League of America, a credit information association, reports that the older an account becomes, the less likely it is to be collected. They report that 98% of the people you invoice will pay within 30 days. But from there the numbers drop off fast. When an account hits the 30-59 day age group, the odds of collecting drop to 93%. When the account hits the 60-89 day bracket, odds drop to 85%. At this point, banks will not consider any account older than 90 days for short term loan collateral. When you see the CLL's statistics, you'll understand why they don't want the risk: the odds of collecting a 90-119 day invoice are 73%; 57% for a 120-180 day invoice; 42% for an invoice six months to a year old; 13% for a year old to two years old; 11% for two to three years old accounts; and 9% for all the rest.

A dealer who has, let's say, $364,000 on the accounts receivable list may end up having to write off as much as $89,000 of this amount, depending on how it is spread out in the aging columns. That's a terrible hit to have to survive in any year! Pushing the collection effort up earlier into the aging cycle improves the odds of collection and can result in shrinkage dropping from $89,000 to as low as $21,000 or lower (a savings of $68,000 in uncollectible accounts!).

Once the money has been collected, it needs to be handled safely. I am appalled as I consult with dealers, many of whom are quite large, and see that their *cash management* systems are not much better than a coffee can full of cash in the broom closet! Safe cash management practices include safeguards on the checking accounts and how invoices from suppliers are paid, among other things. (For example, it is a good policy that the person who reconciles the checking account NOT be the one who has access to it and can write checks. And it is also a good policy for the owner or someone in upper management to review EVERY checkbook reconciliation.) If there is one area where a dealer is subject to highway robbery, it is in this area, where fraud by people with access to the money can siphon off years of profit and success in weeks.[15]

15 I was once involved with a dealer on a consultation. When I graphed his fiscal performance in a number of key areas over a two year period, month by month, I noticed some sudden and sharp changes in the graph. I asked him if he could think of anything unusual during that period. He thought for a while then blanched when he realized he had a bookkeeper on the payroll during that time that he had let go. As it turns out, she had created some false vendor accounts and written checks to them, actually putting the money into her own account. Because she also did the reconciliation, no one could see her doing this. It cost the dealer about $25,000. That dealer now has a different cash handling policy! The dealer contacted his attorney about it and after checking into the former employee, decided to drop it as she did not have enough assets to restore what she had stolen.

On the pages that follow, I include a Gant Chart that shows the different things that successful businesses need to have in place as they grow. For instance, a firm in its first year of business does not yet need all the sophisticated procedures in place that a twenty-year old $10 million firm needs. As you work with your dealers, see where they fit on this chart and help them determine if they have in place now what they need to remain successful, and can develop what they will need in the future to remain successful.

Dealer Development Chart

Procedure or Issue	Size of Dealership (in Employees)			
	1-4	**5-9**	**10-19**	**20-49**
Incorporated or Limited Liab?	■	■	■	■
Outside board of advisors				■
Organization chart		■	■	■
Written job descriptions		■	■	■
Written operating procedures		■	■	■
Employee handbook[8]		■	■	■
Written marketing plan			■	■
Written business plan[9]	■	■	■	■
Healthy financial ratios[10]	■	■	■	■
Mgt oversight of cash mgt	■	■	■	■
Cash needs forecast weekly			■	■
Bank deposits made daily	■	■	■	■
Checking account safeguards			■	■
Written credit/collection Policy			■	■
Written terms of sale			■	■
Credit checks run		■	■	■
A/R aged monthly	■	■	■	■

[8] The company manual should be called an Employee Handbook, not the Employee Policy Manual. The term "policy manual" is pregnant with legal implications, whereas "handbook" allows for a much more loose legal restriction.

[9] It does not have to be long or elaborate, but it *does* need to be on paper.

[10] See Chapter 15.

Procedure or Issue	Size of Dealership (in Employees)			
	1 – 4	5 – 9	10 – 19	20 - 49
Lien laws known, used	■	■	■	■
Offer retail financing	■	■	■	■
Bills okayed before paying		■	■	■
Written operating budget for year				■
Centralized purchase order system		■	■	■
Section 179 used when applicable				■
Adequate insurance	■	■	■	■
Relationships with lenders	■	■	■	■
Adequate lines of credit	■	■	■	■
Customer feedback process		■	■	■
Written pricing procedures			■	■
Complete and accurate job take-offs and quotes			■	■
Job costing				■
Annual advertising budget				■
Advertising planned 90 days out				■
Advertising constantly monitored for effectiveness		■	■	■
Service department established		■	■	■
Service dispatcher		■	■	■
Service manager			■	■

Procedure or Issue	Size of Dealership (in Employees)			
	1-4	5-9	10-19	20-49
Service agreements			■	■
Service run COD		■	■	■
Callback rate less than 2%		■	■	■
Computerized service dispatching				■
Unbillable time under 10% for service				■
Standard service truck inventory set				■
Parts inventory controls				■
Service street rate correct		■	■	■
Flat rate pricing for service				■
Sales forecasts for the year		■	■	■
Sales commission plan				■
Job survey form		■	■	■
Professional sales training			■	■
Computer-generated proposals		■	■	■
Job flow control board in place	■	■	■	■
Job staging system in warehouse				■
Full time job foreman				■
Daily job checks				■
Incentive pay for installers			■	■
Equipment inventory system				■

Procedure or Issue	**Size of Dealership (in Employees)**			
	1 – 4	**5 – 9**	**10 – 19**	**20 - 49**
Annual physical inventory count		■	■	■
Inventory on accrual accounting basis		■	■	■
Quality control procedures				■
Problem resolution procedure		■	■	■
Uniforms, photo ID badges		■	■	■
Written customer satisfaction pledge		■	■	■
Delegation of management responsibility			■	■
Legal and adequate personnel files				■
Written job performance Standards				■
Exit interviews				■
Performance review process			■	■
Robust training policy and schedule		■	■	■
Retirement plan in place				■
Manpower needs forecast Annually		■	■	■
Daily time tickets		■	■	■
Written chart of accounts for HVAC businesses		■	■	■
Computerized accounting System			■	■
Monthly financial statements	■	■	■	■
Departmentalized P&L			■	■
Statements done by the 10th of the month	■	■	■	■
Monthly "dashboard" ratios report				■

Procedure or Issue	Size of Dealership (in Employees)			
	1 – 4	5 – 9	10 – 19	20 - 49
Monthly break-evens known		■	■	■
Weekly cash reports				■
Vital documents protected		■	■	■
Daily computer backups	■	■	■	■

Review Questions for Chapter 9

1. The three key pillars for success in the HVAC trade are:

   A) money, location, and product

   B) product, people, and pricing

   C) psychology, capital, and systems

   D) psychology, people, and pricing

   E) none of the above

   Answer: _______

2. Which of the following is ***not*** an element of the psychological makeup of a dealer?

   A) entrepreneurial drive

   B) engineering ability

   C) intelligence

   D) people skills

   E) they are all elements

   Answer: _______

3. To sustain a $3,000,000 business would require about how much capital investment?

   A) $450,000

   B) $300,000

   C) $150,000

   D) can't say—I don't have the working capital figures

   E) can't say—I don't know the local median household income

   Answer: _______

4. As a general rule, a dealer's line of credit should be large enough to get him through his _____ weakest months of cash flow.

   A) six

   B) five

   C) four

   D) thrcc

   E) two

Answer: _______

5. If I divide a dealer's current assets by his current liabilities, I have just computed his

A) working capital

B) current ratio

C) leverage ratio

D) debt to equity ratio

E) probability of survival

Answer: _______

6. A dealer complains he is losing sales. A check of his current ratio to quick ratio shows the result is 0.54. What might be a major cause of his drop in sales?

A) he has too much inventory

B) he doesn't have enough inventory

C) his prices are too high

D) his salesman is too lazy

E) he has the wrong inventory in the shop

Answer: _______

7. True or False. A financed inventory order does not go on the dealer's books. It only hits the books after it is all sold.

A) True

B) False

Answer: _______

8. A UCC-1 form

A) forces the dealer to cede to your distributor all his personal property if he goes bankrupt

B) puts a lien on the dealer's house or other personal asset(s) to cover the risk for an inventory financing loan

C) protects your distributor in the event the dealer goes bankrupt

D) guarantees you will be paid when the dealer places an inventory order

E) none of the above

Answer: _______

9. What goes in the blanks?

"Labor brings in the ___, but Management makes it ___."

A) dough, slow

B) work, go

C) jobs, profitable

D) dough, go

E) cash, hash

Answer: _______

10. One of the most important things a Tier One TM can bring to his or her dealers is

A) good processes

B) lots of leads

C) better pricing

D) good employees to hire

E) none of the above

Answer: _______

11. A dealer is really committed to service agreements when she has about _____ or more of them in force.

A) 100

B) 200

C) 300

D) 400

E) 500

Answer: _______

12. Susan Porkelvitch owns an HVAC company. Her top service tech makes $32 an hour, plus $10 an hour in benefits. As a general rule, what should Susan be charging for service labor on the street?

A) $168

B) $126

C) $84

D) anything over $42 an hour

E) nothing over $75 an hour or she'll lose business

Answer: _______

13. Your dealer asks you how much he should spend on advertising after co-op. What is your answer?

A) 3% of sales

B) 8% of sales

C) 5% of sales

D) no more than 10% of sales

E) it depends on his market focus and business mix

Answer: _______

14. A dealer's potential market is

A) everyone in the area

B) only those who have actually bought from him

C) his "target" or "demographic"

D) usually much larger than he thinks it is

E) none of the above

Answer: _______

15. Most successful dealers get financial statements

A) once a year

B) once a quarter

C) every month

D) every week

E) every day

Answer: _______

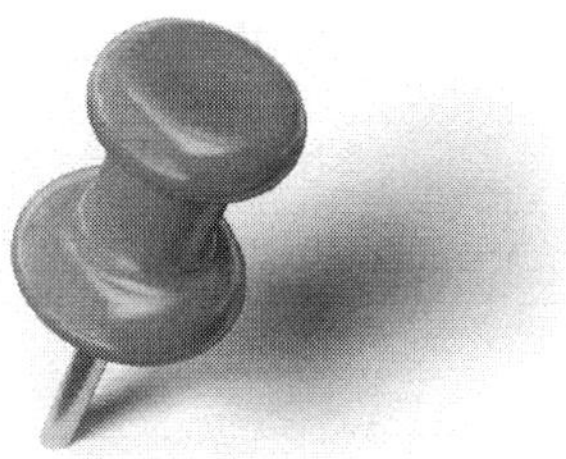

Chapter 10: Finding New Dealers

One of the most shocking facts about the HVAC trade is that the number of businesses in the trade does not change very much from year to year— there are roughly 85,000 HVAC contractors in America right now. But research shows that nearly **one third** of them are new every year! This suggests that each year, about 1/3 of the HVAC firms in America go *out* of business, often resurfacing with a new name, or as entirely new companies and owners entering the field.

So unless you are constantly devoted to finding and developing new dealers, odds are that eventually you will be holding the short straw.

Setting Up New Accounts

Branded dealers (dealers who identify with one or more national brands) usually have a lower turnover rate because the TMs who set them up are a little choosier about who they sell to, and so the better fish are chosen to make it upstream. But even if you were lucky enough to have an account list with only 10% turnover, that would still mean three to four accounts a year for the average dealer-oriented territory manager. That means, on average, you need to pick up one new account every quarter (and since dealer conversion in the summer is virtually unheard of, you must pick up slightly more than one new dealer per quarter).

For that reason, I favor what I call a $6P + 3C^2$ plan. It means:

Six **P**rospects on the list at all times; three **C**alled per week with a goal of **C**onverting three of the six.

Such a recruiting regimen would take about three hours a week to work and could result in four to six new dealers per year being added to the account list. (You would obviously need to double up in one or more of the quarters since dealer conversion in the summer is very difficult to pull off.)

Since the idea is to experience a net *gain* of four to six dealers a year, a TM may have to recruit at a slightly faster pace if the current attrition rate is more than four dealers a year.

The process I am about to outline is one way to do it. There are other ways too. The main thing is that you find what works for you and then stick with it (but always alert for ways to make it better).

When I was a territory manager, I believed in making several sales calls before ever discussing price. In this method, you won't discuss price until the fourth or fifth sales call. Compare that to the common practice among TMs today!

There was a reason for this. I wanted to be sure that the contractor, who I may not have known well at all, would be a good representative of my brand and my distributorship, and that the other dealers I had as customers would be proud to welcome him aboard as a comrade. (See the "Radical Recruiting Idea" sidebar.) I also wanted to be sure that he chose me for what I could bring to him, not because my price was hot. I learned over time that any dealer I could convert on price I could also lose on price. (In fact, if you drop off a hot price to a prospect, I can guarantee you that before you can turn the key in your car's

A Radical Recruiting Idea

When I was ready to recruit a new dealer, if I had a dealer in that area already or one who worked that area frequently, I would first meet with my dealer to explain the situation. I would prepare a share of market projection and show my dealer that his business gave us X share of market points, but that my marching orders required me to get Y points this year. The gap could be translated easily enough into boxes of equipment to move, so I would ask the dealer, "This is a pretty steep jump. Do you think you could bring in that much more new business in the next twelve months?" I never had a dealer say they could do it—many said they could get *some* of it, but not all of it. I would then say, "That's great! Let's work toward that then. Meanwhile, I need to find another dealer to help us get the share we have targeted. I need to ask you a very important question. Who do you respect in this area but do not compete with on jobs?" I would then wait while the shock wore off and then let the dealer answer. I always got two or three names when I asked that question.

And what names did I get? The names of dealers my dealer respected but did not run into on jobs. It would be a grave error to set up a new account that my present dealers did not respect. That would be an insult to them and could result in a mutiny. It would also do me no good to set up a hot competitor. I might win the prospect over but lose my existing dealers, so I may have no net gain at all.

In one case I even had my dealer ask if he could go along on the sales call to the prospect. I agreed, and when we met with the prospect (at a restaurant for breakfast), I ate my breakfast while my dealer sold the prospect on joining our team!

ignition when you leave, his current brand has the new pricing and is reacting to it.)

Here's a process I recommend for new dealer recruiting:

Step 1: Find some good prospects

First, develop a good list of possible conversion prospects. There are many sources you can use to develop a good list. Here are a few:

- Yellow Pages
- Parts Counter customers
- Supply House (observations of daily traffic)
- New dealer inquiries received at the distributor
- Service trucks on road
- Utility marketing representatives
- Permit filings • Dealer referrals (from my present dealers)
- Builders
- Competitor websites (dealer locators)
- Better Business Bureau
- Chamber of Commerce
- ACCA/NCHACCA/SMACNA/ASHRAE/RSES, etc.
- Competitive newspaper ads

However, in my opinion, one of the best sources of prospecting leads is a database such as the type you can purchase from database warehouses, such as InfoUSA. The HVAC contractor databases you can purchase from InfoUSA contain a wealth of great information that is useful for prospecting. You can order just a few counties or the entire nation. The larger the database, the more it will cost, of course, but the lower the price per record. I know some territory managers who annually buy an update for their territories out of their own funds because they believe in this type of data so much (and on a territory level, the cost is only a few hundred dollars).

I cannot show you any examples of an InfoUSA database because the ones I have are technically owned by my clients. I formatted them and made them usable for their TMs, but they own the databases and formats, and by the rule of client confidentiality, I am not at liberty to display any of their databases.

But I can tell you what they contain and how they work. They are set up in Excel workbooks and utilize the Excel AutoFilter option, a handy little way to rapidly extract from a huge pile of data only those records that meet your requirements. I can, for example, filter a national list for just those contractors located in Colorado, and then filter down to Arapahoe County, and then filter down to the city of Englewood, and see that there are thirty-two contractors in the database. For each contractor listed, I can view the company name, address, owner (contact) information, Yellow Page data, age of the company, size in terms of employees, approximate sales, and a host of other things, *including a credit rating.*

Suppose I wanted to find prospects that did $1 million a year or more in sales and that had credit ratings of A or higher. My thirty-two Englewood, CO contractor list shrinks to fifteen names, eight A+ credit ratings and seven A ratings. Most people would admit that this makes the task of finding six prospects for the hot prospects list a lot easier than calling on each one in town, one at a time, just hoping to find a few good keepers.

But once I had narrowed my list down to six or more prospects, I would do one additional step before making a sales call. I would ask my credit manager to order credit reports for the ones I had chosen. Most distributors belong to credit reporting agencies and get big discounts on credit reports, so this is not an expensive step to take. It may cost as much as $25 per report, and for six prospects, that's $125 invested. But if even one of those reports comes back showing that the prospect I thought was a diamond in the rough was really a chunk of gravel in the rough, I saved far more than $25 worth of my time finding that out the hard way! (Reports can be obtained from Dun and Bradstreet, and other vendors.)

But Cold Calls CAN Work!

Having made my stand against cold calls, I will also tell you that one of my most successful conversions was a result of a cold call.

I was in a small Missouri town looking for a new dealer. I stopped by at the local bank to ask the banker who he would hire if he needed a new system for his home. Or bank. In both cases, he gave the same name. Two tellers did the same thing. Even a customer in the lobby said the same!

So I dropped by to see this dealer. He handled a popular brand at that time and when I came in and told him who I was and that I was scouting out the area to find a dealer to handle our product line, he grabbed me by the arm and almost drug me into his office and closed the door! You see, just that week, his brand had set up its THIRD dealer (in a town of 12,000 people) and this guy—the younger of the two dealers the brand already had, and by far the bigger of the two —was upset.

When I told him what I was looking for and had to offer in return, he said he'd convert 100% that week. And he did!

Step 2: Make Initial Contact

Some TMs like to make cold calls—calling on a prospect without an appointment in the hopes that he or she will be available and can give them a few minutes of time.

A First-Call Tip

On the first sales call, I advise TMs to use a card-stock tent card that is folded down the middle and is printed on both sides with this text:

1. **Can I trust you?**
2. **Do you have my best interests in mind?**
3. **Will you be there for the team?**

As the first call gets underway, the TM places this card on the dealer's desk and points out that it has the same questions on both sides, meaning that both of us must evaluate what we do together in light of these three questions.

This sets the stage and puts the bar pretty high for what you expect of the dealer and what he can expect of you in turn!

Personally, I don't like doing cold calls at this level of sales because to me a cold call almost says, "I don't care about your time or needs; I just want to get in front of you and push my stuff on you." When you set an appointment, you are telling the prospect up front that you are professional, you respect their time—that you are different from the other Tier Four TMs who darken their doors on a regular basis, lugging their squeaky little red wagon full of junk to sell.

I normally advise TMs in my workshops to compose a brief letter explaining who their company is, who they are, and what brand they represent. Then they should say that they are looking to set up a new dealer in the area and from what they had gathered via research, the prospect may fit the bill. But, the letter goes on to say, working together successfully in a supplier-contractor relationship means both parties must be improved by the relationship, and that is why the TM would like a few minutes of the prospect's time—to see if there is a good fit that could lead to profitable business for both parties. The letter concludes by asking the contractor for an appointment.

I then counsel that in many cases, a contractor won't call—he'll be too busy, or that's just not his style, or he never sees the letter because a gatekeeper round files it, and so on. So be prepared to call the dealer a week later to see if he got the letter. If he did, ask him what he thought of it and see if he wants to set an appointment. If he did not, explain what the letter said and ask for the appointment. If he says "No," take him off your prospect list. If he says "Yes," go see him on the agreed-upon date and time.

Step 3: The First Call

Whatever you do, ***be on time***!! If you are running late, call ahead and say so and ask if the appointment is still okay to keep, or should you reschedule?

Second, *honor your time commitment*. If you asked for fifteen minutes for the first call (and that's a lot for a first call), don't go beyond fifteen minutes, unless the prospect is really interested and *wants* you to stay.

Third, leave your squeaky little red wagon at the office. Take only a note pad, a credit application, and some general product catalogs, as well as your business card and a personal résumé. (The résumé is not to use as part of a job application; it is only a single-page sheet listing your credentials as a TM and listing some bragging points about how you have helped your other dealers grow and be more successful. And leave your cell phone in your car, don't just turn it off!).

So what is your purpose for this visit? *To see if this dealer and your distributorship can make a good team!* Nothing more, nothing less.

On your first visit, use your ears and mouth in proportion to their numbers. Ask a lot of questions, and then shut up and let the dealer talk. As he talks, write down what seem to be major points and concerns he has. Ask clarifying questions. *Don't* paraphrase him (you'll see why in Chapter 23). Write down what he says in his own words, not yours.

Here are some good questions you can ask:

- ★ Where do you want this business to be in five years? Ten years?
- ★ What are you most proud of as a dealer?
- ★ What has been your best installation job so far? Why?
- ★ What sorts of things make you uneasy about the future?
- ★ Do you have any family members who would like to develop their careers here?

You are looking for a good philosophical fit between the prospect, you and your distributorship. It doesn't matter how big the dealer is and how much business he can send your way—if he marches to a different drum beat than you and your company, it will not be an enjoyable parade.

If, after ten minutes or so, you sense a good philosophical fit, bring out the product catalogs and just place them on his desk. Don't go through them right now. If he wants to see more, he'll start thumbing through it immediately; if he does not, he'll let it sit on his desk until later. Also, hand him the credit application and ask him if he'd be willing to fill out the credit application and mail it to your distributorship? If he balks, find another prospect.

At the end of your visit, it doesn't hurt to say something like, "Well, the fifteen minutes I asked for is up, and I don't want to over stay my welcome! May I come back next week and continue this conversation?" Then set a time and date. If he does not want to meet again, find a new prospect. And if he asks you if you can stay a while longer and talk some more, do so if you possibly can.

When you get back to the office, take three minutes and *hand-write* a personal thank-you note. Mention how grateful you were for his time today and how you are looking forward to your next meeting (and list the date and time you agreed on.)

Step 4: The Second Call—What Does He Need?

On the second sales call, be sure to ask for more time; up to an hour or so if the dealer will give it to you.

Your purpose on the second call: *to find out what his needs are so you can start to build a business proposition based on mutual needs relief!*

Again, take your note pad and a good set of ears. Also take along one good business idea you can leave behind—perhaps a copy of a magazine article on something that came up on your first visit, or a simple spreadsheet you wrote, or some other value-added freebie that shows you know how to bring to the table things that will help him grow.

Ask high-gain questions—questions that require more than a "yes/no" response, or a number.

Over the years, as I have gained more and more skill with it, I avidly recommend you learn how to ask SPIN© questions as described by Neal Rackham in his two outstanding works, *SPIN© Selling*, and *The SPIN© Question Field Book.* Both go into more detail than I will here on how to ask these powerful high-gain questions, and of the two, the *Field Book* is the more practical of the two. Get it, read it, and do the exercises. You'll be a stronger TM for having done it.

SPIN stands for something.

S stands for **Situation Question**. This is the easiest type of question of all to ask and most TMs are already quite good at it. Here are some examples:

- ★ Do you offer service agreements?
- ★ How many installers work for you?
- ★ How long have you been in business?
- ★ Where did the idea for the name of the company come from?

Most of these questions can be answered with a number or a very short answer, and don't reveal a whole lot more than what the question asked about. They are okay for starter questions, but the TM who stays at this level is doomed to be a lowly order taker on a milk route the rest of his career.

P stands for **Problem Question.** Most TMs are fairly good at this type of question too. Its purpose is to probe and see if the dealer has any problems he is facing. Here are some examples:

- ★ So what makes you say your advertising program this year is weak?
- ★ Why do you think the turnover in the service department is too high?
- ★ So what would you say is keeping you from having 1,000 service agreements?
- ★ Do you have to pay freight to get equipment delivered to you?

So far, so good. Most TMs can handle the S and P questions pretty well without any additional coaching. It is the I and N questions that may be new to you.

The I and N questions are devoted to one goal: making a dealer's problem so large in his own mind that he *must* take action to solve it, and take action *now*. The fact that a dealer may have a problem (or many problems) that he is living with is an indication that in his own mind, they are either not serious enough to really solve at this time, or their solution is beyond his skills and understanding. Either way, the emotional temperature of the dealer's soup is lukewarm at best. You need to get the soup to boil.

The **I** question is an **Implication Question.** It is the hardest type of question to ask because it must, out of necessity, let the dealer realize that the problems he is living with are costing him far too much (in time, in money, in prestige, etc.). They are, by their very nature, downers. They make a person feel uneasy. Therefore, how and when you ask them is vitally important.

The best time to ask an I question is right after a P question has uncovered what you think may be a major issue. It is important to use a soft tone of voice and empathy at this time (although I have seen sales people use a little more edge and force at this point with great success).

Here is an example to show what I mean. Suppose your conversation has gone like this on the second call:

You: So how many service trucks do you run? (S question)

Dealer: That varies, but anywhere from six to ten.

You: Why the variance? (P question)

Dealer: Well, my guys come and go a lot. I lost two techs last week just because Schplotz Heating across town offered them 25 cents an hour more to work there.

Do you think the dealer has just revealed something important to you? You bet he has! He has significant turnover in his service department. Yet, he has not done much about it, since he still runs a wide variance in the number of trucks on the street in any given month. Here is how you can build up to the I question:

You: That must hurt! Tell me, are there any other causes of service techs leaving that you don't mind sharing with me?

Dealer: Why?

You: Because I am trying to determine if we can be of help to each other or not, and this may be an issue we can work on together in the future.

Dealer: Oh, I see. Well, I've had to let three guys go this year because they didn't show up for work and didn't even bother to call in. And one guy was let go because he drove over a customer's dog and killed it and refused to own up to it. And one failed a random drug screening a few months back.

You: Ouch! Well, do you mind if I ask you a pretty tough question?

Dealer: I guess not.

You: If we don't address these issues, what do you have to look forward to in your service operations?

Did you catch that breath escaping of out of the dealer's lungs with that last question?

That's the impact of an *Implication Question*. It paints a picture of a future that does not solve the present problem. It forces the dealer to stop and contemplate what might happen if he plays ostrich with this issue.

A couple of things about Implication Questions. One, don't ask them if your product or dealer service offering package cannot address the issues. You'll look really stupid if you do. (For example, asking how a lack of local service training might impact his service success when your own distributor does not offer service training to dealers is not a good move.)

Second, a dealer may not always answer the question with words. Because the Implication Question drives a stake into the emotional heart of the issue, the dealer may not have words to express how it makes him feel. He may just frown, or narrow his eyes, or press his lips tightly together; you may see his nostrils flare open a little; or he may redden and blush, or sigh, or go, "Ugggh!" When you ask the Implication Question be very vigilant to pick up any cues you can (verbal and non-verbal) about how it may be affecting the dealer.

If you have done a good questioning sequence up to this point and the Implication Question was well formed, you can be sure that now the dealer's emotional soup is near boil, if not already boiling.

But he will be upset at his *situation*, not at you. Don't be afraid to ask an Implication Question when you've done good questioning to get to that point. The dealer's angst will be directed at his own issue (and perhaps even blaming himself for being a fool), but he won't be mad at you—unless you ask the question rudely.

A third point to keep in mind about the Implication Question: let the dealer have an emotional "Ugghh!" but don't leave him there for long. After a little time in the emotional pit, you need to lower a rope to him.

And the **N** question does that—the **Needs Pay-off Question.**

The Needs Pay-Off Question offers a *generalized* solution to the problem just uncovered by the Implication Question, but it does so in a non-selling mode. And this will be the hardest thing to contain as a sales professional using SPIN questions for the first few times: you will be tempted to say to the dealer, "Well, we can solve that issue for you!"

That would be the **wrong** response to make to the dealer's Implication Question answer. It is wrong for important psychological reasons. (And believe me, sales is psychological more than anything else. It certainly is *not* a logical enterprise!)

A dealer has to find his or her own internal emotional release when an Implication Question causes his or her soup to boil over. You cannot step in and take the pot off the burner for the dealer. They need to have the freedom and joy of doing that themselves, and the Needs Pay-Off Question does that.

Here is how we could continue our dialog with a good Needs Pay-Off Question:

> **You**: I see that struck a nerve. Let me ask you this, then. What could it do for your business if those turnover problems with the service department were solved?

After asking the question, sit back and shut up. Watch the dealer's face and listen as he answers. You'll see a dramatic change come over him. He may brighten, he may talk a little faster, and he may even smile.

John Ruskin

John Ruskin (February 8, 1819 – January 20, 1900) is best known for his work as an art criticand social critic, but is remembered as an author, poet and artist as well. The following quote is from one of his essays and crystallizes the issue of price better than almost anything else ever written!

"It's unwise to pay too much. But it's worse to pay too little. When you pay too much, you lose a little money, that is all. When you pay too little, you sometimes lose everything because the thing you bought was incapable of doing the thing it was bought to do.

The common law of business balance prohibits paying a little and getting a lot. It can't be done. If you deal with the lowest bidder, it is well to add something for the risk you run. And if you do that, you will have enough to pay for something better.

There is hardly anything in the world that someone can't make a little worse and sell a little cheaper and people who consider price alone are this man's lawful prey."

Notice how the TM did not pull out the squeaky red wagon and start selling his snake oil. He merely asked the dealer to imagine life with that problem addressed, and the dealer liked the picture! Later, the TM will come back and put his stuff into that new picture so the dealer will be drawn to making the change that must happen for the dealer and TM to work together.

What you do next is, in my opinion, absolutely critical. You stop and ask the dealer something like this: "Wow. I think we just hit on something very significant. Do you mind if I write this down before going on?"

Then **write down what the issue is** (and use the dealer's own words as much as possible). Write in detail what the dealer revealed to the P question and his response to the I question. If possible, use his own words for the N question response. This may take a minute or two to do, and you may feel awkward with the silence as you write, but if you do this now, your next sales call will be a slam dunk.

My advice is to go for as many significant issues as you can on the second sales call. At least four, and maybe up to eight if you can. The more you uncover that you can address, the better your odds of recruiting the prospect!

After your appointment, thank the dealer for his time and candidness and ask for a new appointment. When you get back to the office, send another *hand-written* thank you note.

Step 5: The Third Sales Call

Wow! Look at this. You are on your third prospecting call with this dealer and you have not talked about product or price yet! What kind of TM are you, anyway?

One of the best. On your way to becoming a Tier One TM, or a master if you already are on Tier One.

On your next visit, you are almost ready to close the deal, but not quite. You have a little more work to do.

On this visit, **your primary purpose** is to *show the dealer how you, your product, and/or your distributorship can address the issues* he revealed on your last sales call.

Between the time of the previous sales call and this one, you've had a few days to review your notes and take in the dealer's issues. In particular, you have had time to prepare a powerful presentation (see Chapter 26) that will address the issues you uncovered on the second visit.

On your third call to the dealer, after your opening dialog, pull out your legal pad with the issues on it and the dealer's responses to the Implication and Needs Pay-Off Questions. Hold it in your hand and say something like this: "The last time I was here we had a rich time in discovering some of the issues that have you concerned. I captured those issues on this pad and wanted to know if you'd be willing to look it over to make sure I got it right?" (I cannot think of any reason why a dealer would say "No" to this question!)

Hand him the pad, and say, "Would you review the list and make sure I have it right?" (Whose words will the dealer be seeing? His own!) After a few seconds, ask this important question: "Does the list look okay to you?" (If not, make the changes he recommends.) Then say, "Is there anything else that has come to mind since last week that you'd like to add?" If so, discuss it and add it to the list.

Hand the pad back to the dealer now and say something like this: "As I told you on the first call I made here two weeks ago, I wanted to explore the *possibility* of us doing business together. Frankly, unless you have needs I can fill, we have no need to do business together, right? So what I'd like to do now, if it is okay by you, is show you how working with me and my company can help you address all these issues. Will that be okay?"

Now on your second call of the discovery process, you found those issues in a more or less random order as you went fishing for dollars. You have no idea which one is most important to the dealer, and if you start your presentation now with the first item, you may (or may not) start off with the dealer's hottest issue and thus have his highest attention. So you ask this bold question: "Which issue do you want to hear about first?"

What will the dealer pick? Probably his hottest issue!

You then make your presentation, using whatever tools you prepared (such as videos, DVDs, spreadsheets, brochures, booklets, and so on). As you present, do frequent "Are we together?" checks and when you are done, ask, "Well, how do you feel about that issue? Was that enough information, or do you need some more to work with?"

After the dealer is satisfied, ask him to take a pen and check off that issue. Then ask him to pick the next issue, and repeat the process until you are done with the entire list.

When you have completed your presentation, you can say something like this: "One a scale of 1 to 10, where 1 is you want me to leave and never come back and 10 is you want to sign on right way, where would you say we are?" Hopefully, the dealer will say 6 or higher, and the higher the better! If you earn a 5 or lower, you are probably history. At best, you'll be a back of mind brand he may offer on an occasional sales call.

By now, you have probably used up all your agreed upon time for the call, so set the next appointment. But this time, you want the dealer to come to your distributorship. (If it is a long trip, offer to arrange the transportation.) Tell him that before he decides to sign on, you'd like him to see your operation to make sure he is satisfied with making a decision to work with you. (If he already knows your company and is satisfied, you can skip this step.)

Step 6: The Distributor Visit

The fourth sales call is held at your distributorship. Here, he will meet the key players (please make sure they will all be in town that day to meet your prospect!), see your awesome mountain of inventory, watch as your warehouse guys ship out load after load of hot merchandise, meet your service department team, see your training facility (if possible, schedule the visit on a day when you have a class going on), kick the tires on your service training lab complete with live bugged units for techs to work on in classes, and so on. Make sure you have a nice lunch with the distributorship principals (at the very least, the sales manager).

Near the end of lunch, the management team member should set up the conversion with a question like, "Well, John, what do you think so far? You've met Tom four times now and have seen our operation up close. What do you think? Can you see yourself working with us?" Usually at this point, the dealer will say he does. At this, you should step in and say something like, "Great, John! I love to hear words like that! Why don't we talk it over in detail back at our offices and then see what the next step might be?"

Upon returning to the distributorship, take the dealer into a small conference room, perhaps with your sales manager, and get his feedback (again) on what he has seen and experienced today. Ask if he thinks he'd like to join the team.

If he does, set an appointment for next week to complete the process. If not, ask what is holding him back and try to bring him back to a sign-on.

It is not uncommon at this point for a prospect to say, "Well, I'm really impressed with what you've done so far, and all, but I have no idea how much you are going to charge me for my products. What will my pricing be?"

Explain that you will go over that in detail on the visit next week and assure him at this time that you will be competitive. Don't promise to be low, but just to be competitive.

Again, a *hand-written* thank-you note after this visit is a good idea. Also try to get your distributor principal and other key players to write a letter thanking the dealer for coming by and offering to help him feel at home as a new player on the team.

Step 7: Closing the Deal

On this (hopefully) final prospecting call, take with you the pricing you want to use for this dealer along with an order form for his first order. Also, if your distributor requires it, take a dealer agreement letter for him to sign.

I do not know how your distributor operates, but I can tell you that mine had tremendous intelligence on our competitors in the market place, and that included copies of competitor price sheets to their dealers. (And I am sure my price sheets were in *their* files too!) You also know, from your careful calls so far, what type of equipment the dealer normally likes to sell. From that, you'll have a pretty good idea of what he is paying for his equipment.

What I did at this point was open up by saying, "The final step, as I see it, in teaming up is to be sure that our pricing is at a level you can be comfortable with. Do you mind if we explore pricing now?"

I then would ask the dealer what his bread and butter condensing unit was. (Of course, I already knew from my observations, but the question is good to get him involved in the process.) He might say, "A three-ton 14 SEER unit." I would then get my price sheets out and turn to the 14 SEER pages and find the 3 ton unit and say, "Okay, I have a price here. Just out of curiosity, what are you paying for that unit now?" He may say, "I'm not going to tell you until you tell me yours!" To which I would reply, "I understand. My price is written down on this sheet and I cannot change it, so whatever you tell me is just what it is. So what is your current cost?"

He gives an answer. I then say, "Our price on that model is $X." Now "X" might be a little higher than what he is paying (but not too much higher). Of course, if there is a world of difference in quality between his model and yours, you can reasonably command a bigger differential in pricing.

He may wrinkle his brow when he gets your price, but just go on. "And what coil do you match that up with?" He'll give an answer; you ask his price on it and then offer him your price—if possible, be at his current brand's coil price, or maybe even just a little under it. Just enough to make him satisfied that on a bones-to-bones comparison, you are in the ballpark. Do the same question for furnaces, heat pumps, or package units.

Bottom line: your overall system price should be about 1% to 5% higher than what he is buying now. This will catch him off guard. He was probably thinking you'd be the same pricing level (or lower) to what he has now. He will probably say something like, "I don't get it. You want me to handle your product line, but you're $50 a system higher than what I have now! I don't get it!"

That's when I would smile and get out my note pad from our first two visits together. I would also have the John Ruskin quote (see sidebar) ready. I would then hand him the pad (with his check marks still on it) and say, "In our previous visits, you said these are the things that are causing you some pain right now. You agreed earlier that if this pain could go away, you'd have a much better life. Well, that $50 a system is the price of pain relief." I would then hand him the Ruskin quote and say something like, "It looks to me like you've tried the risky way Ruskin spoke of. Are you ready to try the better way?"

In all my years of converting dealers, I only had one prospect dig in and refuse to go along because my price was a little higher than what he had from his present supplier. I finally said, "I understand your feelings. So here's the deal—either pay about $50 a system to take away your pain, or if you want your old pricing levels, keep your present brand—and the pain. It's your choice." After a few seconds of a stunned look, even this tough old bird said, "Well. Now that you put it that way. I guess it's okay." And he signed up!

Once agreement is reached on pricing, ask the dealer if he'd be willing to finalize the process. He'll probably agree but want to know what that involves. This is where you bring out a dealer agreement letter (if your distributor uses one) and ask him to sign it.

My practice was to use a very nice ball point pen with the brand's logo on the clip for the signing ceremony. When done, I would get the pen's box out of my briefcase and put the pen in it, and then hand it to the dealer with my compliments! That always put a smile on their faces! A strong handshake usually came next.

Then ask the dealer if he's ready to put in his first order. Have one in mind for him (explaining why if necessary) and get his okay on your order pad. Then tell him that when this equipment arrives, you want him to call you so you can come out to his shop and explain to his sales force how to sell it. You also want to show his installers and service techs how to install it and perform a start-up on the unit. (If necessary, take your service advisor along. Make sure to buy the service advisor a fine dinner when you are done.)

If you have a dealer starter kit, this is a good time to get it out. (This could include a literature rack and a starter kit of literature; decals for his doors and trucks; patches for his uniforms; ball caps; lighted clocks for his showroom; and other items.)

Step 8: Orientation

When his first order arrives, go to his shop at a convenient time for his sales people, installers and service techs, and orient them to your equipment as it pertains to their tasks. This could take anywhere from an hour to half a day, so advise your new dealer of the time constraints so he can tell you the best time to have his people come in for the orientation.

After the orientation meeting, tell the dealer that as soon as half of it or so has been installed, you'd like him to call you so you can return for a debriefing.

Step 9: Debriefing

After half or more of the initial order has been installed, meet again with the sales people, installers and service techs, with the dealer principal present, and get their feedback. To the sales force, ask, "Was it easy to sell this equipment?" Accentuate their positive experiences and coach them if they had problems. To the installers ask, "How did it go when you installed it?" And to the service techs, "How did start-up go for you?" More than likely, all involved will be positive about the new line and back you up by their enthusiasm. Thank them for their time, and then in private with the dealer principal, ask, "Well, you heard it. What do *you* think?"

He'll probably be on board too. Now is the perfect time to ask him if he's ready for his second order.

From this point on, you have a new dealer. In many ways, he will be like a new child (at first, anyway). He will need help with how to interact with your company. You'll need to patiently show his staff how to use the internet for business, who to call for various problems, how to file a warranty claim, how to file advertising co-op forms, and so on. Make it as easy as possible for your new baby to grow and become strong and healthy.

If you do, he'll take good care of you in your old age!

Review Questions for Chapter 10

1. A territory manager has forty dealer accounts. In any one year, 10% of them will leave his customer list (either through attrition or changing brands). If this TM wants to grow his territory with the $6P + 3C^2$ plan, how many dealers does he need to convert this year?

A) 8

B) 6

C) 4

D) 7

E) none of the above

Answer: _____

2. One of the best sources of leads for new dealers is

A) the Yellow Pages

B) dealer locater links on competitor web sites

C) your parts department counter people

D) customer databases from commercial sources

E) the Internet

Answer: _____

3. Once you have selected some prospects to convert, you should

A) call or write each of them for an appointment

B) run credit checks on each of them

C) make your first visit a short one and test for alignment of values and vision with your distributor

D) all of the above

E) none of the above

Answer: _____

4. A good I question would be

A) How many service agreements do you have?

B) If your warranty filing was easier to do, how could that help your business?

C) So if you don't pick up a deep commercial product line to back you up, how will you reach your goals in that market segment?

D) So how does not having an integrated controls line affect you on commercial jobs?

E) None of the above

Answer: _____

5. When should you demonstrate to the prospect that you and your distributorship have what he needs to grow?

A) on the first call

B) on the second call

C) after you have uncovered his deep needs

D) in your introduction letter

E) none of the above

Answer: _____

6. Why should your pricing be just a little bit higher than his present pricing?

A) because you're worth it!

B) because any dealer converted on price can be lost on price

C) because the increment is the price of pain relief

D) all of the above

E) none of the above

Answer: _____

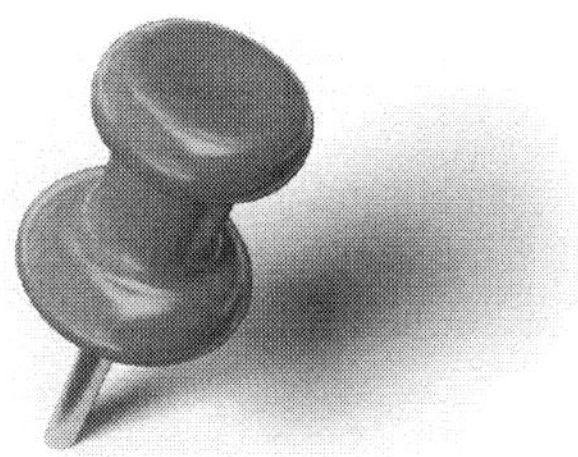

Chapter 11: Helping Contractors Develop and Mature

Most of the people who are in the HVAC contracting trade are there because they have a knack for it. They are good at repairs or forming sheet metal or installing equipment, or a host of other skills. Most of them are *very* good at it.

Yet most of them have never learned (formally) how to run a business. As a result, many contractors stumble through day to day trying to find their way, like a blind person trying to find a restaurant on a busy New York street at noon.

A territory manager who is well versed in how to analyze where his or her dealers are and what they need to do to grow as quickly and painlessly as possible is in a position to offer his or her clients help that will be tremendously appreciated and highly valued by the contractor.

What's In a Name?

I have found over the years that most dealers don't like the term "dealer development." They object to a term they feel patronizes them. They will tell you that they want help in organizing and growing their businesses, but developing it?

I once worked for a major manufacturer in a small team that was called The Dealer Development Group. Being the only person on the team with contractor and territory manager experience, I pointed out that this term was demeaning to many dealers. (An older team member who had been around for several years thought this was also true based on his interactions with dealers as a trainer.) Our team leader decided to check it out and contacted about twenty dealers by phone to get their reaction and learned we were right. So we changed the name of the team.

So whatever you call it in front of a dealer, try to avoid the term "dealer development." Since this is a term that is common among manufacturers and territory managers, I will use it in this chapter, but I repeat—try to avoid it in the presence of dealers.

They All Need a Road Map

As we discussed in Chapter 9, most dealers need help in growing their businesses as they encounter various obstacles to smooth growth. They need your help to get around these obstacles. In essence, they need a good road map.

The Gant Chart at the end of Chapter 9 can give you a good starting point to see what a dealer needs to have in place at various stages of development and what he needs to work on to prepare for the next stage of his growth. I suggest you develop a series of questions (call it a Mega Needs Analysis) to help your dealers determine if they have in place what they should have now to stay successful and if they can develop the tools for future success.

Your road map will probably contain two phases—the Present and the Future. In the *Present phase*, you want to be sure to address any practices or processes the Gant Chart says the dealer should have in place but does not yet do. For instance, from the get-go, a dealer really needs to have a written business plan. This does not have to be the formal ten-chapter treatise that a management course at Harvard Business School might require (although such plan formats can be outstanding), but it does need to be written down.

For dealers who want to write the full-blown Harvard B-School type of plan, there is software on the market that can be used to build a plan using standard boiler plate templates. Most of it is surprisingly good stuff. The joy of a business plan is not in the plan itself but in thinking about what you want the business to do and how it is going to do it. (This includes the research most plans call for.)

A simple plan (it usually takes no more than four or five pages to write out) is to complete a simple seven-step process. The dealer should:

1. Identify his or her most pressing problem(s)
2. Review what has happened so far—what created this/these problem(s)
3. Sort out the causes and look for common factors
4. Do a SWOT analysis on the factors (SWOT stands for strengths, weaknesses, opportunities, and threats)

5. Review the results with others (especially the TM)
6. Assign people in the organization to attack the problems.
7. Monitor progress on the plan

There are various ways to determine causes of the problems a dealer has. One of my favorite tools comes from the Japanese quality control movement and is sometimes called a "fishbone" diagram (or more formally an Ishikawa Diagram, named for its advocate, Kaoru Ishikawa). A fishbone diagram analysis of causes to problems begins with a drawing like this:

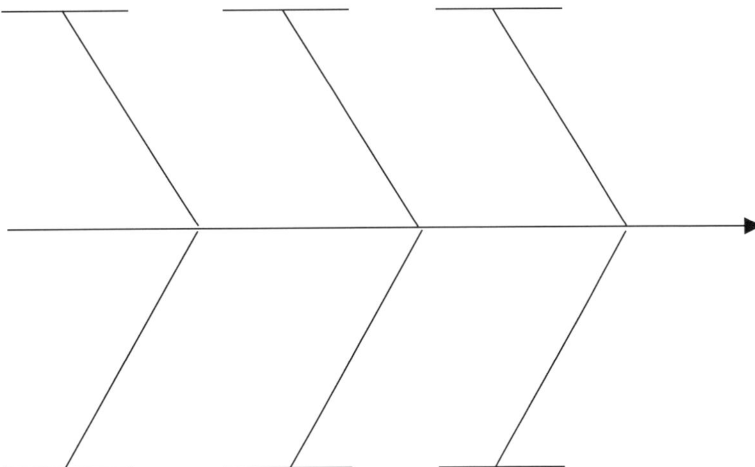

The horizontal arrow carries the name of the problem. For instance, the dealer may decide that this year, he wants to raise the profits in the replacement sales division. So on the horizontal arrow, he would write "Profits in Repl Sales too low."

The dealer should then get with some of the knowledgeable people in the company—people who might have knowledge about why the profits are so low and brainstorm what may be causing the profits to be so low. Let's say that after twenty minutes of brainstorming, the problem team has come up with several possible causes:

★ Pricing set too low to start with

★ Material costs have risen more than the estimator realized

★ Labor came in too high compared to estimate

★ The departmental P&L for installs is inaccurate

★ Complications arise on jobs that eat up time and materials

The next step is for the dealer (or a scribe she appoints) is to add these possible causes to the ribs of the fishbone. Here is a sample to show the process so far):

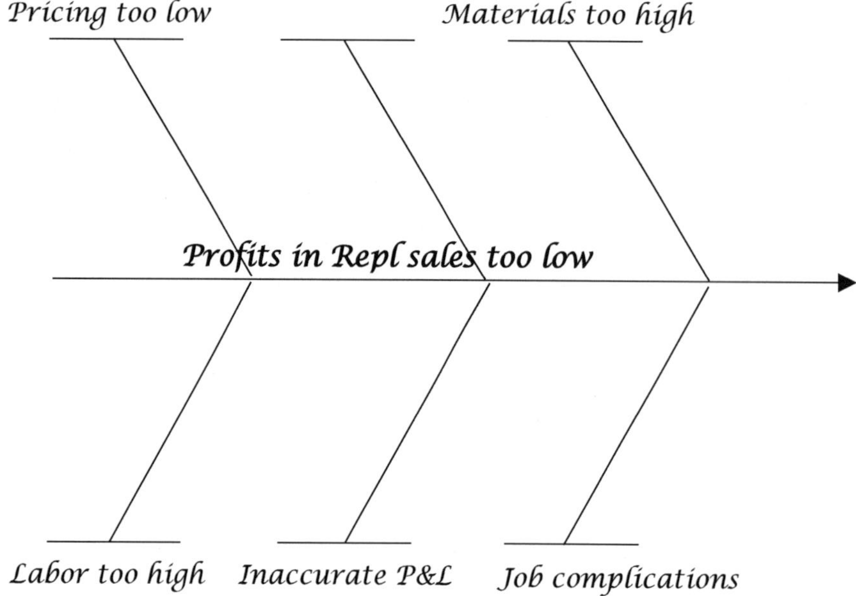

The next step can get quite involved (and noisy!). The team now takes each rib in turn and explores it as thoroughly as possible with new questions. "Why would pricing be too low?" There may be four or five answers to that question (use of wrong overhead, use of too low a profit goal, tendency to sell on price and not quality, and so on). Each cause for the rib's issue can then be sketched on to the diagram as sub-ribs, as the example here shows. When completed, a fishbone diagram could be very elaborate and scary looking, and just full of information that can help the dealer improve her business!

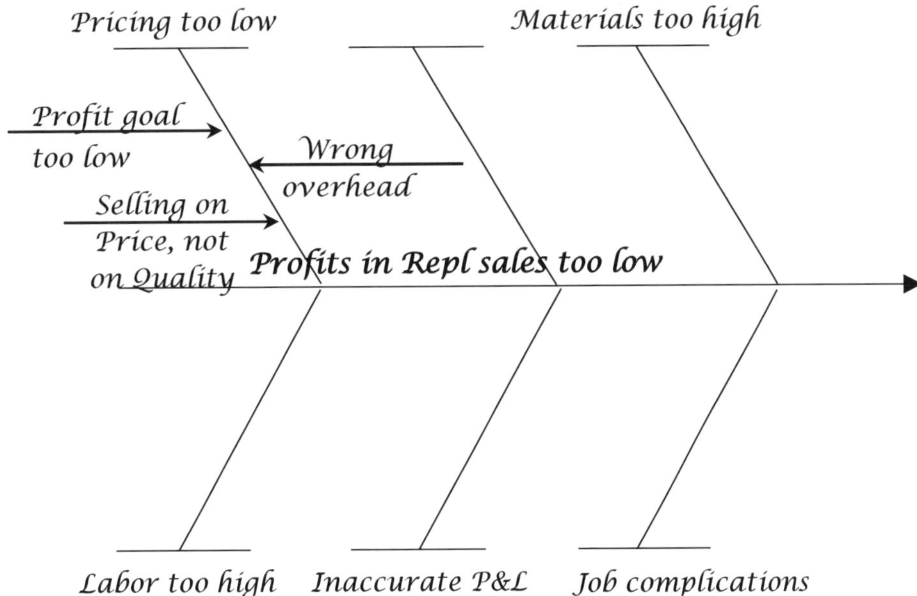

A completed fishbone diagram for a dealer could take up several poster-sized sheets and can get very complex. But it is a critical road map that shows what is blocking the growth of the company in the selected area (in this example, low profits in replacement sales).

At this stage, steps four through seven can be completed for each element of the fishbone.

What a Plan Should Focus On

Any good business plan should, in my opinion, focus on three key elements. If a part of a business plan cannot be tied back to one of these three elements, delete it!

The first element is ***The Plan Must Focus on Processes***. What this means is that most dealers get into messes in their businesses because they don't have good processes in place to help all the employees pull together to get a job done efficiently. There is often an awesome amount of waste in a shop as people pull and tug in different directions trying to solve the team's problem in their own way, and not realizing that the contribution they are making is really messing up the work someone else must do to help bring the project to harvest. A procedure is nothing more than a detailed recipe for how to do a job. It specifies who does what and when. When followed, a job gets done as planned and on time. If people ignore their responsibility in the procedure, it is impossible to predict what will pop out at the end.

For example, suppose that the dealer principal who developed the fishbone diagram on the previous page assigned the "Wrong overhead" sub-rib to an office employee who has some accounting skills. This person might then write a procedure on how to correctly set up a P&L for the replacement department so the overhead is correctly stated. Following that procedure every month will insure that accurate overhead data is available to estimators as they compile job prices.

Second, ***The Plan Must Improve Productivity***. That is, everything the plan outlines should contribute to generating more sales dollars per employee in the company. If it does not increase productivity, that plan element should be deleted.

As an example, suppose that on the rib labeled "Labor too high," the person assigned to that rib decides that the way installers are paid should be revised. If his plan actually leads to less work being done per week, the idea is bad and should be scrapped immediately. But if his plan yielded significant gains in weekly work done, it is a good move and should remain part of the company's DNA. (However, be aware that many times a dealer won't know if a plan is increasing productivity for several weeks or even months. Remember that step 7 is to constantly monitor the plan and if it is seen that an element of the plan takes the company backwards, it should be amended immediately.)

Third, ***The Plan Must Have People at its Core***. No plan should ignore the fact that human beings must make the plan happen, and as someone once said, "If you think you can build a fool-proof system, you obviously don't know the creative power of fools."

If success in executing a plan requires someone with an advanced degree in nuclear physics and you have no nuclear physicists on the payroll, the plan will probably not succeed. The plan has to allow for the talents of the people who must do it. It might require that those people get extra training along the way, but it cannot go much beyond their abilities or the plan will not succeed.

The plan should also make allowances for the emotional impact plan success can have on people, as well as the downer a failed plan can produce. For that reason, I don't have a problem with a dealer including celebrations for hitting a plan in the plan itself, nor do I have an issue with a dealer allowing for morale recovery when a plan backfires. People under inspired leadership have been known to achieve amazing feats in times of stress. Likewise, poor leadership can doom even the best team to a loss before the game even starts. Good leadership allows for the people element in the plan and works the plan accordingly.

As an example, suppose the dealer principal in our example told her team, "If we can hit 12% pre-tax profit by the end of the year, we'll have a special year-end party," or she said, "If we hit 12% pre-tax by year-end, I'll set aside a special bonus pool of 2% of our profits that you will all share in." Such carrots might get those tired old donkeys to pull the cart hard enough this year to make the plan work!

Putting Rubber on the Wheels: Making a Plan Work

Let's suppose you've done a superb job of asking great high-gain questions to determine where your dealers are now and have helped most[16] of them create strong and workable business plans. You and they are diligently working on the *Present phase* of their success. What do you do now to work on the *Future phase* of each dealer's growth—implementing those things he or she will need for continued growth and success?

You must know the complete menu of what your distributor and manufacturer can bring to the party! You must understand all the programs available to dealers and how to help them get the most out of them. (This will include pre-season stocking programs, pre-season advertising programs, in-season advertising programs, travel incentive programs, training programs, and on and on.) You must also be an expert on your product line(s) and how to apply those products (the right product on the right job installed the right way). In short, you must become a walking encyclopedia about everything.

This can be a daunting task! Some manufacturers have such a rich menu of programs (and many distributors are equally strong in adding their own local rich program menus) that it is almost impossible in some cases for a TM to master all the programs and still call on the dealers in her territory. Because of that, I am seeing more and more progressive-minded distributors adding a marketing support specialist position to their payroll. This specialist's job is to support the TMs in their work. The specialist is in charge of the annual training calendar, of the annual pre-season events, and all the other myriad of things that a thriving and strong distributor-manufacturer team can offer. The specialist communicates directly with many of the dealers and is always on call to any TM who wants their help in developing strong dealer development plans for their dealers. If you are fortunate enough to have such a person backing you up, you should be able to go to him or her and say, "I have this dealer who needs help in the following areas..." and that specialist should be able to help you lay out a detailed step-by-step plan to get the dealer to his goals using the programs available from the manufacturer and from your distributorship.

As an added bonus, not only does the marketing support specialist take a lot of the burden

16 I say "most" because not all dealers will want to work with you in this process. Work with those who do and just maintain the business with the rest.

off the TM's shoulders—their work also makes it possible for the TM to spend more time in front of dealers, a fact we know leads to higher sales performance.

As with any good needs analysis, you must establish a clear linkage between a dealer's growth need and the program (or programs) you want to bring to bear on that plan with the dealer. If you don't establish a clear linkage, the dealer won't see where you are helping him.

I suggest that you take the detailed needs analysis along with the programs you think will help the dealer achieve his goals and take them to the dealer on a sales call. Advise him before going that on this sales call you want to go over the needs analysis you did with him and show him what you think would be a workable plan to make progress on the goals.

You then present your recommendation and check the dealer's buy-in. If he has buy-in, you are ready for the next step. If he does not, you need to secure it before going on, because any dealer development plan built on weak buy-in is not going to work very well. If needed, find out what is preventing complete buy-in and try to accommodate your dealer on his issue.

Once buy-in has been established, you and the dealer together need to decide on a road map and mile posts. What item should you focus on first? And what do you think will be the time frame for completing that item? Then what comes second, and so on.

Draw up the road map in a document (a single-sheet memo should work for the map for any one year) and give a copy to your dealer.

Then, ***on every sales call in the following year***, cover some part of the plan with the dealer. If part of the plan requires that the dealer attend a training session your distributor will sponsor, attend with him and, if possible, sit by him. On each sales call, check progress on the goal and see what bottlenecks, if any, exist. Offer to help blow out any bottlenecks so the dealer can realize his goals on time. Keep track of the progress with notes in the dealer's file. On the following page is an example of such a plan element and accountability system from my *Stages* workshop:

Centralized Purchase Order System

A good purchase order (PO) system can help you get control of materials costs.

What is a **good** PO system?

It begins with a *materials requisition* from either a mechanic or job foreman. On service calls, they originate with a phone call **from** the tech that needs to get a part or supplies from a local vendor **to** a person in the office who has access to the **central** purchase order log.

For installers, the procedure should involve some sort of written request (a "materials requisition form"). (Such forms are available from most business form printing company like NEBS and Reynolds and Reynolds.) The requisition form is given to the warehouseman or parts counter control person to see if the requested item is in stock. If it is, company stocks are used first. If it is not in stock, the PO system kicks in.

If the item is not in stock, a PO is issued to a vendor by the company purchaser. (This will probably be a person who wears a dozen other hats!) The key point is that there is only one PO log and one person who controls it— the purchaser. Giving a PO book to each mechanic is about as practical as giving them your checkbook!

The PO log should have a specific number for the PO (which you should instruct your vendors to refer to on their invoices; "no PO number, no remittance"). The log should also record the job (name or number) the purchase is applied to. It should also log the description of the item(s), including part numbers, descriptions, and quoted prices.

Vendor invoices should be okayed by the purchaser before payment based on a review of the log to be sure the invoiced amount agrees with the quoted amount.

When the material is to be shipped in, a *receiving report* should be generated so the purchaser can cross check what was received against what was ordered. The receiving report should include the date the item(s) was/were received, the PO number, who shipped the item(s), how they were shipped, condition they arrived in, number of boxes, method of billing, who received it, quantities, weights, and descriptions.

The receiving report should also be routed to data processing so inventory files can be updated. (Receiving reports are also available from business form suppliers, or you can use the shipping papers that came with the item).

The PO process for standard restocking begins with a materials requisition form filled out by a manager who is ordering stock for future use. Otherwise, the procedure should be exactly the same.

This may seem like a lot of work, but look at it this way. No major successful company has achieved its success without a system like this!

Implementation Plan

Area: Centralized Purchase Order System

Goal: Practice sound cash management

Benefits: Less wasted effort and mis-spent cash.

Task	Assigned To	Time to Do	Start Date	Completion Date
Implement a centralized PO system		1 month		
Assign control of the PO log to one person		1 day		
Develop (or purchase) material requisition forms		1 month		
Develop (or purchase) receiving report forms		1 month		
Check all invoices against POs		Ongoing; 1 hour/day		Perpetual

The text that comes before the plan matrix is material that can be left with the dealer to explain what is needed to create a centralized PO system. The matrix then allows you and the dealer to put names and dates in the chart; you can then use this chart on subsequent sales calls to monitor progress on the plan.

You Don't Have To Always Carry The Ball

Walter Payton was a great running back for the Chicago Bears—one of the greatest in the game of football. But even "Sweetness" did not carry the ball on every play! On some plays, the quarterback handed off to other running backs; on still others, he passed to various receivers. No football player can be the focus of every play in every game.

You don't have to be the answer guy for your dealer all the time either. There will come times when your dealer needs expertise in an area that you have none in. Don't panic, and certainly don't try to fake it. You'll look like an idiot if you do, and possibly damage your dealer's business. Rather, admit that you don't have expertise in that area… but there is someone in your distributorship who does (and there almost *always* is a knowledge expert on almost any field at any distributor). Ask if it would be okay to bring that person into the planning and implementation process.

For example, the dealer needs help with setting up a good chart of accounts for his new computerized accounting system, and you don't know enough about charts of accounts to even look dumb. But perhaps the accountant at your distributorship is a whiz on this topic. Why not bring her in on the dealer's plan, even offering to take her out to the dealership on a sales call if that's what it takes?

One year, I had several dealers who were struggling with credit and collections issues and all of them were in the dark about how to use the lien laws of our state. I knew enough to be dangerous, so I asked our credit manager (who most of the dealers at that time did not particularly like) if she would come to our branch office some evening and put on a three-hour credit law class? She agreed, I announced the class, and that night, 80% of my dealers showed up! She did a brilliant job and afterwards, more than one dealer made comments to me about how helpful her information was and that she was not such a bad person after all!

On your distributor's payroll is centuries of experience and talent. Tap into it. As legendary basketball coach John Wooden once said, "It's amazing how far a team can go if no one cares who gets the glory."

Review Questions for Chapter 11

1. How is dealer development like Johnny Cash's song, "A Boy Named Sue"?

   A) it isn't; this is a trick question

   B) call it partnering, call it coaching, call it anything but "dealer development"

   C) it has a catchy ring to it

   D) none of the above

   Answer: ________

2. True or False. A good business plan will have ten chapters in it.

   A) True

   B) False

   Answer: ________

   Now, why did you choose the answer you did?

3. A good tool for helping a dealer get to the root of some of his problems is

   A) Chinese water torture

   B) a Toyota diagram

   C) a fishbone diagram

   D) a Five-Why diagram

   Answer: ________

4. The three P's any business plan must address are:

   A) product, pricing, promotions

   B) pricing, promotions, publicity

   C) people, places, products

   D) processes, productivity, people

   Answer: ________

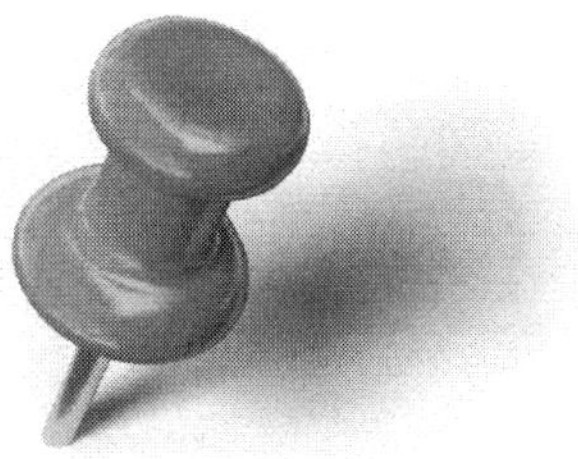

Chapter 12: Account Segmentation

Not every account in your portfolio will have the same value to you. Some accounts will be worth much more than others. A good account segmentation system can help you spot your best accounts quickly and even help you develop general approach strategies to maximize your results with each account you have been assigned without working any extra hours in the week.

The Pareto Principle

There is a principle in mathematics known as the *Pareto Principle*. Named for the Italian economist Vilfredo Pareto (who, in 1906 observed that 80% of the income in Italy went to 20% of the population). It states that in general (for many events), 80% of the effects come from 20% of the causes. Generalized to business, it has come down to us as the old rule, "80% of your sales come from 20% of your clients." In the 1940s, Dr. Joseph Juran attributed the 80/20 rule to Pareto, which was technically a mistake since Pareto was working on the Italian economy, not quality control. But ever since, Pareto's Principle has become a mainstay of modern business theory and management.

> "The 80/20 Rule means that in anything a few (20 percent) are vital and many (80 percent) are trivial. In Pareto's case it meant 20% of the people owned 80% of the wealth. In Juran's initial work he identified 20% of the defects causing 80% of the problems. Project Managers know that 20% of the work (the first 10 percent and the last 10 percent) consume 80% of [their] time and resources. You can apply the 80/20 Rule to almost anything, from the science of management to the physical world.
>
> You know 20% of your stock takes up 80% of your warehouse space and that 80% of your stock comes from 20% of your suppliers. Also 80% of your sales will come from 20% of your sales staff. Twenty percent of your staff will cause 80% of your problems, but another 20% of your staff will provide 80% of your production. It works both ways."

How can this be applied to your account portfolio? Hopefully, it is now obvious that 80% of your success will come from only 20% of your dealers (however you measure that success). That means that 80% of your account list will not help take you toward your goals! They may be nice people, they may buy at a high gross margin level, they may be fun to be with, but they won't make those really big numbers you need to become a Tier One TM. Ouch!

Doesn't it then suggest itself to you that if you are to become a Tier One TM you must learn how to spot the productive 20% of your accounts? Does it also suggest itself to you that you must spend your time with the productive 20% differently than the fun and friendly 80%?

The Bell Curve: It's Not Rat Poisson

The sub-title here is not misspelled. I meant to say "Poisson", not "Poison", because in statistics, the familiar "bell curve" is actually known as a Poisson Distribution (named for the French mathematician Siméon-Denis Poisson, 1781–1840). The famous curve looks like this:

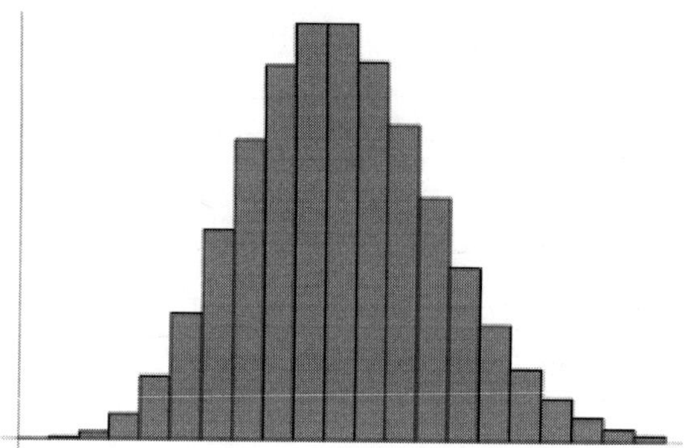

This mathematical principle has taken on tremendous power in modern mathematics. It helps explain a great many things and is a useful tool for tracking and predicting success in various endeavors.

In quality control, you hear talk of six sigmas. The six sigmas come from the fact that in statistics, a *standard deviation* is depicted by the symbols (the Greek letter sigma). A standard deviation is a useful measurement of how closely data that at first appears random actually falls into patterns. The six sigmas come from the fact that in quality control processes, engineers use six standard deviations, three on either side of the middle of the humped curve. Statistically, 99.73% of all possible outcomes occur inside six sigmas. This graph shows it well:

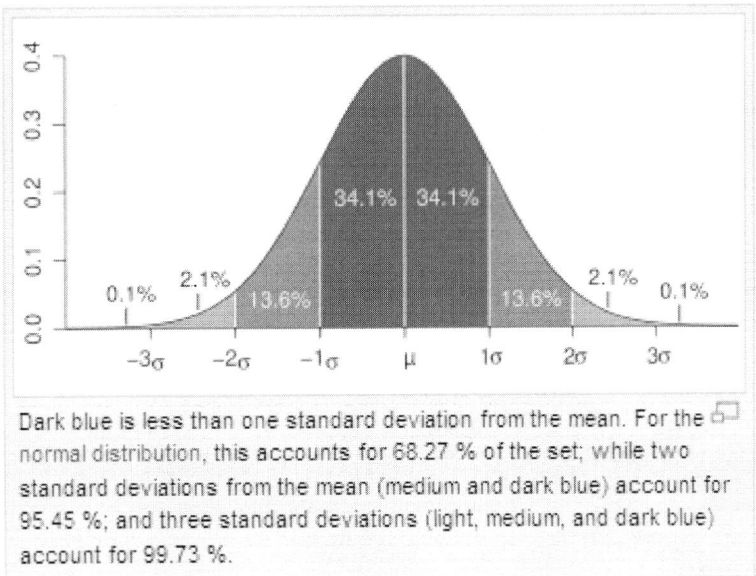

Dark blue is less than one standard deviation from the mean. For the normal distribution, this accounts for 68.27 % of the set; while two standard deviations from the mean (medium and dark blue) account for 95.45 %; and three standard deviations (light, medium, and dark blue) account for 99.73 %.

The two right-most standard deviations make up 15.7% of the total population, which is almost the 20% of the Pareto Principle. So if you were to plot a graph of sales dollar brackets or buckets on the horizontal axis and the number of dealers in each bucket on the vertical, you might get a graph similar to the one above. For instance, if you used $50,000 buckets, you might have on the horizontal axis $0-$50,000; $50,000-$100,000; $100,000-$150,000; $150,000-$200,000; $200,000-$250,000; and $250,000-$300,000. You could then plot the number of dealers in each bucket and end up with a curve with a hump in the middle. (Although I have seen territories that did not plot out quite that way, they were the exception to the rule; most territory plots produce a humped curve.)

So what's the big deal?

The big deal comes from the fact that in most training scenarios, *giving all the members of a population the same training opportunity changes the shape of the curve, but not in the way you might expect.*

For instance, suppose this is the curve of your sales portfolio now:

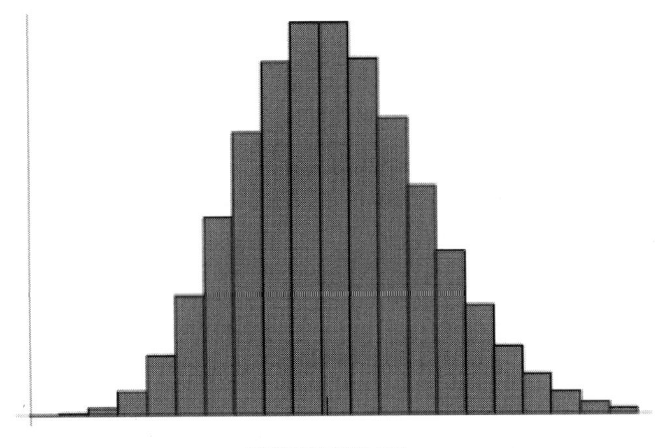

You might then suppose that by working with all of your accounts with equal force and zeal, you could make your portfolio do this:

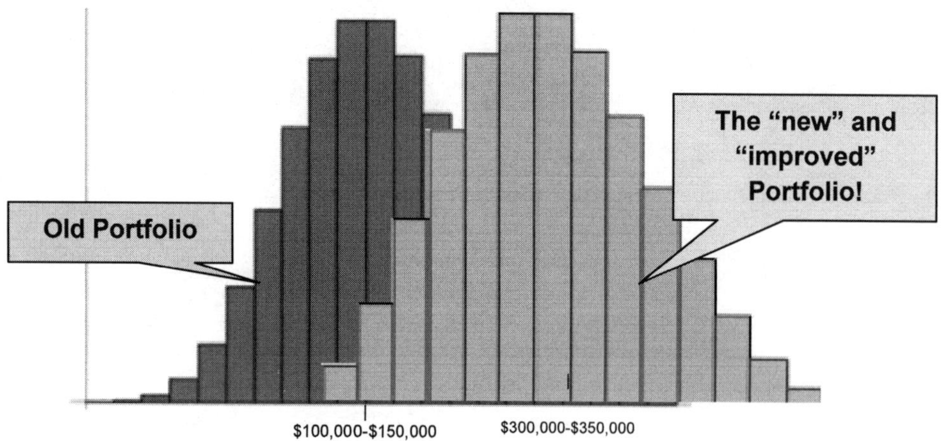

You might expect that your efforts would result in the entire portfolio moving in lockstep to the right, each dealer buying more and growing his or her business.

But that is just not the case at all! Sadly, research shows us that people are where they are in the curve for various reasons (most of them psychological) and moving them in the Poisson Distribution is well nigh impossible. Here is what training research shows us about the effects of working with people in a Poisson Distribution:

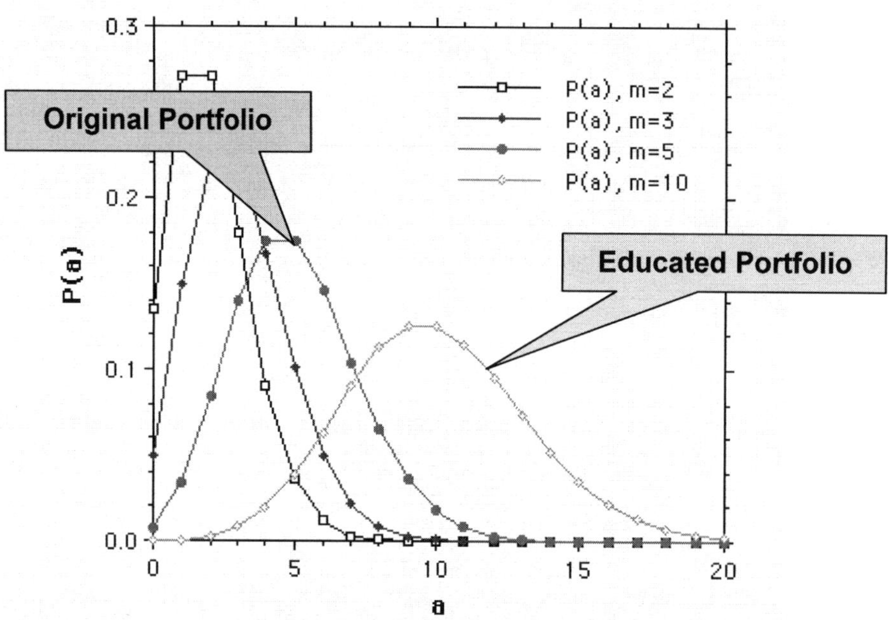

Note first the curve moves to the right some, but it also loses some height! The *area* under the educated curve will be greater than the *area* under the original one (a measure of how much the portfolio grows in dollars overall), but there is no lockstep march to the right.

Note the typical migration paths for dealers along the original portfolio plot. Those who are on the left end of the curve are still on the left end of the curve after the development effort; those who were in the center still stay more or less in the center; and those to the right of the hump remain to the right of the hump. But more importantly, notice the amount of movement. *The farther to the right of the original curve a dealer is, the farther to the right he ends up on the new curve.*

Do you grasp the significance of this? It means that your better dealers, with training, can become outstanding dealers, while your weakest dealers, with training, still end up as weakest dealers. You can kiss those frogs on the left end of your curve all you want—they'll still croak, catch flies with their tongues and go ribbet when you speak to them. And those who are princes on the right end of your curve will go on to become kings.

Where to you think you need to spend your time? With the frogs or the princes?

Enough Math and Theory! What's the Payoff?

Okay, enough of the math, graphs and theory. I had to build my case for what most sales people say is counter-intuitive, something that seems to break all the rules.

Forget about trying to take all of your dealers up the development mountain as a group. You cannot do it. They won't all go with you.

Some will. Some will make a little effort. And some will tell you where to go. (And it is not the summit of Mount Development!)

You must find those two right-most sigmas, that 20% or so of your portfolio who really want to grow (and can) and climb Mount Development together.

Does this mean you abandon the rest of your accounts?

Not at all. You still call on them (though maybe not as often) and you still sell to them (their money is just as good as the top sigmas). But you don't invest a lot of effort into turning them into princes. They are frogs, and frogs they shall more than likely forever be.

Enter Account Segmentation

The process of account segmentation is nothing more than organizing your account list in such a way that you can solidly identify the princes and turn them into kings. It also helps you identify the frogs and keep them fed, wet and happy. (But you won't turn them into princes.)

Size is not the only consideration in segmenting your account list. Years ago, I worked for a manufacturer who told its TMs to sort their dealers by size from largest to smallest and then draw a line at the top 20% of sales dollars and live with those accounts. The rest could be seen as needed.

The problem with this approach was that once the top 20% figured out they were the 1200 pound gorillas; they began acting like it, dictating to the distributor (and even manufacturer) how things should be. It is usually not a good idea to have a passenger jet being flown by a fork-lift truck operator!

Another Approach to Consider

Every account on your list has potential in three areas—they are *size, profit contribution,* and *strategic importance.*

Size is self-evident. A dealer can be a large one on your list, or a small one. Generally, I would say that if you ranked your accounts from largest to smallest and found at what point the top accounts made up 80% of your sales, you could draw a line and say, "This is my cross-over point between being a significant account and being a smaller one." Now that may or may not be 20% of your dealers, but it will be 80% of your volume and that is the key.

Next, is each dealer on your list profitable? Probably not. Some will contribute healthy gross margins and require little support in return, so they will be very profitable. Others will contribute little in gross margin but require a great deal of support and end up costing you money to work with. *Note that it is not the gross margin percent that matters, but rather the gross margin dollars.* A small account with high gross margin percents may generate fewer gross margin dollars than a large account with a lower gross margin percent.

> **Example:** Dealer A is a small dealer, buying $100,000 a year from you at an average of 27% gross margin. He contributes $100,000 x 27% or $27,000 a year in gross margin dollars to your company. Dealer B is a big hitter, $700,000 in sales, at 16% gross margin. Dealer B has a much lower margin rate, but he is putting $112,000 gross margin dollars in your distributor's bank account every year. Remember, it's dollars that go into the bank, not percentages.

Determining whether or not a particular dealer is profitable to your distributorship on a *net profit* basis is not easy to do. (Gross profits are easy to measure by contrast.) You will probably need to have someone at your distributorship who has access to more information than you do to help you determine which accounts you have post a positive net profit and which ones post an annual net loss.

Finally, does each dealer possess *strategic value* in your territory? Again, probably not. As for the meaning of strategic, consider these questions:

- ★ Does having this account give me a competitive edge in the market?
- ★ Does this account carry influence and prestige in the contractor community?
- ★ Am I proud to have my product associated with this account?
- ★ If I lost this account permanently to a competitor, would the consequences be drastic?
- ★ Would losing this account cause me to lose traction in the market?
- ★ Does the PR value of this account warrant special efforts on my part to keep it?

If you answer "Yes" to most of these, the account should be considered strategic in nature!

So there are three areas where we can answer yes or no for each dealer:

1. Is the dealer a significant contributor of my total sales?
2. Is the dealer profitable?
3. Does the dealer have strategic value beyond the score cards?

There are only eight ways to answer these three questions:

Size	Profits	Strategic
N	N	N
N	N	Y
N	Y	N
N	Y	Y
Y	N	N
Y	N	Y
Y	Y	N
Y	Y	Y

We can now affix labels to each category to help us determine an account's overall value to us.

Size	Profits	Strategic	Label
N	N	N	Loser
N	N	Y	Non-financial player
N	Y	N	Profit gem
N	Y	Y	Revenue laggard
Y	N	N	Diamond in the rough
Y	N	Y	Profit laggard
Y	Y	N	Financial-only player
Y	Y	Y	Winner

The value to the labels is that they let us easily class an account and then open up to us different approach strategies.

On the next page is a matrix showing what I would consider to be solid strategies to have for each account on the list. As you can see, you need to be prepared to have different conversations with each dealer—one plan won't fit all!

Dealer Types and Strategy Matrix

Dealer Type	Main Issues	Strategies
Loser	Does nothing for you; why is it still an account?	Make it ATI (available to the industry); reassign to inside sales; stop wasting time calling on it
Non-financial player	Nice prestige account; does not buy much	Can you turn it on to your brand and products? What is keeping you from being a major player in his game?
Profit gem	Small insignificant account with good profit margins	Cash cow; feed it and keep milking it. It will probably never become a big account (but it could), so explore if growth is an option; if so, migrate down the type list.
Revenue laggard	Profitable and strategic account; just small in size (rare combination)	Does he want to grow? If so, help him and migrate down the type list. If not, continue high service and enjoy the profits.
Diamond in the rough	Big but unprofitable and non-strategic account	Can this sow's ear become a silk purse? (Not likely!) Can a mix shift change the profit picture and at least migrate him to a profit laggard?
Profit laggard	Large and strategic account; but not profitable	Can you cut your servicing costs? Will a mix shift bring up the margins? Not advisable to make ATI unless horrible relationship.
Financial-only player	Large and profitable account, but of no strategic value	Wonderful cash cow; keep it and grow it. Never mind about the strategic issue.
Winner	A dream account!	**PROTECT IT!**

A Word About Pruning a Portfolio

Many TMs find that as they gain skill with account segmentation methods there are accounts they find they really don't want to work with any more. They want to fire them (make them ATI).

Before you decide to de-select an account, talk to your boss about it. There are cases where an account may be a Loser or a Diamond in the Rough and you want to can it. But what you may not know is that the principal is the cousin of your distributor owner's best friend. If you were to can that dealer (not knowing the behind-the-scenes politics), you could end up being canned yourself!

Always build your case carefully and then take it to your sales manager. Explain why you want to drop an account—you are willing to either turn it over to house coverage or drop it altogether. Then ask for your sales manager's advice. (He had better ask you first off, "Who do you have in mind to replace it?") If he reveals that there is information you don't have that makes the account valuable to the company for non-financial reasons, and you still don't want to cover it, ask if it can be assigned to another TM, even if that means that TM must cross a border into your territory for sales calls. It is better to keep the company well-related to its customer base than placate you in a bad situation and lose business.

Review Questions for Chapter 12

1. The idea that 80% of business comes from 20% of the customers is a statement of

A) the Peter Principle

B) the Poisson Principle

C) the Pareto Principle

D) the law of diminishing returns

E) none of the above

Answer: ________

2. The princes in a territory portfolio occupy which portion of the Poisson curve?

A) the far left side

B) the middle

C) the far right side

D) they can be anywhere on the curve

E) none of the above

Answer: ________

3. True or False. Working with all your dealers with zeal and energy can move the entire portfolio to the right in lock-step style.

A) True

B) False

Answer: ________

Now, why did you choose the answer you did?

4. Billy Bob Nuckledragger owns Royalty Heating. He is a large account (one of your three biggest), but an account analysis from your IT department shows he runs at a net loss of -2% a year. He is not the kind of account the community looks up to. What account type would you say Royalty Heating is?

A) Diamond in the Rough

B) Loser

C) Financial-only player

D) Winner

E) None of the above

Answer: ________

7. What would be a good overall call strategy to use on Royalty Heating?

A) make him ATI

B) keep milking it and try to help it grow

C) try to change his purchase mix and see if he can become stra- tegic

D) protect it

E) none of the above

Answer: ________

Chapter 13: Keeping Score

Can you imagine a PGA event where the officials did not keep score? Or a Super Bowl where the scoreboard was turned off and the officials did not keep score?

What about yourself? Do you jog? Bicycle? Fish? Hunt? Shoot archery? Do you keep score? If not, why not? If you do, why?

Those who keep score usually do so because they want to get better at whatever it is they are keeping score in. Pros come to the practices, and pros keep score.

To be a Tier One Territory Manager, you will need to keep score too and track some basic numbers.

Personal Score Cards

More than likely, you already get some type of score card from your distributor on a monthly basis—your monthly sales report. The exact format and content of your report will depend on your distributorship's accounting system and reporting capabilities, but as a minimum, I like to see the following information on each monthly report:

- ★ Detailed sales for each account for that month. (Detailed sales would mean that a complete listing of everything the account bought is on the report, from contactors to condensers, showing model numbers and part numbers, as well as order and invoice numbers.)
- ★ Summary year to date (YTD) sales for each account
- ★ Summary YTD sales from last year for each account.

- ★ Total sales dollars and gross margin dollars for each sales item reported, including a summary sales and GM report for each account.
- ★ Co-op advertising accrual dollars for each account, both for the month and YTD.
- ★ Accrual of incentive trip funds for each account for both the month and YTD (if your distributor provides incentive trips).
- ★ Accounts payable aging report for each account, showing amount that is current, 30-60 days old, 61-90 days old and over 91 days old.
- ★ Inclusion of any credits the account received (such as advertising co-op, warranty, concessions, etc.)
- ★ A grand summary showing sales by basic product category for the month and year to date and comparison to last year to date. (Product categories might be such broad groupings as compressor-bearing units, furnaces, coils and air handlers, small packaged units, parts and supplies, accessories, larger commercial units, refrigeration equipment, ice machines, and so on.)

Such reports might run several pages of the famous green-bar paper, but in my opinion, they are worth every penny to the Tier One TM. (Mine would get bound into a large computer report binder each month and kept on a special shelf in my office.) Such information tells me at a glance who is buying what and at what gross margin levels; who is actually using their co-op marketing funds; who is possibly having problems with warranty (or whether we have a product problem), who is paying their bills on time, and whether or not I am making my sales goals by product category.

If your present reports do not supply you with this level of detail, you may want to see if it is possible to get reports like this.

Score Cards for Dealers

Most of the information on the monthly sales report is not designed for dealer eyes. The report is for *your* eyes, to tell you how *you* are doing.

Dealers should get score cards too, but with different information on them. The CD that accompanies this book has one that I used when I was in the field ("Monthly Dealer Score Card.xls"). Since it is not a protected sheet, you can modify it if you wish to convey the information you want to convey.

The report format on the CD is one that most IT departments should be able to generate for you from the company's central computer system. In my case, I was the first (and for several years the only) TM in my company who wanted such a report, and it would have been cost prohibitive to have our software vendor program the report into the system, so I ended up creating my own on a spreadsheet. It would take me about ninety minutes a month to prepare the report (I only prepared reports for my top twelve dealers), but the use of the report made this time investment more than worth it.

So that you can better understand the report and how to use it, I will take you through a sample step by step.

In the upper left hand corner, I set up the dealer name and tracking year:

	A	B	C	D
1	Fester Bestertester and Clyde Fonebone Inc.			
2	2008 Purchases Summary			
3	Purchases Target for this Year:		$280,000	
4				

I enter the dealer's name on A1, the year of the purchase summary tracking on A2, and the sales quota we agreed upon for that year in C3.

If you then scroll to the right, you'll come to the distributor setup area. Make sure to fill it in too:

	A	K	L	M	N
1	Fester Bestertester and		Golden Opportunity Distributors		
2	2008 Purchases Summary		Sharon Lyons		
3	Purchases Target for this				
4					

With the exception of the dealer's name and sales quota, the information you have entered so far automatically copies to all the other worksheets in the book.

Next, we recapture the sales history of this account:

	A	B	C	D	E	F	G
1	Fester Bestertester and Clyde Fonebone Inc.						
2	2008 Purchases Summary						
3	Purchases Target for this Year:		$280,000				
4							
5	History						
6	Month	Jan	Feb	Mar	Apr	May	Jun
7	2007	$13,000	$10,400	$15,600	$17,000	$22,000	$35,000
8	2006	$10,900	$11,200	$13,800	$19,000	$19,800	$33,000
9	2005	$9,000	$10,400	$12,000	$14,000	$16,000	$36,000
10	Weighted Average	$11,633	$10,667	$14,400	$17,167	$20,267	$34,500
11	Percent	5%	5%	6%	8%	9%	15%
12	Percent YTD	5%	10%	16%	24%	32%	48%
13	Average YTD	$11,633	$22,300	$36,700	$53,867	$74,133	$108,633
14							
15	Target	$14,258	$13,074	$17,649	$21,040	$24,840	$42,285
16							

This will be the most tedious part to set up (at least the first time you use the Score Card). However, once history has been input, in the following years, you can simply select the data you still need and copy it, then paste it (using the Paste Special option, set for Values) and you are ready to go in about thirty seconds for a new year.

Here, we report what the account's total purchases were by month over the last three years. On line 10 you see a weighted average number. This method gives more voice to the most recent years, assuming that if there is a trend, the weighted method will pick it up better than a simple average.

The monthly percents are then reported, and YTD data is accumulated.

Line 15 shows you (and the dealer) what the sales should be for the current year by month if the quota is to be achieved.

Then, each month, as you get your sales reports from your IT department, you update the monthly sales detail section:

	A	B	C	D	E	F	G
1	Fester Bestertester and Clyde Fonebone Inc.						
16							
17	This Year						
18	Month	Jan	Feb	Mar	Apr	May	Jun
19	Major Brand Equipment	$9,654	$8,876	$16,934	$17,334	$15,334	$39,461
20	Other Equipment	$967	$1,376	$1,872	$1,605	$907	$7,654
21	Air Treatment/Zoning	$486	$211	$687	$883	$1,116	$2,746
22	Refrigeration Equipment	$0	$0	$0	$0	$0	$0
23	Ice Machines	$0	$0	$0	$0	$0	$0
24	OEM Parts	$764	$1,169	$634	$644	$709	$2,126
25	Generic Parts	$633	$964	$701	$1,164	$645	$0
26	Supplies	$217	$116	$309	$716	$317	$0
27	Tools, Instruments	$188	$0	$46	$0	$77	$0
28	Miscellaneous	$96	$32	$0	$37	$101	$0
29	Totals	$13,005	$12,744	$21,183	$22,383	$19,206	$51,987
30	Total, YTD	$13,005	$25,749	$46,932	$69,315	$88,521	$140,508
31	Target YTD	$14,258	$27,332	$44,981	$66,022	$90,862	$133,147
32							
33	This Mo vs Avg Mo	112%	119%	147%	130%	95%	151%
34	This YTD vs Avg YTD	112%	115%	128%	129%	119%	129%
35	This YTD vs Target YTD	91%	94%	104%	105%	97%	106%

Lines 19 through 28 are those product category sales summaries I said I wanted to get on my monthly sales report, and this shows why. I pass this information along to the dealer. If a dealer is normally active in one of those categories but I am showing no sales in that category (as is the case on lines 22 and 23), I may want to talk with him about it and see what I have to do to earn some of those refrigeration and ice machine sales.

The monthly sales are totaled and YTD figures calculated. Then, a key part of the report—the month and YTD are compared to the targeted goal to see if the dealer is ahead of plan, on plan, or behind plan.

Next comes the Fund Status report and it looks like this:

	A	B	C	D	E	F	G
1	Fester Bestertester and Clyde Fonebone Inc.						
36							
37	Funds Status	Jan	Feb	Mar	Apr	May	Jun
38	Advert Co-op Earnings	$212	$205	$376	$379	$325	$942
39	Claims	$108	$124	$370	$520	$800	$400
40	Balance	$104	$185	$192	$50	($425)	$117
41							
42	Incentive Trip	$106	$103	$188	$189	$162	$471
43							

The advertising co-op earnings are reported. By default, the earnings rate is set on the Instructions tab of the workbook and is 2% by default. You can change the Instructions tab to whatever earnings rate your dealer receives. If he earns different rates on different product classes, you will have to enter his earnings manually off the earnings report as this worksheet does not go to the complexity of tracking earnings by product family.

Advertising claims that have been paid by the distributor are reported with the marketing funds balance shown on line 40. You want to make sure your dealer uses his funds during the year, so if this line starts building up a large positive balance, it is time to have a chat about the power of advertising.

The report then shows incentive trip accrual (if you have an incentive trip program). Cell H34 of the Instructions tab sets the accrual rate (the default is 1%). If necessary, enter the trip accrual manually if the dealer earns trip points only on certain products. (The worksheet assumes that all purchases accrue trip funds at the default rate.)

The next section is one that a lot of TMs get squeamish over, but a Tier One TM will spot the value in it immediately and use it to powerful advantage on sales calls. It is the Accounts Payable report. Most lower level TMs feel that accounts payable is not their domain—that's why the distributor has a credit department. But a Tier One or Tier Two TM understands that working closely with a dealer who gets into account arrears can build powerful bonds for future development and growth and cement life-long relationships.

Here is what this section looks like:

	A	B	C	D	E	F	G
1	Fester Bestertester and Clyde Fonebone Inc.						
43							
44	Accounts Payable	Jan	Feb	Mar	Apr	May	Jun
45	Current	$12,550	$11,960	$20,003	$22,383	$17,356	$46,795
46	30 Days Old	$1,276	$756	$4,503	$2,007	$3,497	$637
47	60 Days Old	$0	$0	$756	$1,247	$0	$0
48	90 Days Old	$0	$0	$0	$0	$0	$0
49	120+ Days Old	$0	$0	$0	$0	$0	$0
50	Total Due	$13,826	$12,716	$25,262	$25,637	$20,853	$47,432
51							

I see that in March and April, Fester got behind a little on his A/P—not in serious trouble, but enough to cause me to raise an eyebrow. So what did Fester and I spend a minute or two discussing on my March and April sales calls? Collections! I can even offer to help in any way necessary to help him get his money from his customers faster. (After all, he can't pay me if his customers don't pay him.)

The Warranty Status report looks like this:

	A	B	C	D	E	F	G
1	Fester Bestertester and Clyde Fonebone Inc.						
43							
44	Accounts Payable	Jan	Feb	Mar	Apr	May	Jun
45	Current	$12,550	$11,960	$20,003	$22,383	$17,356	$46,795
46	30 Days Old	$1,276	$756	$4,503	$2,007	$3,497	$637
47	60 Days Old	$0	$0	$756	$1,247	$0	$0
48	90 Days Old	$0	$0	$0	$0	$0	$0
49	120+ Days Old	$0	$0	$0	$0	$0	$0
50	Total Due	$13,826	$12,716	$25,262	$25,637	$20,853	$47,432
51							

When I see warranty expenses rising above 3% of purchases, I get very nervous! Two percent is bad enough, but 3% suggests either a product problem we need to stay on top of, lack of skill on the part of the dealer's installers or service techs, or the dealer is in a sales and/or cash flow slump and is looking for some easy cash flow. (You must mentally factor out any concessions you grant on a special case basis, as these are usually a major product problem that is not the fault of the dealer.)

If I see the warranty expenses rising above the 2% trigger point, at some time during that month's sales calls I will talk about warranty and what is causing it. If the dealer reports that all of the coil line set connections are leaking, I may want to call my service advisor, or even the factory engineers (if the local advisor is not aware of any problem) and verify if they are getting similar reports elsewhere. If not, I may suspect installation skill deficits. That can be addressed at the local level.

The dealer will probably never own up to the idea that he is using warranty to pad weak cash flow. Instead, he'll give some weak excuses about those new circuit boards being no good and so on. Again, checking with the local or factory service people can help determine if that is a legitimate issue or a smoke screen. If it is a smoke screen, what do you think the dealer and I will discuss on those sales calls that month? How I can help him improve his sales and/or cash flow situation! I am not going to chastise him for cheating with warranty. He is probably uneasy about it any-way. Instead, I'll use it as a learning and development opportunity.

The next section of the score card is the Throughput Summary. Here, we want to see if the dealer is raising his productivity through solid throughput practices:

	A	B	C	D	E	F	G
1	Fester Bestertester and Clyde Fonebone Inc.						
57							
58	Throughput Analysis						
59	Equipment is what percent of sales?			31.40%	(average is 31.4%)		
60	How many employees does the dealer have?			9			
61	How many sales people does the dealer have?			1			
62							
63	Month	Jan	Feb	Mar	Apr	May	Jun
64	Estimated Sales	$41,417	$40,586	$67,462	$71,283	$61,166	$165,564
65	Throughput	$4,602	$4,510	$7,496	$7,920	$6,796	$18,396
66	Going rate sales	$813,332	$840,073	$930,389	$936,200	$868,749	$941,021
67	Going rate throughput	$90,370	$93,341	$103,377	$104,022	$96,528	$104,558
68	Sales throughput	$813,332	$840,073	$930,389	$936,200	$868,749	$941,021
69	*Aim for a throughput rate of at least $136,600 per year.*						
70	*The average replacement sales person does $788,000 per year in throughput.*						
71							

First, the footnotes on lines 69 and 70. Be sure to adjust those numbers for your state (as you learned how to do in Chapters 4 and 5).

You will next enter the dealer's average percentage of sales that goes toward the things you sell. (Be sure to track his percentage against only what *you* sell. If you record what he spends on equipment and material and you don't sell all the things he uses, your report will be overstated.) At this level of reporting and communication, any dealer who gets this report should have no problem giving you that information.

Next, on lines 61 and 62 enter how many total employees he has and the total number of full-time comfort consultants (sales people) he has. (If the dealer does the selling, he is part time. Enter a decimal here, such as 0.5.)

The worksheet then projects annual throughput using a going rate computation (which you learned about in Chapter 5). This way, you and the dealer can track whether throughput improvement strategies are paying off. (And I advise that every key account be on a throughput improvement program of some kind every year.)

Finally, the score card generates several graphs that help you capture all this data in an easy to understand pictorial form. I won't reproduce the graphs here, as you can see them easily enough on the score card.

Use of the Dealer Score Card

Only my top twelve or so accounts received this report from me on a monthly basis. When it came time to deliver the monthly report, all of them looked forward to it with eagerness!

First, before delivering the report, I would print two copies—one for them and one for me. On their copy, I would use a green pen and jot notes on it, like "Hey, way ahead of plan! Great job!" or "I'm getting nervous about the A/P trend; let's discuss."

We would then go over the report item by item. You can't imagine the way I felt when a dealer would look at his numbers and become proud he was ahead of his plan, or take on grim determination to get back on plan so as not to let me down. With my Big Twelve, I hardly ever had to ask to crank up the sales effort—they did it themselves because they wanted to beat their own forecasts!

In all my years in the territory I only had one case where the A/P report deteriorated badly and the dealer started to clam up. I sensed we were heading for a crisis and started to take steps to head it off by protecting our investment, but I was too late. Within three days of my final visit, he filed Chapter 7 (immediate closure due to bankruptcy) and left the area. I never heard from him again, and was left holding the bag for $35,000 in inventory. (And no, this is one dealer who refused to sign a UCC-1 form. From this lesson, I learned to never again let a dealer get away with that.)

So whether you use the form on the CD or design your own, consider using monthly score cards with your best accounts in this way. You'll be delighted by the results and your dealers will show extra pride that they chose to work with *you*!

Review Questions for Chapter 13

1. The primary purpose of a personal sales score card is to

   A) put pressure on poorly performing accounts

   B) constantly improve yourself

   C) be able to boast at sales meetings about how good you are

   D) make sure your commission checks are the right amount

   E) none of the above

   Answer: ________

2. The primary purpose of a dealer score card is to

   A) put pressure on poorly performing accounts

   B) help the dealer constantly improve his operation

   C) make sure you are getting paid on time

   D) make sure the dealer is not dinging you for weak sales

   E) none of the above

   Answer: ________

3. Below, write how you would use a dealer score card to help you improve your relationship with your main dealers.

Chapter 14: Got Dealers?

How many dealers do you have in your territory? Too many? Too few? How can you tell?

A Tier One Territory Manager has a strong idea of how many accounts it will take to dominate the territory, and they set out to establish that number and in the right places and right types to get the job done.

One Possible Case

Let's begin by seeing how a TM might go about setting up new construction and add-on/replacement coverage ratios for a territory.

Let's suppose that a careful analysis of the territory (see Chapter 5) shows that a TM's territory is 57% new construction oriented and 43% add-on and replacement oriented. Further, her analysis reveals that the territory should have a total residential and light commercial yield of $89 million. There are 525,000 people in this territory. How many dealers of each type would she need to maintain a given share of market?

That will depend on the share of market that is her target and the average size of her dealers.

Suppose that the TM's share of market target is 6%. This means she must capture 6% of $89 million, which is $5.3 million in business. Last year, she sold $4.7 million in equipment and materials.

Now, let's assume that this TM has forty-one accounts. (Research shows that TM productivity peaks at around thirty-four dealer accounts, so forty-one accounts is certainly a manageable load, although our TM may find herself working long hours many weeks.) If that is the case, her average dealer purchases 1/41st of $5.3 million, or about $130,000. If the typical dealer's retail sales are three times his purchases, her average dealer has sales of about $500,000. In per capita terms, she has one dealer for every 12,804 people.

We have already determined that 57% of the territory is residential construction oriented and 43% is residential replacement. We don't know the split out on commercial, but if we assumed it paralleled the residential numbers, we could not be too far off. So about $51 million of the territory purchases are for new construction (57% of $89 million) and about $38 million are for replacement.

If our TM were to log onto the U.S. Census Bureau web page (www.census.gov), she could follow the links to produce maps that can help her see what is happening in her territory. Here is the Census Bureau's map showing homes built since 2000 in Arizona:

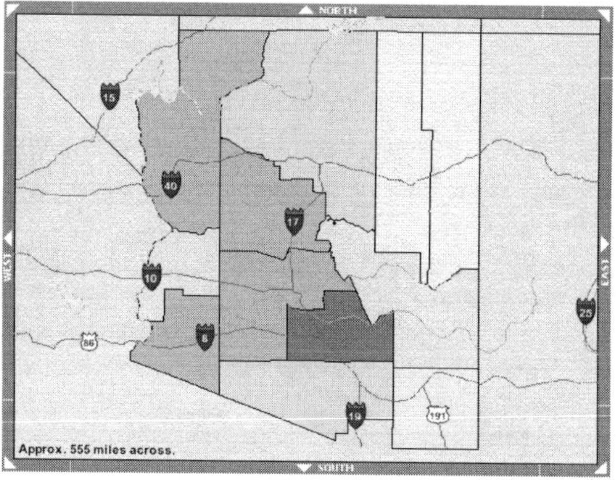

The darker the area, the higher the percentage of homes. The darkest area shown is the Southeast Phoenix metroplex (Tempe, Mesa, Chandler, etc.) and shows that about 25% of the homes in that area were built since 2000! The next lighter shade means 15-18% of the homes were built since 2000. This includes Western and Northern Phoenix as well, and includes the corridor leading up through Prescott to Flagstaff.

If our TM wanted to focus on new construction accounts in her territory, she would want to concentrate her efforts on the Southeastern Phoenix area. (However, I would also advise her to talk to local realtors and the local HBA to find out where the hot building trends are going so she does not miss a great opportunity because of dated information.)

How many dealers does she need in a given area to reach specific sales goals? Now we can answer that question with intelligence because we have done our homework.

If she does not want to change her share of market, the answer is none. She already has enough to hit her current share.

But suppose that in one county, she has only a 4% share of the residential market and that she wants to double it to 8%. She already has three dealers there buying a total of $400,000 a year from her. Doubling her share means a doubling in sales, so she needs $800,000 in sales from that county. Her three dealers can probably get *some* of that $400,000 increase, but not all of it. So she has to add dealers. She has to add probably four dealers. Overall, her territory is 57% new construction and 43% replacement, but in this particular county, the numbers are 31% new construction and 69% replacement. So among the four dealers she adds, she needs to select one new construction dealer and the other three should be add-on and replacement dealers.

How about a reverse analysis? Suppose she has a town with 22,000 people in it. She has one dealer there now. She gets an inquiry from a dealer who probably buys about $400,000 a year from suppliers. Should she take him on?

It depends on how big her existing dealer is. If he is a typical dealer, buying $130,000 and serving about 12,800 people, the answer is Yes, she should bring on the new dealer. (Unfortunately, in a town that small, the new dealer will probably run into the existing one on jobs; she may lose her existing dealer, which runs contrary to my desire to set up new accounts that my existing ones respect and don't compete with. In a small town, that combination may not always be possible.) The small existing dealer may end up leaving, but if the TM can fully convert the new dealer, she will make up for the loss three times over. A good move, in my book!

But suppose her existing dealer was bigger than her average dealer—that he purchased $300,000 a year from her. Would bringing on the $400,000 dealer be a good move?

That one's a little trickier to answer! In a town of 22,000 people and dealers who average $130,000 in purchases for every 12,800 people, there is $10 to be had from every person in the market. Her present dealer is giving her $13.60 per person, and if she could capture *all* of the new dealer's business, her total business would rise to almost $32 per person. She would have about 19% share of market.

This brings up an important point. *How much share of market* can a TM maintain over the long haul? (The key is "over the long haul.") The answer, from my experience and talking with platoons of the nation's best TMs, is *somewhere around 25% to 30%.* Over 30% and you will find your dealers meeting each other on the same jobs, so someone (or several) start picking up alternate brands to escape the me too trap. So 30% is achievable, but it will take some fancy footwork to maintain! What if, in this small town, the new (and bigger) dealer begins to muscle in on the existing one's turf? What will be her net gain?

At best, she would only gain $100,000 in sales. But she might also damage her reputation with her other dealers or with the trade in general in the area. This is a scenario that has no clear cut answer, but the decision whether or not to add the $400,000 dealer will take some soul searching and hard thinking on the part of the TM! Personally, I would not do it.

Now, if the new dealer was a replacement dealer and her existing one a new construction dealer, the case is less difficult to decide, isn't it? These two should rarely compete with each other, so bringing on a new large dealer in a small market under these conditions should be workable.

But What If One Dealer Wants to Change His Focus?

Fine. We bring on the new account to handle the replacement business while we keep the old to do the new house market. Everyone is happy.

Until the housing market hits a slump (which it does every seven to ten years). What might happen then? The $300,000 new construction account may try to jump into the replacement market to survive the drought. Is this a good idea?

Rarely!

New construction dealers rarely succeed in the replacement market, and for a number of shocking reasons. First, their crews normally don't have great customer skills and respect for property like those of a replacement dealer. After all, when all you do is rough-ins on a house that is not finished (there is no ivory carpet to track up!), and you work all day with other trades people, most who talk like sailors on a wharf, it is a little shocking when such a crude crew shows up to work in an existing home to change out some equipment or modify some ductwork. Homeowners often get nervous when such people show up in their beautiful clean homes.

Second, the person who does the selling often uses the builder sales model, where price,

price, and price are the three deciding factors. A new construction dealer can really mess up a thriving replacement market by jumping into it with both feet and undercutting the legitimate replacement shops on price.

So what to do?

I only had one account that was strong in new construction. We had a housing slump over a two year span and he wanted to jump into the replacement market to ride out the drought. I advised him not to do it. I suggested that if wanted to do this then he should set up a *separate company*, with a *separate name*, with its *own sales force and installers*. They could still use the parent company's warehouse, shop and back room people (accountants, purchasers, etc.) to keep costs down, but he needed special skills in such a replacement operation in order to succeed. He frowned, and rejected the advice. He plunged head first into the replacement market with red-hot pricing (and rough workmanship). For about nine months he caused no small amount of turmoil in that market—then things quieted down as he pulled back out of it, nearly bankrupt and shaken by the experience.

I have also seen cases where new construction dealers did it right—setting up separate operations with their own sales and installation staff (sometimes even in separate buildings), and it worked well.

So back to our TM's dilemma. If I were her, I would talk to my new construction dealer and tell him how a replacement dealer was going to pick up the line too, and that this should not affect his business in the least. I would warn him, however, that if he ever hit a slump and wanted to play in the replacement market where the new dealer would be entrenched, that he needed to do it with a separate team.

My Own Experience

When I was covering a territory, I used the coverage ratio of 25,000 people per dealer. If I placed dealers in my territory at that density, I would hit around 30% share of market (which I maintained for six years). It made the decision about letting a new dealer join the team (or purging a poor one) easier.

It was also a good conversation piece when recruiting. I once picked up a very strong replacement account because in a town of 12,000 people, his brand had just placed its *third* dealer. I told him that my math suggested one dealer (about $200,000 in purchases) per 25,000 people was more realistic. He dropped his present line and joined the team, and I never set up another dealer in his coverage area. He appreciated that, and I appreciated his business!

Obviously, if I had a $400,000 dealer in one town (I did, in fact, have two that size) I could figure that such an account could cover 50,000 people at the 30% share level. In a town of 100,000 people, I had two such dealers. I could not bring anyone else on without jeopardizing my two heavy hitters, and they knew it, and several dealers who approached me about taking on our line learned it too.

You always protect your big, heavy producers!

As long as they produce.

Review Questions for Chapter 14

1. A TM has thirty-two dealers purchasing a total of $3,670,000 in a territory of 440,000 people. If the per capita purchases for residential and light commercial equipment in this area is $180, what is this TM's share of market?

A) 4.6%

B) $8.35 per person

C) $114,688 per dealer

D) all of the above

E) none of the above

Answer: ________

2. The largest city in the territory of the TM in question 1 has 175,000 people in it. How many average size dealers does this TM need to achieve a 12% share of market?

A) you can't tell with this information

B) 33 dealers

C) 275 dealers

D) none of the above

Answer: ________

3. Which option offers a new construction dealer the best chance of surviving in the replacement market?

A) hiring a good replacement sales consultant

B) having installers who are especially skillful and tactful

C) having high quality tools for the crews to use

D) run the replacement operation as a separate entity

E) A, B and E

Answer: ________

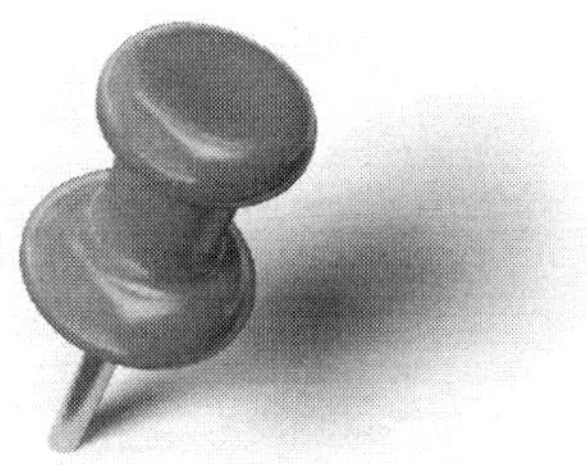

Chapter 15: Basic Contracting Financial Management

The number one thing that comes to the top on surveys of contractors about what they would like to see in local training is financial management. It consistently places at the top of the list in surveys conducted anywhere in the country.

With it being such a vital topic, the territory manager who has at least a good understanding of the *basics* of financial management is in a position to offer his or her accounts solid counsel and advice that can lead to incredibly strong business bonds through the years.

Before we dive into this subject, it is time for the famous disclaimer: *this chapter is not designed to turn you into a financial management expert.* No one chapter in a book can do that, and mastery of this subject takes years and years of experience, practice and mistakes. You will not become a financial expert because you read a chapter from a book or have a year or two of experience under your belt. Therefore, when you give financial advice, give it only after great thought and consideration, and, if necessary, talking it over with someone wiser than yourself. Bad advice you give in this area can destroy your dealers, and you should be very, very aware of that and proceed with care.

The Basics: The Books

Financial management begins with what dealers usually call the books - the accounting reports they get from their accountants (whether in-house or outside professionals makes no difference). There are three reports each dealer needs to get on a regular and frequent basis.

They are:

1. The Income Statement (or Profit and Loss, or P&L)
2. The Balance Sheet
3. The Cash Flow Statement

These reports should be **prepared monthly** by an accountant (hired, or on staff). Anything less is not frequent enough to allow a dealer to wisely manage his or her business. I often get small dealers squealing that such a frequency of reports would cost too much. I always reply, "Okay, so what if you just get one a year—and find yourself broke before you even know it?" Because a smaller business is much more subject to the volatilities of the market it is even *more* important for a smaller dealer to get monthly statements.

These monthly reports need to be in the hands of the dealer **by the 10th prox.** What this means is that the financial reports need to be completed and delivered by the tenth of the month following the close of the current month. For example, a dealer should have his April statements on his desk no later than May 10. Anything slower means the dealer is trying to drive his high speed car down a curving road by looking in the rear view mirror. The sooner the reports are on his desk, the sooner he can make adjustments to the monthly business activity to recover a loss or exploit an opportunity.

Clean Books?

I was once involved on a consultation where the dealer of a large company brought me in because for all his millions in sales, he was only turning 2.7% pre-tax profit.

I went over the books with him and found a number of anomalies: $21,780 in casual labor (another term for part-time help). I said that was a lot of casual labor. What made it up? He replied that this was his son's pay. And when did the son work there? During the summer, when he was out of college. And he got paid $21,780 for three months of work??? The dealer sheepishly grinned, and said, "Well, actually, that's his tuition at college."

There were similar bloated numbers in other places which turned out to be start-up funds for his wife's new business, as well as new cabinets and carpets for their home. When we added all these little take-outs back into the P&L, the dealer was making closer to 10% pre-tax, which made him happy.

But I had to warn him that if he was ever audited, his padding of the books could cost him dearly. If a dealer wants to provide his wife a new luxury car every two years (and she does not work for the firm), he can, but he needs to do that by writing himself a dividend check at the end of the year, not burying it in the company's expenses and reducing his tax liability thereon.

Finally, the books need to be **clean**. That means business information only on them, no personal finance.

Introduction to the Income Statement

When I ask dealers which of the three documents is the most important, they always say it is the income statement (or P&L). I always reply that this is true if you want to review company activity. But what if you wanted to review the company's worth, or its cash situation? Then the other two reports are more important, are they not? So the income statement is no more important (or less) than the balance sheet and cash flow statement. Don't let me listing it first make you think otherwise.

The income statement is supposed to be a simple document, and in most cases it is. The difficulties arise when dealers try to split hairs and wrangle over where to put sometimes trivial amounts of money.

Here is the basic format of an income statement:

Income (sales)

<u>Less Cost of Sales</u>

= Gross Margin

<u>Less Overhead</u>

= Net Margin

Let's review each section in some detail.

Income (or Sales)

Here, the accountant shows the total of all sales for the accounting period (usually one month). Sometimes, accountants will call this section Revenues or Receipts instead of Sales or Income, but it is the same idea—money comes to the company from customers, and this is where it gets recorded.

Cost of Sales

Sometimes called Cost of Goods Sold, here is where the accountant places expenses the company incurs because it got jobs, and *only because it got jobs*. As I tell dealers, this is where the things you use on a job go. This includes material (like equipment, sheet metal, pipe, wiring, refrigerant, thermostats, concrete pads, and the like) as well as direct labor, permits, fees, freight, and other various and sundry items. Here is a little quiz for you. Place a check mark in the boxes of the items you think should go in the Cost of Sales section of an income statement:

- ❑ warranty expenses
- ❑ sales salaries
- ❑ cost of a furnace
- ❑ fuel for trucks
- ❑ withholding taxes
- ❑ subcontractors
- ❑ sales commissions
- ❑ advertising
- ❑ labor to install a unit
- ❑ unbillable time
- ❑ owner's salary
- ❑ business license

To see if you got them all correct, turn to the next page.

Here is what you should have checked:

☑ warranty expenses	☑ sales commissions
❑ sales salaries	❑ advertising
☑ cost of a furnace	☑ labor to install a unit
❑ fuel for trucks	❑ unbillable time
❑ withholding taxes	❑ owner's salary
☑ subcontractors	❑ business license

If you got them all correct, go on to "Gross Margin" on page 246. You don't need what is on this page.

Warranty expenses definitely go into Cost of Sales, because Cost of Sales only contains costs a dealer gets because he gets jobs and only because he gets jobs. If he did not get jobs, he would have no warranty exposure.

Sales commissions go into Cost of Sales because commissions are expenses a dealer incurs because he sells a job and only because he sells a job.

Sales salaries, however, get paid whether the sales consultant sells a job or not. Since Cost of Sales is tied directly to jobs, sales salaries do not go in this section.

Advertising, although a legitimate business expense, cannot be tied to any one job or even a set of jobs. It does not go in the Cost of Sales section.

The cost of a ***furnace***, ***labor to install*** a unit, and ***subcontracts*** are all costs a dealer incurs when he does jobs, and only when he does jobs. If he did not have the jobs, he would not have labor on the job, nor equipment, nor the need of a sub to do work for him.

Everything else cannot be traced directly to a specific job or set of jobs, so they don't technically belong in Cost of Sales.

Often, dealers will argue that fuel for trucks should go in Cost of Sales because without the job, the truck would not have to drive out to the site, but I always counter with, "What about those times the truck is not driving to a particular job site? And how are you going to tell how much fuel and oil a truck uses on a drive to a job site?" It is impossible to measure, so we don't track it under Cost of Sales. Unbillable time, by its nature, is not chargeable to a job, so it does not go in Cost of Sales. A business license is required to do work in general, but not any one particular job. Withholding taxes are applied across the board, not just to any particular job. And the owner's salary is only chargeable to Cost of Sales to the extent the owner actually works on jobs. The time he spends doing other things goes elsewhere.

In short, if it goes on a job ticket (either as a time card entry or a material use ticket), it goes in Cost of Sales.

Gross Margin

Subtracting the Cost of Sales from Sales leaves Gross Margin. (Some dealers call it Gross Profit, but we don't know yet if it is a profit. It could be a Gross Loss! The term Gross Margin is neutral, so it is better to use it.)

Overhead

Overhead contains those expenses a business incurs whether it gets jobs or not. Two pages ago, several items in the checklist were of this nature (sales salaries, advertising, withholding taxes, unbillable time, owner's salary, business license). Other examples of overhead costs would be rent, utilities, office worker salaries, management salaries, shop labor (unless the dealer has his shop people code their time cards to individual jobs, in which case it goes where?), and the like.

Net Margin

Subtracting Overhead from the Gross Margin leaves the Net Margin. If this is a positive number, the dealer made a profit. If it is a negative number, he sustained a loss.

Check Your Understanding

To be sure you've got the idea so far, let's check your understanding. Melody Toon owns a dealership where sales last year were $1,100,000. Cost of Sales came to $624,000 and overhead was $329,000.

What was Melody's Gross Margin? $________________

What was her Net Margin? $________________

Did she make a profit? ☐ Yes ☐ No

Turn the page to see the answers.

Melody's Gross margin is $1,100,000 – $624,000 = $476,000. Her Net Margin was $476,000 – $329,000 = $147,000. Yes, she made a profit (because the Net Margin is positive).

Often, accountants will also show each expense (or expense group, like the Cost of Sales) as a percentage of sales. To find the percentage, simply divide the expense by the sales.

In Melody's case, what is her Gross Margin percent?

$476,000/$1,100,000 = 43.3%.

And what was her Net Margin percent?

$147,000/$1,100,000 = 13.4%.

What was her Cost of Sales as a percentage of Sales? 56.7%.

And her Overhead as a percent of Sales? 29.9%.

Other Columns on the P&L

Accountants often will show the current month's numbers and then the year to date (YTD) numbers side by side on a P&L, with both numbers also expressed as percents of sales of their respective sales figures.

A few go on to give their clients two more columns—the same month and YTD data from *last year*. This lets the dealer compare the current year to last year to see if he is growing or not.

But one column that all dealers should get (and very few do) is what I call the *rolling twelve* column. (You'll learn why this is so vital in a few more pages.) The rolling twelve column reports a complete fiscal year on each P&L. For example, a dealer's May statement will show the data for May and for the YTD of his current fiscal year, and may show the same May and YTD from last year. If he has a rolling twelve, he will also see the data from June 1 of last year through May 31 of this year. His August statement will likewise show a rolling twelve that spans September 1 of last year through August 31 of this year. Each P&L captures an entire fiscal cycle.

Statement of Income and Expenses for
Moe, Larry and Curly's Comfort Shop
Fiscal Period Ending Dec. 31, 20xx

Sales			
Residential Replacements	$530,000		
Commercial Replacements	$220,000		
Custom New Homes	$150,000		
Service Sales	$190,000		
	Total Sales	$1,090,000	100%
Cost of Sales			
Equipment and Material, Res Replacement	$175,000		
Equipment and Material, Comm Replacement	$80,000		
Equipment and Material, Custom Home	$38,000		
Parts and Material, Service	$38,000		
Labor, Residential Replacements	$90,000		
Labor, Commercial Replacements	$32,000		
Labor, Custom Home	$40,000		
Labor, Service	$44,000		
Permits, fees	$2,000		
Subcontracts	$10,000		
Warranty Expenses	$22,000		
Callbacks	$2,100		
Vehicles	$44,000		
Freight in	$1,500		
	Total Costs	$618,600	57%
Gross Margin		$471,400	43%
Overhead			

Fixed Overhead:			
Salaries and wages, office	$150,000		
Sales salary	$22,000		
Sales Commissions	$30,000		
Service Dispatcher	$24,000		
Service Manager	$40,000		
Payroll Taxes and Insurance	$87,000		
Insurance, General Liability	$36,000		
Rent	$18,000		
Other fixed expenses	$24,100		
Total Fixed Overhead	$431,100		39%
Variable Overhead:			
Advertising	$20,000		
Telephones	$6,800		
Other variable overhead	$3,000		
Total Variable Overhead	$29,800		3%
Total Overhead		$460,900	42%
Net Profit/(Loss)		$10,500	1%

Look over Moe, Larry and Curly's statement carefully. Moe never bothers to look at it critically, but you should. Is it accurately set up? If not, what do you spot as errors? Before you get into a hurry and skip past this white space, cover the text below it with your hand and try to figure it out and write your discoveries here.

There are errors, and here they are:

- ★ Vehicles should not go under Cost of Sales as it is impossible to say how much of each vehicle's cost should be charged to any one particular job.
- ★ Sales Commissions should not be in Overhead because the commissions only get paid when a job is sold.

If you were to reassign these numbers to their proper sections, does the Net Margin (the bottom line) change? No, not at all. But what does change? The total Cost of Sales (and hence the Gross Margin), and the Overhead. The change is not very large—only about 2%. But it can be serious, as you are about to see.

The income statement is a vital document to an HVAC dealer for two reasons: (1) it tells him how well he is playing the game, much like a scorecard can tell a golfer which holes he needs to work on, and (2) it is the document that provides the foundation for his job pricing. We will come back to the first point later in this chapter. Right now, we want to focus on how the income statement impacts job pricing.

I have produced Moe's *corrected* income statement on the next page.

Statement of Income and Expenses for
Moe, Larry and Curly's Comfort Shop

Fiscal Period Ending Dec. 31, 20xx

Corrected

Sales			
Residential Replacements	$530,000		
Commercial Replacements	$220,000		
Custom New Homes	$150,000		
Service Sales	$190,000		
	Total Sales	$1,090,000	100%
Cost of Sales			
Equipment and Material, Res Replacement	$175,000		
Equipment and Material, Comm Replacement	$80,000		
Equipment and Material, Custom Home	$38,000		
Parts and Material, Service	$38,000		
Labor, Residential Replacements	$90,000		
Labor, Commercial Replacements	$32,000		
Labor, Custom Home	$40,000		
Labor, Service	$44,000		
Permits, fees	$2,000		
Sales Commissions	$30,000		
Subcontracts	$10,000		
Warranty Expenses	$22,000		
Callbacks	$2,100		
Freight in	$1,500		
	Total Costs	$604,600	55%
Gross Margin		$485,400	45%
Overhead			
Fixed Overhead:			
Salaries and wages, office	$150,000		
Sales salary	$22,000		
Service Dispatcher	$24,000		

Service Manager	$40,000		
Payroll Taxes and Insurance	$87,000		
Insurance, General Liability	$36,000		
Rent	$18,000		
Other fixed expenses	$24,300		
Total Fixed Overhead	$401,100		37%
Variable Overhead:			
Advertising	$20,000		
Vehicles	$44,000		
Other variable expenses	$9,800		
Total Variable Overhead	$73,800		7%
	Total Overhead	474,900	44%
Net Profit/(Loss)		$10,500	1%

The Price is Wrong

Unlike the old television game, *The Price is Right*, most contractors today do not set the right price on their jobs as evidenced by the fact that the average net profit before tax is dismal in this trade. In this section, you will learn how the income statement bears on job pricing. (The fact that most contractors see no relation between the income statement and their job pricing is the main reason most don't make adequate profits.)

Let's consider the case of Moe, Larry and Curly, whose corrected income statement you saw on page 252. Moe has to bid a job today. He does a good takeoff and figures he'll need $5,000 worth of material and equipment to do the job. He also figures sixty-four man-hours of labor (Moe always bids in eight hour increments since most installers only think in terms of eight hour days. A few can handle four hour half-days.) Since his installers make $20 an hour, this comes to $1,280 in labor. He also figures another $300 to handle freight, permits, and a sub to do a small part of the job. He wants to make 12% net profit on this job. Given his overhead of 42%, what should the job be priced at? Figure out the price to the best of your ability and write it in the box below. Then, after you have turned in your bid, read on beyond the box to see how you should have solved it.

My bid is:

$

Here is how to solve the job pricing problem.

Imagine the job as a pie chart, like this one:

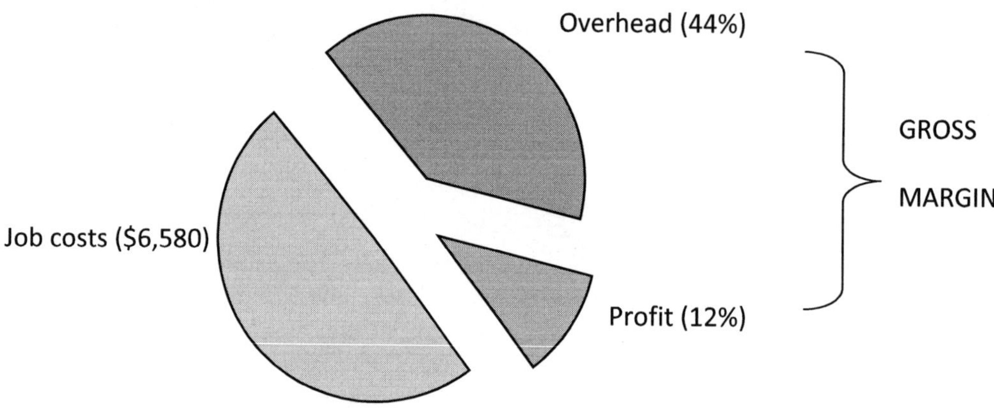

Every job bid must cover the job costs (material, labor, subs, permits, freight, etc.), some overhead, and create some profit. The job costs come directly from the job take-off (the bill of material and estimate of time the bidder thinks the job will take). Most contractors are pretty good at this part of the process. Profit is pretty obvious too. But the overhead piece is where most contractors drop the ball. If a company normally uses, let's say, 10,000 man-hours of direct labor a year on jobs, it should be obvious that each hour used on jobs should carry 1/10,000th of the overhead. So this job must carry overhead in proportion to the labor on it. Moe's accountant tells him that historically, his overhead runs 44%. So, 44% of what? Of Moe's *sales*. Moe's overhead runs 44% of his *sales.*[17]

17 That's a pretty high overhead, as it turns out.

So 44% of the job's asking price should go to overhead; $6,580 to job costs (like material and labor); and 12% of the asking price should be how much is left after all the bills are paid (the profit). The problem is all we have are the job costs and some percentages—no asking price. So how do we get the job asking price?

Easy, actually. Look back at the pie chart above. Overhead is 44% of sales and the Net Profit goal here is 12% of sales. Together, this is 56% of sales. So what must be left for the Cost of Sales slice of the pie?

If you said 44%, you are right!

Now we have this fact: $6,580 is 44% of the job's price. Can we solve that problem? Sure! We need a ratio to do it. Here is how it goes:

The Job Price is to 100% of the Job Price as

$6,580 is to 44% of the Price.

Since this is a ratio, we can write it like this:

$$\frac{\text{Job Price}}{100\%} = \frac{\$6,580}{44\%}$$

Any percentage can be expressed as a decimal, so this ratio can be re-written like this:

$$\frac{\text{Job Price}}{1.00} = \frac{\$6,580}{0.44}$$

Now you should know that any number divided by 1.00 is the number, so the left side of the equation reduces to merely the Job Price. The Job Price is equal to $6,580 divided by 0.46, or some $14,955 to the nearest dollar.

The $6,580 figure is the ***total job costs*** (as estimated by the estimator). But where did the 0.44 (or 44%) come from? It is the difference between 100% and the sum of the Overhead and Net Profit. Look back at the basic income statement outline on page 243. Do you see what would be another name for Overhead and Net Profit?

How about Gross Margin? Because indeed, that is what the sum of Overhead and Net Profit is.

So we can now write a general job pricing equation based on the income statement. It is simple and easy to learn. Here it is:

$$\text{The Right Prie} = \frac{\text{The Job Costs}}{100\% - \text{Gross Margin }\%}$$

Where it Comes From

You (and all your dealers) should know this job pricing formula by heart. The Job Costs come from the estimator's take-off. (Obviously, experience is important here!) The Gross Margin comes from two elements—the Overhead as shown on the income statement, and the net profit the dealer wants to make on this job.

And what determines how much profit a dealer should make on any job? I like to look at jobs as projects with differing amounts of risk attached to them. Like investments, low risks result in low yields. High yields come at high risk. If the job is simple—if *any* clown in town could do it—a dealer would be lucky to make even 5% profit on it. (And, in fact, the job may go for what would amount to a *negative* profit—a loss—to the dealer in some markets.) But if the job is complex and the dealer is the only one in town that can do a job like that, why not make 14%, or 18%, or 22% net (or more) on this job? No one else can do it and it is risky, so the dealer has a right to earn high profits on the job.

So here are the three sources of information needed to do a job price:

(1) The Job Costs (from the takeoff)

(2) The Overhead (from the income statement)

(3) The Net Profit (based on risk assessment)

Proof of the Right Price

Let's double check to make sure that $14,955 pays all the bills and leaves Moe with profits equal to 12% of the sales.

Here is the math:

The Job Sells for…	$14,955
The Job Costs come to…	$6,580
Resulting in Gross Margin of…	$8,375
Overhead is 44% of sales, or…	$6,580
Leaving us a Net Profit of…	$1,795

If we now divide $1,795 by $14,955, we get 0.119966, which is close enough to 12% to make me happy.

How Much Wiggle Room Is There?

Often, a dealer will find himself drawn into a bidding war with a competitor and will reduce his price to remain in the game and (hopefully) get the job. How much wiggle room does Moe have on this job?

How much could Moe cut his price before he hurt his company? (Be careful before you answer. Think carefully here!)

The answer will shock you.

Moe cannot cut his price one penny! If he did, would he be making 12% on the job? No. He might make 11.9996%, but not 12%. If he wants 12%, he must get $14,955 for this job, or live with less than 12% net profit.

It often shocks dealers to hear this. But when I go on to explain why, they understand it. Most dealers would like to make 10% net profit for the year. (Few ever achieve it, mostly because they don't set the price correctly to begin with.) If a dealer takes a 5% cut on his profit margins to save a job today, he'll have to make 15% profit margin on a future job to get back on the 10% road he wanted to travel this year. Yet how many 15% jobs come along? Some, but probably not enough to save the dealer's bacon.

Here's another question to ponder. How much could Moe cut his price before he began to lose money on the job?

If you said, "His profit margin of $1,795," you would be correct. Any price reduction that goes beyond $1,795 means Moe is taking dollars out of the job that should pay for job costs and the overhead. Now we know that $1,795 is 12% of Moe's price. How many times do dealers find bidders on jobs that are more than 12% below them? Quite often! So on many jobs, Moe could give up all his profit margin and *still* be high.

Dealers can never win in the long run on price alone. Most don't know that and have to prove it to themselves by going bankrupt.

Moe will have to learn how to sell on something besides price (like value) if he wants to survive, and if you are a Tier One or Tier Two TM, this is the kind of dealer you are looking for!

Can They Make It Up On Volume?

Suppose that on this job, Moe was beaten by a dealer who had the same costs and overhead as Moe (a very unlikely possibility, but work with me here for a moment). Suppose this other dealer bid the job at $10,000 (figuring that with costs of $6,580, he has $3,420 to play with. That should *surely* be enough to live like a king off this job!

Well, let's find out. Our low-ball competitor does the job for $10,000 and when it is done, his accountant hands him the job cost report:

The Job Sells for…	$10,000
The Job Costs come to…	$6,580
Resulting in Gross Margin of…	$3,420
Overhead is 44% of sales, or…	$4,400
Leaving us a Net Profit of…	-$980

Ouch! Bob Boogeyman ended up losing $980 on this job!

But since Bob Boogeyman's accountant is as stupid as Bob is, he does not realize that the true overhead is the overhead Moe had to allow for ($6,580), not the 44% of the actual sale Bob made. Bob's overhead then is actually $2,180 more than he (or his accountant) thought it was, so Bob actually lost $3,160 on this job! And he can't make that up on volume!

To understand this, go back to the original setup—that Bob Boogeyman has the same overhead and costs as Moe. If Bob's overhead and costs are identical to Moe's, the overhead his jobs must carry must be identical to Moe's too, not the $4,400 he thought it was. (In fact, if Bob kept bidding jobs like this all year, his sales figure would drop behind Moe's, and with the overhead staying the same, his overhead as a percentage of sales would actually ***increase***. He would still end up having to raise his prices dramatically to say in business. But by the time Bob learns this, his shop will have become the property of some other business.

The Devil Is In the Details

Moe's income statement on page 249 is based on an actual contractor. (As they say in documentaries, only the names have been changed to protect the guilty.) As we have seen, it was not set up correctly and the corrected version on page 252 gave a different overhead—it was 2% higher than Moe had thought.

This is not much of a change—just 2%. But look at its impact on Moe's job pricing. With the old (wrong) P&L, Moe should have bid the job this way:

Job Price = $6,580/100% - (42% + 12%) = $6,580/100% - 54%

= $6,580/46% = $14,304

Notice that this is $651 less than Moe's correct bid. If Moe used his wrong P&L to price jobs, he would not make 12% net on his jobs. He would make a profit, but not 12%. (He might make 10% net, not 12%. I leave it for you to prove it to yourself by checking the math.)

This is not much, but what if this happened on every job Moe bid this year? If he had plans to make 12% net for the year, he could never, ever get there with his old income statement and its errors.

This is why I always advised my top level dealers to make sure their income statements were properly structured, with each account in its appropriate section. Otherwise, at the end of the year, the numbers they hoped to see just wouldn't be there!

Moe's statement also lacks some important data that I like to see dealers get on a monthly basis. One thing his statement lacks is a "This Month" column. All we have is the "Year to Date" (YTD) data. A dealer needs to be able to see on each monthly statement his sales for the month and a growing accumulation for the entire year so far.

Moe should also have the same two columns from last year—last year's current month and last YTD as well.

Finally, Moe should have that Rolling Twelve column I mentioned earlier. This is important because if Moe uses his statement Overhead percentage to drive his job pricing, his Overhead will vary from month to month (because Overhead, as dollars, does not change much month to month, but sales do). As a result, he would be changing his job pricing math every month, resulting in confusion for his sales force and errors. The Rolling Twelve shows the Overhead for a full year every month. It may move from month to month, but usually by only a fraction of a percent. This gives Moe a much more stable number to use for his job pricing.

More Than One Business

Not only did Moe have an error on his income statement (a small one, but one that would cost him 2% net profit over the year—only some $20,000!). Moe also should *departmentalize* his income statement. This is the process of breaking up a single-column income statement (like the one on page 252) into a statement that shows the incomes and expenses for each department in Moe's company.

Moe obviously has at least two departments—Installation and Service. (One could build a good argument for *four*—Custom New Home, Residential Replacement, Commercial Replacements, and Service. But for now, let's keep it simple and just do a gross breakdown between Installation and Service.)

In creating a departmentalized statement, a dealer must know his Sales and direct costs (Cost of Sales) by department. Luckily for us, on page 252, Moe has already done this. A dealer also has to know if any of his overhead expenses are properly the responsibility of any one division or if all the divisions share in that expense.

Any division-specific overhead expenses will be charged to those divisions in their own overhead reports. But the expenses that all divisions must support must be spread among the divisions in an equitable manner to get an accurate picture of whether or not each division is making money on its own two feet.

But how to allocate the shared overhead expenses? Some off-the-shelf accounting programs split up the overhead in direct proportion to the sales dollars, but this is not accurate for our purposes because the difference between costs and sale price is not uniform across all departments. (Service departments, for example, should set prices that are much higher than costs compared to installation departments.) Other systems allocate shared overhead on the basis of the square footage of the shop occupied by each department, but there is clearly no direct link between a department's floor space and overhead in an HVAC shop like there is in a retail store.

The only reliable way to split up shared overhead is to allocate it on the same basis that is the cause of overhead. When you think about it, why does a dealer have overhead at all? The ultimate answer is, *"To get his field people out to the jobs so they can work as fast and efficiently as possible so he can repeat the cycle as often as possible and maximize his income."* In other words, overhead exists to facilitate the job of field labor to be productive.

This gives us the key we need to unlock the shared overhead allocation. If 70% of the labor in the company is on the Installation payroll, we can give Installation 70% of the shared overhead, with the balance (30%) going to Service.

On the next page, you'll find a form (it is on the CD-ROM) to help departmentalize a statement by hand.

Departmentalizing Worksheet

	A	B	C	D	E	F	G
		Original		**Installation**		**Service**	
2	From the Income Statement...	Dollars	% Sales	Dollars	% Sales	Dollars	% Sales
3	**Sales**	$	100%	$	100%	$	100%
4							
5	**Cost of Sales**	$					
6	- Labor	$		$		$	
7	*% of Labor*			%	*D6/B6*	%	*F6/B6*
8	- Parts	$				$	
9	COS Left	$		$			
10	*(B5 - B6 - B8)*						
11							
12	**Gross Margin**	$	%	$	%	$	%
13		*(B3 – B5)*		*(D3–D6–D9)*		*(F3-F6-F8)*	
14	**Overhead**	$	%				
15	- Sales Salaries	$		$			
16	- Serv Salaries	$				$	
17	OH Left	$					
18	*(B14 - B15 - B16)*						
19	Overhead Allocated			$	*B17 x D7*	$	*B17 X F7*
20							
21	Dept Overhead			$	%	$	%
22				*D15 + D19*		*F16 + F19*	
23	**Net Margin**	$	%	$	%	$	%
24		*(B12 – B14)*		*(D12 – D21)*		*(F12 – F23)*	

Here are detailed instructions.

Line 3: Record the total Sales for the entire company in B3. Compute the sub-totals for Installation and enter in D3, and for Service in F3.**Line 5**: Record the Cost of Sales for the entire company in B5.

Line 6: Record the total labor in B6; Installation labor only in D6; Service labor only in F6.

Line 7: Compute the percentage of direct labor that was used by Installation by dividing D6 by B6 and expressing as a percentage. Put this in D7. For Service, divide F6 by B6 and express as a percentage in F7.

Line 8: In B8, record the cost of parts and repeat this in F8.

Line 9: Subtract B6 and B8 from B5 and enter in B9. Copy to D9.

Line 12: Subtract B5 from B3 and enter in B12. For Installation, subtract D6 and D9 from D3 and enter in D12. Divide D12 by D3 to get percentage for E12. For Service, subtract F5 and F8 from F3 and enter in F12. Divide F12 by F3 to get percentage for E12.

Line 14: Record the company's Overhead in B14.

Line 15: Record all sales related salaries (installation manager, salesman salary) in B15 and copy to D15.

Line 16: Record all service related salaries (service manager, dispatcher) in B16 and copy to F16.

Line 17: Subtract B15 and B16 from B14 and record in B17.

Line 19: For Installation overhead, multiply B17 by the percentage in D7 and record in D19. For Service overhead, multiply B17 by the percentage in F7 and record in F19.

Line 21: For Installation, add D15 and D19 and record in D21. Divide D21 by D3 to get percentages for E21. For Service, add F16 to F19 and record in F21. Divide F21 by F3 to get percentages for G21.

Line 23: Record the Net Margin for the entire company in B23. For Installation, subtract D21 from D12 and enter in D23. Divide D23 by D3 to get percentages. For Service, subtract F21 from F12 and enter in F23. Divide F23 by F3 to get percentages.

Now, on the next page, I show you this form filled in for Moe's business using his now-corrected Income Statement.

	A	B	C	D	E	F	G
		Original		Installation		Service	
2	From the Inc Statement...	Dollars	% Sales	Dollars	% Sales	Dollars	% Sales
3	**Sales**	$1,090,000	100%	$900,000	100%	$190,000	100%
4							
5	**Cost of Sales**	$604,600					
6	- Labor	$206,000		$162,000		$44,000	
7	*% of Labor*			79%	*D6/B6*	21%	*F6/B6*
8	- Parts	$38,000	→	→	→	$38,000	
9	COS Left	$360,600	→	$360,600			
10	*(B5 - B6 - B8)*						
11							
12	**Gross Margin**	$485,400	45%	$377,400	42%	$108,000	57%
13		*(B3 – B5)*		*(D3–D6–D9)*		*(F3-F6-F8)*	
14	**Overhead**	$474,900	44%				
15	- Sales Salaries	$22,000	→	$22,000			
16	- Serv Salaries	$64,000	→	→	→	$64,000	
17	OH Left	$388,900					
18	*(B14 - B15 - B16)*						
19	Overhead Allocated			$307,231	*B17 x D7*	$145,669	*B17 X F7*
20							
21	Dept Overhead			$329,231	37%	$145,669	77%
22				*D15 + D19*		*F16 + F19*	
23	**Net Margin**	$10,500	1%	$48,169	5%	($37,669)	-20%
24		*(B12 – B14)*		*(D12 – D21)*		*(F12 – F23)*	

Notice the shocking difference this makes for Moe's business! Moe finds that his overhead in the Installation side of his business drops from 44% to 37%. This will result in lower job prices than before (though, of course, if Moe can still get the old prices for jobs, he should). It also means that Moe has a serious problem to solve in the Service department.

(Do you see where we could now take the Installation column and run this form again, this time splitting the report into Residential and Commercial installations, then run it once again with the Residential installation data to produce Custom New Home and Residential Replacement details?)

How does this impact Moe's job pricing now?

With the original (incorrect) income statement, Moe's job price was $14,304. With the corrected statement it is $14,955. But with the new overhead data for Installation, it should have been set at $12,902 (run the math to prove it to yourself, or see the footnote).

Obviously, if Moe thinks the job would actually go for $13,500, he should bid it at that number and, if he gets the job, make more than 12% net profit. But if he has stiff competition on the job, it may take $12,902 (or even less!) to get the job.

Departmentalizing Spreadsheet

The CD-ROM that comes with this book contains an Excel worksheet that helps you quickly departmentalize a dealer's books. Below is a screen shot to show you how easy it is to set up and use:

Departmentalizing Worksheet

Company Name: **Moe Larry and Curly**

Fiscal Period: **Fiscal Period Here**

From the Income Statement....	Original Data		Installation		Service	
	Dollars	% Sales	Dollars	% Sales	Dollars	% Sales
Sales	**$1,090,000**	100.0%	**$900,000**	100.0%	**$190,000**	100.0%
Cost of Sales	**$604,600**	55.5%				
Labor	**$206,000**	18.9%	**$162,000**	18.0%	**$44,000**	23.2%
Labor percentages			**78.6%**		**21.4%**	
Parts	**$38,000**	3.5%			**$38,000**	
Remaining C. O. S.	**$360,600**		**$360,600**			
Gross Margin	**$485,400**	44.5%	**$377,400**	41.9%	**$108,000**	56.8%
Overhead	**$474,900**	43.6%				
Sales specific overhead	**$22,000**		**$22,000**			
Service specific o'head	**$64,000**				**$64,000**	
Overhead left	**$388,900**					
Overhead allocation			**$305,834**		**$83,066**	
Departmental Overhead			**$327,834**	36.4%	**$147,066**	77.4%
Net Margin	**$10,500**	1.0%	**$49,566**	5.5%	**-$39,066**	-20.6%

You only need to enter the information in the input boxes and the worksheet does the rest.

A Dealer's Life Is Never Easy

Now that you understand how the income statement drives job pricing and you know the job pricing formula, it is time you learned that a dealer's life is never easy. What you are about to learn must be taught to your best accounts (actually, all of them would benefit from this, but only your best will use it). If you do, they will make a lot more money and you will too!

Let's take a job off the norm. Let's go back to Moe's original job on page 253. This time around, we'll leave material at $5,000 and miscellaneous costs at $300, but instead of sixty-four hours of labor at $20 an hour, Moe thinks this new job is going to be a much harder case, so he estimates three times as much labor ($3,840). Using Moe's departmental overhead of 37% and a profit goal of 16% (harder job!), what should Moe's bid be? Work it out and write it in the box.

My bid is:
$

If you got $19,447, you got the right answer. (Total costs of $9,140 divided by 100% less (16% plus 37%), which simplifies to $9,140 divided by 0.47.) That's the right answer, and it is the answer most dealers who have been properly trained in how to set a job price would price it.

But if you got $19,447, you are wrong—as are about 98% of the dealers who bid a job like this.

Here's why: Why does a dealer have overhead in the first place?

The answer I get most often from dealers in workshops is, "To make money." But ***how*** does overhead help a dealer make money? It actually costs money, so how can it help a dealer *make* money?

But as we discussed earlier in this chapter (page 261), overhead exists to support the efficient use of labor.

All overhead must ultimately support getting labor onto jobs efficiently and quickly so the dealer can maximize his productivity. ***Overhead exists to support labor utilization. Period!***

If a dealer has an overhead expense that cannot be shown to directly support the efficient use of labor in the field, he does not need it as a business expense.

But how can a dealer use this knowledge to accurately price jobs? The income statement contains the answer. It lies in the form of the ratio of overhead to labor. With a *properly structured* income statement, the ratio of overhead to labor gives us a COWL factor. (COWL stands for **C**overing **O**verhead **W**ith **L**abor.)

Look at Moe's corrected income statement on page 252 where the total overhead came to $474,900 and the total labor was $206,000. The COWL factor for Moe's overall business would then be $474,900 divided by $206,000, or 2.31. What this means is that for every dollar of labor Moe has on a job, he also has $2.31 in overhead on that job.

Do you see that if a dealer has a good idea of how much labor a job should take, he will have a good way to estimate how much overhead that job has to carry? He can simply multiply his labor estimate (in dollars) times the COWL factor to get the overhead amount.

That being done, the dealer will now have all the pieces of the job price except the profit. He will know the costs of material and equipment, as well as the cost of labor and the cost of overhead. All he needs to allow for is the profit in the job.

In the original job pricing formula on page 256 everything in the job carries overhead—equipment, material, and labor. All the job costs are on the top of the equation and that total is divided by 100% less the Gross Margin %, and the Gross Margin % contains the overhead as an element.

But now, the dealer will *know* the overhead going in. He takes it out of the divisor (where it was buried) and this is what he ends up with:

$$\text{The Right Price} = \frac{\text{The Job Costs (with overhead)}}{100\% - \text{Net Profit }\%}$$

So, going back to our unusual job on page 266 we can get the right job price by taking $5,000 for equipment and material, $300 for subs and permits, $3,840 for labor, and for overhead, we use 3840 x 2.31, or $8,870. This makes the total job costs come to $18,010 (already almost equal to our "right price" bid). To make 16% net profit, we divide that by 0.84 to get a bid of $21,440 (which is $1,993 *more* than the right price formula says it should be).

Did you see what happened here? The dealer had a heavy labor job to bid and he used his normal job pricing method to bid it. But that job pricing method makes *everything* in the job recover overhead, and this includes stuff that does not cause any significant overhead, like equipment and material. So he is pricing a risky job with a method that is blind to the realities of overhead recovery! Do you think he is aware of that when he prepares his bid?

Probably not. And when he turns in his $19,447 bid and finds he is the low bidder, he rejoices for getting a nice job. He does the job and on paper appears to make 16% net profit.

But only because his bookkeeping system is lying to him! In job costing a job under right price methodologies, it is *assumed* that the overhead is the percentage of sales that the income statement shows it to be. If the job is a normal job, this would be a fair assumption to make. But if the job is abnormal—like this one, with its extra dose of labor—that assumption will not be right.

His job cost report looks like this:

The Job Sells For…	$19,447
The Job Costs come to…	$9,140
Resulting in Gross Margin of…	$10,307
Overhead is 37% of sales, or…	$7,195
Leaving us a Net Profit of…	$3,112

And indeed, if we divide 3112 by 19447 we get 0.16.

But the error lies in *assuming* that overhead is 37% of sales. Actually, overhead is a function of job labor, is it not? So the job did not return 16% in profit. The overhead is not $7,195 (which is what 37% assumes), but rather $8,870 (the job labor times the COWL factor). If we change the $7,195 overhead number in the job price checking math to $8,870, we find that the net profit drops to $1,437, which is 7% of sales, not 16%.

Now if we use the departmental data for Moe, we would actually get a different COWL factor. Going back to page 264 and dividing the Installation Overhead we see there by Installation Labor it gives a new COWL of 2.03. Using this new COWL and the same costs and margins as before, the job would now price at $20,161 ($1,279 less than the old COWL result). Do you now see the importance of departmentalizing the income statement?

I am now going to make a crucial business point, but before I do, I need to create a couple of definitions to make the point easier to understand. First, let's call the job pricing method given by the formula on page 256 the SID method (where SID stands for single divisor). And for the COWL method, we'll simply call it the COWL method.

Because SID recovers overhead with *everything* that goes on the job (including material), it can overstate the overhead for high material jobs. It calculates too much overhead burden for the job because equipment is so high, and yet equipment does not cause any appreciable overhead.

Conversely, when equipment on a job is low (and labor high), SID won't recover *enough* overhead, and the job price will be understated.

In bid terms, a high material job (the kind that dealers dream of) will be overpriced with SID, while a high labor job (the kind every dealer dreads) will be underpriced. The dealer will end up getting stuck with the high labor jobs while his competitors run off with the high material jobs. Not a good place for your dealers (or you) to be in!

On the other hand, COWL pricing works exactly the way we want it to on jobs of different material to labor ratios. If the job is high in material and light in labor, COWL only recovers a little overhead. The job price will be lower than the SID price. Conversely, if the job is labor-intensive, COWL will impute a lot of overhead to the job, so the job will be priced high. Dealers who consistently use COWL pricing will get more than their share of high material jobs and tend to never get high labor jobs.

Let's prove that with two hypothetical jobs using Moe's departmental data from page 264 (where the COWL is 2.03 and overhead is 37% of sales).

A High Labor Job (Low Material)

As an added tool in looking at jobs before they are bid, consider the ratio between material and labor on Moe's departmental statement on page 264. The material costs (all Cost of Sales except labor) are $360,600 against labor of $162,000. Moe's historical Material to Labor ratio is then 360,600 divided by 162,000 or 2.23. This is the ratio of Material to Labor, not Overhead to Labor, so don't confuse it with COWL. It's a totally different number. But it is a benchmark we can use to look at jobs and predict which method (SID or COWL) will work best.

Briefly, if the job's Material to Labor ratio (M to L) is above the historical ratio, COWL will be the best bet to set a winning price and get this high material job. If the job's M to L ratio is lower than the historical ratio, SID will produce the lowest price, but then the dealer should not want to win a high-labor job. So again, COWL is suggested. ***Either way, the dealer should use COWL.***

Suppose now that Larry has to bid a job for Moe. Larry figures $18,000 in material on the job. Normally, such a job would require about $8,072 ($18,000 divided by 2.23) in labor. But Larry finds this job is going to be harder than usual, and estimates it will need $13,500 in labor. What is the job's M to L ratio? 18,000/13,500 or 1.33. This is well below the historical benchmark of 2.23, so SID will give a low price. Larry wants to make 11% net profit on the job. Let's see how SID prices this job.

Using the SID method, Larry gets a price of...

($18,000 + $13,500) / [100% - (11% + 37%)]

= ($31,500) / ([100% - 48%]

= $31,500 / 0.52

= $60,577

The same job using COWL would price out like this:

($18,000 material + $13,500 labor + ($13,500 x 2.03 overhead) / (100% - 11%)

= ($18,000 + $13,500 + $27,405) / 89%

= $58,905 / 0.89

= $66,185

Note that Larry assumed he'd make 11% profit on $60,577 in sales if he uses SID, but since his SID bid is $5,608 lower than the COWL bid, his profits are not 11% of $60,577 ($6,663), but only $1,058 (1.7%).

A High Material Job (Low Labor)

Curly has a job to bid for Moe where the material comes to $23,000. Labor is only $2,700, giving a whopping job M to L ratio of 8.52. Curly thinks he can get 12% net for this job.

SID would price the job like this:

$25,700 costs / [100% - (12% + 37%)]

= $25,700 / [100% - 49%]

=$25,700 / 51%

=$50,392

COWL would give this price:

($23,000 material + $2,700 labor + $5,481 overhead) / [100% - 12%]

= $31,181 / 88%

= $35,433

Now suppose Curly thinks that in his market, given his known competitors on this job, the job might go for something around $42,000. Should Curly bid it at $35,433? Probably not. He could probably bid it up around $41,000 or even $41,500 and still be the low bidder and win it. Note that if he does, he does not make 12% net profit—he makes a lot more than that!

Suppose the job went for $41,500. How much profit would Curly make on the job, assuming labor came in as estimated? Here is the job cost report:

The Job Sells For…	$41,500
The Job Costs come to…	$25,700
Resulting in Gross Margin of…	$15,800
Overhead is …	$5,481
Leaving us a Net Profit of…	$10,319

This is a whopping 25% net profit! Yet, had Curly used SID, he would never see a contract to sign on this job!

By now, I hope you see how important the income statement is to the dealer. Later in this chapter we will return to it to see what to look for in terms of normal numbers and abnormal numbers, but first, I want to open a whole new can of worms.

Mass Confusion: Margin versus Markup

Somewhere along the line, someone came up with the idea of ***markup***. Ever since, HVAC shops have been in trouble.

The methods you have seen so far—SID and COWL—are both ***margin*** methods. They divide the costs by a divisor to get the sell price.

Some people don't like to do division (even though on modern calculators it is easy to do). They prefer to multiply instead. So the invention of the idea of markup.

The problem is, the multiplier that a dealer needs to use to derive a job price is not intuitively obvious, and most dealers think it is.

Let's take an example. Suppose a dealer runs overhead of 30% and wants to make 10% net profit on a job. This is a gross margin of 40%, right? So, most dealers would take the job costs and multiply them by 1.40. But this won't work. Let's see why.

Suppose the job costs are $100 (just to keep it simple). Using the dealer's approach, the job would sell for $140. But using SID, the job would sell for $100/60%, or $167. To make 40% gross margin, a dealer cannot use a multiplier of 1.40. He must use a multiplier of 1.67. But where does the 1.67 come from? From the factor, 1/ (100% - GM%)! Just like SID!

In other words, to make 40% gross margin, a dealer has to multiply his costs by 1.67. What if a dealer wanted to make 34% gross margin. What would his markup multiplier be? Before reading on and finding the answer, run the calculation and see what you think it should be. Write it here:

Markup should be _________

The answer is 1.52. (Take 1 / (100% - 34%), to get 1 / 0.66).

I can appreciate the idea that some folks would rather multiply a cost by a factor than divide. But the confusion that markup has caused has cost many a dealer his fortune, even his business!

There is a critical reason why margins and markups are different. Imagine that the dealer's business is like a 100-floor skyscraper. The ground floor is where the costs come in. The dealer must put these costs on the elevator and send them up to the right floor for pricing. But what button would he push?

The percents on the income statement (the percents that define overhead, gross margin, and all the other metrics) are numbers based on sales (the 100th floor of the skyscraper). But the dealer approaches every job from the costs (1st floor). If the dealer punches in "40" on the elevator keypad to take his job to the 40th floor for 40% gross margin, he'll be several floors short because he is dealing with costs and trying to express a number based on the sale price he is trying to derive! It is maddening!

Bottom line? If I were you, I would forget all about markup and tell your dealers to do the same. If they *must* use markups, at least give them a table like this:

		Net Profit Desired								
		8%	9%	10%	11%	12%	14%	16%	18%	20%
Overhead	**20%**	1.39	1.41	1.43	1.45	1.47	1.52	1.56	1.61	1.67
	22%	1.43	1.45	1.47	1.49	1.52	1.56	1.61	1.67	1.72
	24%	1.47	1.49	1.52	1.54	1.56	1.61	1.67	1.72	1.79
	26%	1.52	1.54	1.56	1.59	1.61	1.67	1.72	1.79	1.85
	28%	1.56	1.59	1.61	1.64	1.67	1.72	1.79	1.85	1.92
	30%	1.61	1.64	1.67	1.69	1.72	1.79	1.85	1.92	2.00
	32%	1.67	1.69	1.72	1.75	1.79	1.85	1.92	2.00	2.08
	34%	1.72	1.75	1.79	1.82	1.85	1.92	2.00	2.08	2.17
	36%	1.79	1.82	1.85	1.89	1.92	2.00	2.08	2.17	2.27
	38%	1.85	1.89	1.92	1.96	2.00	2.08	2.17	2.27	2.38
	40%	1.92	1.96	2.00	2.04	2.08	2.17	2.27	2.38	2.50
	42%	2.00	2.04	2.08	2.13	2.17	2.27	2.38	2.50	2.63
	44%	2.08	2.13	2.17	2.22	2.27	2.38	2.50	2.63	2.78

Figure 1: Markup Table

The Balance Sheet

Whereas the income statement is a report on the activities of the business for a specified time (usually a month), the balance sheet is a picture of the business's health as of that moment *from the time it started.* A good comparison would be that the income statement is a video, while the balance sheet is a snapshot.

The purpose of the income statement is to show the owner how work that period resulted in billings and expenses that lead to a profit (or a loss). It is the job of the balance sheet, though, to show the owner just how much the enterprise is worth at that moment.

Balance sheets are named for the fact that they contain two sides and both sides must have the same totals, or be in balance.

The general format of the balance sheet is fairly simple. It looks like the one on the next page.

ASSETS	LIABILITIES
Current Assets	Current liabilities
Fixed Assets	Long-term liabilities
Other Assets	***Total Liabilities***
Total Assets	
	EQUITY
	Stock
	Dividends
	Retained earnings
	Total Equities
	Total Liabilities and Equity

In a balance sheet, the total of the Assets must equal the total of the Liabilities and the Equity. Otherwise, the sheet does not balance.

Another way of looking at the balance sheet is to say that the Assets side (left side) shows what the company *owns*. The Liabilities and Equity side (right side) shows *who* owns it. Thus we have *things* on the left side and *people* on the right side.

Whereas many general accountants might construct an income statement incorrectly for a contractor, they rarely make errors with the balance sheet. This is because the balance sheet is a much more stable format than the income statement and has evolved over the centuries to a form that is very useful in banking and business. A full-blown balance sheet for Moe, Larry and Curly appears here.

Balance Sheet Summary
Moe, Larry and Curly's Comfort Shop
Fiscal 20xx

Assets		
Current Assets		
Cash	$21,764	
Accounts Receivable	$364,217	
Inventory	$63,867	
Work in progress	$14,734	
Prepaid expenses	$1,864	
Total Current Assets		$466,446
Fixed Assets		
Fixed assets	$196,348	
Depreciation	($110,347)	
Net fixed assets	$106,001	
Real estate	$0	
Total Fixed Assets		$192,002
Other Assets		$11,364
Total Assets		$669,812
Liabilities		
Current Liabilities		
Accounts Payable	$97,634	
Accrued Liabilities	$38,167	
Notes payable	$28,671	
Other Current Liabilities	$2,679	
Total Current Liabilities		$167,151
Long-Term Liabilities		$93,568
Total Liabilities		$260,719
Net Worth / Equity		
Stock	$35,000	
Dividends	$150,140	
Retained Earnings	$176,659	
Cur year retained earnings	$47,294	
Other	$0	
Total Equity		$409,093
Total Liabilities and Equity		$669,812

What the Parts Mean

The parts of a balance sheet have odd-looking names. Let's take a moment to explore what those names signify.

Any time you see the word *accrued*, it means that moneys have been recognized as having been received or spent *before* the cash actually hits the bank account. For example, Accrued Liabilities are debts the business has as of this moment even though a check has not been written for them yet. (Examples could include payroll taxes that have been withheld from paychecks but not yet paid to the government, and union dues that have been withheld but not yet forwarded to the local.)

Accounts refer to any entity the business deals with, either its customers (Accounts Receivable) or its suppliers (Accounts Payable).

Work in Progress represents inventory that has been earmarked for a job but not yet installed or not yet billed out. Many contractors like to use this account since it reduces the *Inventory* account which in turn makes some banking ratios look better.

Depreciation is how assets (the things the business owns) decrease in value over time, due to age, wear, tear, and so on. For example, a dealer might buy a new pickup truck today for $30,000. The moment he drives it off the automobile dealer's lot, it loses $6,000 in value since it is now used. Over the next several years, the accountant will reduce the value of the truck by means of special depreciation tables provided by the Internal Revenue Service. It is possible, of course, to have an asset that has been depreciated to $0 value but still in good condition and capable of doing useful work.

Current Assets and Liabilities are those that are normally cycled day to day in the normal course of doing business. *Fixed Assets*, on the other hand (and *Long Term Liabilities*) extend beyond the day to day cycle of business. For example, a sheet metal shear is a fixed asset since it is not used up on jobs—its work can be spread out over thousands of jobs for decades. Other fixed assets would include furniture, vehicles (even though they tend to be replaced every three to five years), computers, buildings, tools, and radios. Long Term Liabilities are those debts that go beyond the current year, such as multi-year vehicle loans, loans for the building, and so on. Normally, the accountant records here the unpaid principal of the notes.

Stock represents the original start-up investment of the owner(s) to start the company. Stock laws are complex and it is not necessary for you to be an expert on them to be a Tier One TM. Stock rules affect taxation and ownership after the original owner retires.

Dividends are funds the owners can pay themselves at the end of the fiscal year as rewards for running the business. Tax law limits the amount of compensation the owners may take as dividends, but dividends are a wonderful way for owners to reward themselves and limit their tax liabilities at the same time, since dividends are not subject to FICA (Social Security) and Medicare withholdings.

Retained Earnings are allowed only in corporations. These funds are any left-over profits after all expenses and dividends have been paid. In a type-C corporation, these earnings are not taxed until the owner withdraws them. In a type-S corporation, the profits are taxed and then what is left may go into Retained Earnings. Note that Retained Earnings are not necessarily present as cash in the bank. A company may show $200,000 (or more) in retained earnings, but have only $20,000 in the bank account! Retained Earnings are basically accumulated profits and show outsiders (such as lenders or buyers) how much the owner has built the value of the firm over the years. Whether or not the owner can get that much money for the Retained Earnings is another question.

The Cash Flow Statement

The third document a dealer needs to get on a monthly basis is the cash flow statement. It is a report that shows where the month's money came from and where it went. Dealers who don't get cash flow reports are usually in cash flow problems because they are not aware of what contributes to cash flow (or stops it up). A cash flow report is a great way to spot the problems and fix them before they become crippling.

A simple cash flow report is shown on the next page:

Weekly Cash Report

For week ending ____________ Prepared by _______________

Beginning Cash on Hand (start of the week)

Petty cash	$	☜ Box 1	
Checking acct #	$	☜ Box 2	
Checking acct #	$	☜ Box 3	
Payroll acct	$	☜ Box 4	
Savings	$	☜ Box 5	
Other accounts	$	☜ Box 6	
Total beginning cash (add boxes 1 thru 6)		$	☜ Box 7
Probable Accounts Receivable coming in this week		$	☜ Box 8
Other cash collected		$	☜ Box 9
TOTAL CASH AVAILABLE FOR THE WEEK (add boxes 7 thru 9)			$
			☝ Box 10

Cash Outlays for This Week

Total Payroll	$	☜ Box 11	
Accounts Payable Due	$	☜ Box 12	
Loan Payments	$	☜ Box 13	
Other Cash Outlays	$	☜ Box 14	
Total Outlays For the Week (add boxes 11 thru 14)		$	☜ Box 15
ENDING CASH FOR THE WEEK (Box 10 – Box 15)			$
			☝ Box 16

Estimated Cash Needs for Next Week

Starting Cash (Box 16)	$	☜ Box 17	
Accounts Receivable collected	$	☜ Box 18	
Other	$	☜ Box 19	
Total available for the week (add boxes 17 thru 19)		$	☜ Box 20
Payroll	$	☜ Box 21	
Accounts Payable due	$	☜ Box 22	
Loan Payments due	$	☜ Box 23	
Other	$	☜ Box 24	
Total due out for the week (add boxes 21 thru 24)		$	☜ Box 25
PROBABLE ENDING CASH FOR NEXT WEEK (Box 20 – Box 25)			$

What Makes for Good Numbers: The Use of Ratios

Dealers often come up to me during workshops at breaks and show me their financial statements and ask, "How do these numbers look to you?" To me, they look like numbers on a page. Just numbers. I often get people to do a double-take when I say, "I can't tell you if these are good numbers or not because I don't know what you do day in and day out to post these numbers to these pages. The problem is not with your numbers; the problem is with your processes. It's the things you do that put these numbers on these sheets."

There are, though, some *general guidelines* we can use when looking at a dealer's financial statements (and here we are speaking mainly of the income statement and the balance sheet—the cash flow statement is rarely a document that requires much analysis).

Over the years, financial houses such as banks and services like Dun and Bradstreet and others have compiled statistics about businesses. Over the years, a huge amount of data has been collected, and analysts have pored over this data and combed it for the outstanding performers, average performers, and poor performers and have found consistent patterns in the values the numbers have for outstanding, average and poor firms. These values are often called *ratios* and knowing them can help a dealer tell whether or not his operation is outstanding, average or poor.

Summaries of financial data can be purchased annually from Dun and Bradstreet (and other commercial data sources), or obtained free every five years from the U.S. Census Bureau (as the "Economic Census"). What I have found is that the numbers change *a little* from year to year, but not very much. A Dun and Bradstreet report you buy in 2009 is probably going to be very close to one you buy in 2012.

What do the ratio reports tell us? A lot of things!

We know, for instance, that **actual gross margins** in HVAC businesses decrease as a percentage of sales the larger the firm gets. Here are some typical numbers:

Sales Volume	Typical GM %
$0-$200,000	34%
$200,001 - $600,000	29%
$600,001 - $1,000,000	26%
$1,000,001 - $2,000,000	22%
$2,000,001 - $4,500,000	20%
$4,500,001 and up	15% and down

Does this mean that the bigger a dealer gets, the more price driven he becomes? Not necessarily. A lot of this has to do with the type of work he does. Smaller shops tend to stick to residential work where the larger ones are usually active in commercial work and industrial projects, where low price is the trump card.

Bear in mind that the numbers in this table are the *averages*. The best performing dealers will be way above these gross margin percents, and the poorest will be well below them.

A stunning thing arises out of the data analysis. When we factor in the net profit after taxes, we find that the smaller shops actually have a *higher* ***overhead*** *relative to sales* than the bigger shops do. This often stuns smaller dealers to hear this, but often the overhead in a small shop will run 28% or more of sales, while the larger ones shown above will be down around 11%

or 12% of sales. (Of course, 12% of $100,000,000 in sales is still a lot of overhead!) The point here is that the smaller dealer has a lot more overhead than he may think! If he does not get good financial statements, he won't know for sure, and all the job pricing in his critical first few years will be off because of it!

The **owner's salary** is usually a higher percentage of sales in a small shop than a big one—much higher. In a small business, it could run as much as 8% or 9%, while in a large one it may only run 2% or less. These are, remember, the *averages*. A dealer who sells $600,000 a year and pays himself $48,000 is average, and poor! Why shouldn't a dealer make $180,000 a year or more from his efforts? (Of course the bigger the sales, the easier it is to take $180,000 out of the operation. But strong incomes are possible even with smaller firms if the owner will focus on that.)

Measuring Outside the Box

Before I get to the traditional financial ratios that are important in this business, I want to remind you of the measures of productivity and throughput that we discussed in Chapter 4. Although not technically financial ratios, the measures of throughput are as valid as signs of success as traditional metrics, and they have the advantage of focusing your dealer's attention on the things he does with his labor pool that can make or break his business.

I tell dealers to watch three types of ratios. I call these ratios (1) the Measures of Activity and Process, (2) the Measures of Solvency, and (3) the Measures of Managerial Efficiency.

Measures of Activity and Process

These measures are tied to throughput and day-in, day-out activity and as such are a good indicator of how well (or poorly) the dealer is managing his daily opportunities.

The first ratio I list under this category is the **Productivity Ratio** of Chapter 4 (page 41). The current U.S. average is $159,644 per employee, but you must adjust this value for the state as described in Chapter 4.

Also from Chapter 4 is the **Service Sales per Service Truck Ratio**. (See Chapter 4, page 44.) In Chapter 4, we said a value of $160,000 per truck per year was good for residential service trucks, and $190,000 per truck per year for commercial trucks.

I would also include in this group the **Service Sales as a Percentage of Replacement Sales** (see Chapter 4, page 47), which for a replacement driven shop ought to run between 25% and 50% of sales.

Another non-financial ratio I would list in this category is the **Material to Labor Ratios** for each division of a company (assuming the income statement is departmentalized properly). There is no right value to these ratios, but generally the higher the ratio, the better the dealer's odds are of making a profit, since dealers tend to make more profit dollars per hour when they sell material as opposed to selling just time. It is not unusual to see service-oriented divisions run low ratios (1.50 or even lower), while it is also common to see commercial divisions run high ratios (4.0 or higher). Obviously, shifting a dealer's product mix toward the top tier products will move his M to L ratio up as well.

We will now look at a few of the more important ratios.

Activity and Process Ratios

Age of Accounts Receivable

I include several traditional financial ratios in the Activity and Process group. The first of these is the **age of accounts receivable**. This is a measure of how fast the dealer collects the money that is owed to him. It is calculated by using this formula:

$$\text{Age of A/R} = \frac{\text{Accounts Receivable}}{\text{Annual Sales}} x 365$$

We can run Moe's Age of A/R by referring back to his financial statements on pages 252(income statement) and 276 (balance sheet). Digging out the numbers called for, you can calculate the Age of A/R. Do so now and write your answer in this box, then read on to see if you are correct.

Age of A/R is:
days

The answer (based on sales of $1,090,000 and accounts receivable of $364,217) is 121.96 days.

So what should it be? No more than forty-five days, and preferably down around thirty or less. Would you say Moe has a collections problem? If so, he probably has a cash flow problem too, since the two are normally linked. If your dealer is slow in paying you, he probably has too many days in A/R. Ask him what his days in A/R is. If he knows, and he reveals that it is more than forty-five days, find a way to help him collect his money so *you* can get paid! (Your credit manager can be a big help here too.) If he does not know, offer to help him compute it and then go from there.

Age of Accounts Payable

A similar ratio to the Age of A/R is the **age of accounts payable**. It is computed the same way as the Age of A/R, except we use the value of Accounts Payable from the balance sheet instead of the Accounts Receivable. Use Moe's data now to compute his Age of A/P:

Age of A/R is:
days

The answer you should have gotten is 32.7 days. A value of thirty days is considered adequate, and anything less than thirty days indicates a very liquid condition (that is, bills are easily paid as they come due).

Average Age of Inventory

Another good number to keep a close eye on is the **age of inventory** (sometimes called the average age of inventory). It is easy to calculate, and you use this formula:

$$\text{Age of Inventory} = \frac{\text{Average Inventory x 365}}{\text{Annual E \& M Costs}}$$

Here, E&M stands for equipment and material.

To properly calculate this ratio, you need to know the starting inventory and ending inventory. The starting inventory would be the inventory as shown on the final balance sheet of the *prior* fiscal year. The ending inventory will be the inventory on the *current* year's final balance sheet. The Annual E&M Costs come right off the year-end income statement.

In Moe's case, we don't have last year's balance sheet, so we cannot do a pure age of inventory calculation. We could use the balance sheet inventory as it is now and be in the ballpark, but not precise. (If we did that, we would get $63,867 of inventory *plus* $14,734 from work in progress or a total of $78,601. We multiply by 365 and divide by the total cost of equipment and material of $331,000. The result is 86.67 days.)

But suppose Moe got out his year-end balance sheet from last fiscal year? Now we can run a precise calculation. Suppose his balance sheet shows inventory and work in progress totaling $61,304? How would we run the calculation now? First, we must find the average inventory. We do this by adding $78,601 to $61,304, and dividing the result by two. This produces an average inventory of $69,953. Multiplying this by 365 and dividing by $331,000 gives us 77.14 days.

What should the value be? *For equipment, an age of forty-five to sixty days* is considered good. Less than forty-five days is acceptable if your dealer is near a well-stocked branch and you can get equipment to him fast. Over sixty days suggests that the dealer has slow-moving inventory in his barn. This will do neither him nor you any good. If you find yourself in that situation, do what you can to help the dealer unload the slow-moving equipment. If the units are still current models and in their original cartons, you may be able to take them back in exchange for new units for the current season (for example, taking back some unsold furnaces in April and exchanging them for an equal dollar value in condensing units).

For parts, sixty days or less is good. And for floor plans (inventory orders that are financed over longer windows of time, like six months), the age could go as high as seventy-five days or so.

Remember, if your dealer's barn is stuffed with slow-moving inventory, you are going to have a hard time moving more iron through his doors.

Other Good Ratios To Track Frequently m(But Not Lose a Lot of Sleep Over)

The ratios that follow now are still part of the Activity and Process group, but are not as vital as the ones we have examined so far.

The Age of Conversion

This is not a religious term. The **age of conversion** is a hybrid ratio that measures how fast the dealer can run the cycle: order → inventory → sale → invoice → collection → pay bills → order again. The faster the dealer can repeat this cycle, the more work he can do per year (and the more you will sell her). It is simply the sum of the Age of A/R and the Average Age of Inventory. In Moe's case, we are talking 122 + 77 = 199 days.

But this is just a number. What does it mean? It means that Moe is really running a sloppy operation! How do I know that? Because if we use the *ideal* values of the Age of A/R and Age of Inventory (45 days and 60 days respectively), we get 105 days, some 94 days faster than

Moe turns the cycle!

Here is what that means to Moe (and why making his cycle faster should be a major objective). The value of his A/R ($364,217) and Inventory ($78,601) is $442,818. At an age of conversion of 199 days, this means he has tied up $442,818/199 or $2,225 per day in his slow cycle. If Moe could trim his cycle to 105 days, he would free up 94 days worth of daily money—in other words, he would have 94 x $2,225 or $209,150 freed up for use as capital in other areas! This would be possible because of greatly improved cash flows and less bad debt write-off.

If your dealers are running ages of conversion over 105 days, they too are suffering from inefficiency. Some guidance on your part (especially on how to collect their A/R) can help them stabilize what could be a rocky ride!

Inventory Turns

A spin-off from the average age of inventory is **inventory turns**. To find the inventory turns, merely divide 365 by the average age of inventory. In Moe's case, we divide 365 by 77 to get 4.74. Most experts would advise that Moe should run *six to eight turns a year*. Because his number is so low, he must have a lot of slow-moving inventory in his barn (or too much inventory in general). Either way, until the slow or excess stuff leaves the barn, he can't bring in new stuff from you to keep the pipeline full, right?

Current Ratio

Of importance to bankers (and distributors) is the dealer's **current ratio**. It is found by dividing the Current Assets by the Current Liabilities. In Moe's case, this means $466,446 divided by $167,151, or 2.79. Lenders like to see this number be *1.5 or higher*, meaning the firm has more than enough liquidity (ability to raise cash) to cover any short term debt it incurs. Moe is in very good shape here, but only because his A/R is so bloated. When you have a dealer below 1.5, you may have a dealer who will not be able to pay you when bad times occur. Any time you have a slow paying dealer, you may want to figure out his current ratio and, if it is below 1.5, teach him how to reduce debt while raising cash. (Your credit manager and sales manager should be able to help you with this.)

Quick Ratio

Similar to the current ratio is the **quick ratio** (sometimes called the acid test ratio). In this ratio, the creditor removes inventory from the current assets and in essence asks, "If I had to call this guy's note, could he pay me back with cash and receivables quickly?" (Hence the name of the ratio.) This number *should always be 1.0 or higher*—in other words, for every dollar a dealer owes, he should have a dollar in cash and A/R to cover it. If yours does not, you had better hope that he never runs into rough economic times!

The Inventory Test

The relationship between the current and quick ratios allows us to set up a **quick test for inventory** too. To run the check, merely divide the current ratio by the quick ratio. The value should lie *between 1.5 and 2.0*. A value greater than 2.0 suggests there is too much inventory, while a value less than 1.5 suggests there is not enough. (But be careful here; a well-stocked local branch that can deliver to your dealer quickly could mean that a value of less than 1.5 is perfectly normal.)

Days in Inventory

Also spinning out of the inventory age ratio is the **days in inventory** ratio. It is simple to compute once you know the age of inventory. Just take the inventory value and divide it by the value of equipment and material (from the Cost of Goods Sold) and multiply by 365. For Moe, this means $78,601 divided by $331,000, and then multiplying by 365 to get 87 days. Most experts advise *thirty to sixty days* for this ratio. Moe has too much inventory (which we already knew; this is just one more piece of confirming information).

Days in Cash

Days in Cash is an important ratio, and one that is often overlooked. To calculate it, simply divide the cash on hand (shown on the balance sheet) by total annual sales, and then multiply by 365. For Moe, this means $21,764 divided by $1,090,000 then times 365, which gives 7.3 days. Most experts advise an HVAC shop to carry *fifteen to eighteen days* in cash. Any amount over eighteen days should be invested in an interest-bearing instrument. Moe is about half of the minimum—not good. And when you consider his bloated A/R, you will know why. He needs to go on a collection drive! Then his cash will improve and he'll have less pressure from vendors wanting to be paid!

The Pricing Test

The final measure of Activity and Processes is what I call the **pricing test**. It is a simple ratio to determine if the dealer is marking up his jobs adequately. Simply divide the value of Accounts Receivable by the value of Accounts Payable. The number should be 2.0 or higher. If it is not, the dealer is not setting his prices high enough and you need to have a job pricing session with him!

Measures of Solvency

The solvency measures are also important to know, but most dealers don't need to keep a very close eye on them. Looking at them every other month or so should be adequate to steer the company well.

Two measures of solvency have already been covered—the current ratio and the quick ratio.

Working Capital

A very important measure of solvency is **working capital**. Working capital is a measure of how many fluid resources the firm has harnessed to produce revenue. It is found by taking the difference between the Current Assets and the Current Liabilities. In Moe's case, this means $466,446— $167,151, or $299,295.

The benchmark for working capital is that it should be *10% of next year's sales*. How does Moe look? If we divide $299,295 by $1.1 million (his approximate sales next year), we get 27%. Moe has plenty of working capital (a rarity as it turns out). But this is not necessarily good since so much of Moe's Current Assets are tied up in accounts receivable.

The guideline of 10%, is based on an average HVAC shop. If a dealer is heavily involved in slow-paying work (like large commercial projects or residential new construction), he may need *more* than 10% of sales in working capital simply because the payment windows get drawn out so long but the payroll and supplier bills still come in on a regular basis. Conversely, a dealer who does a lot of his work in fast-paying areas, like service (run COD) and replacements (due upon completion) may get by with less than 10% of sales in working capital. Keep this in mind as you work with your dealers to improve their working capital.

Debt to Equity

When you were a child, did you ever play on a see-saw on the school playground? If so, the see-saw probably consisted of a large board (2x10 or so) about twenty feet long with scallops cut for your thighs and a handle to hold. The rig probably laid across a large steel pipe and had three semi-circular bearings on the board to let you offset the center to allow for different weights of the see-sawers.

The D to E ratio (as it is usually abbreviated) is a measure of how close to the owner the fulcrum is on the see-saw. If it is closer to the debtors, they have the leverage and can move the dealer a lot with a little action. If it is closer to the dealer, he has more control.

To compute it, divide the Total Liabilities (on the balance sheet) by the net worth (Equity) of the business (also shown on the balance sheet). For Moe, this means dividing $260,719 by $409,093 which gives us 0.64.

This ratio should have a value of *1.0 or less*. In other words, the firm should owe less than it is worth! Moe looks good on this ratio.

Whenever the D to E ratio rises above 1.0, lenders and suppliers get nervous. The firm owes more than it is worth, and if a disaster occurred, someone would not be paid!

Current Debt to Equity

Similar to Debt to Equity, this ratio divides the Equity into the Current Liabilities. For Moe, this means $167,151 divided by $409,093, resulting in a value of 0.41. *For a smaller company, this number should be less than 0.67. For a larger one, the value should be 0.75 or less.* Obviously, Moe is fine here too.

What the ratio means if it is too high is that the short-term creditors (like your distributorship) have more at risk with the dealership than its owners do.

You won't normally know the Debt to Equity and Current Debt to Equity ratios for your dealers (unless they share their balance sheets with you every month). Your credit manager might not even know these ratios. But if your dealer is in the slow pay group, chances are that his D to E and CD to E ratios are out of kilter too!

To strengthen a ratio that is not good, a dealer needs to retire debt and/or build equity. This is not a quick fix problem. It will take months, if not years, for a dealer with weak D to E and CD to E ratios to become healthy again. If you get involved in a ratio fixing effort, be prepared for a long, stressful process.

The Z Score

Originally developed by Edward Altman (hence its alternate name, The Altman Score), the Z Score is a predictor of bankruptcy for large companies. In my experience as a consultant, however, I find it has a lot to offer smaller firms too.

Its computation is very involved and I will not go into it here. If you are interested in the formula, see the footnote to this page![4]

The benchmarks for the Z Score are *3.0 or higher to be safe*. A value of *1.81 or lower means the firm will probably be bankrupt within two years!* I don't recommend you compute the Z Score for your dealers unless you are worried they may be in a tail spin from which they cannot pull out. If the result is under 1.81, act fast to protect your company because you may be left holding the bag for some inventory and the accompanying accounts payable.

I have only seen one dealer with a score under 1.81 pull out and save his company, and it almost destroyed his health and marriage to do so. So 1.81 is not a guarantee of bankruptcy—but it comes pretty close!

Measures of Managerial Efficiency

These are great measures to compute about once a quarter or so, although many dealers don't like them because they are like report cards for how they are doing as business people, and all too often they don't do very well!

4 Z Score = [(6.56 x Working Capital as a % of Sales) + (3.26 x Retained Earnings) + (6.72 x Pretax Profits) – Interest Expense] ÷ [Total Assets + (1.05 x Equity)/Total Lia-bilities].

Return on Investment

This may be the best overall indicator of business skill because it reports what the dealer has done with his investment. Has he made money with it and built a strong operation, or has he wasted opportunities and resources? This number will tell.

There are three approaches to the issue and all yield different results (but only because they are looking at different things). First, one can calculate the return on sales. This is found by dividing the net profit before taxes by the sales (both from the year-end income statement). For Moe, the numbers are $10,500 in pre-tax profits and $1,090,000 in sales, giving a return on sales of only 1%. There is no benchmark for this number *per se*, but obviously the higher the return on sales, the better.

The other measure is known as the return on total assets and it measures how well the owners are using the firm's assets to make money. To compute it, divide the net profit before taxes by the total assets. For Moe, this means $10,500 divided by $669,812. The result is 1.6%. A vibrant HVAC dealership should be able to run *15% or more* (and 33% and up are easily within reach).

The third approach measures how well the firm turns a profit compared to the owner's equity and is sometimes called return on equity. To compute it, divide the pre-tax profit by the equity. For Moe, the result is 2.6%. Again, there is not a magic benchmark, but the higher the better. Vibrant companies run numbers of *33% and up.*

Current Assets to Total Assets

As its name implies, you divide the current assets by the total assets. For Moe, the result is 70%. The value should be in the range of *80% to 90%*, meaning that 80% to 90% of the assets are current assets—the ones that make it possible to do jobs quickly and efficiently. Moe is a little low here. He should probably collect some of his receivables and use the cash (after paying off the bills) to improve his vehicle and/or tool base.

Fixed Assets to Equity

Again, the name tells you how to compute it. The value should be *under 33%*, since anything over that suggests too many fixed assets to support the sales being generated. Moe's ratio is 47%, way too high! Moe has the potential to do more sales than he is (he has the fixed assets to support it), and if he did that and retained some of the earnings at the end of the year, he would see his fixed assets to equity number improving. This is a ratio that takes a long time to heal, so if your dealer embarks on a campaign to improve this ratio, be patient.

Sales to Equity

This ratio measures how well the business utilizes its resources to generate revenues. A value of six to ten is typical of a strong company. Moe's number is only 2.66.

The precise nature of Moe's inefficiency cannot be found by this ratio alone, but the fact that he is very inefficient is obvious. A Tier One TM would now do an intense discovery process to help Moe uncover all the factors that are contributing to his anemic performance, and then help Moe lay out a plan of action to fix them.

Using Financial Tips to Deepen Relationships

You now have a gold mine of information that can help your dealers grow and thrive. The question is how to use it and get your dealers to use it too?

First, don't try to be a financial consultant. That is a very complex area and you don't have enough information (in this book, at least) to be adept at it. But you can talk about financial matters without being a world-class expert on them!

Second, look for creative ways to open up conversations that will involve the dealer's financial statements. Then try to craft your questions and explorations in such a way that the dealer is willing to open the books and let you help him solve a challenge.

For instance, let's suppose you don't think your dealer is pricing his jobs the right way. How could you work your way toward a conversation on job pricing?

There are many ways this could go, but here is one:

> **You**: "I just heard the other day that the average dealer's net profit is less than 3%. Can you believe that?"
>
> **Dealer**: (sigh) "Yeah, I can believe it."
>
> **You**: "Oh, are you in that group?"
>
> **Dealer**: "Yep."
>
> **You**: "Hmm. I see. Well, you know, there is some pretty simple math involved here: SALES – COSTS = PROFIT. So if your profits aren't where you want them to be, there can only be two causes —not enough dollars in the SALES bucket, or too many dollars in the COSTS bucket. Do you have any idea which it may be?"
>
> **Dealer**: "I'd like to see more dollars in my SALES bucket, but it's hard enough to sell these jobs at the prices I'm at now. I don't see how I could raise my prices and still sell jobs."
>
> **You**: "Well, if you don't, what does the future hold for you?"
>
> **Dealer**: (growls)
>
> **You**: "Look, do you mind if I pass on to you something I learned the other day about job pricing? It might help you more than you think, and if needed, I'll help you learn how to sell it to your customers. Heck, I'll even go on some sales calls with you to demonstrate what I'm talking about. What do you say?"
>
> **Dealer**: "Well, I guess it couldn't hurt."

What happens next is up to you, but the dealer has opened his inner door to you. Maybe you give him a sample job to price and see how he gets the answer. That is, if he can get an answer. Or maybe he uses the wrong method. (Something like this: "Can you put a price on this job? The costs of material are $2,500 and labor is $600. You want 10% net profit. I want you to use your overhead. What is the right price?")

Once I visited one of my key dealers and he met me at his door with a scowl on his face. When Charlie scowled, it was not a good sign. I said, "Charlie, you look worried. What's up?" He replied, "I need a price cut." Now to any Tier One TM, those are fighting words. So I smiled and said, "Hmm. What makes you say that?" He replied that he was losing jobs to another major brand over the last month and that therefore (he thought) the other dealer had better prices than he did. He needed parity.

I pursed my lips, rubbed my chin, then looked him in the eye and said, "Okay, let me see your financial statements."

He shot back a look of surprise to me and said, "Why?"

"Because," I said, "I make my living off commissions for what I sell you. You are asking me to sell to you for less money. That means I am going to have to give up some income, and if I'm doing that, I just became an investor. Before I invest, I want to see your books."

Stunned, Charlie said, "Well, okay."

To make a long story short, I found some errors on Charlie's income statement, plus it was not departmentalized. We took about two hours to collect the data needed to departmentalize the books and then I had Charlie take any job he had lost and refigure it with his new overhead (he knew how to use SID). He did and was dumbfounded—he was now $150 under the other guy!

"Charlie," I cajoled him, "you don't need a price cut. You need better accounting." And that's where we left it— no price cuts, and because Charlie was losing his shirt on service, he ended up hiring his son to be the full-time service manager (the son was a good service tech but was getting tired of running calls). In the end, Charlie did well on both installation and service (thanks to his son's good guidance of the service department).

Or ask him how he set his street rate for service labor. You then help him determine a profitable street rate. The process is somewhat involved. But the dealer has to open his books to you while together you and he put together the numbers it takes to set a profitable street rate. More than likely he'll need to go onto flat rate pricing (if he is not already) and you can have a whole sales call devoted just to that later. The point is, by asking a loaded question; you can usually get the dealer to open up to you his closest secrets. As a result, you grow in your relationship together and your dealer's business grows more successful. Just what a Tier One TM does for a living!

Review Questions for Chapter 15

1. What are the three financial reports a dealer should get on a regular basis?

1) ________________________________

2) ________________________________

3) ________________________________

2. How often should a dealer get his financial statements?

3. The dealer needs to have his statements in his hands by what date?

4. When we say a dealer's books must be "clean", what do we mean?

5. Another term for overhead plus net profit is ______

6. Given overhead of 27% and a profit goal of 13%, what price should a dealer set on a job with costs of $4,768? Use SID.

7. With a COWL factor of 1.86 and job costs of $26,889 for equipment and material, $3,678 for labor, and a goal of 8% net profit, what is the correct price for this job? Use COWL.

8. The main drawback with SID is how it handles high labor jobs. What is that drawback?

Chapter 16: Knowing Your Stuff

It may seem strange to some that I don't talk about the technical side of being a territory manager until Chapter 16, but that is because too many territory managers are technical wizards but virtual imbeciles when it comes to the first 15 chapters. My experience shows that ***people really don't care how much you know until they know how much you care.***

Engineers or Generalists?

Is a territory manager called to be an engineer? Or a generalist?

Engineers know a great deal about a specialized area. They draw upon their experience and deep knowledge to design solutions to complex problems. In our business, mechanical engineers can design incredibly complex systems to keep any building comfortable in a stunning array of conditions and do so with minimal energy use.

But you are not called (primarily) to be a mechanical engineer. You will need *some* engineering skills, but you do not need to worry that you will be expected to do things that are normally done (and done better) by licensed professional engineers.

Nonetheless, you must know how to do certain things if you are going to help your dealers build strong, profitable businesses, because this trade is, like it or not, strongly engineering in its characteristics.

Basic Skills

There are basic engineering skills that I think any TM from Tier Three on up should have. It is very difficult to be a Tier One TM without these basic skills.

Math Skills

First, a strong TM is fairly ***good in math***. This does not mean you have to be able to work integral equations or solve differentials for heat loss. But it does mean you need a good sense with a calculator or computer. You should be able to use a calculator or a computer to compute such things as the answer to an equation, or to find the heat load on a given structure, or the size of a section of ductwork to deliver a specified quantity of air at given conditions.

When I began my career as a TM, laptops were not yet invented (I would eventually become the first TM in our company to use a laptop). I had to be able to compute the basic heat loss/gain calculations, duct sizing equations, and fan curves by hand using a calculator or slide rule. (Yes, Virginia, there really were things called slide rules.)

In those days it was not unusual for a TM to be able to sketch out a duct design for a residence in twenty minutes using some basic principles and basic math. The things I did then on a calculator I can still do, but I must admit that computer software makes it so much easier (and precise) to do today!

Those math skills should also include the ability to *construct a simple spreadsheet* that can do something basic, like figure a job price or price an order.

Having a major in mathematics, I was not cowed by databases, so early on when I got my first laptop, I created my own database to track my job quotes and successes and failures. You do not need to be proficient with databases, as many of the tracking programs I would use today are already on the market in commercial packages. But the ability to track all my job quotes and know where they were and which ones I had won (and which I had lost, and by how much) allowed me to build a powerful knowledge base that later let me get amazingly close to my competitors on commercial bids.

These math skills in turn will be put to use in several areas.

Load Calculations

Most of the time, your dealers will be supplying equipment for jobs where a load calculation does not have to be done (because someone else did one earlier and made the result of the load calculation part of the job specifications). But sometimes, your dealers may get involved on a job where there are no plans or specifications. Then they may need your help to prepare a load estimate.

Fortunately, there is a large library of strong load calculation programs on the market today to help you do this. All of the better load calculation programs today give accurate results and are not that difficult to run.

You should be able to help your dealers determine the load on any structure they are likely to become involved with. This could include upper end, large homes (often with unusual floor plans, window design, or internal loads such as swimming pools or tanning beds). It could also include small stores and restaurants, and even small manufacturing facilities.

If your load estimating package is robust enough, it should give you a complete *psychrometric solution* for the job, including entering air and leaving air conditions (which in turn let you select coils properly), and be able to show the loads in a multi-room structure on a room-by-room basis and then show the maximum simultaneous load so you can properly size the central plant. The package should also indicate CFM (both total and by room) to help you lay out an efficient duct design. The program should be able to handle loads caused by outdoor air, such as makeup air systems and fresh air economizer systems as well as infiltration.

You need to know that in the United States, heat is measured in British Thermal Units or BTUs. A BTU is defined as the amount of heat needed to raise the temperature of one pound of water at normal atmospheric pressure one degree Fahrenheit. It is roughly the amount of heat given off by a large wooden kitchen match as it burns up. Sometimes, you may be required to figure a load in watts (primarily for utility companies). There are 3.414 BTU in a watt (so a 10,000 BTU load would be equivalent to 10,000 ÷ 3.414 watts or 2,929 watts).

Psychrometrics and Coil Selection

A good load calculation will dictate the *psychrometric solution* for coil selection purposes. (Psychrometrics means air measurement.) Psychrometrics involves the behavior of air at various conditions—how much energy it can carry at various combinations of temperature and humidity, how much moisture it can carry at various dry bulbs, and so forth. It is a complex science, pioneered by Dr. Willis Carrier.

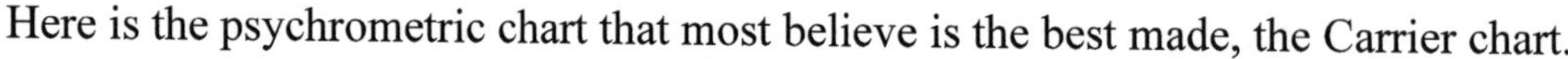

Here is the psychrometric chart that most believe is the best made, the Carrier chart.

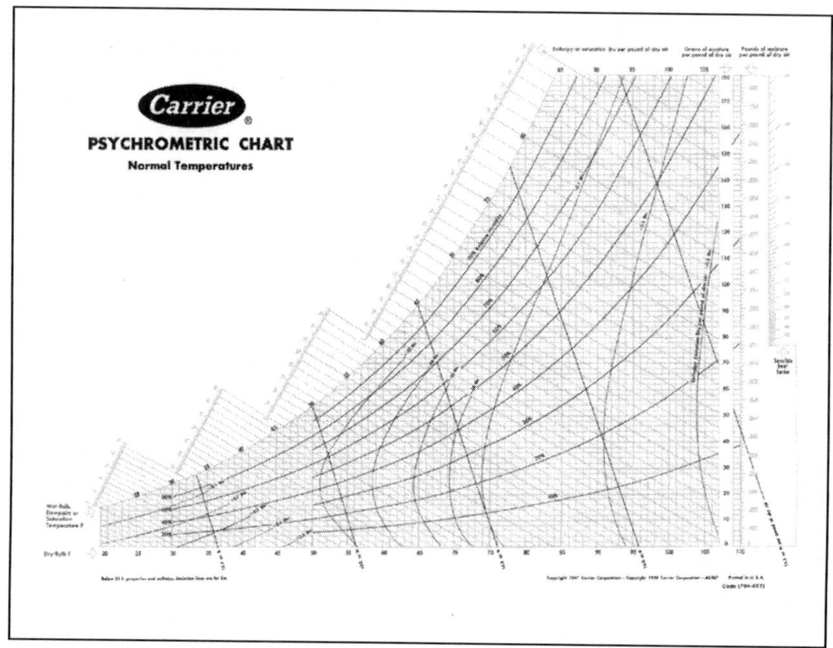

This chart's unique feature—the one that makes it the most accurate one —is the fact that Willis Carrier discovered that the diagonal lines running from lower right to upper left—the enthalpy lines—are not straight lines, but very slightly curved. (This is easier to see on a large scale chart.) The Carrier chart shows a very slight bowing of the enthalpy lines when a straight-edge is laid against them.

At first glance, the psychrometric chart looks staggeringly complex, but when you learn what the lines represent, it becomes about as easy to read as a simple road map.

Let's take a few minutes to learn the parts of the chart. (If you already know your way around a psychrometric chart, you may wish to skip ahead to page 307.)

Let's begin by showing the two most fundamental lines on the chart—the dry bulb lines and the wet bulb lines.

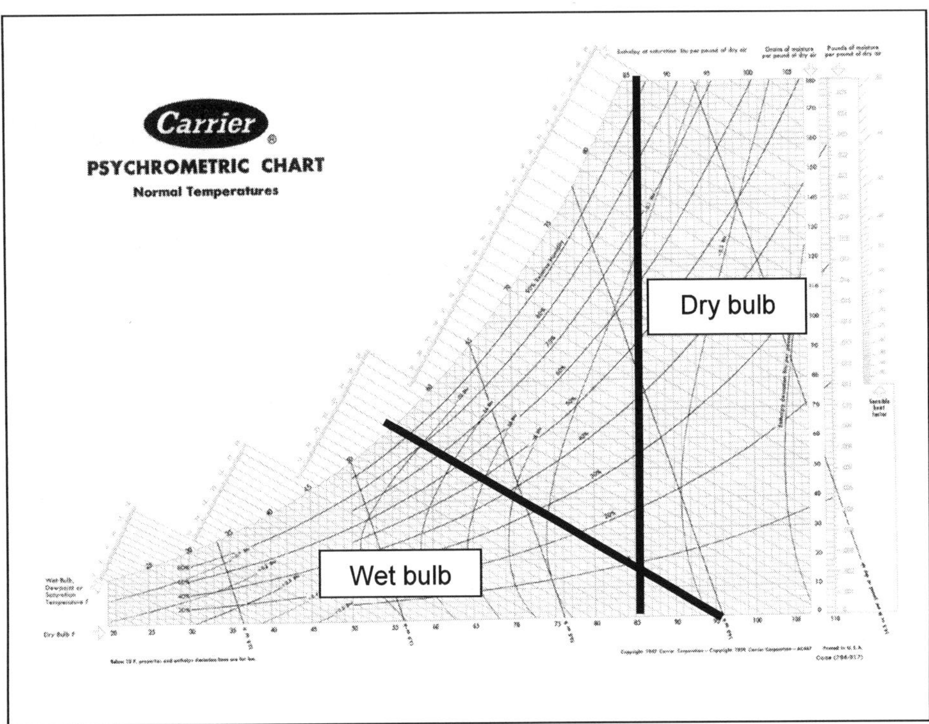

The dry bulb line is the line you would select based on the temperature of the air as shown by a dry bulb thermometer. (This is the temperature normally quoted on weather forecasts, when they say that today it will be 107, or 26.) The wet bulb line is the temperature that would be recorded (for the same air) by a *sling psychrometer*, a thermometer with a wet wick over the sensing bulb that is whirled in the air by means of a chain or some other device. As the wet wick moves through the air, the water in the wick evaporates, cooling the wick (and thus the sensing bulb). The dryer the air, the faster the water evaporates and the cooler the wick becomes.

The nature of any air sample can be given by just these two readings! That is the power of the chart. For instance, if the weatherman tells you that the temperature (dry bulb) is 93 right now and the wet bulb is 74, you can plot a lot of information about that air from just these two data points, which you'll see in a moment.

But the fact is that the weatherman does not give the wet bulb reading in the forecast—she gives the relative humidity. Where does she get that? From the chart! Where the dry bulb and wet bulb lines intersect, in fact.

See those curved lines that run more or less parallel to the left curved edge of the chart? Those are the lines of constant relative humidity.

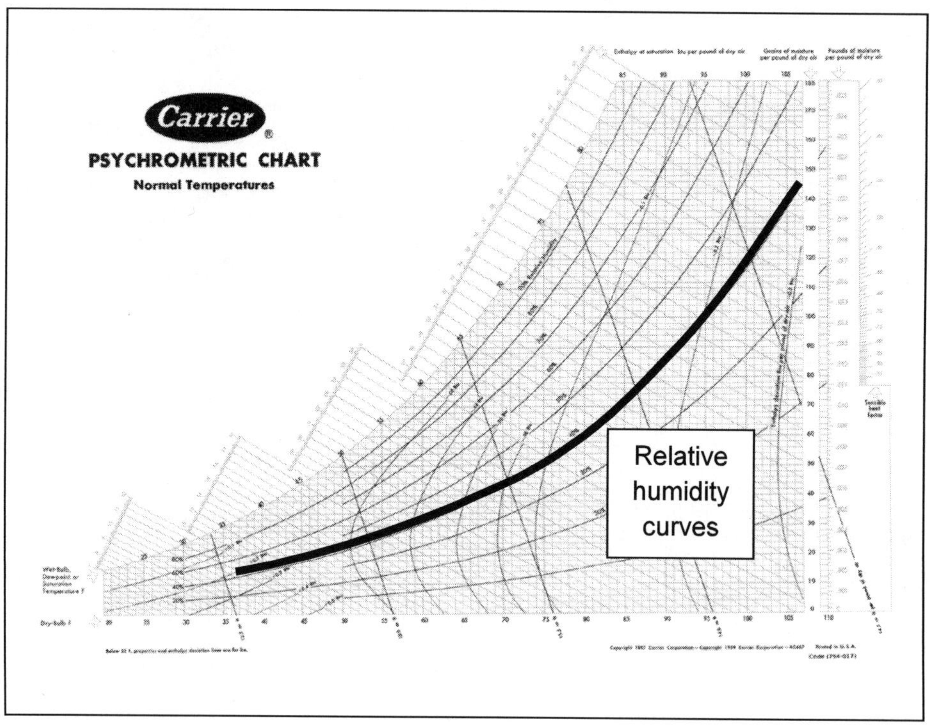

Knowing this, we can now determine the relative humidity of the air sample just cited (93 dry bulb and 74 wet bulb; or, in common shorthand, 93DB, 74WB). These two lines meet at about 40% relative humidity.

Here is that solution drawn on the chart:

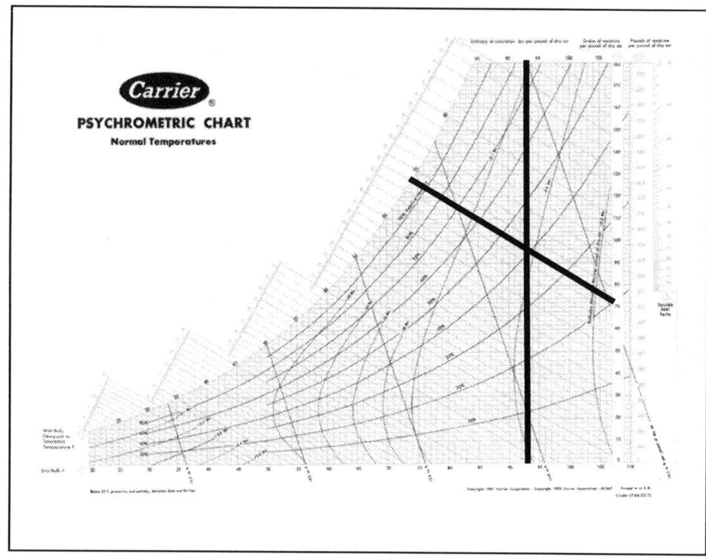

From this point now flows a lot of information about the air we have just measured. If we draw a horizontal line to the left from the intersection of the DB and WB lines to the left edge of the graph, we will obtain the *dew point* of the air. The dew point is the temperature at which the moisture in the air would begin to drop out of it as condensate. Obviously, if we wanted to air condition this air and remove some of its humidity, we'd need a surface at least that cold or colder. Drawing such a horizontal line on the chart shows that the dew point for this air is just a little above 65 degrees.

Drawing a horizontal line from the intersection of the DB and WB lines and extending it to the *right* brings us to the right axis of the graph where we can read the actual moisture content of this air sample. The units are given in grains of moisture per pound of air. In this case, there are 94 grains of moisture per pound of air. (A grain is a small measurement, it takes 480 grains to weigh one ounce!) Thus, we can deduce that each pound of this air carries 0.20 ounces of water (94 grains divided by 480). That may not sound like much, but in a typical residence of 2000 square feet, this air would hold 14 *pounds* of water vapor! That's almost two gallons of water!

The psychrometric chart also shows how many cubic feet of air this one pound takes up. There are five black diagonal lines on the chart, running roughly from a 5:00 o'clock to 11:00 o'clock angle. See them? Those are the air volume lines. Our sample (the intersection of 93DB and 74WB) is almost halfway between a line that reads 14.0 cu ft and one that says 14.5 cu ft, so we could say that this one pound of warm, moist air occupies about 14.25 cubic feet of air.

If we have a fan that can move 1,600 cubic feet of air per minute, how many pounds of air flow over the coil each minute? Easy!

1,600 cfm / 14.25 cf/lb = 112.3 pounds of air per minute. (Surprised?)

Amazing that from just two readings (DB and WB) we can pick up four vital elements of data about the air: relative humidity, dew point, grains of moisture per pound, and cubic feet per pound.

But like the Ginsu knife commercials say, "But wait! There's more!"

Part of a good psychrometric solution to a load calculation will not only express the *entering* air conditions (as we just did), but also the *leaving air conditions* that will be required to satisfy the load calculation.

Suppose the load program we ran showed that we needed to supply air to the space at 62DB and 61WB. If we plot these two lines on the chart, we see that the air leaving the coil must be at 95% relative humidity (air leaving coils is almost always near 100% saturation). The dew point will be about 60.2F and there are 79 grains of moisture per pound of air. A pound of discharged air will occupy about 13.4 cubic feet.

Every pound of air going over the coil must give up 15 grains of moisture (the difference between 94 grains and 79 grains), or about 0.031 ounces of moisture. If the load program calls for 1,800 cfm of air we can find the total moisture load dropped at the coil. 1,800 cfm of leaving air, at 13.4 cubic feet per pound, is 134 pounds of air. The moisture load dropped at the coil is then 134 pounds x 15 grains per pound or 2,010 grains per minute. This is a rate of 120,600 grains per hour (251.25 pounds). That's over 30 gallons of water!

This gives engineers the data they need to specify the coil's *latent capacity*. The latent capacity of a coil refers to how much water vapor it can remove under given conditions. It gets its name from the fact that removing water does not change the temperature of the air (so the moisture load is invisible or hidden, hence latent), but it does have a hellish effect on the refrigerant in the coil. Published coil performance tables show both *latent* and *sensible* capacity. Sensible capacity is how much the coil can change the temperature of the air. Since a coil can only do so much work on air, the capacity used by the removal of moisture is *not* available to cool the air. Failure to allow for this in coil selection can result in disastrous indoor environments and lead to such things as mold growth.

To remove one pound of water vapor from air takes 970 btu! So to remove 251.25 pounds of water per hour our coil must absorb 251.25 x 970 btu worth of heat, or some 243,713 btu (roughly 20 tons). Obviously, by picking out DB and WB numbers at random, I have created a psychrometric solution that would be virtually impossible to solve with commercially available equipment (1,800 CFM is not quite 5 tons worth of air), but the point to this exercise is to show that the psychrometric chart can tell you a great deal about system performance prior to system selection. Good choices up front mean fewer callbacks and job headaches later!

One final gem from the psychrometric chart involves a special point indicated at the center of the chart. On the next page, I have plotted the entering and leaving air conditions and drawn a line (sometimes called the process line) between the two points so designated. By placing a ruler at the dot at the center (highlighted by the circle) and drawing a line parallel to the process line, and running it to the far right of the chart, I can find the *sensible heat factor* the coil must be capable of if we expect to cool the air properly.

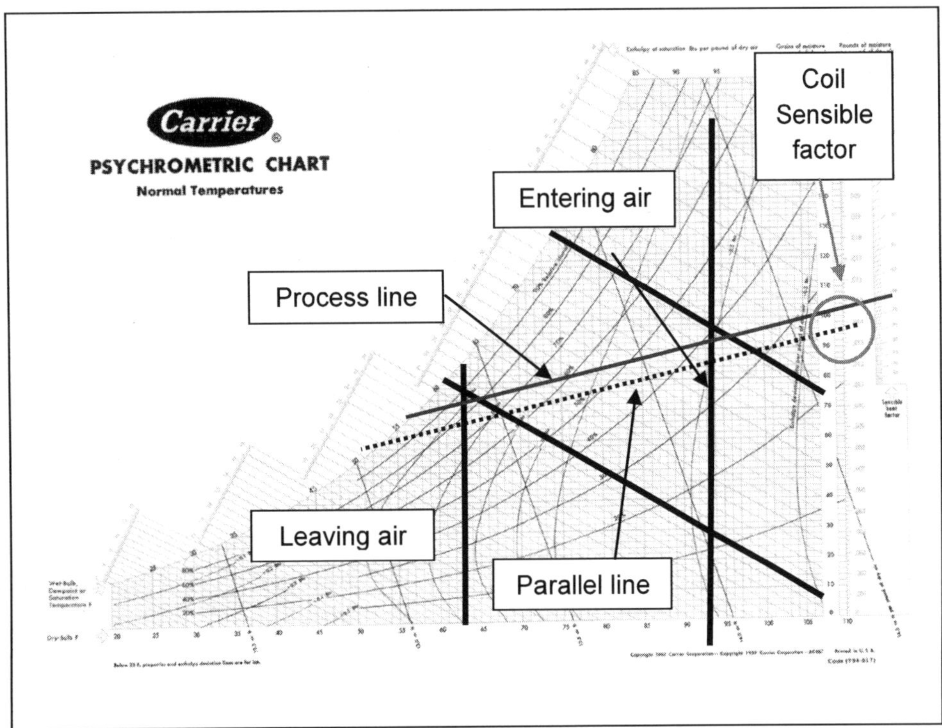

Here, we find that the coil sensible factor must be 0.72 for this system to work properly. If you or your dealer selected a coil that did not deliver a 0.72 SHF (as the sensible heat factor is often abbreviated), you could be in for a very unhappy experience and an upset customer.

The point is that when the psychrometric solution is specific and precise (like it will be with software load programs), you cannot just select a 5 ton coil and assume you'll get five tons of performance out of it. You must verify that the coil can do the latent and sensible jobs the load calculation calls for or you will be in serious trouble.

Basic Duct Design

Notice I said *basic* duct design. You don't need to become a whiz at duct design, but you do need to know what makes for good design and how to spot problems (and avoid them).

Different parts of the country seem to have different preferences for duct systems, so you should learn the prevalent type in your area and what is considered to be good practice. But most all of them agree on the basic design rules for residential ductwork—large enough ducts to limit pressure losses to 0.10" water column of static per 100 equivalent feet for supply ducts, and 0.08" water column of static per 100 equivalent feet for return ducts. (An equivalent foot is the length of straight duct that would have the same pressure drop as a fitting. For instance, an

8x24 supply duct would have one equivalent foot of length per foot of duct, but an elbow that is only twelve inches long may have a pressure loss equal to ten feet of straight pipe.)

I spent many years in the Midwest where most houses had basements and ductwork was built using a main trunk line with runouts. The main trunk would be rectangular (usually eight inches tall by varying widths) and the runouts would often be made of six-inch round pipe running between floor joists and feeding floor grilles. Return ducts likewise were located high on interior walls and fed into a main return trunk back to the air handler or furnace.

Good Specs Blow the Competition Out of the Water!

I was once involved with a dealer on a complex commercial job. The psychrometric solution of the load program indicated we needed a 12-row, 14 fins-per- inch coil to do the job, so I assembled a custom air handler package for the 20 ton job. The dealer's bid came in at $77,000, *ten times the bid of the other dealer the owners called.*

We were asked to explain ourselves, so I asked the client to have their engineers attend a meeting. I went over the calculations and psychrometric solution and showed why a 12-row, 14 fins-per-inch coil was needed, and that the other guy's standard rooftop unit with 4 rows and 12 fins-per-inch would be a disaster.

My dealer got the order!

To quickly field-size a main supply trunk, I'd begin with an 8" x 2" duct and add 2" of width for every 100 cfm the trunk had to carry. (Thus, a 1,200 cfm trunk had to be 2" wide plus twelve 2-inch additions, or 26" wide by 8" high.) For return trunks, I'd take the supply trunk rule of thumb and add two inches to the width.

But where I live now (Phoenix, Arizona), the practice is that few homes have basements, so ductwork is run overhead. Most homes have a central box right off the air handler or furnace, with flexible duct runs going to ceiling grilles in the various rooms, much like an octopus, with one central return grille (usually a filter grille) in a hallway. A basic rule of thumb we found helpful was that six-inch round pipe would deliver about 100 cfm of air to a grille, and an eight inch pipe about 150 cfm. (If six-inch flex duct is used, the delivery will be slightly fewer cfm at the same pressure loss, or a higher pressure loss for the same cfm. In badly hung flex duct, it can be *much* lower air flows and higher pressure drops!)

The point is that no matter what system is used in your area, you need to know how to size the ductwork for various cfm rates and pressure drops. Once a good load calculation has been run—one that shows how many cfm of air each room needs—it is not too difficult to figure out how many runs to bring to the room to deliver that amount of air. Your best bet is to consult duct sizing tables from the manufacturers of ductwork in your area.

You also need to know that ductwork introduces two negative factors into the system—pressure losses and noise. Most residential air handlers and furnaces can safely handle up to about one inch of static pressure drop in the system. If your duct system has more than one inch of pressure drop in it, some rooms will not be adequately conditioned, and in a worse case, you could damage the furnace or compressor.

Likewise, air velocity (which will vary with the pressure) creates noise. The standard design rate of 0.1 inches of static loss per 100 equivalent feet of duct should produce noise levels that are not objectionable for most residential jobs, resulting in air velocities in the range of 500 to 700 feet per minute (fpm). But for areas where noise may be an issue (such as a home entertainment center), air velocities in the ducts should be kept below 600 fpm with outlet velocities below the same value. (Most grille manufacturers produce tables showing how much noise their grilles produce at various outlet velocities. For critical noise jobs, these tables must be checked to be sure the proposed design will not create excessive noise and that the resulting air flows will still permit good mixing of conditioned air with room air.)

For some commercial applications, air velocities are even more critical. None is more critical, perhaps, than a broadcast studio, where duct velocities should be kept under 500 fpm and outlets in the range of 300 to 500 fpm, with return air grille velocities below 500 fpm. I saw the plans a dealer drew up once for doing a church auditorium where the main trunk velocities were going to exceed 1,200 fpm and the grille velocities 1,000 fpm! I warned him that this would create a space with a roaring wind sound. The solution was to redesign the system with many more runouts, thus reducing runout velocity and grille velocity to under 600 fpm, and then oversize the main trunk to keep its velocity under 750 fpm. It cost the church more to install, but at least they could hear their pastor. (I suppose that was okay with them!)

System Efficiency Ratings

You should know how such things as SEER, HSPF, and AFUE are generated and how system factors can affect these ratings.

In its simplest guise, SEER is defined by the Department of Energy as the "ratio of the cooling output divided by the power consumption. It is the BTU of cooling output during its normal annual usage divided by the total electric energy input in watt hours during the same period. This is a measure of the cooling performance for rating central air conditioners and central heat pumps.[18]" When manufacturers rate their equipment for SEER, they do so by setting up operating equipment in a carefully controlled laboratory environment and carefully measuring system capacity compared to power input. The higher the number, the better in terms of less energy usage.

If anyone should ask you, SEER replaced an earlier term, EER, because EER was a rating at a static set of conditions. Because of this, many manufacturers worked hard to produce units that were highly efficient *at those conditions* but less so at other conditions. The SEER system measures the *system efficiency* over a broader range of conditions and is a better measure of the system's actual efficiency.

HSPF is a similar measurement but it is used on heat pumps to measure their seasonal heating efficiencies. A good definition of HSPF can be found at http://tva.apogee.net/res/rehhspf.asp where we find:

> HSPF is calculated by taking the total annual heating requirements, including all energy inputs (defrost and back-up heating energy included) divided by the total electric power used.

Since HSPF uses BTUs for the system outputs and watts for the system inputs, the number is lower than SEER numbers (because there are 3.414 BTUs in a WATT). Still, the higher the HSPF rating the more efficient is the heat pump. (You may also recall that HSPF replaced its static-condition predecessor, COP, or coefficient of performance.)

AFUE is a rating of furnace seasonal efficiency. The Department of Energy defines AFUE this way:

> The measure of seasonal or annual efficiency of a furnace or boiler. It takes into account the cyclic on/off operation and associated energy losses of the heating unit as it responds to changes in the load, which in turn is affected by changes in weather and occupant controls.

A furnace's AFUE is measured in percentages, the higher the number, the more efficient the furnace. A furnace with an AFUE of 94% means that 94% of the BTU content of the gas the homeowner buys ends up being transferred to the air going over the heat exchanger.

---

18 See http://www.eia.doe.gov/glossary/glossary_s.htm.July 25, 2007.

Know When to Say "When!"

There is a down side to being a technical wizard (or at least the man behind the curtain who knows which levers to pull): your dealers can come to see you as their in-house engineer and start asking you to do more and more of their engineering for them.

That is *not* your job! You need to know *how* to do these things so you can help your dealers install good jobs, but it is *not* your job to do the designs (except in a few cases that I will come to in a moment).

If you find yourself being pulled by your dealers into doing their engineering, you may need to do what I did when I found myself being asked to do more and more designs for my dealers. You will have to wean them!

There came a time when several of my lower tier accounts started expecting me to do all their loads and duct designs and I said I could not do that, nor would I do that. But I would do this: on a certain date, I would teach all my dealers how to do loads and duct design in an evening course at our branch warehouse. Those who did not come would not find me being very supportive when they needed advice on loads and ducts; those who did come would have my free second opinion on the designs they came up with, but they were still going to be responsible for their own loads and duct designs.

On the specified night, all but one dealer showed up for the class and all did well with it. The following week, I made a sales call on the one who did *not* attend. Early in the call he handed me a roll of blueprints and said, "I need a load run on this house." I replied, "I don't do loads anymore." He frowned and asked why not. I pointed to the announcement I mailed him about the loads and duct class we did the week before—it was still tacked to the bulletin board on his wall, and said, "You were invited to the class and did not show up. Do you see what it says at the bottom of that flier?" He read it (probably for the first time) and came to the part where it said that after that class I would no longer be doing loads or duct layouts for them, since they would know how to do their own.

He drew up, went, "Harrumph!" and added, "Well, Brand H will do my loads for me." I said, "Fine! Let Brand H do your loads then." And he became a Brand H dealer. (Which was fine by me since I wanted to find a way to cut this dealer off without causing trouble, which given his political connections, could have been delicate.)

As the old proverb says, "Give a man a fish today, and you will have to give him another tomorrow. Teach him how to fish today, and he can feed himself."

The *only* exceptions I made to my no loads/no duct design rule were for (a) large and complex commercial jobs that were often beyond the skill level of even my best dealers to calculate, and (b) complex or unusual custom new homes that presented special challenges to sizing and/or design. But for really complex problems, I would ask the dealer's permission to hire a mechanical engineer (that he would pay for) to do the really tough jobs. Most had no objection to this and it helped them nail down some very nice design/build jobs that otherwise might have gone the cut-throat plan and spec route!

Review Questions for Chapter 16

1. A Tier One TM is comfortable with technical issues without having to be a (n) ___

A) know-it-all

B) engineer

C) good salesman

D) generalist

E) none of the above

Answer: ________

2. Use a psychrometric chart of your choice and tell what the relative humidity would be for air entering a coil that is 78F DB and 66F WB.

A) 74%

B) 13.7 cubic feet

C) 60 F

D) 53%

E) none of the above

Answer: ________

3. A heat pump's heating efficiency is measured by

A) HSPF

B) AFUE

C) SEER

D) EER

E) COP

Answer: ________

Chapter 17: Information Management

If any chapter in this field guide will quickly become obsolete, it will be this one. Information management and its technology is changing so rapidly today that what even the industry leaders are writing about as being the next big thing is history next week.

Yet, there are some fundamentals that should transfer across any kind of information management platform you use, and mastery of those fundamentals can give you an edge in a tough market.

A Mobile World

More than ever, we live in a mobile world where a sales professional is never really out of reach of her clients—or her office. You now have at your command cell phones, laptop computers, portable printers, PDAs, DVD players, USB drives, Blackberries, i-phones, and a long list of other new high-tech gadgets, all promising to make you more productive and help you get ahead of the competition (and to lighten your wallet).

But all the technology in the world will do you no good if you don't know how to use it to deliver the one thing that is becoming the measure of good customer service today—information. When I teach classes of new territory managers how to become Tier One TMs and see them come to class with more gadgets than ought to be legal, (but many of them having no ability to use them for anything other than texting their friends and playing games) I know that a certain portion of that class is doomed to failure eventually. The gadgets are not the measures of your success or even of your brilliance. They are merely tools, keys that help you unlock the treasure troves of knowledge and information your dealers need in order to grow and succeed.

Like It Or Not, You're a Filter

Manufacturers, and distributors—can put out an awful lot of information to the channel that is not always relevant to every position in the channel. One of the hardest (and most important) jobs you have as a TM is to know what to pass on to your dealers, and what to block. In short, you are a filter of information flow, in particular *two-way flow*.

For example, the factory announces a newly-discovered trouble issue on a certain product and spells out a fix for the problem. Do you pass this information on to *all* your dealers? Or only to those who have installed any of the subject units?

Or the distributor rolls out a new marketing program for the spring that uses a consumer offer to get customers to call, and Old Jedediah, your dealer in Possum Trot, never participates in marketing programs because everyone in the county knows and trusts Jedediah. Do you take the marketing program to him too?

The same thing holds for new product rollouts. Some dealers will not get on the bandwagon for, let's say, ductless splits. So do you burn up sales call time going over something they don't believe in (and probably won't ever endorse) or do something more productive?

You see, not everything that comes out of the factory—or even your own front office—needs to be heard in every dealer's office. You must learn how to determine what information is relevant for each account and then be sure each account gets what they need to stay informed.

You Have to Stay Personal

In this high-tech, high-gadget age, it is easy to become impersonal in communications. Just send someone a fax, an email, a text message or a Tweet. That's all you need!

Sometimes that is fine. But sometimes, it is not enough. Did you know that only 7% of your communication is the words you use? The other 93% is the inflection and cadence you use when you say them and the body language you display as you say them. (More on that in Chapter 23.) Personally, I abhor email as a medium for detailed and intimate communication because it just does not lend itself to that type of dialog because the recipient cannot read your tone or cadence or see your body posture. (They will force their own tone and cadence onto your words, sometimes with disastrous results.) At least with a hand-written note, you can indicate emotions by the size of your writing and the pressure you use as you write on the paper. But in email, you are just typing letters—each letter the same precise digital representation of an alphabetic character, with no way to show emotions (other than the ubiquitous ALL CAPS SHOUTING MODE). If you have a very important message to deliver to a dealer, use the telephone and *call* her. Let your voice communicate what email cannot. Better yet, if it is a really vital issue, see the dealer in person.

The same can be said for automated attendant phone systems. Personally, I dislike them as I have to listen to a recorded voice give me options (and over half the time what I want to do is not covered by the bloody options!). I realize they save companies money as it is much cheaper to buy a computerized phone system with synthesized voice that does not require health benefits, vacation pay, or even having to worry about having a bad day. But I wonder if in our drive for cost savings we have not lost sight of a bigger and more important element of doing business?

Use the New Technology When It Is Good for Both Parties

I am not against new technology. I love the gadgets almost as much as anyone else. It's just that my years of business have shown me that despite our technological advances, at heart we are all still people, and people don't change very fast. If I could put you into a time machine and transport you back in time 500 years to the days of Galileo or Kepler, you may not know the languages (Italian or German), but you would find that you could still communicate as if they were modern Europeans. Or if I sent you back 5,000 years to the pyramid builders, you would probably find them just as human as your next-door neighbors (other than the fact that they spoke Old Egyptian). The point is, people have not changed that much as human beings in over 5,000 years despite the blinding speed of our technological change. The things that motivated people while they were building the pyramids still motivate people today (and ditto for what makes them afraid). Technology changes all the time, but human nature is not nearly so adaptable!

So use new technology when it is good for both parties and shun it when it is not. If your dealers are comfortable doing business over the internet, let them check your inventory and place orders without your involvement, and spend your time with them building their business! (It doesn't take a Tier One TM—or even a Tier Three TM—to be an order taker!)

If your dealers are comfortable filing warranty claims and advertising claims on-line, let them do it. And if they are not, make sure they get them in by hand on time and properly filled out.

I was the first TM in our distributorship to use a laptop. Back in those days (can you hear the squeaky voice of an old prospector here?), there was no software to support a TM in his job, so I wrote my own programs to assemble job quotes and track jobs, and then later generate an order off the stored job data. When I would go into a dealer's office and he needed a quote, say, for some rooftop units for a job he was looking at, I would open the laptop, assemble the quote, print his copy on my portable battery-powered printer, and store the quote automatically on the hard drive. If the dealer later called with a purchase order, I would retrieve the quote, execute the order generating command, and send an order to our purchasing department. The whole process was a huge time saver and eliminated errors on quotes.

Today, most major manufacturers provide this type of software to their field sales forces. If you have access to it, you may want to learn how to use it because the time it can save you can be spent on more important matters (like face-to-face conversations with your dealers about what steps should be taken next to grow their businesses).

Your top tier dealers should all have web pages. If they don't, encourage them to develop a web presence. Most major manufacturers have programs for dealers to help them get started with web pages. However, most of these factory-sponsored plans are basic ones—basically a brochure type of web presence. Such sites are okay for starters, but you want to encourage your dealers to have interactive pages as soon as possible—pages where customers can download information, contact the dealership, set up a sales appointment, or even set up a service call or purchase items like service agreements or filters.

There is a growing body of service dispatching software available today that have GPS capabilities. Such programs help a service tech find a house quickly and efficiently, and they also provide the service manager important information about how the techs drive and where their trucks are 24/7. (This makes it hard for a tech to moonlight, or spend part of an afternoon in a bar, as a few have discovered in recent employment termination cases!) Such programs can also help a dealer spot reckless drivers and take action before insurance premiums skyrocket.

How many of your dealers are using bar code scanning systems? (For that matter, is your *distributorship* using bar code scanning yet?) Bar code scanning is an incredibly powerful way to track product movement, consumer trends, and other details that are important to a dealer or distributor. Linking a bar code scanner to a customer database makes building a customer record as easy as waving a scanner over a label!

Are your dealers starting to use PDAs, tablet PCs, I-pads, or net-books for some of their service techs? Though still a young technology, these new tools hold tremendous promise for service departments as some manufacturers now offer software to run on these systems that helps a tech troubleshoot a system, using video lessons (even in bi-lingual mode!). Thus, a young tech with limited experience can sit in his truck for a few minutes and learn how to fix a problem he has not seen before and look pretty good before the customer as he fixes the unit!

Some hand-held devices can also be set up to read diagnostic codes from a circuit board. The hand-held device can display the fault codes and history of the unit when it is not working properly.

And this is nothing compared to the incredible breakthroughs in controls technology over the last decade as more and more manufacturers are developing control systems that can monitor system performance and then dial out on a telephone line to the contractor's monitoring computer to report problems—before the owner is even aware they have a problem! Imagine how it can affect a customer when a service tech shows up at their home some morning with a part under their arm and say they have come to fix the air conditioner. The customer says, "But it's working okay!" The tech replies, "Yes, sir, it is—for now. But this morning, the unit called our shop and said it was starting to experience a problem, so we are here to fix it before it causes you an inconvenience!" Now *there* is value-add you can charge for!

And I have not even tapped into the new fields of smart houses, predictive diagnostics, smart chips, and other technologies either under development or already available that have the potential to change forever how we do the business of HVAC.

Managing Information

But this chapter is about information management, not just the technology of information.

So how does a Tier One TM do information management?

First, a Tier One TM recognizes that *information flow is a two-way street.* Not only does she have to pass information down the channel to her dealers; she must also collect information from her dealers and pass it up the channel to people who need to know it. Say, for instance, that one of Jane's dealers just ran into a rebate program from Brand X that no one back at the home office knew about. Jane should gather all the data she can about the program and pass it along to the sales manager or marketing manager (by a phone call, fax, or email). She is also responsible to pass information along horizontally (when it is verified to be accurate). In such a case, Jane would pass along to her other dealers the scoop she picked up on Brand X's rebate program so they could be ready to counter it if it shows up in their markets.

Second, a Tier One TM must be *skilled in the use of communications software*, such as Word, PowerPoint, Excel, Outlook (or their equivalents), and other programs. Finesse with Adobe Acrobat (the program that creates PDF files, not the one that merely reads them) would also be good to possess. (The Microsoft Office 2010 Suite has a downloadable PDF maker that is free and very good!) Good communication skills (and the ability to use software to convey them) are every bit as important (in my opinion) as the "hard" engineering skills discussed in Chapter 16.

Third, a Tier One TM communicates to each dealer what each dealer specifically needs. Shotgun communications are easy and fast, but rarely as effective as customizing the message for each receiver. When I covered my territory, I had a file drawer that I called my Take file. Each dealer had his or her own folder in the file hanging from a Pendaflex rack system. During the week, as I came across articles or items that I thought would help a particular dealer, I would make a photocopy and put it in his or her Take file. Often, I would jot a short note on a pad at night after dinner as a new idea to discuss with him hit me. Then, on my sales calls, I would take the Take folder with me and deliver its contents to the dealers, discussing each item I had in the folder as I did. Consider creating a take file system.

Fourth, I would advise you to buy a decent *digital camera* (or cell phone with a camera built in) and keep it with you. Use it to photograph your dealer employees in terrific action scenes. You will be amazed what it can do for employee morale and your relationship with a dealer when you hand the receptionist a photo you printed of her on the phone and the caption, "Here is what a top-notch receptionist looks like at work!" Or the impact it has when you hand a service tech a photo of him beside his truck and you remark as you hand it to him, "I seldom see techs show as much pride in their trucks as you do. I'll bet your boss is proud of you too!"

You can also use the camera to photograph outstanding job workmanship a dealer executes, and then show other dealers what a really great looking piping job looks like, or how to arrange four condensing units on a slab for a mega-home, and the like.

Of course, you can also use the camera to document bad jobs and use them in discussions with your field service team or the dealer to discuss ways to do a better job next time around.

Sometimes, when you get to a dealer's office for your appointment, he is busy—either on the phone with a foreman discussing a job problem that just came up, or trying to put out a fire on a job that developed a delivery problem, or dealing with an irate customer. Often, you may have to wait several minutes while he finishes what he is doing. When that's the case, you can communicate with other employees in the office to see how things are going and to get a second set of eyes looking at your performance.

One thing I did to help in such situations was get my key dealers a *plastic wall rack* like the ones doctors sometimes use in their exam rooms. (It mounts on the wall and comes out at an angle. The nurse puts the patient's file in it so when the doctor comes in to see you, he has your history at his fingertips.) I gave each of my key dealers one of these to which I had affixed a large adhesive shipping label with a cartoon of a cowboy about to draw his guns in a shootout, and a label under the cowboy, "Stuff for Harshaw." I told my dealers that during the time between my sales calls, things would come up that did not require immediate attention but to which they would like answers next time I was in. They could then jot it down on a slip of paper and drop it in the Stuff folder and go on about their business. On my next sales call, I would go over each item and make sure the dealer had his questions answered in full. (I also did this for any employee in the business; if they had a question they needed an answer to, they could drop me a note and I would find them and give them the answer, or call them later if they were on a job at the time.) I would then use my waiting time to go over these issues and prepare answers.

If your sales call is at a time of day when a meal is usually taken, don't overlook the *power of the business lunch* (or breakfast or dinner). Often, getting a dealer away from the office for an hour while you chow down on a burger or steak can lead to better communication (because of fewer distractions) and can well be worth the cost of the meal. In my case, I had a standing deal with all my dealers. If we went to breakfast, lunch, or dinner, I would buy on odd-numbered days. They would buy on even numbered days. I did not buy all the time and I recommend that you don't fall into that trap either. You and your dealer are a partnership, and partners share the costs as they go.

In managing information flow, don't forget *the other employees at the dealership*. It may surprise you, but a Tier One TM knows that he is relating to *all* of the employees at a dealership, not just the dealer principal. Be careful about overlooking the receptionist as a key communicator, the service technicians, or even the lowly installers. Often, they will tell you things the boss won't and what they tell you can reveal things you were not even aware of.

Review Questions for Chapter 17

1. Regardless of the changes in technology, the most important thing for a territory manager to do with his customers is

A) stay one step ahead of them in communications technology

B) communicate clearly the information the customer needs

C) never take a cell phone call while talking with a dealer

D) send them informative emails at least once a week

Answer: _______

2. In our wondrous age of high-tech communications equipment, it is vitally important to

A) be concise

B) be precise

C) be personal

D) all of the above

Answer: _______

3. You have a dealer (Roscoe) who is not computer literate and no-one in his office is particularly skilled either. For the coming pre-season program, your distributor offers your dealers a 3% bonus co-op split (53/47 rather than 50/50) for a dealer who files his advertising claims on-line. Roscoe appreciates the gesture, but neither he nor his staff is enthusiastic about filing his claims on-line. What should you do?

A) give him the co-op bonus anyway

B) train him and his staff and train them and train them until they

are comfortable with the idea

C) not force the issue

D) do his claims for him

Answer: _______

4. How many of your top accounts need to have interactive web sites?

A) all of them

B) at least half of them

C) 25% of them

D) leave them alone—if they want a web presence, they'll build one

Answer: _______

5. In a healthy distributor/TM/dealer relationship, communication should be

A) happening constantly

B) a two-way street

C) in writing **and** electronic

D) done by the Internet as much as possible

Answer: _______

6. Which of the following is a good use of a digital camera?

A) taking flattering photos of dealer employees

B) taking photos of outstanding jobs

C) taking photos of bad jobs

D) all of these are good uses

Answer: _______

Chapter 18: Doing the Grind

In this chapter, we will talk about doing the grind—the daily, weekly, monthly routines of being a top tier territory manager without getting ground up in the process. In particular, we will talk about having short term plans and working them.

"Gentlemen, this is a football..."

With these words, it is said, the immortal football coach Vince Lombardi would start his annual training camp with the Green Bay Packers. Lombardi was not insulting his players. He was stressing to them that success in professional football comes as a team masters the basics. His tenure as the head coach of the Packers in their glory days proves his wisdom!

The difference between being at the top of your field and being second is not much. For example, did you know that in the 1980 Winter Olympics at Lake Placid, the gap between the first and second place finishes in the 15km Cross Country Ski Race was only *three inches*! Likewise, in 1992, Al Unser Jr. crossed the finish line at the Indianapolis 500 race only *25 feet* ahead of Scott Goodyear for one of the closest finishes in the history of the Indy 500. Only *0.043 seconds* separated the pair after 500 miles of racing!

Do you remember who was the first person to walk on the moon? If you said Neil Armstrong, you'd be right! But who was second? (Does anyone remember Michael "Buzz" Aldrin?) Or who was the first man to climb Mt. Everest? It was Sir Edmund Hillary, in 1953. Do you know who was second? (It was his Sherpa guide, Tenzing Norgay.)

So what's the point of this first place/second place talk? Only this: The difference between coming in first and coming in second—between winning and not winning, between fame and mediocrity; is not usually a matter of *big* differences but of *little* ones. You don't have to be a *lot* better than the competition... just a *little* better!

One story tells about two territory managers hiking together in Alaska. One day, they came into a glade in the woods and startled a ten foot-tall Kodiak bear on the other side of the clearing. The bear reared up on its hind legs, roared, and charged after the TMs. One TM pulled his backpack off immediately and started putting on his running shoes. His partner said, "You fool, why take up your time doing that? You can't outrun a Kodiak! They can run at thirty-five miles per hour!" The other TM shot back as he was tying his laces, "Oh, I don't have to outrun that bear. I just have to outrun *you*!"

So Is This Job Drudgework?

With a title like *Doing the Grind*, one might think so! And, in fact, some Tier Four TMs see it that way.

But what I am speaking of is the fact that this job requires some discipline if you are going to operate at Tiers One or Two, and this discipline means that certain things should be practiced regularly to help you do all you have to do easily and quickly. I found my days as a TM to be some of the most exciting and challenging of any job I have ever held and loved it immensely (on most days, anyway!).

Being a Tier One TM is a job that demands a great amount of attention to detail. You cannot wing it and sustain performance at Tier One for long. You must have a plan and work it routinely.

A Simple Aid: The Call Planner

One of the simplest things you can do to be sure you are paying attention to the right details at the right time is to use a simple call planner. A call planner is a form that helps you spell out what things you want to cover on a sales call with a dealer, and in what order. (I know a few Tier One TMs who no longer use a call planner, because they have become so good at their jobs that the process is unconscious to them. They do a great job at covering their territories and don't need a call plan sheet to do it. But for anyone operating at less than a Tier One level, I strongly recommend they use a call planner.) On the next page is a simple call planner I developed (you'll find a copy of it as a Word document—so you can modify it—on the CD that came with this book):

Call Planning Sheet

Account: ____

Appointment: M T W Th F S at _______ am/pm Date: ________

1. Old Business
o Old job quotes to follow up:
o Submittals to deliver:
o Approved submittals to pick up:
o Issues from last visit:
2. New Business
o Programs:
o Advertising:
o Catalog updates:
o Pricing updates:
o Quotes / Jobs:
o Other:
o Other:
3. Problems to Resolve
o Billing errors:
o Credits:
o Service problems:
o Warranty issues:
o Back orders:
4. Orders to Ask For
o Specials, promotions:
o Specific job orders:
o Monthly floor plan:
o Other:
5. Intelligence to Gather
o What the competition is doing:
o What is happening in construction:
o Rumors:
o Other:

To use this form, you should *call ahead and set an appointment.* I am surprised when I teach TM workshops at how many TMs do *not* call ahead and set appointments for their sales calls!

By setting an appointment with a dealer (even one you only see once a quarter), you are saying to him or her, "I respect your time and know you don't like unplanned surprises. I also value my time and don't like to waste it trying to find someone who is busy that day." It is a compliment to a dealer to acknowledge that you respect his or her time and don't want to surprise them with an unannounced call.

The appointment also gives you a chance to go over briefly what you will be covering on the sales call—new product info, quotes, submittals, new marketing programs—whatever it is that makes it important for you to spend time with that dealer.

I always recommend that after you finish the call for the appointment that you fax or email a confirmation to the dealer and recap (in general terms) what it is you will be going over together during that call.

If you are running late the day of your appointment, *call the dealer* and let him or her know. Ask if being late will cause a hardship and if so, offer to reschedule.

The call planner forms were always filed in the dealer's permanent file so I had an outline history of every sales call I made for that dealer.

The Tickler File

In the last chapter you read about my Take file system.

I also had a thirty-one day accordion file on my credenza that was labeled TICKLER. In this file would go notes for follow-up with dealers on issues.

You'll notice that the form on page 327 has an area called "Problems to Resolve." If the dealer needed an issue to be addressed, and I could not address it on the spot, I would place his Call Planner sheet in the TICKLER file three days before I had promised him an answer. I would also add the item to my To Do list and go about getting an answer for my dealer.

I would check the TICKLER file every day to see what I had promised and by what date. By having the tickler surface three days before the promised date, I had the chance to get the dealer an answer before my promised time, a big point earner with most dealers! Once I had the answer, I would fax, call, or write the dealer with the answer he needed. (We did not have email at that time, but today I would add email to the avenues of communication.)

The Bedrock Basics

The call planner, Take and TICKLER file ideas are good ideas to help you run a territory with fewer fumbles, but they are just tools and don't really address the bigger issue. The bigger issue—and this is the one that in my experience really separates the Tier One TMs from the Tier Three and Four ones—is a fierce devotion to personal management and self discipline. You cannot really do well in the big leagues until you come face to face with these two areas and tackle them.

In Chapter 3, you learned what your time was worth per hour. In Chapter 27, you will learn some practical ideas to help you become better at time management. But in the meantime, there is something you need to know, something that can really set you free in the area of self-management. Here it is:

There is no such thing as "time management;"
You cannot manage what you do not control.
There is only self-management and discipline.

I often have TMs ask me how they can get better at time management (a common complaint among all Tiers of TM). When I give them this answer, they often frown, shake their heads, and look at me like I have three heads.

But it really is true. Time is an attribute of space, like the three dimensions we are familiar with (length, width, height). Like gravity, it is an inexorable thing, going on whether you want it to or not. You can no more control and manage time than you can control or manage gravity. It is beyond your abilities. Hence, time management is a myth.

But managing yourself *in time*, so that you are efficient and effective *in the here and now* is within your power, and that's the little secret that can set you free from the guilt of poor time management and open the door for you to become a productive powerhouse every day.

Discipline means that there will be days when you'd rather not make your rounds and see the same old customers and discuss the same old issues and hear the same old complaints. But you do it anyway because you know that in the long haul, it is the person who is consistent that wins. It is an old cliché, but true nonetheless, that the tortoise beat the hare because he was consistent and steady, while the hare ran in furious bursts but without an overall sense of purpose.

To an extent, you will probably have to regiment your life a little more than you thought necessary. (This is a bitter pill for some people who just are not psychologically wired for it. They can still make excellent sales people, but they must really use a lot of props to help them stay consistent and steady in their work routines.)

I believe you should see your "A" accounts—your elite group—often, perhaps once a week or more. (But in every case, you should establish a sales call frequency that the *dealer* wants. If an "A" account only wants to see you every other week, that should be fine with you.) Your "B" accounts can be seen every other week or even once every three weeks; and "C" accounts once a month or less.

If a dealer says he'd like to see more of you, offer to trade your time for purchases and growth. I did this, and it quickly separates those who really want to spend time with you for growth and development purposes from those who just want to tie up your time.

If you territory is large, you may need to establish a milk route agenda, driving to some parts of it in certain weeks, trying to minimize travel time and fuel expense without sacrificing critical development time. (To a limited extent, I had two milk routes in my territory—one running north that I traveled every other week, and one running south that alternated with the north route.)

All Work and No Play Undoes Jack

I have seen TMs dive into their territories with zeal and gusto. So much zeal and gusto that they forgot to spend time recharging their batteries and being with their families. Usually, these folks burned out in a year or two and ended up as the type of sales rep that give all of us in sales a bad name.

Remember this: you are in a marathon, not a sprint. You must pace yourself for the race is long and difficult.

Don't be a Rabbit!

Learn to *pace yourself* so that you can get a maximum amount of work done without knocking yourself out doing it. One year, I experienced chest pains as I lay in bed. Thinking it may be the precursor to a heart attack; I made an appointment with a cardiologist and had a series of tests run. All the tests came back negative. I did not have a heart attack or anything close to it, but I was showing signs of acute stress. (The fact that I was working about seventy-six hours a week was probably not helping any.) The doctor advised that I get rid of the stress in my life. I asked him with a tone of irony in my voice, "Yeah, and any idea how to do that?" He just smiled and said, "Oh, you'll find a way… or die."

On Sprints and Marathons

Before I entered the HVAC field, I was a high school teacher. One of my duties was to serve as a timer at track meets in the spring.

Our high school had a girls' 4x440 relay team. One particular girl on this team had the nickname "Rabbit" because she would always run her lap as if it were a 100 yard sprint. Since she was the first one to run on her relay team, she was impressive to watch—until she hit the far end of the first curve.

Then, along the back straightaway, the other girls would start passing her until she was dead last by the time she stumbled to her handoff.

That poor girls' team did not win a single relay that year, and it was because Rabbit would not listen to anyone's advice to pace herself for her lap and not burn her legs and lungs out in the first 200 yards.

So I found a way. I cut down to fifty-five hours a week on the job (some weeks less than that) and learned to leave it all behind me at 5:00 pm on Friday and not take it up again until 7:00 am Monday. I started developing new interests and hobbies, which lead me to start building model ships from scratch, and astronomy. Both hobbies require strong discipline if you expect to achieve noteworthy results.

Perhaps that is about the best advice I could give you—*find a hobby or a pastime that will demand discipline of you.* Then do it and stick with it. Maybe for you that would be golf. Learn to play and play so that when you scrub a shot after a beautiful putt you don't throw your clubs across the fairway. Jog. Ride a bicycle. Climb mountains. Fish. Hunt. Backpack in the wilderness. Take up photography. Do martial arts. Serve food at a homeless shelter. Do something not at all related to your work and determine to become *really good* at it. Set high goals and bust your ass reaching them.

If necessary, *become accountable to someone for your self-discipline*. It does not hurt to hire a good personal performance coach if she can help you toe the line and acquire the habits of effective self-management. Whoever you tap for this task, make sure they have the guts (and your permission) to tell you when you are full of manure and the timing to praise you when you start to get it right.

Keep a diary or a journal. You don't have to be eloquent or even use very many words. Some days, I just wrote a line or two. Other days I'd fill two or three pages. And none of what I wrote would be usable even for a cheap magazine. But it does not have to be. You are not writing for the world to read. You are writing to show to yourself how you have grown over time and what lessons you learned along the way.

Many of you will discover that you are spiritual creatures. If so, *don't leave your God out of your development*. Worship, prayer, meditation— all of these can help you bring an unruly life under control and make it submitted to a higher will.

The nineteenth century English essayist James Allen wrote a wonderful little book whose title was based on a verse in the book of Proverbs in the Bible. The book is titled *As A Man Thinketh*. I have read it numerous times because its truths come into my mind and heart like new electricity to recharge my batteries from time to time. Get it and read it. And while you are at it, try to find a copy of Bob Beuss's little gem, *Favor, the Road to Success*. (It is out of print now and may be very difficult to obtain.)

For that matter, develop the habit of *reading every day*. I don't care what you read. Just read an hour or more a day (besides trade journals and emails). I like to read about the American Civil War and astronomy. Others find mental muscle in good fiction; others in mysteries; others in poetry. Some like to read books on business and finance. Whatever it is, find a topic and major in it. After ten years, you'll be amazed at how much you will know about that topic.

<u>There Are No Secrets</u>

In short, there are no secrets to becoming a Tier One TM. It takes time and discipline. Master the fundamentals, the basics. Learn the little things and take the time to learn how they fit together and inter-relate. Then you'll be amazed at how strong you can become in your field!

If there was a short cut, do you think I'd be writing this book? This book contains solid things in every chapter to help you reach Tier One status, but there is no silver bullet that will kill your werewolf in one shot, no magic potion that will change you into Superman or Wonder

Woman overnight.

As Zig Ziglar has said, the way to the top is through the stairwell. The elevator is broken!

Review Questions for Chapter 18

1. To be the best in your territory, you need to be

   A) the best you can be

   B) at the top of the sales reports every month

   C) better than the second-best territory manager

   D) on time for all of your appointments

   Answer: ________

2. To be a Tier One territory manager, you need to

   A) pay attention to detail

   B) dress well every day

   C) master the use of a computer

   D) keep good records

   Answer: ________

3. A call planner is

   A) a bad idea for most territory managers

   B) a good idea to keep sales calls on track

   C) a good tool to help plan a sales call

   D) a good way to keep a record of every sales call

   E) B, C and D

   Answer: ________

4. What kind of file can you use to remind yourself of future promises and commitments?

   A) a future file

   B) a tickler file

   C) a take file

   D) a reminder file

   Answer: ________

5. The big secret to being a Tier One territory manager is

   A) self-discipline and personal management

   B) to be good at time management

   C) to know when to take time off to recharge

   D) to have an accountability partner or coach

   Answer: ________

6. If you have trouble managing your time, your best solution would be to

   A) start the day an hour earlier or work an hour later

   B) cultivate self-discipline in your life

   C) use a day planner of some type

   D) make a "To Do" list every morning

   Answer: ________

7. One of the best ways to become an "expert" on any topic is to

   A) take a college course on the topic

   B) write a magazine article or book on it

   C) read about it all you can for years

   D) hang out with people who really know a lot about it

   Answer: _________

Chapter 19: Sales Reviews

Most distributors have regular sales reviews. Some do it monthly. Some quarterly. Others once a year or never.

Yet a regular and methodical sales review can be of immense help to the Tier One territory manager and the company he or she works for. In this chapter, we will consider what a regular sales review can do to make you a more potent TM.

Dark Days of Fear, Dread and Trembling

I have known TMs who approach sales reviews with a high degree of fear and trepidation. They just know they are going to be put on the spot and made to look stupid before their peers. (Sadly, some of them do! But as Forest Gump so often said, "Stupid is as stupid does.")

Maybe you have an immature sales manager who enjoys making some of his sales staff look stupid or incompetent. If you do, I feel sorry for you. Maybe you should try to find a company where the sales manager is more supportive. (I'll have more to say about the Sales Manager role in Chapters 28 and 30.)

Most sales managers are not vindictive ogres crouching in the shadows waiting to pounce upon a hapless victim who wanders by their lairs. Most are good and decent men and women who want to see their sales team excel at their jobs because when their teams do well, *they* do well.

A sales review should not be viewed as a time to be feared (unless you have one of those Attila the Hun managers). It is a time to learn how well you are playing the game and to learn what you can do to get even better.

Do you think Tiger Woods is content to shoot four over par at a practice session?

Sales Reviews: What They Should Cover

I have seen sales reviews that were conducted one-on-one (just the sales manager and the TM, to discuss results and recommendations for improvement) and I have seen them where they are a group therapy session. Both can be effective if done correctly.

First, your sales manager should have a form of some sort (usually a computer printout) and should have sent a copy to you ahead of time. (Not all will do this, but I find it works better if the sales person is prepared for their review and not ambushed.)

The report should show two sets of numbers—your sales plan numbers and your actual numbers. The actual numbers should be your year-to-date (YTD) numbers, with another set of *projected* numbers.

Here is an extremely simple example of such a report:

TM: Susan Merginthall			Month: May 201x
	Sales Plan	Results YTD	Going Rate Results
Sales	$5,700,000	$2,137,433	$6,412,299 112% of plan
GM	$1,254,000	$438,174	$1,314,521 105% of plan
18SEER	$520,000	$160,345	$481,035 93% of plan

To compute the Going Rate Results, the sales manager must know what percentage of the annual business the distributorship does in each month. Then, the sum of those percentages becomes the divisor for the YTD numbers.

> **Example**: For Susan's company, the fiscal year starts in January. By May, 33% of the year's business is done on average. So to get the Going Rate Results, her sales manager (or the computer program the company uses) divides the Results YTD for May by 0.33 to get the Going Rate Results.

The Going Rate Results data shows where Susan should end up if she continues the rest of the year at this pace with no changes in her territory or sales call behavior. A sales manager can usually tell as early as April whether or not a TM is going to hit their sales goals for the year. Here, we see that Susan is 12% over plan for sales total dollars, but only 5% over plan for gross margin dollars. Is she pursuing high volume work at the trade-off in gross margin? There is nothing wrong with that, but if she is not careful, she could fall into a trap that is steep and slippery. She is also 7% behind plan on selling high end equipment. Could this be part of the reason her gross margin dollars are down? So you see there are two different factors at play reducing the gross margin dollar performance. Which is it? Or is it a combination of the two? Or could it be something else entirely? A good sales manager will talk with their territory managers and try to find out and then take steps to help their territory managers make their numbers for the year.

Besides the numbers, a good sales report will also have subjective performance "grades" as well. For instance, on the next page is one possible report format:

3rd Quarter Reviews

Scale: 1-5, 1 = low, 5 = excellent

Criterion	Susan
Performance	
Sales YTD	5
Quarterly review	4
New sales generated	3
Old sales grown	4
Gross margin	3
AVERAGE	3.8
Weight	3
Weighted Average	**11.4**
Competency	
Selling skills	4
Mastery of sales cycle	4
Qualifying skills	2
Customer knowledge	5
Relationship management	4
Presentation skills	5
Negotiating skills	3
Personal confidence	4
Professionalism	5
Prospecting skills	2
Product knowledge	5
Channel management	3
Mentoring	1
Business acumen	3
Information management	3
Leadership	4
AVERAGE	3.6
Weight	2
Weighted Average	**7.2**
Frequency	
Calls per week	3
Quotes per week	3
Executive calls	5
Prospects per week	1
Focus on "A" Accounts	3
Reports in on time	1
Calls on key accounts	3

Time management	2
AVERAGE	2.6
Weight	1
Weighted Average	**2.6**
Total of all Weighted Sections	**21.2**
Perfect Score, All Sections	30.0

This form reviews a great deal of critical sales behavior, so let's take a moment to see what it covers and why.

The Performance section is based on the numbers report we saw on page 338. Susan's sales manager has given her his subjective rating on the five criteria he wants his sales team to focus on. Her only two weaknesses, and they are mild ones at that, are the generation of new sales and the gross margin performance. More than likely, her sales manager will want to work with her on developing new sales, perhaps offering to ride along on some new dealer recruiting calls or existing dealer calls to open up new lines of sales opportunity.

Mentoring

Some companies have formal mentoring programs where a skilled veteran is paired with a rookie for a set period of time. The two meet at least twice a week (one of those days being a ride along by the rookie in the veteran's territory and the other being a reciprocal ride by the veteran with the rookie) and the veteran teaches the rookie all he or she can about being a Tier One TM.

For this effort—which takes considerable time for the veteran, time he or she might rather spend with customers—the company often gives the veteran a bonus or a significant piece of the rookie's sales commissions.

The Competency area covers those fundamentals of selling every Tier One TM has in strength and that other TMs are developing. All of the factors listed here are covered in various chapters in this book, so I don't think I need to spend a lot of time explaining them. I do, however, want to focus on how Susan's manager rated her and what might flow out of that rating.

She has a few areas of significant weakness: qualifying skills, prospecting skills, and mentoring. The first two are strongly linked. The last one is an indicator of Susan's ability and willingness to help other TMs learn the ropes.[19]

Susan is just six years out of college and in her fourth year as a TM. She does not feel she can mentor anyone else, but her sales manager sees tremendous talent and good communication skills in her so he may want to start nudging her toward some mentoring assignments—perhaps pairing her up with a new TM to show him how to do a dealer development plan (a skill at which she excels), and so on.

19 [1] "Learning the ropes" is a naval phrase going back to the days of sail. When a new sailor joined the crew, he had no idea which rope controlled which sail or yardarm. So experienced sea dogs would teach him the ropes so he would know what rope to haul if the master gave the order to reef the fore top g'alt sail or let go the main top.

The other two issues—qualifying and prospecting—are simply areas where Susan is weak and needs some specialized training. Her sales manager might do some ride alongs with her and show her by example how to improve these two areas, but the best solution would probably be some formal training.

The Frequency report shows how well Susan is doing with those things that should be done often or in a timely manner. Most of the data for this section comes from Susan's call reports (which are combined with the company's expense report forms to simplify the TM's job). Overall, Susan is about average (2.6 is just above the midpoint of 2.5). She does a great job of getting to the dealer principals, but other than that, she does not manager herself in time very well. (If she did, she would be doing all the other things on the list adequately.)

Susan's overall rating of 21.2 (out of a possible 30.0) is a little above average. She is doing well overall, but there are skill deficits that she has that if she does not address them, before long will end up holding her back from becoming the Tier One TM she really is capable of becoming.

A sales review, being a one-on-one event, should probably last less than fifteen minutes (although there are times when it may be necessary to spend more than that on the meeting). If the meeting is going to be positive and upbeat, the sales manager can do it in almost any venue, including the office, a restaurant, or at a lunch setting. But if the meeting is going to be a time of adjustment for the TM, it is best to meet in a private location (the sales manager's office, a conference room, etc.).

Sales Meetings: A Related Topic?

Most distributors conduct sales meetings for their TMs on a regular basis. Some do it monthly, others every other month, quarterly, or even less often. Personally, I lean toward the monthly general sales meeting with weekly mini-meetings among sub-teams in between.

The purpose of a sales meeting is *not* to evaluate each TM's individual performance, but rather to report to the group how the company as an entity is doing. The sales manager (or sometimes, the CEO) should report overall performance to plan YTD and report on any significant events or circumstances that could have an impact on the group hitting (or missing) its plan for the year. A sales meeting is, in some ways, a miniature State of the Union Address.

But it goes beyond that and should cover more. It should be a time for management to communicate to the TMs product changes (such as new products due out, or phase out schedules as products are undergoing change), service bulletins, marketing programs, intelligence on competitive products and/or programs, and so on. It is a time to gather and refine the group's collective knowledge and conduct sales and skills training.

How Long Should Sales Meetings Last?

Weekly mini-meetings among team members should last no longer than an hour, and preferably less. The main thing here is to review the state of business for that week. The commercial department should have a representative present to describe commercial bids due this week that the TM's accounts may be involved in. The commercial rep can also report on how the company did on previous bids.

I suggest that the weekly mini-meetings be held in a conference room with those chest-high tables like one sees in bars and restaurants—the type that are at a comfortable height while standing. No chairs. The sales manager wants to convey a sense of in-and-out for the meeting, and chairs don't send that message very well. I also advise sales managers to announce up front that the minutes for the meeting will be written up and posted via email to the group by the end of the week, but that the person who will be responsible won't be named until the end of the meeting.

Monthly sales meetings (where all the teams assemble at one location, or meet via an online service) should probably last half a day. This gives ample time to cover the state of the sales report and cover new intelligence. If the meeting starts at 10:00 a.m. and ends by 3:00 p.m. (allowing an hour for an on-site lunch), most of the out-of-town TMs can drive in that morning and drive home that night, saving on hotel bills.

Special sales meetings (perhaps twice a year?) will probably require a full day to two days to conduct and will definitely involve extensive travel costs, so to justify the expense; the content had better be first rate!

Taking Initiative

If you are experiencing problems in your territory that may require help beyond your skill level, *don't wait until a scheduled sales performance review!* Go to your sales manager and say, "I need some help in my territory, and I need it soon." Asking for help is *not* a sign of incompetence; waiting too long and then having to explain lousy sales numbers *is*.

You should never be afraid of going to your manager and asking for help. If he or she is the kind of person who will ridicule you for it, then I feel sorry for you and would not blame you if you did *not* ask for help, but I find that such troglodytes are rare in the sales management field today.

You might also talk to a fellow TM who is good at the kind of problem you are facing. If they are the type who would not mind at all helping you, ask them for some advice. If possible, they might even ride along with you in your territory to address the problem you are having. (Some TMs would never do this, seeing it as stealing their precious face-to-face time with their dealers. Others would welcome it because they realize that when the water in the company's harbor goes up, all the boats rise with it!)

If you are a sales manager and would like a memo on doing territory manager "ride-alongs" (where you ride with the TM for a day and evaluate his performance in front of dealers), contact me via my web site and I'll send you a PDF file that contains helpful tips on how to do ridealongs.

Review Questions for Chapter 19

1. Suppose your sales through the end of July this year are $2,358,912 and that historically, your distributor does 62% of its business by July 31. What is your going rate for the year?

A) $3,821,437

B) $3,804,697

C) $6,207,663

D) Not enough information to determine it

Answer: ________

2. A territory manager has a sales quota for the year of $6,000,000. By April 30, she has sales of $1,236,800. Her distributor typically has 24% of the year done by April 30. Is she on track to hit her quota?

A) Yes

B) No

Answer: ________

Now, explain why you chose the answer you did.

3. A territory manager has a sales performance review. During the review it is determined that he is on track to hit his sales quota, but he is only at 90% of his gross margin goals and 70% of his high-efficiency system sales goals. Furthermore, his call reports show he is not calling on prospects very much (only two calls a month). If you were evaluating this TM's performance, what do you think might be at work here?

A) pursuing sales at the expense of margin by using lower prices

B) avoiding the "harder" selling of higher efficiency by selling the

"easy" low-end stuff

C) both A and B

D) A and B, plus setting up too many small volume accounts

E) none of the above

Answer: ________

Chapter 20: Marketing and Advertising

A Tier One territory manager is a person who also has a good grasp of the fundamentals and techniques of marketing and advertising. In this chapter, you will learn some powerful concepts that can help you as you help your dealers grow their markets and increase their sales.

Is It Working?

Before a dealer can plan an intelligent marketing and advertising program, he has to know if his present efforts are working. The TM who can help a dealer determine this and then spend his advertising dollars in the best places to get the best results will have a contractor more apt to succeed than the TM who is in the dark on these issues—and one more likely to take the TM's advice.

The first thing a dealer needs to do is train whoever answers the phone and sets up sales appointments to ask a crucial question, and the question that should be asked is *not*, "Where did you get our number?" Ninety-four customers out of one hundred will say, "The Yellow Pages." So the dealer could get the idea that the Yellow Pages is *the* medium to advertise in (just like the phone book people tell them)! But the question itself is wrong. People go to the Yellow Pages to find a dealer's number *because they cannot remember it.* But they decided to call that dealer for a different reason.

The question that needs to be asked is, "We are very glad you called us today. May I ask you what lead you to call us?" This is the question that gets to the root of their motivation.

I advise dealers to use a weekly tally sheet like this one to track the answers the receptionist or sales administrator will get:

Weekly Lead Source Score Sheet

For the week of ___________________________

Lead Source	Sunday	Monday	Tuesday	Wednesday	Thursday	Friday	Saturday
Date							
Prospecting							
Referrals							
Service dept							
Shows							
Newspapers							
Direct mail							
Yellow Pages							
Internet							
Radio							
Television							
Telemarketing							
Other							

If a dealer does not use a particular medium (like television), he can obviously delete that line from his form. As the customers answer the question, the receptionist/administrator can place a tally mark in that box for that day. (The reason we want to track tallies by day is to see if a particular ad—say, a newspaper ad run on Tuesday—produces any hits that day or the day after.)

The weekly tally sheets should be collected and kept for batch analysis. When the dealer has an adequate number—twelve to fifteen sheets—he can do a batch analysis. This is a process in which the dealer totals all the lead sources and then cross-references the leads to sales results.

There is software on your CD that does this automatically once the data has been entered. The dealer needs to be able to go to any sales lead (whether the job was sold or not) and tell where that lead came from. He must also be able to pull out the cost of the lead medium (if it was purchased—some media are free, such as referrals). Finally, he needs to be able to total the sales by lead type. Once all this information is collected, a report can be generated that shows which leads end up with the most sales. These are the leads the dealer wants to strengthen with more budgeting. He can also measure how much each sale cost to obtain and thereby spot the best lead types for generating sales. Again, those lead types should be fed more, the others less.

The bottom line from using the Advertising Analysis workbook on the CD is that when the dealer is done, he will know which types of advertising to do, which to drop, and how to focus his efforts where the results are the best.

When you consider that some dealers spend $60,000 a year or more in advertising (a decent salary!), it is amazing that more of them don't demand an annual report of how this "employee" is doing his job! Deep analysis often reveals that as much as half of a dealer's advertising budget is wasted.

How Much Should a Dealer Spend?

This is where the second worksheet of the Advertising Analysis workbook comes into play. I cannot begin to tell a dealer how much to spend on advertising until I know his sales plan for the year by market segment and how much advertising clutter is already in his marketplace. The form on the next page was developed to help a dealer decide how much he may need to spend on advertising in his market. (This form is also part of the Advertising Analysis workbook on the CD.)

Commercial Sales	Sales Budgeted	Advertising as a Percentage of Sales [1]	Advertising Budgeted
Plan and Spec	$	0%	$
Negotiated	$	0%	$
Design/Build	$	1-2%	$
Service	$	2-5%	$
Service Agreements	$	0-1%	$
Other	$	n/a	$
TOTAL COMMER	$		$
Residential Sales			
RNC[2]- Tract homes	$	0%	$
RNC- Custom homes	$	1-2%	$
RNC- Multi-family	$	0%	$
Add-on/Replacement	$	3-8%	$
Service	$	3-10%	$
Service Agreements	$	3-5%	$
Room Air	$	3-8%	$
Other	$	n/a	$
TOTAL RESID	$		$
		TOTAL ADVERTISING BUDGET	$

Note 1: Suggested budget guidelines. Note 2: RNC = residential new construction

To use this form, help your contractor fill in the sales budgets for each of the market segments shown and then decide what percentage of those sales to devote to advertising and promotion. (Note that for certain markets, such as the commercial design/build market, the advertising budget will probably *not* be spent on advertising as such, but in the production, for instance, of a brochure that explains how the contractor is a professional at design/build. It could also include such things as entertainment expenses for builders or key clients, especially in the custom RNC home market.)

The budget derived by this form will be a pre-co-op budget—in other words, the total dollars the dealer *should* spend on advertising in his market. His out-of-pocket expenses will be less since he will be able to claim back *some* of these costs to manufacturers for co-op dollars.

How Far to Plan Ahead?

Like it or not, a lot of this business is *weather-dependant*. That being the case, given our inability to forecast weather three days out (let alone thirty), long-range advertising plans are not always a good thing to develop. However, I do firmly believe that a dealer needs to have a *general* plan for the year broken down by quarters, with detailed plans set at least thirty days out (if not ninety).

I recommend that dealers advertise *with* the weather patterns, not against them. What I mean by this is that traditionally, manufacturers pour a lot of money into *pre-season* advertising, and dealers usually allocate their funds in that same time frame to piggy-back onto the manufacturer program to maximize penetration of the market at a minimal cost.

But let me ask you something. Which makes more sense—buying a bucket of fish bait for $10 and catching no fish all morning, or buying a bucket of fish for $20 and catching your limit in an hour?

Dealers need to advertise the way fishermen fish—when the fish are biting. The fish aren't biting in the pre-season. (And those who do are usually looking for a good deal.) They bite in the season, when they turn on their unit and it does not fire back. They are uncomfortable so they call someone for service and learn their system is kaput. *Now* they are ready to buy, and time is of the essence. The luxury of shopping and getting eight bids is not realistic when it is 105 outside (or -10).

So why do manufacturers advertise so heavily in the pre-season? It goes back to the history of this trade to the days when most manufacturers had their dealers put in large *stocking orders* for the pre-season. It was common, thirty years ago, for distributors to have their dealers place large orders for equipment in February or March (and again in August or September). This has several advantages for everyone.

1. For the Dealer, it means he has equipment in stock when the customer needs it. He can install a new unit that afternoon, and if he is the only guy in town with that unit, he can leverage his inventory for a good price.

2. The distributor wins because the dealer's barn is now full of their stuff and the odds of a dealer bringing in a lot of brand X's stuff are now greatly reduced.
3. The manufacturer wins because the pre-season windows were usually during the times of greatest dealer cash flow. Dealers felt confident and went along with hefty orders, thus unplugging the end of a full pipeline, letting the manufacturer cram more product into the pipe.

So the dealer has a full barn of equipment which must be paid off in six months (the normal pre-season financing window). And what happens? For the first couple of months, *the phone doesn't ring*. So what does the dealer start to do? Sweat and worry. At this point, the cavalry arrives in the form of the manufacturer and distributor running pre-season advertising designed to make the phone ring. The dealer feels better and all is right with the world again.

Except that most pre-season sales campaigns have mediocre success at best, and many are downright dismal (especially those that heavily promote rebates—you mean, you were over-priced to begin with?). Because the fish aren't in a biting mood when it is too warm for the furnace and not hot enough for the A/C. It is beautiful outside, and no one is thinking about what is yet to come.

When does a dealer want a customer to call him? Any time, but especially when the customer turns on the unit and it does not work. That normally occurs during the season because after 1,806 starts for a badly maintained unit, the 1,807th start rips open a winding in the compressor or all that moisture finally produces enough acid to lead to a grounded compressor, or whatever else the season's stresses have laid on the loyal unit.

When the customer calls the dealer *in season*, and the service tech finds a dead (or dying) unit and recommends a new unit (or, better yet, system), the homeowner, who sees the service tech as a hero in a white hat, tends to go along with him, whereas the evil sales person is trying to sell them something. Service techs who sell equipment usually have stunningly high success rates compared to professionally-trained sales people just for that reason—they have the trust advantage!

Yet I often hear dealers argue that to advertise in season is suicidal because they can't get to all the calls anyway.

What a problem to have! Tough, isn't it?

Do you know what happens when a dealer's business capacity is full? He has the luxury of raising his rates, because more than likely everyone else in town is swamped now too and *no one* has any idle capacity to throw at a new customer.

I advise contractors to look at their historical sales and determine what percentage of their business they do every month (which, of course, lets them calculate their business by quarter as well). Then I advise that they allocate their advertising budget along those lines.

For example, suppose that Phinehas T. Korndingle has an advertising budget of $40,000 and that his quarterly sales run like this: 1st quarter, 16%; 2nd quarter, 20%; 3rd quarter, 47%; and 4th quarter, 17%. Phinehas should then allocate about 16% of his budget (or $6,400) to the first quarter; $8,000 to the second quarter; $18,800 to the third quarter; and the balance ($6,800) to the fourth quarter. These being general guidelines, Phinehas should be free to add to or subtract from a quarter as circumstances dictate (for example, an early summer).

For the current quarter, the dealer should have a good idea what theme he wants to promote in his advertising, and if possible, lay out a detailed plan for the next month. He should know week by week what he will be saying in the media and what media he will be saying it in. But if he is not careful, he will find himself being drawn into the Advertising Vortex. To prevent that, I recommend…

Using an Advertising Agency

Some distributors use a local advertising agency that they also make available to their dealers (due to rate concessions or other special treatment). Some manufacturers do the same. If the local agency is a good one, I am all for the dealer jumping on that band wagon and working with the agency. But if they are not, I have no problem with advising a dealer to buck the trend and find his own agency. The key here is compatibility—is there a good fit between the dealer and the agency's people? If not, I don't care how good the agency is, the dealer will not have a good experience.

The purpose of an advertising agency is to help your dealer (a) plan a general promotional theme; (b) plan detailed short-period themes; (c) design good ad copy that achieves the first two objectives; and (d) place those ads in the best places to maximize the dealer's lead generation for the dollars invested.

That sounds easy. It is not.

The dealer who thinks he can be his own advertising agency probably has an idiot for an agent.

Why Marketing Programs Fail

There is a lot of confusion about the differences between marketing and advertising. Marketing is devoted to developing the messages that will attract specific buyers. Advertising is creating and delivering those messages. They are very similar, but marketing is more of the strategic side of the coin while advertising is the tactical side. Marketing asks the "who" and "why" questions. Advertising addresses the "what", "where", "how" and "when" questions.

Most dealers don't stick with a marketing program long enough to get good results. The following is adapted from the November 20, 1995 issue of *Air Conditioning, Heating & Refrigeration News* and addresses the top ten reasons marketing programs fall apart.

1. Failure to direct the right message to the *right audience.* This is perhaps the most fatal of all flaws. Most dealers have never actually carefully defined who their audience is. Most will say, "It is everyone out there." They are wrong. Only certain people will want (or can even afford) what the dealer offers. Who are they, where do they live, and how much do they have to spend? These are the hard questions a good marketing firm will force a dealer to grapple with before they design any sort of marketing or advertising plan.

2. Failure to match the *goals* to the budget. In other words, not spending enough where it is needed, or spending too much where it is not. I covered this on page 350.

3. Failure to make a *significant effort* (not enough bullets fired). Most dealers want to see results right away. They advertise on Tuesday. Where are the Wednesday phone calls? Or they mail out 2,000 direct mail pieces, and get back only three responses. They think, "To hell with this approach! It's a waste of time!" Good marketing and advertising takes time to get into the customer's mind (where you want your image and message to be).

4. Failure to use the right *techniques* and methods. A good advertising agency can recommend the best techniques and methods based on the target audience ("demographic" in the jargon of the trade).

5. Failure to be *consistent.* An advertising campaign should not be changed week by week just because last week got no leads. When a dealer changes the message all the time, the customer never has a chance to build a solid connection from Fact A to Fact B in their mind.

6. Failure to *grab attention.* Most dealer advertising I see (and sadly a lot of manufacturer copy) is so boring, I tune it out immediately. Everyone on this planet broadcasts and receives on *two* radio stations, WII-FM and MMFG-AM. You probably already know the FM station—"What's in it for me?" But you may not know the AM station—"Make me feel good about myself." Advertising that fails to hit *both* stations in the first five seconds or so of the ad (or the opening line of the print) is not going to generate many leads!

7. Failure to *understand* the customer. Due in part to the fact that the dealer has never carefully defined his target demographic.

8. Failure to be on the *cutting edge.* Face it—novelty gets remembered. Run-of-the-mill messages get lost in the Dull Stuff file. Good ads are not good because they are cute or funny (although that often helps)—they are good because they get remembered.

9. Failure to use *research.* See points 7 and 1.

10. Failure to recognize *results.* Too often, dealers want the ads to *sell* the jobs for them. That's not the purpose of advertising. Its only purpose should be to get the phone to ring. From there, the dealer turns the contact into an intensely personal and rewarding experience for the customer.

Creating an Advertising Philosophy

I suggest you take your key dealers through a six-step process that when completed, can help an advertising agency work with them in the best and most efficient way possible. Here are the six steps of crafting an advertising philosophy:

1. The first sentence tells the main purpose of the advertising.

Example: "The purpose of Stellar Heating's advertising is to motivate people to call requesting a quote."

This should be easy. And it may be necessary to craft a purpose sentence for each market segment the dealer wants to advertise to.

2. The second sentence should spell out the main benefit the dealer will offer.

Example: "The main benefit stressed will be the outstanding customer care Stellar Heating provides to its customers."

This gets a little tougher. What main benefits will the dealer want to promote for each of the market segment purpose sentences he creates?

3. The third sentence lays out the secondary benefits that will entice customers.

Example: "We will also stress the high quality and energy savings of our systems and workmanship, including our total satisfaction promise."

4. The fourth sentence states the target audience (demographic) you are seeking.

Example: "Our target audience is homeowners in the thirty to sixty year age bracket with household incomes of $45,000 and up with homesthat are ten years old and older."

This is where your territory analysis (Chapter 5) can be of help to your dealer. In some cases, larger advertising agencies will have good research in-house and readily available to use.

5. The fifth sentence says what you want your target audience to do. Example: "The action to be taken by our audience is to make an appointment for a comfort consultant to visit their home and do a comfort analysis."

6. The last sentence describes the personality of your company as you will express it in your ad. Example: "We will convey an image of honest people who can be trusted in our customers' homes; people who do quality work right the first time and who genuinely care about our customers."

Here is where a good advertising agency can shine. If they have talented people, they can often come up with an idea or an image your dealer can convey that will work well for her. For instance, I had a dealer who used to place his own fifteen-second tags on the manufacturer and distributor-placed TV spots. In his tag, he was pictured standing in a crisp clean uniform with a white towel draped over his arm, and he'd smile warmly and say, "XYZ Heating—the dealer with white towel service." The image he was conveying, of course, was one of clean work, and given the demographic he targeted, that was a very powerful image to plant! I know, because he had a disproportionate share of the high-dollar business in town.

How To Speak "Advertising"

Or, A Brief Primer on Advertising Terminology and Methods.

Newspapers

They allow you to *respond rapidly* to market conditions. (This requires that the dealer sign a wait order, in which a pre-composed ad is held in the paper's files until he calls them and tells them to run it or until a pre-arranged trigger, such as the forecast high.)

They are also full of advertising *clutter*. It takes a lot of ad space (or costly color) to be noticed. (The average newspaper is 64% advertising copy!) And it is worse in the Sunday papers.

Also, newspaper *circulations are down,* as more and more people are getting their news through alternative sources.

In choosing a paper, the advertising agency should ask for the **ABC Report figures**. The ABC Report is the main source of information about a newspaper's circulation. They should look for three key numbers: net *paid* circulation, circulation *area*, and how much of the circulation is *home-delivered*. The higher the paid circulation and home delivery numbers, the better.

Newspapers measure ad space in *column-inches*. A column inch is a space one column wide by one inch tall. An eight column inch ad, for example, could be one column wide and eight inches tall, or two columns wide by four inches tall, and so on.

There are *different rates* available from most newspapers. The lowest rate is the run of paper (or ROP) rate. This lets the editor place the ad on any page they want—your dealer may not get prime reading space because of this. The next rate up in quality (and cost) is the preferred position rate (PPR), which lets your dealer specify the location for his ad. The top of the pyramid is the insertion order (IO), which allows the dealer to specify the date, size and location of the ad.

For **co-op**, most distributors and/or manufacturers require proof that the ad was run by means of *tear sheets*. A tear sheet is where the newspaper supplies the dealer with the entire page on which her ad ran. This shows the name of the paper, the date, and so on.

What size ad is best? It depends, and varies with budget capacity, but generally, a ***quarter-page ad is the best all-around*** ad size. Even better would be a five column by fourteen inch ad (seventy column inches), but the prices can get very high as ad size grows.

Newspaper Advertising Summary

★ Rapid response

★ Buy column inches: ROP, PPR, IO

★ Submit tear sheets

Radio

Radio lets your dealer target a *precise audience* since radio markets are so finely fragmented today. The dealer can also respond very quickly to market conditions with radio ads.

Before buying radio, your dealer needs to define her target demographic carefully. For example, does she want to cater to people aged twenty-five to forty-five with household incomes of $35,000 and up, or would she prefer to focus on people in the forty to seventy age bracket with household incomes over $60,000, and so on. A good advertising agency should be able to help with this vital step.

Once the target demographic is identified, the ad agency should ask the radio station for a *ratings report* and look for its penetration of the demographic group selected. Let the ad agency do this, as these reports can be very complex and difficult for the layman to read.

Radio advertisers speak in terms of *vertical* and *horizontal* saturation. Vertical is intense, short-term, heavy burst advertising that is repetitive and works best for *specials*. Horizontal saturation is less frequent and more low-key, focusing on *image* more than a hot deal.

Like newspapers, radio has different *rates* for different frequency of placement and time of day. There is the standard contract rate (also called the rate card)—so many dollars for so many spots. If your dealer contracts with a station for enough time in a given period, she might qualify for the end rate, which is a significantly lower per-minute rate. A third rate is the adjacencies and fixed times rate, which runs her ad at a fixed time each day or before or after a particular event (such as a weather forecast or sporting event). Adjacencies cost more than other ads, but may be a better buy if the target audience is listening at that time.

To help determine the best radio buy, have your advertising agency find out the *gross rating points* of the station. A gross rating point applies to listeners twelve years old and up. One rating point is 1% of all the listeners of a given demographic group. One GRP (gross rating point) is the rating points times the number of times the spot runs. The more GRPs your dealer buys, the more of her target audience she will reach.

> For instance, suppose a sports program on the radio appeals well to the target audience and it has fifteen rating points. The dealer buys five spots on the show.
>
> The GRPs therefore are 15 rating points x 5 ads = 75 GRPs.

To build your *image*, figure on 50 to 100 GRPs per week. For *sales* or specials, concentrate the GRPs in shorter bursts of time.

Tell the station in advance that your dealer will need *notarized scripts*, affidavits of performance, lists of run times, and detailed invoices for co-op purposes.

Radio Advertising Summary

- ★ Precise aim
- ★ Buy Gross Rating Points
- ★ Rate tiers (SGR/RC,ER, A/FT)
- ★ Notarized scripts

Television

Its tremendous cost can be more than offset by its awesome *reach*.

As in radio, start by carefully defining the target demographic. Then decide on a vertical or horizontal approach.

Next, have the ad agency check with the stations and ask to see their share of market reports for the demographics that were chosen. The *Nielsen Station Index (NSI)* or the *American Research Bureau* (*Arbitron*) are well-known and reliable sources.

Generally, dealers should avoid home-made spots. They should hire a professional firm to do it right! And this will be expensive. It can cost upwards of $25,000 for each minute of ad shot (and some agencies or producers charge even more!).

TV time is sold in *day parts*. A day part is a particular time of day and the volume of viewers during that time. Typical day parts are:

- Early morning news (6:00 a.m. to 9:00 a.m., M-F)
- Daytime (9:00 a.m. to 4:00 p.m., M-F)
- Early fringe (4:00 p.m. to 6:00 p.m., M-F)
- News (5:00 p.m. to 6:00 p.m. and 10:00 p.m. to 11:00 p.m., but varies with the football season)
- **Prime time (7:00 p.m. – 10:00 p.m. every day)**
- Sports (noon to 6:00 p.m. on weekends)
- Primer sports (special events, like the World Series)

If the dealer buys time on a *pre-emptable* basis, it will cost less, but he also gives the station the right to sell his slot to another advertiser who will pay more for it. If he gets bumped, he should ask the station what their make-up policy is.

Your dealer can buy a *run of the schedule*, which specifies a time slot, but does not require the station to run the ad in highly desirable slots, like the news.

Television uses the same GRP system as radio, but without a lower age limit.

As a rule, television should be used to *reinforce* other advertising.

TV's strong suit is building a dealer's *image* (it **is** a visual medium), and for that purpose, the dealer should consider 50 to 75 GRPs per week for three or four months. For specials, he should run higher GRPs over a shorter period.

Cable TV is a new way to fine-tune a demographic. With broadcast television, the dealer's message goes into every home the signal can reach, even if some of those homes are well beyond the dealer's normal service radius. With cable TV, the dealer can usually buy his ads in certain circuits or parts of the area, not the entire audience.

Before signing a contract, have the ad agency get a written promise of product protection. This is a pledge that the station will not run a competitor's ad within, say, fifteen minutes of your dealer's ad.

For co-op, be sure to obtain the notarized documents that radio should supply.

Get Your Taxes Worth!

One powerful feature of the U.S. Census web site is the ability to generate color-coded maps of an area showing such things as age, income, home ownership, and other data sets. From the Bureau's home page, select "Maps" and you will be prompted through a series of screens to determine the data you want mapped.

Television Advertising Summary

- ★ Reach!
- ★ Target your audience
- ★ Buy day parts
- ★ Reinforces other media efforts
- ★ Visual, visual, visual
- ★ Get protection

Direct Mail

The most *personal* form of advertising. (According to the US Postal Service, **78%** of all direct mail advertising gets opened and read! But then remember the source for this statistic.)

If a dealer wishes to use a postage-guaranteed return response card or envelope, he will have to purchase a *permit* from the Post Office.

Dealers may buy mailing lists from a number of sources, but one of the best is InfoUSA (on-line at InfoUSA.com).

Direct mail historically has low response rates (around 3%), but with a large volume of pieces mailed, that can be a heavy dose of leads. The key to success in direct mail is staying with it. It takes seven mailings to generate critical mass in the minds of the demographic, and most dealers give up after three or four mailings.

Billboards

Use them to *reinforce* the other advertising.

Billboards are sold in *poster panels.* Poster panels are 12’ 3” by 24’ 6” in size. There is space on a poster panel for three poster sizes— twenty-four sheets (8’ 8” by 19’ 6”), thirty sheets (9’ 7” by 21’ 8”), the bleed (10’ 5” by 22’ 8”) and the painted board (14’ by 48’). A new innovation is the pre-printed plastic or Mylar graphic panel.

The ad agency should focus on promoting the *big idea* of your dealer’s service or offer. If possible, no more than *seven words*! And make the message personal (either in words or pictures).

As for color, black on yellow is best, but stick with the *primary colors* for best results.

Building a Marketing Plan

The rest of this chapter will cover some of the information that should be covered in a written marketing plan. Marketing plans take a lot of time and work to write, but if they are done right, the dealer will generate a significantly higher number of better quality leads, and that should show up in the check book balance!

1. The Present Market

Describe your dealer's business as it is now and the market as it is now. Include demographic data (how many people in the target demographic; where they are located, and so on). You may find it helpful to fill in this chart:

	Number of People	Percent
Total population		100%
Ages birth to 20		%
Ages 21 to 40		%
Ages 41 to 55		%
Ages 56 to 65		%
Ages 66 and over		%

If possible, get the *median household size and income data* (available from www.census.govand other sources). Try to get this data for each of the "tiers" shown in the table above.

Since income is positively correlated to education, determine the *education level* of the target. See if you can estimate the total residential HVAC market in dollars. (Remember Chapter 5?)

Describe the *business climate* of the area. What business(es) dominate? What are their future outlooks? (If there is a state university extension office in the area, they can probably provide economic outlook reports to local businesses for free or a very low fee.)

Describe the *housing* in your area. How many homes are there? What percentages of them are occupied by the owners? How old are they? What are they heated and cooled with?

Who are the *competitors*? Where are they? What lines do they handle? What markets are they in (residential, commercial, service, etc.)? How many people work there? Estimate their sales (using what you learned in Chapters 4 and 5).

What are your dealer's *strengths and weaknesses*? He should be honest, and specific.

As a summary to your research, what is the *most lucrative market* to be in for your dealer's area? Which market is the easiest to *defend* from intruders? The most *difficult* to enter? Which market would be the easiest for your dealer to become the *major player* in? Can your dealers marshal the forces needed to make these moves? How? When? Who?

<u>*2. Your Dealer's Present Company*</u>

What is the dealer ultimately *living for*? What does he *want out of life*? How is his company going to make this possible for him?

What primary strategy will your dealer employ to achieve his goals? (Example: He will be known as the high quality leader, or he will be known as the cheapest clod on the block, etc.). What will be his primary *management philosophy* to achieve this? (Example: He will design systems and procedures that make his business as automatic as possible so he doesn't have to put out all the little fires.) How will he deploy his management philosophy through his people?

What do his *employees* think of their company? (Surveys, surveys, surveys…) What do their customers think? (Again, based on surveys, please.)

What challenges do his employees give him? How is he going to address them?

What challenges have his customers given him? How will he address them?

How do his *suppliers* see him? Do they give him any special challenges? If so, how will he deal with those challenges?

Does his company's organization reflect accurately the way he wants it to be *perceived by the community?* If not, what does he have to change?

How about his *facilities*? How do they look? Do they efficiently support production, or does he need to make changes? How about his vehicles and major tools? Same for them!

How good is his *location* for supporting his efforts with his target market? If it is not good, what will he do to improve it?

How is his ongoing *selling effort*? What is his *success ratio* (percent of sales calls that end up in orders)? How long do sales calls take (on average)? How many *dollars per hour of sales calls* does he generate? How many profit dollars per hour? How many *leads a day* does he get (on average)? Where do they come from?

Has he done a thorough *advertising analysis* yet? If so, what did it teach him? Is he advertising in the *right media* and in the *right way*? How much will he *spend by medium next year*? *What* will he say? *When* will he say it? How does he constantly *monitor* ongoing advertising effectiveness?

Describe your dealer's *sales force*.

What is his *breakeven volume* (annual, monthly, weekly, daily)?

Does he have a *company brochure or video* (or DVD)? Does he use a *presentation book* in sales calls? Does he use *retail price pages*?

If he is in the replacement market, *how many service technicians* does he have? How many *service calls a year* do they run? A month? A week? A day? How many *calls per man* (same time brackets)? How many *sales leads a week* do they turn in (on average)? Have they been trained in sales procedures and how to set up a sales call for the comfort specialist?

How well does he utilize his *labor pool*? How much *unapplied time* does he have? What is his plan to reduce it? How much time is spent in fixing mistakes? What is the plan to reduce this time?

Review Questions for Chapter 20

1. The best question to ask of customers when measuring lead generation effectiveness is

   A) Where did you get our number?

   B) Who suggested that you call us today?

   C) What lead you to call our company today?

   D) Did you find us in the Yellow Pages?

   E) None of the above

   Answer: ________

2. A good advertising budget for a dealer would be ____% of sales.

   A) 3%

   B) 5%

   C) 6%-8%

   D) over 8%

   E) it depends on the dealer, his business mix, and his market

   Answer: ________

3. How far ahead should a dealer plan his advertising?

   A) A full year

   B) A year for general budget, and detailed plans by quarter

   C) B plus a specific plan for the next thirty days

   D) You can't plan far ahead due to the weather

   Answer: ________

4. When should a dealer advertise?

   A) All the time

   B) When the customers are most likely to buy

   C) In the pre-season

   D) Right after he gets his stock order in the barn

   E) None of the above

   Answer: ________

5. True or False. A dealer would be wise to use an advertising agency.

A) True

B) False

Answer: ________

Now, why do you say that?

6. Probably the main reason marketing and advertising programs fail is

A) due to a lack of money

B) not doing it enough

C) not carefully defining the target demographic first

D) poor co-op rates from manufacturers and distributors

E) bad advertising agencies

Answer: ________

7. What do we call the statement that can guide an advertising agency in creating a powerful marketing and advertising program for a dealer?

A) The advertising philosophy statement

B) The Master Plan

C) The purpose statement

D) The mission statement

E) None of the above

Answer: ________

8. A dealer in a mid-sized market wants to use radio to build his image. How much advertising should he probably buy?

A) Ten 60-second spots a week

B) Twenty 30-second spots a week

C) An insertion order

D) 75 gross rating points a week or more

E) None— radio is terrible for building image

Answer: ________

Chapter 21: Sales Skills—They Ain't What They Used to Be!

For a long time now a particular selling model has held sway in American sales training. It served us well for decades, but recent developments in psychology and market research are showing us that that old selling model is deficient in several key areas. In this chapter you will learn about how the old model came to be and where the new model departs from it.

The Work of Edward K. Strong

Edward K. Strong (1884-1963) was a professor of psychology at Stanford University in the 1920s when he wrote a groundbreaking book, *The Psychology of Sales and Advertising*. The book is no longer in print, although used copies can be obtained on eBay and other sources. I was fortunate enough to find a copy at the Washington University (St. Louis) library and was able to arrange for a one-month loan of the book.

The book marks the first time that the then-new science of psychology was applied to sales and it became an overnight sensation in sales training. Chances are very good that you have attended a course that was built, at least in part, on the work of Mr. Strong. If you ever had training on feature/benefit selling, you were benefiting from Strong's work. If you have ever been exposed to trial closes, you were influenced by Strong and one of his most devoted advocates, J. Douglas Edwards.

Most of the sales training developed since Mr. Strong's publication has used his data as the framework on which various systems of selling have been built. Whatever their modern titles may be, most sales courses today are repackaged variants of the truths Strong discovered.

In the 1980s and 1990s, several major corporations with big-ticket products found their sales forces having varying degrees of success in their sales careers. Many of them hired the same consulting firm to get to the root of their problem with their poor performers—they hired The Huthwaite Company, a New England-based group led by Neil Rackham and John DeVincentis. Rackham and his team accompanied sales reps from these firms (the likes of which included such names as Motorola and Xerox) on 35,000 sales calls and recorded observations. Analysis of the data revealed a stunning pattern.

Whereas all of the reps being studied had attended the traditional sales training courses based on Strong's work, none of the top performers were using what they learned! They had found their own system and it worked brilliantly for them.

Puzzled by this, Rackham and his team dove into what was different about the top producers and their approach versus that of the rank and file who were not hitting their numbers. The problem they found was in the sales model itself.

Strong's work is based on what we would today call relatively small ticket sales—things like calculators, cameras, tires and the like. Items that don't cost a great deal, but for which some consideration must be made to make a good decision. But the big-ticket items being sold by firms like Motorola and Xerox (where a single high-end copier can run $2 million or more) don't fall into the same class of product.

Nor do their buyers.

And *that* was the key difference! People approach a small ticket purchase much differently than they do a large ticket purchase. Traditional sales training did not even realize there *was* a difference, and so did not teach it.

So here is the bottom line for us in sales today—if you are selling small ticket items (like cameras, electric shavers, tires, or computers), the Strong feature/benefit and trial closes model works well. (Strong's research was well-grounded; he just did not study large ticket sales when he did it.) But if the product is a high-end, big-ticket item, features and benefits and trial closes *actually get in the way of the sale* and can torpedo it.

The top producers that Huthwaite studied did not use feature/benefit presentations and only asked for the order one time. The more reps asked for the order, the lower the closing rate (directly the opposite of the trial closes model). And the more the reps talked features/benefits, the more the prospects argued and the less they bought.

Let's apply this to the air conditioning business. When a dealer aligns himself with a major line, is that a big-ticket decision or a small one? Most dealers would consider it to be a major decision. So the way a sale is approached—in our case, getting the dealer to sell our stuff—would best be made by using a method that is different from what most sales people are taught.

Likewise, when a dealer's comfort consultant presents a new system to a homeowner, a system that could cost upwards of $20,000 or more, this is probably not in the league of the small-ticket sale either. If the comfort consultant uses traditional pressure sales techniques, she will probably not succeed. (The fact that most comfort consultants admit to closing rates of under 40% is proof of that.)

Advocates of Strong's methods and the courses they have produced will jump up at this point and shout at me, "But Strong sales methods don't have to be pushy! Most aren't!"

That misses the point. The point is that the psychological forces at play in the prospect's mind are different in a large-ticket sale than in a small-ticket one. It has nothing to do with being pushy (or soft). It has everything to do with how the client thinks and feels through the process. And the traditional methods tend to focus more on the presentation of the proposal than on discovering and satisfying true customer needs.

This is why I am such a strong advocate (no pun intended) of a sales approach that is needs-analysis focused and does not involve the sales person dragging his little red wagon of goodies in the door on every sales call. How can a prospective dealer decide that he needs you and your stuff if you don't take the time to find out what *he* needs and then align your presentation to *his* needs? It's not about features and benefits at this point, or even trial closes. It's about assembling a superior package that clearly wins and leads the dealer to wanting to do business with you.

So Where Do We Go From Here?

The rest of this field guide will explore in depth those things that make for a powerful and effective sales system. The field is far too complex to handle well in one chapter. It will take many chapters to do it well.

As we explore these issues in the chapters that lie ahead, ask yourself whether or not you think what you read will contribute to the psychological comfort of the dealer and whether or not it could be the engine that propels strong buying behavior for your dealer as your customer.

Selling is first and foremost psychological and emotional. It is not rational.

When I say that in seminars, many people stop me and ask me to explain, because that is not what they are taught (especially in some of the sales models being offered to this trade today).

Think back to the last time you were in a store to make a major purchase. (It may have been an appliance, like a refrigerator or a large-screen TV.) As you stood on the showroom floor pondering the models being offered by the store, did one of the store's clerks (clad in the store-issued smock) walk up to you and say the famous line, "Hi, may I help you?"

And what did you say in response? Probably the second-oldest lie in history: "No, just looking." It's a lie because you are there to ultimately make a decision and you need information to support that process. But we all know that salespeople want only to get into our pockets and sink their cash vampire fangs into our wallets, so we brush them off with the "just looking" line.

Funny. And we are all in sales for a profession!

I once met a clerk in a store who came up to me in a scenario like that and handed me his card and said, "I'm Tom. If I can be of any help to you, I'll be over there." (And he pointed to a spot on the showroom floor several respectful feet away.) I smiled and thanked him, and after a few minutes, called him over. He proceeded to do a masterful job of questioning me to determine my needs and helped me make a good decision on a purchase that day.

Notice that he did not *sell* me anything. He *helped me make a good decision on a purchase.* Even as a sales trainer, I inherently don't trust sales people. But this guy was not a sales person. He was a needs consultant, what Richard Bandler calls a decision engineer.

No one likes to be sold things (especially big-ticket things); but people *do* want to make good decisions (ones that won't make them look stupid later). It is the job of every Tier One TM to know this and learn how to do it day in and day out. This is what you will learn from this point forward in the Field Guide.

Sales is intensely psychological, more so than logical. Have you ever made a purchase that made you intensely happy? How does the memory of that purchase or that thing make you feel now? Warm? Bright? Colorful? Pleasant?

Now, have you ever made a purchase that, at the time, you knew you should not have made but you did it anyway? Does that memory evoke the same warm feelings of the pleasant one? It's different, isn't it? Feels funny, odd, out of kilter. Cold. Dark. You probably are not proud of that purchase even to this day.

Now at the time you made the decision to buy the good thing, do you recall running through a logical checklist of why you should buy it, or did you just say to yourself, "Cool! I like it! I'm going to buy it!"

I had a contractor in a sales workshop in Boise, Idaho. He said that my idea that sales is emotional, not logical, was a bunch of bull manure. (I am cleaning up his language a little!) I stopped, looked him in the eye, and said, "You may be right!" His brow wrinkled. "Tell me," I said, "have you bought a major thing in the last twelve months?"

"Sure!" he answered.

"What was it?" I asked.

"A new truck!"

I rubbed my chin and said, "Hmm, good. Tell me about it." And he went on for two minutes singing the virtues of this truck—its towing capacity, its horsepower, its off-road capabilities, its comfort, its extended cab, and so on. When he finished, I said, "One more question. At what point in the test drive did you decide you just had to have that truck?"

He paused for a moment, then frowned, and said in a low voice, "You S. O. B!" I smiled and said, "That decision was not logical, was it? You decided to buy the truck because it made you feel good, didn't you?"

"Yep," he sheepishly replied.

The decision to buy is an emotional one. We collect information in getting to that point, and we weigh that information with logical filters, but the decision to buy is an emotional one, not a logical one. We will justify our purchase with logic (like the Boise contractor did), but we don't primarily buy something just because it fills our needs perfectly. It has to feel right too. That's why you have memories of buying things you know you should not have bought at the time but did anyway, and why today they still feel bad. You ignored your heart.

Tier One TMs know this. Above all, they make sure that the contractor has a right feeling about doing business together. And they know that this point is reached emotionally, not logically.

Review Questions for Chapter 21

1. One of the key attributes of Edward Strong's sales process is

A) deep needs analysis

B) feature/benefit presentations

C) setting the right price

D) asking for the order one time

E) none of the above

Answer: ________

2. True of false. To make a good decision, we have to gather some information and evaluate it.

A) True

B) False

Answer: ________

Now, why did you select the answer you did?

3. True or False. If a contractor does not have a good feeling about working with you, he can still be a major player in your portfolio.

A) True

B) False

Answer: ________

Now, why did you select the answer you did?

Chapter 22: Deep Communication, The Key to Amazing Sales

Every person on this planet has a unique and particular way of looking at things. This in turn results in each person having a unique and particular way of making decisions, especially buying decisions. This chapter will teach you some of the skills you will need to decode another person's way of evaluating their world and how they reach a decision within their frame of reference. If you can figure out then how to get **into *their*** frame of reference and speak to them in such a way that they hear you speak **their** way of making decisions, what do you think happens to resistance and objections?

Getting To the Center of Sales

When you drill down to the very core of what sales is all about, you will find emotions. Most of us have to have some feeling of good—trust, relatedness, honesty—before we are ready to buy something from someone. Most of us will not buy something (no matter how badly we may want it) if we think the person offering it to us is not to be trusted. Whatever trust is, (and it is very difficult to define), it is an emotionally rich thing. As territory managers, we want to be sure that our dealings with our customers engender a sense of trust and confidence so our dealers are more willing to buy from us. If we give off an aura of self-centered ambition, many dealers will be leery of opening up to us very much, and it is that poker player mentality that often gets in the way of so many territory manager/contractor relationships!

Think for a moment about your personal relationships. Chances are good that you have at least one person on this planet with whom you are close—close enough to enjoy each other's company, close enough to have really deep and personal conversations— conversations where you may occasionally finish each other's sentences, or even say the same thing at the same time. If you have a person (or several people) with whom you can relate like that, you know what I am talking about. It is deep and special.

This deepness, this specialness, has a name. We call it *rapport*. Rapport means that I demonstrate to you (by my words and actions) that I fully understand where you are mentally and emotionally right now and I can get into that world with you and communicate with you deeply and significantly. I may not even be aware of it at the time I am doing it, but we both know the moment when it arrives!

In sales, rapport can be defined as demonstrating understanding of the other person in such a way that you earn the right to help influence their decision.

As a Tier One territory manager, I don't want to sell anything to my dealers. I want to help them make great decisions that will be of benefit to them and their families for years to come. To help them make such decisions, they have to sense my partnership with them emotionally—they have to sense a true and deep rapport.

Here is the good news: you already know how to establish true and deep rapport (if you have someone you can relate to like I described a few paragraphs ago). It is something you already know how to do instinctively. In this chapter, you will learn how to establish true and deep rapport intentionally so you can help your dealer make great buying decisions!

We Are Sensory People

Every person on this planet has senses that he or she uses to interpret their world. As humans, all of us have five (although for some folks one or more may not be working). Those five, of course, are vision, hearing, smell, taste and touch.

Everyone on this planet also has a favorite sensory channel (or blend of channels) that they prefer to use to interpret their world. For example, I prefer the visual channel. I tend to learn fastest (and easiest) through pictures, videos, drawings, maps, diagrams and the like. I visualize ideas in my head.

My wife is more of an auditory person. She learns best by hearing something and/or writing it down and she prefers detailed instructions and descriptions over diagrams. She thrives on talking an issue through. When we use MapQuest to find a location, I look at the map; she reads the step-by-step directions!

Still other people prefer to learn by touching and feeling things, manipulating things, or by movement. (We call this style the *kinesthetic* mode. It is also very closely related to feelings—which is why we often call emotions "feelings"—so people who prefer a kinesthetic channel for interpreting their worlds are often those who process things emotionally rather than logically. They would drive *Star Trek's* Mr. Spock nuts.)

Not too many people operate mainly in the smell or taste modes as primary channels (except, perhaps master chefs or sommeliers), but all of us can use smell and taste.

Most people settle on a primary sensory channel (or blend of channels) by their adolescent years, and certainly our favored patterns are set by the time we are adults.

Do They See What You Are Saying?

One of the most common phrases people use during a conversation is, "Do you see what I am saying?"

Look carefully at that statement for a moment.

Do you detect a blend of two styles? Do you notice the visual component ("Do you see…") as well as an auditory component ("… I am saying.")? People who ask this type of question are often blends of two channels—you guessed it, visual and auditory. But to me, a heavy visual, the question is ambiguous. I really cannot see what you are saying unless you write it on a white board, a flip chart or a piece of paper. Unlike the comics, when people speak, words don't form in the air over their heads in a balloon.

I say this to bring out the fact that in deep communication (the kind you want to maintain with your dealers), you need to be aware of their preferred input channel and speak to them in that channel. If you do not, you run the risk that what you are saying will be filtered out.

Filters Galore

When I speak to you as part of an effort to communicate an idea or concept, I begin by drawing upon my experiences and understanding of that idea. How did that understanding form in the first place?

Probably emotionally, and at an early age. For instance, infants don't yet have a vocabulary—they cannot speak or understand words yet. They process everything through their emotions. It does not take long to realize that a certain face, voice, smell and feel is Mommy and that Mommy feeds us and cuddles us, changes our diapers, and generally makes us glad to be alive! So the very appearance of Mommy's face over our crib is often enough to cause us to kick and smile for sheer exhilaration.

Likewise, the first time our dear Aunt Bertha visits us—you know, the aunt with the big lips and overly-done lipstick, thick glasses, and brassy voice, and walks up to our crib and jabs a bony finger in our side and tickles us and belts out "Oh, look at the pretty baby!", we often pucker up and belt out a loud chorus of crying, because we were scared poopless.

We don't have words for Mommy or Aunt Bertha yet, but we know how they make us feel and we draw on that emotional imprinting early on to express to the world how we feel about it.

Funny thing. As we grow older, the brain never outgrows its ability to encode experiences as emotional images and imprints.

So as I grow up, thousands (perhaps millions) of experiences start to blend together and get stuck together to form my concept of a particular thing—for instance, car.

And as you grew up, your brain likewise encoded thousands (perhaps millions) of experiences that you filed away under the heading car too, and that is what defines (for you) the idea of a car.

Now what are the odds that you and I had the exact same experiences as we grew up, or that we saw them the same way and encoded them in our brains the same way? Pretty slim, right?

So as I communicate to you on the concept of a car, I am drawing upon my integrated experience over a lifetime and try to relay to you what is in my mind in the category car. But I won't necessarily use the right group of words to convey my concept, or even try to convey the entire concept, but only a part of it.

My communication must now go through my mental filtering process and be put into words by my speech system—pronunciation, vocabulary, and so on. More information gets lost.

Now you must receive my communication, and you must do so in an environment that competes for your attention. Some of my words may not even be heard, or may be heard incompletely, or totally mis-heard. You must try to hear me over the noise of traffic outdoors or the dog barking in the kitchen. More information is lost.

Then the message has to get past your hearing system and be interpreted by you and then compared to your concept of car to see if what I am saying makes sense. More information is lost.

The incomplete, garbled message you receive from me about car must now be validated or rejected by your own experiences and value system. If what I say about car meshes with your experience, you will receive it and may even make my input part of your new expanded concept of car. If what I say runs counter to your experience, though, you may totally reject my input altogether and think I am an idiot.

In fact, when you boil it down to the basics, it's amazing that we can communicate at all, isn't it?

How This Affects Communication

This complex filtering process does not just affect communication—it ***is*** communication!

No matter what I am trying to communicate to you and how I choose to do it, you will accept it or reject it as it makes sense (or does not make sense) to you as *you* understand the concept. ***We all evaluate our communication with everyone else on the basis of our own internal biases and representations.*** So when I talk to you, it is imperative (if I want to maximize the odds that we will achieve communication success) that I speak to you the way you like to interpret your world. Anything else runs the risk that your defensive filters will kick in and reject my message, even if it is a good message!

This means that I, being a strongly visual individual, must learn how to communicate to you in your preferred system (visual, auditory, kinesthetic, or a blend). I must learn as fast as I can how you read the world and then put my message into that mode for you so you'll have an easier time receiving it, and hopefully accepting it.

How to Unpack Another Person's Preferences

As it turns out, unpacking another person's representational preferences for information is pretty easy—once you understand the ground rules.

We can begin with the easiest one to master, *the eye movement cues.*

When you ask most people a question that requires a second or two of recall before answering, their eyes will momentary break contact with you and move to a home position for a fraction of a second, then come back to making contact with you as they give their answer. It is this momentary breaking of contact, and the direction their eyes move, that gives us a clue to how they process information.

But for this to work, we must ask questions that require some recall on the part of the other person, and we must be careful to ask our questions in a sensory-neutral way.

Questions that require some recall are those that go beyond the surface knowledge of the other person. Surface knowledge issues are things like one's name (everyone knows their name, right?) or their address or telephone number, and things like that—information that is used frequently and is readily available to the mind for recall.

We must get beyond such softball questions and ask deeper questions to put the other person into deeper recall mode, where the eyes will move and thus divulge how they store their information.

Secondly, we must ask our questions in a sensory-neutral mode. For instance, if I were to ask an auditory person what color their first car was, their eyes would probably move the way a visual person's eyes move, because my question forced them into a visual recall mode. I might then conclude, from watching their eye movements, that they were a visual person (and be totally wrong). Instead, I need to ask the question more along the lines of "Tell me about your first car."

Eye Cues of the Visual People

About 60% of the world's people are visual people—they process information with pictures. This processing appears to be a universal human trait (that is, it does not vary with nationality or location in the globe or gender). But whereas local cultural considerations can impact how much the eyes move, they don't seem to overrule the neural response to move the eyes in a certain way while accessing a visual memory.

Visual people tend to look up when accessing a visual memory. The most common direction is to the upper left (of the accessor's frame of reference), so to someone watching a visual person access a memory, the eyes will tend to move up and to the right of the questioner. Sometimes people will move their eyes up and to *their* right when accessing a visual memory (or creating a visual image to help them frame their answer). But either way, an upward tic of the eyes indicates that a visual access is in process.

A secondary cue for visual people is that sometimes, when you ask them a question, they just look straight ahead, but their eyes squint a little or seem to glaze over or go out of focus. This is because they are watching a video or movie of the memory before answering you. This one is tough to detect because the eyes *don't* move. They simply momentarily defocus, squint or the face becomes more relaxed (or more animated, depending on the video being watched).

Remember, it is just a tic of the eyes! If you are looking at your notes when you ask someone a question, by the time you raise your eyes to watch their response; they have already moved their eyes, accessed their memory, and returned to their normal communication position. It literally happens in the blink of an eye! The key to interpreting someone's eye accessing cues is to stay totally immersed and attentive to the conversation, watching them for any little cue that lets you know how they are processing their thoughts.

Eye Accessing Cues of Auditory People

People who process the flow of information to and from the world around them with their ears (hearing) are *auditory* people. Auditory people, of course, have eyesight and use it (as visual people can and do use their hearing), but auditory people simply prefer to interpret their world through sounds and words rather than pictures.

The way an auditory person's eyes move during memory recall is horizontally—that is, they move toward their ears. Again, this will be a short movement, just a tic of the eyes, but it lets you know that in accessing the memory for the question you asked them, they had to pull up a sound or replay a conversation in order to answer you.

Auditory people on average comprise about 20% of the population.

Eye Accessing Cues of Kinesthetic People

The remaining 20% of the population is in a group we call kinesthetic (from the Latin word for motion). These are people who process the world primarily through their sense of touch (they have to handle or do things to fully understand them) or *they filter the world through their emotions.*

A kinesthetic person's eyes will dart *down and to their right* for an instant when recalling a memory or constructing a thought. The expressions, "That's down right good!" and "That's down right bad!" both have strong emotional implications, and the use of "down right" may not be an accident!

> **Fear of Public Speaking?**
>
> ***Remember this***: if ever you have to speak before someone or a group and forget what you wanted to say, force yourself to look down and to your left, not up to the sky. The sky won't help you. Your speech spooler will!

The Last Quadrant: Eyes Down and to the Accessor's Left

The only direction we have not covered yet is what is going on when a person's eyes move down and to *their* left. What sort of people are these?

Everyone does this! What it tells an astute observer (such as yourself) is that when a person's eyes drop down and to their left for a fraction of a second, they are trying to frame up some more words to complete the answer they are giving you. The down-left eye movement is almost *always* done during a conversation, and is usually accompanied by a brief pause by the speaker (which he or she may fill with an "uh").

So what is going on when this happens? Speech in the human brain is a lot like printing with a computer. When a computer program is told to send output to the printer, the computer quickly fires off the output to a special program called a print spooler because the printer cannot print fast enough to keep up with the blinding speed of even the slowest computers today. So the computer's central processing unit (the CPU, or brain) fires off its output and returns to a ready mode to do more work. The print spooler then feeds the data to the printer at a speed the printer can keep up with and the job prints while you go back to working on your document.

In speech, when we start to talk to someone, our brains likewise fire off some words to a spooler—we can think much faster than we can talk! But the spooler can only contain a few sentences. Eventually the spooler runs out of words, and if the speaker is not ready for this (and most speakers are not), they suddenly find themselves without words to continue. So their eyes drop to the lower left briefly. Internally, the brain is figuring out what to say next and then spooling a few more sentences into the speech spooler. The eyes then come back up to the normal position and the talking continues. Sometimes, the speech spooler has to be reloaded (with the customary down-left eye movement) because the concept is difficult to explain and the speaker must find the right set of words—maybe complex words—to state the thought.

Decoding "Lefties"

One time I was working at decoding a person early in a sales call and found their eye movements to be the opposite of what I expected. Eventually I said, "May I ask you a somewhat personal question? Are you by any chance left-handed?" He said he was and was astounded that I could figure that out by conversation alone and wanted to know how I did it. I told him about eye accessing cues and he was intrigued. He also felt a little vulnerable until I told him that I did this on sales calls in order to understand as fast as possible where my client was coming from so I could be sure to communicate with them in a way that made sense to them, since in sales, good communication both ways is vital. He agreed with that and everything went smoothly from there on.

This may sound odd to you, but I often teach workshops in which I ask territory managers to speak to the group or to answer me in class. Sometimes, they freeze and choke on their words. When they do, they almost always look up to the ceiling and fret and start to feel embarrassment. (Perhaps they are looking for a guardian angel to come rescue them?) I never want to have a student feel this, so I quickly jump in and run to them and snap my fingers in front of their eyes and grab their left hand and say, "No, no, the words are down here. Look here! See the words? Now what were you going to say?" And guess what—they answer fluidly!

Let's summarize the basic[20] eye accessing cues in this table:

Processing Type	Eye Movement	% of People
Visual	Upwards	60%
Auditory	Horizontally	20%
Kinesthetic	Down and to *their* right	20%
Speech spooler	Down and to the left	100%

But remember: when trying to pick up eye accessing cues, be sure your questions don't force the other person into a particular mode, because then the eyes will move the way the answer needs to be formulated based on the question, even if that is not the normal style of the other person. Try to ask questions in as neutral a mode as possible while you are trying to establish the other person's primary sensory channel. Once you have it, you can then use questions that are congruent with that channel.

20 Basic because there are subtle variations of these cues, such as upward-left and upward-right for visual people, horizontal-left and horizontal-right for auditory people and so on. But these subtleties are not significant enough to worry about for a sales career.

Be aware that some folks will be a blend of two (or even all three) modes and will have eye movement cues that indicate more than one mode is at work. This may be spooky to some people, but it really is the norm for a small percentage of people.

Finally, since the eye movement cues for kinesthetics and speech spoolers are directional, don't assume that left-handed people will automatically be the opposite in their directional access. First off, only about 30% of the population is left-handed. And of those who are, 90% of them have eye accessing movements that are the same as right-handed people (this stuff appears to be hard-wired physiologically). So only 10% of the 30% who are left-handed will have reverse-wired accessing movements. It only comes up once every thirty-three people or so!

Digging Deeper: More Clues

So far, we have learned that 60% of the population is visual, 20% is auditory, and the other 20% is kinesthetic. We have also learned that visual people, when digging up data for conversation, usually move their eyes upward (briefly), while auditory people move their eyes horizontally, and kinesthetics often glance down and to their right. (As an experiment, the next time you watch an interview on television, watch the eye movements of the person being interviewed by the host. Watch what happens when especially difficult issues are being discussed, like the death of a friend or an experience in combat. In such cases—in almost every case—the speaker will choke for a moment and look down and to their right! Then they will shift to their lower left and start to answer. Practice decoding eye accessing cues while watching interviews and you'll be amazed at how easy it can become.)

Let's now add to what we have learned and start to form a powerful basis for sales at a level you may have thought was not possible.

More Visual Traits

Besides occasionally looking upwards when engaging in conversation, a visual person has other things they do that are additional cues as to how they process their worlds. First of all, *visual people tend to speak more rapidly than average.* They will also use a lot of inflection and frequently change their volume and pace of speech. There is a good neurological reason for this!

A common expression is that a picture is worth a thousand words. Visual people *think in pictures*. And these pictures often change (and change rapidly). Imagine the brain of a visual person. It sees a picture that helps it compose a statement, and it is spooling about a thousand words to the speech spooler. So far so good. But then the picture changes, and with it, another thousand words go to the spooler. Except the spooler is still reeling out words to the mouth from the first picture! So what happens? The visual person speaks more rapidly, trying to empty the speech spooler of the first picture so it can take on the second picture. And what happens if meantime a third or fourth image forms in the brain? Get the picture?

Visual people also tend to use their hands a lot while speaking. Italians are known for using their hands when speaking, but with visual people it really is an important part of their communication. This is because as the visual person is speaking, she is seeing the action in her brain. If she is describing how she poured drinks for her guests at a dinner party, you will actually see her hands pouring the drinks in the air! Or if a visual person is describing his fairway shot at the seventh tee box, his hands may actually make the swing as he talks about it. The hand gesture is a vital part of the picture the visual person is trying to convey to you.

Visual people also tend to use words that are visual in nature. For instance, when I determine that a person is visual, I will check understanding from time to time by asking questions like, "Is that clear to you?" or "Do you see what I mean?" Other words that can betray visual processing are: colorful, bright, dark, dim, fuzzy, sharp, paint, sketch, draw. This is not a complete list, but it should give you the idea as a visual person tries to paint a picture for you or tries to help you see things as sharply as they do.

Visual people tend to enjoy looking at pictures or movies to acquire information. This means that on a sales call to a visual person, I want to use visual presentation formats, such as DVDs, PowerPoint slides, pictures, brochures (that are full of pictures, not words!), in short any kind of visual presentation I can think of.

Visual people will usually be turned off by high levels of detail. As a result, you may find it difficult to help a visual dealer get excited about a table of numbers (such as equipment efficiency ratings), because as a visual person, he does not normally input new information through charts and lists, but through pictures. This turn-off by detail is not a universal rule for visuals, but it is true more times than not, so be aware of it. If your visual dealer shows signs of boredom when you bring out charts, ditch the charts and find a way to show the same information visually (like using a graph or a sketch).

So what does all this imply for your behavior on a sales call? Plenty! Regardless of *your* normal sensory mode, if you have a visual dealer in front of you, *you will have to flex your communication style to his style if you want to improve your odds of having good communication.* You will want to try as much as practical to match his verbal style (speed of speaking) and your words need to have a strong visual content. You will want to use lots of pictures, movies, or charts and graphs. Try to avoid raw data (like tables and matrices). And unless your dealer shows a strong liking for details, avoid the minutia. If you can become adept at such flexing, you will find the door to more sales with a visual dealer opening wider for you, because by speaking his language, you are showing the dealer you understand his world, and that makes you more trustworthy than someone who does not.

More Auditory Traits

Besides looking horizontally when accessing information for a conversation, *auditory people will normally tend to be very precise (and often slow) speakers*. This is for the opposite reason visual people tend to be rapid speakers. For a visual person, a picture spools up one thousand words. But an auditory person does not begin with pictures. He constructs his concepts and thoughts with words. And not just any words. They have to be *the right words, in the right order, said the right way.*

I often think of the late William F. Buckley when I think of an auditory person. Mr. Buckley displayed these traits so strongly it was hard to miss them. His speech was very well formed, his pronunciation meticulously correct, and his sentences formed in almost monotone chants. There was a precise, almost poetic quality to his speech. He did not use much inflection or change of pitch or pace. He did not need to do these things to communicate because to an auditory like Mr. Buckley, the message is in the words themselves.

Because auditory people are so keenly aware of using the right words in the right sequence to construct thoughts, *they tend to be very good with details*. It is not unusual to find auditory people in such professions as accounting, law, or engineering, where accuracy and attention to detail and a good command of language is vital for success.

Auditory people are most comfortable with auditory words, like these: hear, sound, click, strike a chord, ring a bell, ring the chimes, symphonic, lyric, melodious, pleasing to the ear. When speaking with an auditory client, I will often pause to check understanding by asking questions like, "How does that sound to you?" or "Does that strike a chord in your mind?" Every time I use such a question with an auditory person, they smile! (Because they sense in me one who understands their world. And I am a visual person! I can *choose* to flex to the auditory style when I want to enhance communication with an auditory person.)

Unlike visual people, *auditory people usually don't use many hand gestures or body movements when speaking*. Again, they don't feel they need to. The message is in the words, not the movie (which they usually don't even see in their brains).

Because auditory people are normally good with details, *they won't get as much out of a picture or a diagram as they will a table of data* or a chart showing numbers.

Implications for sales call behavior: when calling on an auditory person, you need to be sure to flex to their communication style. If you are a visual, like me, you must really slow down your rate of speech. You must learn to speak without using your hands, or at least tone down your gestures a lot. You should bring charts and tables to your sales calls and be ready to go into more detail than maybe *you* like so your dealer will be comfortable with a new idea. From time to time, check understanding with questions that have an auditory flavor.

More Kinesthetic Traits

Kinesthetic people are usually some of the slowest talkers you will ever find. Why? Because they process information emotionally, and our language is not very good at letting us express our feelings. We have to stumble around in our inner dictionaries trying to find the right words to convey how we feel, and that is often awkward or time consuming. Hence, kinesthetic people tend to talk slower. They may still use inflection and change their volume often, and even their pitch, like a visual, but usually the pace of the speech will be slower than a visual.

Stacking the Deck

I had a case one time where we were bringing out a new furnace. I asked my dealers to attend a new product rollout at our branch office and one of them was a kinesthetic dealer. That night, we had a drawing for a free furnace and I saw to it that the kinesthetic dealer's name was drawn from the coffee can, because I knew that for him to get excited about it and sell it, he'd have to put one in himself and feel it. It worked like a charm—he became my biggest mover of that new model!

Like visuals,*they will probably use their hands and body gestures a lot* to illustrate what they are describing (because they often process the world through their bodies with movement). They may dance a little as they talk, or shake their hands up and down as they keep beat to an inner drum.

They will use kinesthetic words like these: hard, soft, warm, cold, fuzzy, comfy, peaceful, scary, afraid, courageous, that fits, it feels good, it feels right.

As far as attention to detail goes, I have not detected any clear pattern among kinesthetics. Some I know are very detail oriented; others are not. If you have a kinesthetic dealer, you will soon determine how much detail he is comfortable with. Once you know it, use that level in your sales calls.

Kinesthetic people love to touch things (like product samples) and move and get involved (like helping to measure a building). Some of them will often touch you as they are talking to you. Don't read this as a come on, but simply as their way of maintaining contact with you during a conversation.

Implications for a sales call: when calling on kinesthetic people, there are a few things you can do to enhance communication. *First, be patient!* This is especially true if you are a visual! When you ask a kinesthetic person a question, it can often take them a long time to answer as they feel around for the right words and how to express themselves. Sometimes, I find myself thinking as a kinesthetic talks, "Okay, okay, get to the point!" But for them to feel comfortable in your presence, you must be patient and let them answer in their own mode. Second, *be ready to slow way down* if your dealer is a slow processor. Some kinesthetics will be this way, and if you move too fast, you'll leave them behind. It is not because kinesthetic people are slower or not as bright as others (they usually are as bright if not brighter). It's just that their chosen mode of interacting with the world is not well-suited to conversation.[21]

On a sales call, *if you have a product sample, bring it out and let the dealer play with it.*

Often (but not always—there are few all-the-time rules when it comes to human behavior) a kinesthetic dealer will *need some proof that a product is good to sell.* For instance, he will look at the factory warranties as a sign of the factory's confidence in the new product.

Time for a Recap

The chart below summarizes all we've learned so far about the three main sensory channels and how to communicate with them:

	Visuals	Auditories	Kinesthetics
% of population	60%	20%	20%
Eyes move	Upwards	Horizontally	Down-right
Speech	Rapid	Slower, metered	Can be any pace
Attention to Detail	Usually not strong	Usually very high	Can be either way

21 It is a fact that our schools were once based on *audio-visual* methods. What is left out? The kinesthetic mode. In the past, a child who was kinesthetic may have been labeled as slow or needing special help when in fact they were perfectly normal. Fortunately, in many schools today, this is now being remedied as more and more curriculum finds ways to reach kinesthetic students in relevant ways.

Voice	Inflection, pace	Monotonous (but not necessarily boring; exception: radios DJs)	Can be either way
Sales Aids	Videos, pictures	Charts, data	Samples, guarantees
Words used often	See, picture, frame it, color, bright, dim, focus, paint, draw, sketch	Sound, chord, ring a bell (chime), resonates, sounds right, clicks, music to my ears, symphonic	Hard, soft, warm, cold, fuzzy, cozy, comfortable, scary, peaceful, confident, afraid

Using What You've Learned

Let's suppose that you want to use what you have learned with your existing dealers. (You can always use it on dealer recruiting calls too!) Say you want to figure out how your top five dealers relate to their worlds. What kinds of questions could you ask to pick up the eye accessing cues and what sorts of words would you expect to hear in their responses to indicate their most comfortable mode?

Suppose you ask this question of all five dealers on your sales calls: "Do you remember the first job you ever installed? Tell me about it."

Two of the dealers—Dealers A and B—move their eyes upward before they describe their first job. (Dealer A even moved his eyes after you said "installed" but before you could say, "Tell me about it.")

Dealer C pursed his lips, wrinkled his nose, and looked to the side before speaking.

Dealer D smiled really big and looked down and to his right before he spoke.

Can we determine the main sensory channel of these five with what we have so far? Try it:

Dealer	Type (V, A, K)
A	
B	
C	
D	

Turn the page to see if you pegged them correctly.

Dealer A was a strong V (visual). Dealer B was also V (visual). Dealer C gave signs of being A (auditory). Dealer D appears to be K (kinesthetic).

Suppose that on your sales call today, you are going to discuss a new control option for your product line. This option allows the system components to talk to one another electronically and lets the installer use only two wires to go from any one component to the other. It also has provisions for communicating with a computer over a telephone line (which does not have to be a dedicated line like other systems). In your car, you have the following tools to help you make the presentation:

Item 1: a DVD explaining the new system; the main menu allows you to show highlights or a fully detailed explanation

Item 2: a PowerPoint presentation on your laptop with fifty-eight slides using lots of pictures, graphs, charts, and other material

Item 3: a sample of a circuit board for the condensing units

Item 4: a technical paper (thirty-two pages) on the new system and how it works

Item 5: another technical paper (twelve pages) that is essentially a submittal document, showing dimensions, performance voltages and so forth

Item 6: a web link (URL) to the manufacturer's intranet site (to which your dealers have access) that has other files and information on the new control system

In the pages that follow, list which item(s) you would use with each dealer and explain why you would use them. After the space for your answer, I will list what I would use and why.

There are **no** correct answers to this exercise. Some answers may make more sense than others, but all can have merit on the right sales call.

Dealer A (Visual)

I would use items ______________________________

Because

My answer: Being a visual dealer, I would use item 1 (the DVD) but use the overview option from the main menu (if the dealer wants more information, we can always go back and play the full version). I would also use the PowerPoint show (item 2), but only show the slides I think are relevant for my dealer to see. I would also give the dealer item 6, the URL for the intranet site. I would then tell him if he wants more information I can give it to him (alluding to items 3, 4 and 5). I might ask questions like, "Can you see your customers really liking what this system could do for them?"

Dealer B (Visual)

I would use items ___________________________________

Because

My answer: I would use essentially the same list as I did for Dealer A, but knowing that Dealer B is a little more into detail than A, would probably use more of the PowerPoint slides and Item 5 (the submittal data). A good question to ask would be, "Do you see how this could help you in your service agreement business?"

Dealer C (Auditory)

I would use items ______________________________

Because

My answer: I would probably go with item 1 (the short version), followed by the text portions of item 2 (the PowerPoint show). I would then get out item 4 (the technical paper) and go over it with him in detail. I would then give him item 5 (the submittals) but probably not spend a lot of time on them. I would also give him item 6 (the URL). A good follow-up question might be, "What do you think it would sound like as your customers began bragging to their friends about their new ultra-controls systems?"

Dealer D (Kinesthetic)

I would use items ____

Because

My answer: I would start with the short version of item 1 (the DVD), followed by item 3 (the sample) and item 4 (the technical paper). We would then go to the URL together on the dealer's computer and browse the other data available to him. A good follow-up question would be, "Wow, does this kind of excite you as you grasp the sales possibilities here?"

Unpacking the Decision Processes

The sensory channels are very important. They tell us how the dealer normally interacts with his world, and then helps us determine our best approach to maximize communication and up the odds of a successful sales call.

But there is more to deeper communication than just decoding how a dealer comes to grips with his world. We can also use astute observation and good questions to figure out how he makes decisions. If we then put our presentation into his decision-making procedure, what do you think the odds would be that he would reject the message? Pretty low, right? Because we are presenting him with the information the way he likes it in the way he normally uses to weigh the alternatives and make a good decision. **We become, in short, decision engineers.** We use our eyes and our engine-ears[22] to help determine how to make our message as easy for the dealer to accept as possible. (And by the way—an added benefit is that the number of objections drop off sharply, almost to zero!)

There are three broad personality traits and two decision components that we can easily probe for with simple questions and astute observation. These five elements give, in essence, the wiring diagram for how any person makes decisions. Once we know their decision procedure, we can put our sales message into that procedure and the sale will run more or less on auto-pilot.

Internal and External Standards

The first personality trait we can unpack is where the dealer places his standards for judgment. His standards will be either **internally** held (40% of the people), **externally** held (another 40%), or a mix of the two (the remaining 20%). There are a number of questions we could ask that get to the root of this trait. For instance, we could say, "How would you know when you are doing a good job?" The dealer might answer, "Oh, I just know it. I feel it in my bones." This suggests the dealer carries his standards internally. If he had answered, however, "I'll see it in the P&L," or "My wife will let me know," he is probably more externally geared toward his standards—his standards depend on others or on external feedback to show him he is doing a good job.

We could also ask a question like this: "How would you know that you made a super sale?" He could say something about how it makes him feel or that he knows it when he sees it (both are internal); or he could say that the job price would be among the biggest he's ever sold, or that he'll have a signed contract of huge size (both external indicators).

22 Thanks to Kathleen LaValle of Pure NLP Seminars Group International (Hopatcong, NJ) for this wonderful term!

If a dealer answers with a blend of the two—say, he knows how it feels to sell a super job and the signed contract is proof he nailed it—he is probably one of those blended 20%.

What does this have to do with how we make sales calls?

It tells us how we can present our evidence. If a dealer is strongly internal, there is not much you can do to convince him of your story. He'll be the judge of its merits and all your proof will not matter if his internal filters reject it. So if your dealer is internal, you will need to present your evidence with comments like, "Only you can decide if this is right for you, Tom," or "I found this to be a really great program, but I don't know—you'll have to decide for yourself if it fits your company or not." One thing is for sure—if you approach an internal dealer with an attitude that he *must* do a certain course of action, he probably won't (just to show you he doesn't have to).

An external dealer, on the other hand, needs outside assurances that what you say is right and will be helpful to him. In such a case, you present your proof or evidence, and then you can add assurances like, "When I showed this to Bill yesterday, he couldn't wait to get started. What do *you* think of it?" You know that your dealer respects and likes Bill.) Or you might say, "We rolled this program out ten days ago, Frank, and already, about 80% of our dealers are on board with it. How about you?" You may need to give your dealer some material to read, too, or some other supporting evidence that helps him feel comfortable with the course of action you are asking him to take. He may in some cases just need a little time to get comfortable with the idea. Rushing him can stampede him into a corner where he will feel trapped and probably refuse to sign on.

Options and Procedures

Another vital element of how our personalities influence our decision processes is how a person processes the information in general. This may sound redundant, but there is a subtle magic at work here.

I want to know whether or not my dealer is one of the 40% or so of people who like **options** from which to choose, or if he is one of the 40% who make a decision by following a **process**, or if he is in the 20% who do both.

As with internal and external orientations, there are many questions we could ask to unpack the options and procedures set. For instance, asking a dealer why he chose the location he is currently at can reveal a lot about his orientation. If a dealer starts by listing criteria or traits about the location—"it's close to the highways, it has great visibility, the price was right, it's only two miles from my house," and so on—he is probably in the options group. He listed the things that went into his decision process and none of them are directly related to each other.

If he had told you a story, though, he would probably fall into the procedures group. Here he might say something like, "Well, in 1997, we lost our lease on our old place, so we had to find a new place fast. I called a commercial realtor, and..." and out comes a story (perhaps a *long* story with lots of detail!).

Here's another good question to use: "Hey, new truck! Nice! I didn't even know you were thinking about a new truck. Tell me, why did you select that particular model?" How would a procedures dealer answer you? He would go into some type of story, maybe relating how he got an itch for a new truck and drove by the Ford lot last week and saw a model like his new one on the lot and started talking to the sales rep. An options dealer would say something more along the lines of the features in the truck that appealed to him—its horsepower, towing capacity, extended cab, large bed, diesel engine, and so on.

This has a huge impact on how you do your sales approach. If a dealer is options oriented, you will find it best to present your sales story to him in such a way that he has several options he can choose from. It's not just that he has to sign up for the pre-season program. He can sign up at a basic level, intermediate level, or premier level, each with different benefits to him. But if he is a procedures person, you will probably find it best to present what you think is the best choice for him to make and walk him through the steps of how you arrived at that conclusion.

How you present your call for action is critical!

When presenting a call for action to an options person, your most effective strategy would be to present the optimal course of action as the first option, followed by the middle course, and then the most basic course of action. For instance, you may present an options dealer participation in a pre-season program by offering him the Premium Option at $5,000 (with a truckload, literally, of benefits), then the Standard Option at $3,000 (with fewer benefits), followed by the Seasonal Option at $1,500 (with only a few benefits). Research shows that options people will choose the first or second option a huge percent of the time, with a strong minority going the top end route. (When the options are presented in the opposite order, though—Seasonal, Standard, then Premium—a surprising thing happens; the majority of people still select the first or second option, but now notice which option is first—the Seasonal one! *Always* present your best option first, then your next best, then your least powerful option. The brain is always making comparisons on a sales call, and the first option on the table becomes the standard by which the others are weighed.)

For procedures people, the process is different. If you offer a procedures person a set of options, she will probably have a case of mental paralysis. She may even look up at you and blink a couple of times and say something like, "I don't know! What would *you* do?" This is a dead giveaway that you just tried presenting options to a procedures person. (Shame on you for not figuring this out earlier!)

The reason they suffer a mild case of mental paralysis has to do with how they reach a decision. To a procedures person, there is a map to follow, a set of procedures. Step A leads to Step B, which leads to Step C, all the way to the last step, where a decision is reached. To a procedures person it is *one* decision, one outcome, not three.

Going back to our example a moment ago of asking a dealer to participate in a pre-season marketing program, here is how it might go with a procedures dealer. You might say something like, "Well, Joan, based on what I know about your business and your preferences in equipment and how our program works this season, I think your best bet would be to go with the Premium Option. Here is why I say that." And then you explain your reasoning. When finished, say something like, "Now we also have a Standard Option, as well as a Seasonal Option. If you'd like to hear about either of those and how they might work for you, I'd be glad to explain them. What would you like to do?" If she likes the Premium Option, she'll sign up on that level. If she is interested in the other two, make your presentations, but *one at a time*, not all three simultaneously. If she likes the Premium Option, suggest to her that there is not much point then in dropping down to the Standard Option, since she clearly likes the benefits the Premium Option gives her.

But remember this: when calling for action with a procedures person, *prepare* up to three courses of action, but present them *one at a time*. And do not present numbers two and three if the person agrees with the first one. (Recall that about 20% of the people are a combination of options and procedures; preparing three procedures and presenting them one at a time satisfies the procedure orientation in such people and gives them three options to select from which satisfies their options programming.)

Toward and Away

Another very important facet of decision making in people is how they view the decision—will it enable them to get something they want (what we call a ***toward*** orientation), or will it help them to escape (or solve) a problem they have (an ***away*** orientation). About 40% of the people are toward, another 40% or so are away, and the balance can be a blend of the two.

Normally, you'll be able to figure out as you get to know your dealers better which propulsion system drives them. Some dealers always talk in terms of problems and how they want to solve them. Others talk in terms of attaining a goal or an objective. And some want to do both.

One simple way to figure out how a dealer is wired is to ask him or her an open-ended question as part of the setup for a sales discussion. For example, suppose you wanted to talk to your dealer about a new marketing program you want her to sign up for. You could begin your presentation by asking her a simple question: "Karen, if you could have a perfect marketing program, what would it do for you?"

The question is open-ended. She can answer it as her heart dictates. Suppose she says, for instance, "Well, Brad, if it could make my phone ring, that would be great!"

What do you know so far? Not enough to decide yet, except that she wants the phone to ring more. So you probably need to ask a follow-up question: "I see. Well tell me, Karen—what is so important about making your phone ring more?"

She may look at you like you're nuts, and she may even laugh, but she'll probably say something like this: "Brad, it means I get to make more sales calls, so I can sell more and make more money! Duh!" This speaks of a strong *toward* orientation in her mind when it comes to marketing plans.

Suppose, though, she had said, "Brad, when the phones don't ring, nothing happens; no money comes in, the bills pile up, payroll bloats, and it gets hard to keep things going. Do you understand me?" Now *this* reply bespeaks of problems in her mind that an active phone could help get rid of. This is a typical *away* answer.

Once you know how your dealer is wired (toward or away), you can then frame your sales message in the proper propulsion context. If Karen is toward, you can say, "Then do I have some good news for you! Our new spring program has been designed to make your phone ring more than ever. Want to hear how it works?"

If Karen is away, you can say, "Hey, I feel your pain! But guess what? Our new spring program is designed to help your phone ring so much that those cash crimps are a thing of the past. Want to hear more about how we plan to do that?"

So let's summarize the primary decision influencing forces at work in every human being:

Trait	What it Means	Good questions to check
Internal	Holds standards internally; marches to own drum beat	Only you can decide if this is good for you... You'll have to judge whether or not…
External	Evaluates decisions based on feedback from external sources	Other dealers have liked… 75% of our dealers who have gone on this program have grown…
Options	Likes a menu of options to consider	Present your most powerful option first; then the next one, followed by the weakest last
Procedures	Arrives at a *single* choice after carefully weighing the evidence in a procedure	After reviewing how you run your business, I think the following plan makes the most sense…
Away	Wants to get away from problems	I think you'll really appreciate how this new control system solves that field wiring problem that drives you up a wall!
Toward	Wants to move toward a goal	This new heat pump will certainly set you apart as the technology leader in *this* market, won't it Tom?

Knowing the Convincer System and Avoiding Buyer's Remorse

The matrix above summarizes how people make decisions. There are eight possible combinations of styles,[23] and when you factor in the visual, auditory and kinesthetic sensory channels, things get complex fast! It looks like the simplistic closing techniques taught in many sales courses may not be rich enough to handle all the contingencies.

It is about to become even more complex—but only because human behavior is complex, and those who become great at sales become great at understanding human behavior.

Everyone uses some sort of convincer system as a test of a decision's rightness. There are

23 1) Internal/Options/Away, 2) Internal/Options/Toward, 3) Internal/Procedures/Away, 4) Internal/Procedures/Toward, 5) External/Options/Away, 6) External/Options/Toward, 7) External/Procedures/Away, 8) External/Procedures/Toward.

several convincer systems and if you know the system of your dealer, you can present your sales message in a way that completely satisfies his convincer system and gives him peace about his decision. If you omit this step in your sales call, you run the risk that the dealer will not rest with his decision and may end up with buyer's remorse, that psychological pang of guilt that perhaps a bad decision was made. Often, buyer's remorse ends up in the cancellation of an order!

There are four basic convincer systems people use:

1) They must **see** something
2) They must **hear** something
3) They must **read** something
4) They must **do** something

It might be best to illustrate how these convincer systems appear by giving examples. A great way to unveil a person's convincer system is to ask a question like this: "Sam, a month after this pre-season program kicks off, how would you know you made a good decision to participate in it?"

Notice how we are asking the dealer how he would know in his own mind that he made a good decision by participating in a program. What he tells us next is what *he* would look for by way of results to know he had made a good decision *today* to participate in a program that we would evaluate a month from now.

Let's examine how a **see** convincer might be expressed. Sam says this: "Well, I'd have to see a spike in my lead generation rate for that month compared to last year, I reckon." (Instead of "see", he might also use terms like "notice" or "observe." Or he may have said, "There would have to be an increase in my lead generation numbers for that month.")

You still don't know how much Sam would have to see—that's the other piece of the convincer system we need in order to help Sam get a sense of comfort and closure over his decision. So you could next ask Sam, "Good. Sam, how many more leads would you have to see?"

Sam might say, "Oh, just a few." What is a few? We still don't know, but at this point, it may start to beat a dead horse to ask what a few is. Or Sam might say, "Oh, five or six." Or even something as easy as, "Heck, just one more would be better than last year!"

Here is how to use Sam's convincer system to help him feel comfortable with his decision to buy into the marketing program today. You could say, "Sam, I'll bet this program delivers to you a lot more than a few additional leads! If it delivered even only three or four more, would that be good?" Or, if Sam had answered five or six, you could say, "Sam, I'll bet this program can deliver more than five or six leads! But we'll see. Be sure to track it, will you?" And if he gives you the softball of "just one more lead," a good reply could be, "Well, I can't imagine a scenario where you would not get just one lead, but probably several more! I just hope you love all that new business!"

The point is you want to use the dealer's convincer system and number of cases to help him feel at ease about the decision you want him to make.

How might the **hear** convincer go? Again, we ask, "Sam, a month after this pre-season program kicks off, how would you know you made a good decision to participate in it?"

This time, Sam says, "I'd have to hear the phone ringing a lot more than last year." (Or, "I'd have to hear my comfort consultant griping less that it is too slow in the pre-season." Or, "If friends and neighbors say to me that they heard my ad on the radio that would be nice.") Sam might also say something like, "If I hear Billy Dean using these ads on the radio this year, I'll know it was a good move for me too because Billy seems to really know how to use advertising around here." If Sam has a specific number of instances he would have to hear, you can use that in your assurance statement. (To the Billy Dean statement, you can say, "Well guess what? Billy signed on last week.")

Related to the see convincer is the **read** convincer. To our question about knowing if he made a good decision, Sam might answer, "I know it is good if I read better sales numbers on the P&L in April." Or he may say something like, "When I read the ad in the paper and see how it looks on the page, I'll know." Again, if it is easy to obtain, get the number of times the dealer needs to read it to know he made a good decision and then work that number into your assurance statement.

Finally, the **do** convincer (which is rare) would have our dealer **doing** something to see that he made the right decision. If Sam used a **do** convincer, he might say, "I'd know it was a good decision if I have to order more equipment during that time frame." When Sam has to do a specific thing, he'll know that he made a good decision.

With each convincer system, there are three basic modes, each which is dependent on a particular number of proofs needed by the decision maker to know he or she has made a good decision.

The simplest of these is the **automatic** type. An automatic convincer is one who only needs one example to show that the decision was a good one. When Sam said he'd be happy if he got even one more lead than last year, he was exhibiting an automatic convincer system. With an automatic convincer, you only need to suggest one way to observe the proof and they will probably be fine with a decision.

The next simplest is a **number of examples**. When Sam said he'd need five or six more leads than the same time last year, he was showing a number of examples system. With number of examples convincers, you need to show them how your course of action will benefit them that many times. When Sam said he'd need to see five or six more leads, that can be a hard job to do. You might get by with something like, "Well, Sam, the pre-season lasts two months, so you really have two months to notice a spike in your leads. If you only got three or four more in April but seven or eight more in May, would you be okay with that?" If Sam had said "two or three," your convincer talk could have gone like this: "You normally get more leads when you advertise than when you don't, right? [Convincer #1] And don't you normally get more leads in the pre-season when you use our group ad program than when you sit on the sidelines and don't participate? [Convincer #2] Then doesn't it stand to reason that participating in this program will be a good move for you?"

The hardest convincer system to handle is the **consistent**. A consistent convincer is one that has to be proved every time the person looks for evidence! He is never totally satisfied with his decision, but he learns to live with it. If Sam was a consistent convincer system user, he might say, "Oh, I don't know. I'm not sure I would ever know for sure. I guess I'll just have to try it and see how it works." (Visual consistent!) With a consistent convincer, you cannot show them that two or three more leads was proof they made a good decision. They'll have to see more leads each and every month of the pre-season. Luckily for you, consistent convincers are very rare. You won't run into them very often, but when you do, you'll probably note that they are never fully satisfied with anything.

Summary of Deep Communication Elements

As you begin to see, sales behavior is much more complex than most sales models teach! Human beings are monstrously complex creatures, and it is usually not a good idea to pigeon-hole them with a small set of personality types.

First, there are three sensory channels that 99.9% of all people use to interpret their worlds. We must know our dealer's sensory channel and communicate in it to be maximally effective.

Then there are the propulsion systems for decisions: internal/external, options/procedures, toward/away—six in all.

Next are the convincer systems (four of them: see, hear, read, do), and the number of examples qualifiers (three of them: automatic, number of examples, and consistent).

Three basic sensory systems operating through six different propulsion systems guided by four convincer systems each with three possible sub-variants is a total of 216 possible combinations of elements that can make up any one person's decision process. That's a lot more pigeon-holes than the DISC system allows, or Myers-Briggs. But then, people are complex!

The bottom line here? *You need to learn as much as you can about the psychology of selling and decision making and master what you learn in your communication with your dealers.* If you do, you will find that an astonishing percentage of your message gets across (most communication is less than 10% effective!), increasing the chances the dealer understands your message and also increasing the odds that he will see the benefits in it for himself and make the decision you want him to make. Then—and only then—can you truly call yourself a **decision engineer**.

The Ultimate Goal: Rapport

The ultimate goal behind any high-level Tier One TM sales approach should be the establishment and maintenance of ***rapport***. But rapport does not mean what most people think it means. (We talked about it on page 375, remember? *In sales, rapport can be defined as demonstrating understanding of the other person in such a way that you earn the right to help influence their decision.)* Rapport means you can relate to the dealer in *his* world and see things from his viewpoint. (You don't have to agree with him, but you do need to demonstrate you know and understand where he is coming from.)

Rapport is not established and maintained by ice-breaker conversation. Ice-breakers, as taught in most sales courses, are helpful to get a conversation rolling, but they are inadequate in and of themselves to permit us to emotionally connect to our customers. Frankly, when I am the customer, I get turned off by a gabby salesperson who tries to complement me on my wall plaques or admire my home or anything else that I smell as sales school behavior. It turns me off and if the salesperson does not start to establish an emotional connection with me within one minute, I mentally write him off, even if I let him make his pitch.[24]

One minute. That's all I give him. And I don't think I'm that unusual from most folks when it comes to this. When you go into a big-box store to buy something like a plasma TV or a new appliance, you might stand there and look at the different models on display, and eventually a smocked and/or badge-wearing sales clerk walks over and asks you the ubiquitous question, "May I help you?" And most of us automatically reply (before we can even think about it), "No, just looking."

Why do we do that? It's because we don't trust sales people and their worn-out, threadbare come-ons. So we erect our defensive barriers (we feign disinterest) to get rid of the pest. In the minds of most people, sales clerks are money-sucking vampires with long fangs designed to hook into their wallets or purses and suck all the cash out.

Yet in truth, we go to the store and look at the plasma TV displays because we *are not just looking*—we are gathering information, forming opinions, settling our emotions about the best choice for us.

Rapport gets you past the natural defenses all of us have against sales people and it builds a bridge of trust so that the customer actually *asks* you to help them form a good decision.

Tools to Maintain Rapport

Two techniques for maintaining rapport during a conversation (I'll use that broader term rather than sales call since the laws of rapport work well beyond the sales arena) are *matching* and *mirroring*.

Matching means that we quickly figure out the sensory preference of the other person and then use the words that are congruent with that system. If my client is auditory, I will use auditory words (How does that *sound* to you? Do you *hear* how that comes together? I hope this idea *resonates* with you.). If kinesthetic, I'll use kinesthetic phrases (How does that *feel* to you? How do you *feel* about that part of the program? I think you'll really appreciate how *solid* this new furnace is.)

---

24 And the *worst* offenders, in my mind, are those telemarketers who call me almost every day and open with, "Mr. Harshaw, this is John of XYZ Services Company. Let me assure you right off that this is *not* a sales call. I simply want to give you some information about our new water treatment service…" No company is in the business of just educating people all the time— except private schools. When I hear such a come on, I always stop them and ask, "If this is not a sales call, just what the heck are you doing wasting your company's time and resources by making an education-only call?"

But matching also means that to some extent, I match the other person's manner of speaking and vocabulary. If they talk slowly, I will have to consciously tell myself to slow down and speak at or near the same pace. If they speak in monotones, I will have to watch how much inflection and cadence I inject into my speech. Too much of it and it will be obvious to the other person (on an unconscious level) that we are not exactly alike!

Most importantly, it means *using his or her words and not my own.* I cannot stress this enough! Too many sales classes today teach you to paraphrase the customer to show that you really understand them. But such a move actually weakens rapport! Why?

Because rapport is maintained as the other person senses (unconsciously) that I understand his world and can relate to him in it comfortably. If I now say to her, "Let me see if I understand you. You said that you wanted a marketing program that generates leads for you. In other words, you want your phone to ring more, right?" She says, "No! I want to rack up more sales!" Boy, did I just damage our rapport! And I did so because I forced her to leave her world for a second (where she is most comfortable) and try to enter mine to make sure I understood her. Bad move, very bad move.

Instead, if you are not sure what the client means by a statement, ask them to clarify it for you. For instance, if Susan said to me that she wanted a marketing program that generated more leads for her, if I *assume* that she wants the phone to ring more and then ask her to sign on then because her phone will ring more, she won't see the connection and will hesitate, perhaps even refuse to sign up. So I need to ask Susan, "Generate more leads? Can you tell me more about that?" Then she will add information that lets me figure out that her real intent is to make more sales, not make the phone ring. So when it comes time to ask her to sign up, I should say that by signing up for the pre-season program, she should see a noticeable uptick in her sales. Do you see the subtle difference here?

Never, never, never paraphrase a customer. Always use *their words* and ask them to clarify something when it is not perfectly clear to you, or where the meanings could lead to multiple conclusions.[25]

The other skill that helps you maintain rapport is *mirroring*. Mirroring is often misunderstood by those who don't know what it is all about and therefore put it down as a bad idea. It is not the mirroring that is bad; it is the unfounded opinions about what it is that are bad.

25 I can recall a sales call once where I learned that the customer valued high efficiency. When I proceeded to ask him to okay the sales order since this new unit would help him save lots of money in power costs, he looked at me with a puzzled look and said with some edge to his voice, "That's not what I said! I want a unit that won't break down all the time like my old one did!" Boy, did I blow that one! In my mind, he is really talking about *reliability*. But I am not selling to my mind; I am selling to his, so I should have asked him to clarify what he meant rather than assuming I knew. It cost me the sale!

Mirroring is simply *adopting a similar (but not exactly alike) posture* as the customer has, *but in a mirror fashion.* For instance, the customer may during the sales call fold her arms across her chest. What does that mean? If you attend some of the popular sales or body language classes, you'll come away with a whole page of what that could mean. Is she being defensive? Is she cold? Is she comfortable? I don't know, and frankly I don't have any way of finding out short of asking her an embarrassing question ("Why are you folding your arms like that?"). But I do know this. If, after a few seconds she settles in her new posture, I casually adopt a similar (but mirror image) posture (preferably while I am speaking); her unconscious mind will see a reflection of herself in the mind's mirror. And most people tend to like their reflections!

If during a sales call Susan, my dealer, folds her arms so that her left arm is on top, I will, after several seconds pass, and while I am speaking (so the shift in my posture is more natural), I will fold my arms in a similar way, but with my *right* arm on top (the way it would look in a mirror).

Later, if Susan uncrosses her arms and then leans back in her chair, I will, at an appropriate moment, uncross my arms and lean back too. If she leans toward her left, I'll lean a little toward my right. If her head is cocked to one side, I will cock mine (to the opposite side).

If Susan is restless and changing her posture frequently, I won't try to keep up with her. It could become apparent to her that I am mimicking her and that is never a good place to go with rapport! I will, instead, depend on my matching skills to maintain emotional contact and let the mirroring skill go unused on that call.

I will never forget the time when I was brought in by the manufacturer I worked for to help an independent distributor figure out why his market share was slipping and then devise a plan to get it back into upward growth. In our first meeting, the principal and I had a chat about what my task was and after about ten minutes, I could see he was getting angry. Finally, he exploded, pounding his fist down on his desk so hard the pen holder bounced, and yelled, with veins in his neck bulging, "I am sick and tired of you damn factory people telling me how to do my job!"

What should I do? In most sales courses, you are taught to defuse this customer's anger by adopting an open and non-threatening posture. But that does not build or maintain rapport—it actually tries to force the client to enter *your* world, and not be at peace in his. So I could not try any of those silly defusing gestures. I could only mirror what he was doing.

So immediately, I pounded his desk equally hard and let my anger rise, and my neck veins bulge out, and shouted back, "Well I am too! I think it's a crock! So what are ***we*** going to do about it?!!"

What followed was six seconds of pure silence as the others in the room looked on in shock. Then a smile cracked the principal's lips and he held his hand out to me and as we shook hands, he said, "I think we're going to get along just fine on this project. Where do we begin?"

Deep Listening Leads to Deep Communication

The title of this chapter is "Deep Communication, the Key to Amazing Sales." By now, you should see that deep communication is the byproduct of mastering a few basic skills and learning, above all, how to be a brilliant observer of human behavior. And by observer, I mean paying attention to *everything* the other person is giving you. Because as Richard Bandler, a pioneer in this area of deep communication and sales says,

> *"Open your eyes and ears and all your senses and notice what's going on around you. Your customer has all the information you need to help them. You don't have to go inside your head and figure out what's going on. If you do, you just made the second fatal mistake of any professional communicator. Not only will they tell you and show you what's going on inside their head, they'll even give you the solution opportunities you need.*[26]*"*

How much of your communication do you suppose is the words you use? Take a guess. Write it in the margin of this page.

Research shows that on average, *only 7%* of what we communicate is in the words themselves! The other 93% is in non-verbal communication. About *57%* or so of our communication is conveyed by our body language—our facial expressions, posture, and gestures. And the balance—some *36%* or so—is conveyed by our tone of voice, our pitch, the speed with which we speak and so on.[27]

Because over half of our communication is via body language, that's why it is so important to understand mirroring and to use it properly. I don't have to waste time learning what posture means in your communication as long as I can mirror it and let your unconscious mind feel at

26 From Richard Bandler's book on sales and deep communication, *Persuasion Engineering.*

27 Which is why e-mail is such a poor way to communicate! All it conveys is the 7% verbal part of the message; without a body to see or a voice to hear, most people will read into the message the non-verbals they *think* the writer meant, and usually be wrong as they do. The result is that more feelings have been hurt because of email than *all* the broken romances in history. And this in just twenty years of email!

ease with my presence.

And since over a third of our communication is in the *way* we say our words, that is why matching is almost as important. When I match your words and your delivery style, your unconscious mind is thinking, "Hmm, this guy is okay. He thinks and talks just like I do."

Dancing With Two or More

Sometimes, you will have to make a presentation to two or more managers in a dealership, and these two may well be wired differently. How do you communicate best with each of them?

It will sound funny, but you must learn to say the same thing in different ways and then say that same thing in the way that is best for each participant in the meeting. I like to jokingly call this speaking out of both sides of your mouth, but it really does come down to that. If the dealer principal is visual, for instance, and his office manager is auditory, you will have to present an idea that both need to take action on by using visual terms for the principal and auditory ones for the office manager.

The funny thing is, even though you are saying the same thing twice (just using different words to do it), the principal won't really get what you are saying to the office manager, and the office manager won't really pick up on what you are saying to the principal, because we tend to pick up words that are sent to us on our normal channels.

And once you have presented the idea, do a check question like, "Do you see the benefits to this? And does that sound like it would work for you?"

Steps to Mastery

This has been a long chapter, and a very complex one. It will probably take you at least six months to a year to master what you have just read! But don't give up! The results are well worth the hard work and study you must put in to become good at deep communication.

My advice is that you take all the skills in this chapter and list them—better yet, I've already made a list (on the next page). Then pick *just one skill* on the list and work on it for a while. *Work on it in private at first*; try reading people on television talk shows (like interview participants).

After you think you have it down, *try using it with someone you trust* to give you good feedback about how you are with using it. This might be a co-worker, or your spouse, or a close friend. Tell them what you want to practice on with them and then when you are done ask them how you did.

Next, pick *a safe place to try out the skill*—perhaps with a server at a restaurant, or the ticket agent at the airline counter, or some other place where if you blow it, no one will notice or care.

Then, when you feel comfortable with all the subtleties of the skill, *try it out on three or four sales calls*. Don't give up if the first call or two don't go well. Keep at it. Determine to master this skill and keep on until you do. Then, make it part of your sales skills from that day forward.

Next, add another skill and repeat the process until you have mastered all the skills in this chapter. When you do, you will be selling at a level of deep communication that will produce results that will astound you (and delight your sales manager)!

Deep Communication Skills

- ★ Sensory channel (V, A, K), and traits
- ★ Speech spooler
- ★ Internal/external
- ★ Toward/away
- ★ Matching (no paraphrasing)
- ★ Mirroring
- ★ Filtering systems
- ★ Eye accessing cues
- ★ Lefties don't reverse it
- ★ Options/procedures
- ★ Convincer system (automatic, number of times, consistent)
- ★ Elements of communication (verbal, non-verbal)

Review Questions for Chapter 22

1. The service manager at one of your dealer's shops is soft-spoken and moves his eyes horizontally often while speaking. He also pauses often and looks down and to his right during conversation. He also has a great mind for details and fantastic memory recall. How might he be wired based only on these observations?

A) auditory and toward

B) auditory and kinesthetic blend

C) auditory with frequent speech spoolers

D) kinesthetic with frequent speech spoolers

E) none of the above

Answer: ________

2. You have a meeting with the dealer principal of question 1 and that same service manager in which you are explaining your new on-line warranty claiming system. During your presentation, the service manager remarks how he hopes this new system does away with delays in credits. You ask him why and he says, "Because they tie up our resources for a long time and that hurts our bottom line!" What can you conclude from this statement?

A) the service manager is a pain in the assets

B) he is upset with your distributor and secretly wants the boss to handle a different line

C) he is "away" in his decision propulsion system

D) he wants options to choose from

E) none of the above

Answer: ________

3. Which statement is the best one to make to this service manager at this point?

A) "Well, gee, Mike, why are you so worried about the bottom line?"

B) "Mike, you can do warranties on-line or by paper, whichever way you prefer."

C) "Mike, only you can say what is best for your service department, but to me it looks like a no-brainer."

D) "Mike, this on-line process can shave three weeks or more off our credits turn around time."

E) None of the above

Answer: ________

4. At some point in your sales call, you ask both the dealer principal and the service manager what they like (or don't like) about the warranty filing procedure as it currently exists. The principal says, "I like the ease with which it flows, and the fact that I can field scrap small parts. That saves me a ton on return freight. I also like the DOA allowances you guys have." The service manger answers, "Overall, it's okay, but I don't like the fact that I have to supply so much detail (much of it redundant) on the forms, and if something is not exactly right (like a serial number is transposed), it gets kicked out. Then I have to re-do the form and resubmit it all over again and wait for the next kick out." What do these two statements suggest to you about the principal and the service manager?

A) the principal is an options person while the service manager is

a procedures person

B) both are options

C) both are procedures

D) the principal is toward, the service manager away

E) none of the above

Answer: ________

5. In calling for action (getting the dealer to sign up for on-line warranty claiming), you ask them both this question: "How would you know three months from now that going to on-line warranty was a good move for you?" The principal replies, "I'd see our warranty funds outstanding greatly reduced." And the service manager says, "I'd have to hear from Joann (the dispatcher and warranty overseer) that the claims were being paid faster." What can you conclude from these statements?

A) that the principal uses a "do" convincer while the service manager uses a "hear" convincer

B) that the principal uses a "see" convincer while the service

manager uses a "hear" convincer

C) that the principal uses a “see automatic” convincer while

the service manger uses a “hear consistent” convincer

D) that the principal is away and the service manager is also away

E) none of the above

Answer: ________

Chapter 23: Dispute Resolution

Because no two people on earth have exactly the same way of conceptualizing the world, it is inevitable that from time to time, two people will not reach the same conclusions from the same facts. Sometimes, this results in a dispute or conflict. Sometimes it does not. But when a dispute is the result of juxtaposed perceptions, the Tier One territory managers come out shining with solid agreements because they know how to reposition their proposals in ways that the disputing party finds acceptable.

A Five-Step Approach

The implication could be made that based on consistent and effective use of the principles of rapport covered in the last chapter that disagreement and disputes can largely be avoided. This is because most disputes arise because of misunderstandings between two parties and effective levels of rapport mean that understanding will be greater than normal—but still not perfect. Disputes *will* sometimes arise between even the closest of people.

When disputes arise, there are a few simple things to keep in mind, things that can help you resolve the dispute quickly and fairly.

Step 1: Find Out Why They Want It

First of all, don't just find out what the other party wants in the dispute—*find out **why** they want it*. Everyone is motivated to take the actions they take *for their own reasons*, not yours. When a dealer disagrees with you, it is usually not a personal disagreement with you, but usually a case where the dealer does not see your position as being helpful to his cause.

Consider an example. You decide to set up another dealer in a market of 100,000 people.

You have two dealers there now (giving you a combined share of market of 4.6%) and you know from research that the market can easily support another dealer. When you announce to Karl, one of your dealers, that you are going to set up Jim Jefferson as a new dealer, he becomes visibly upset. He moans and complains, "That's not a good move on your part. If you set up Jefferson, I'll change brands!"

Ignoring the fact that I think this topic was broached in a very unprofessional and amateurish manner (remember the discussion on page 180, where you learned to ask the vital Two-Part Question?), you now have a mini-crisis brewing. What you say next can save your relationship with Karl or destroy it.

Step 2: Find Out Why They are Upset

To save it, *find out why Karl is upset.* For instance, you might say, "Ouch! I see that really bothers you. Tell me more about it."

You have *not* defended your action (which Karl probably expected you to do). Nor have you put Karl down for being too territorial. You have acknowledged his feeling (without criticism) and are asking for more information in your effort to see Karl's world as *he* sees it. He is probably not expecting this tack from you!

So Karl says, "I think Jefferson is scum, that's why! And if you give him access to the line I have, I don't like that association. I'll change suppliers!" There you have it—or at least some of it. He does not personally like Jefferson and feels that Jefferson's having the line he carries will tar him with the same bad brush that he sees Jefferson tarred with.

But what does he have against Jefferson? You need to find out. So perhaps you ask, "Karl, I didn't know you felt that way toward Jefferson. Can you tell me how he ended up so low on your esteem meter?"

Suppose Karl tells you a dark story about the time Jefferson rubbed him the wrong way. It may have been a job Jefferson stole, or an employee. Perhaps Jefferson caused permanent injury to Karl's wife in an automobile accident years ago. It may even be something minor (at least to you). But you can bet your career that it is a *big deal* to Karl.

The next phase **is to try to understand** Karl's feelings and then see if you can (a) either accept them and drop Jefferson from your prospect list or, (b) help Karl see the changes that will come with Jefferson's enlistment as a positive (a process we call reframing).

If your reasons for selecting Jefferson were not well-founded (he only *looked* good on a prospect list, etc.), you need to ask yourself if getting Jefferson is worth losing Karl. You may win the battle but lose the war! Is Jefferson the hill you are prepared to die on? Would you have a net gain or loss in market share if you brought on Jefferson? It's still not too late to ask the vital Two-Part Question, "Who do you respect and not compete with?"

Let's add a complicating factor. Suppose you have blundered and already talked to Jefferson (before talking to Karl and your other dealer) and he is willing to convert (at least partly) to your line. You have two courses of action—sign him up and lose Karl (maybe) or tell Jefferson you have to withdraw your offer (because of Karl's concerns, although you don't need to give him a reason). He may become angry with you, but your job is to manage your territory (that's your title, remember?) and what a non-dealer feels toward you should be irrelevant.

But, suppose you are convinced that Jefferson will be a great new dealer and that you are going to bring him on despite Karl's feelings. Can you help Karl reframe his feelings? Perhaps, and perhaps not. These things are always incredibly complicated, and delicate.

You might say something like this: "Karl, I can see your issues and I understand why you feel this way. But Jefferson stole your service manager five years ago (and he is no longer there anyway). A lot of water has passed under that bridge since then. Jefferson can bring an added presence in this market that will let me justify putting more co-op ad dollars here, and that's bound to help *your* business too. Can you let go of your anger in order to gain momentum?" It's impossible to say what Karl will do, but at least you have tried to reframe the issue from the past so it may be less of an obstacle in Karl's mind.

Step 3: Find Opportunities for the Other Party's Position

But what if Karl still opposes the idea of Jefferson coming aboard? Do the next step—*try to find opportunities in Karl's position.* Sometimes, dealers get very territorial and resent having to share what they perceive as their turf with anyone else. This is a natural feeling, as old as the tribes of man, but in the modern business world, it is often unfounded. In some cases, showing the dealer the numbers may be enough to shock him out of his entrenchment. Many contractors hold highly inflated views of their share of market, thinking they have up to 30% (or more) of the local business. And a rare few do. But most have shares of only 2% to 5%. If a dealer sees himself as a 30% lion, he would probably assume by default that other dealers are likely so strong and there just is not that much room in this market for two or three 30% share dealers! Showing a dealer that his $300,000 in purchases from you—which is a hefty amount—comes to 2.6% of the market may help him see that there is in fact room at the table for others. It depends on how well you prepare your case and present it to Karl in the way he likes to process information.

Sometimes a dealer starts to see himself as the senior statesman of your local dealer organization. For some dealers, this evokes a sense of deep pride, an aura of dignity (usually well-deserved). Bringing on new blood can be about as hard on such a dealer as the birth of a baby brother or sister to an only child. How do wise parents deal with such a situation? By having the older sibling help raise the new baby.

Would Karl respond in a positive way if you were to ask him to help get Jefferson oriented, and see to it that Jefferson represents the brand well? It could be touchy (especially for Jefferson), but it just might work!

Step 4: Help The Other Party Find Common Ground

Sometimes a dealer fears that a new dealer will compete directly with him and thus take away business. This brings up the fourth strategy, *helping Karl find the good and common ground in the deal.*

There is an MBA exercise called *The Commodity Purchase.* In this exercise, one student has 100,000 pheasant eggs to sell. Five other students represent buyers for those eggs, each with different motives and quantities. For example, some want the eggs for chemicals they contain that can be used in the manufacturing of new life-saving drugs; others need them to make cosmetics, and so on. The winning alliance turns out to be the two drug manufacturers cooperating to outbid the other three players and lock up the supply. But one of the drug manufacturers needs 80,000 eggs while the other needs 70,000. Only about one team in twenty figures out the win-win of the exercise: one drug maker needs only the egg whites, while the other needs just the yolks. This being known, the two drug makers can split the costs, each taking what it needs and letting the other extract what it needs. The win-win is to see that the opponents are *not* competitors but symbiotes.

Would this approach work for Karl? Perhaps. If you could show Karl that while he is very successful in residential replacement, Jefferson is adept at residential new construction and light commercial plan and spec, two markets Karl does not work in, it might help. Furthermore, Jefferson does not dabble in residential replacement. Do we have a pheasant egg win-win here?

Step 5: Stay Calm

If, after all of this, Karl still digs in and threatens to leave if Jefferson is signed up, you come to the fifth and last strategy for dealing with the impasse—*you keep on it even if the deal appears to be headed for trouble.* You have to ask Karl, "What will it take for us to reach a peaceable solution?" Karl may not budge. You may have no choice but to set up Jefferson and let the chips fall where they may. But then again, Karl could give you new information that can lead to a breakthrough.

Reframing

If you take a painting and change its frame, the result can enhance or hurt the impression it makes. Take Thomas Gainsborough's masterpiece, *The Blue Boy* (a painting of Jonathan Buttall, the teenage son of a London iron magnate), that is now on display in the Huntington Library, San Marino, California. Copies and posters of this famous work are in many homes. The painting is best displayed in a period frame, meaning one that is heavy, large, ornamental and gilded. In such a frame, the painting looks right and proper. But change the frame to a modern one made of plastic or metal, and most art aficionados would howl with cries of outrage. Reframing a painting can ruin it (or help it, depending on the frame).

Often, helping a dealer see his opposition to a proposed plan of action in a new way can make a bad picture start to look good to him. So how do you go about reframing?

Start by clearly *understanding how, and why, the dealer frames the issue at present.* You'll have to ask lots of questions to do this. When you have a solid understanding of the dealer's framing, you can start to work with it.

One of the things I like to do in reframing is calibrate the *submodalities* that are in the dealer's frame. That's a big word, so let's unpack it.

Submodalities are the way we see our feelings. All people have feelings and with a little guidance and effort, all people can make pictures of those feelings in their mind's eye (even if they are not visual people).

Allow me to play a dialog I had once with a student in a sales class. His job the next day was to demonstrate a certain sales skill before the whole group, what trainers often call the dreaded *role play*. At a group dinner the night before the role play, I sat at the table with this student and five others and he talked about the next day's task. He was clearly falling into dread and fear, so I turned to him and said, "I can see the very thought of this practice demonstration has you pretty nervous."

He said, "Yeah, I *hate* role plays. I never do well in them!"

[Notice how he used "role plays" while I used "practice demonstration?" That is a tip that he sees this thing in a very unhealthy light.]

"'Never'?", I echoed, with an upturn in my voice. He frowned. "Look," I continued, "your mind works faster than you think. And you don't have to actually experience a thing to learn from it. Are you aware of this?"

He answered, "No."

"Fine," I said. "Tell you what. Would you like to slay that dragon of fear for tomorrow?"

He looked at me with a funny expression and said, "What do you mean?"

"I mean, would you like to nail that demo to the class tomorrow like a pro?"

"I guess so," he replied.

"Good! Now close your eyes. Place your feet flat on the floor and your hands on your legs. I promise you, no one will hurt you!" (Laughter around the table.) "Relax. That's right. Just relax. Breathe out and take a deep breath. Hold it a second. Now let it out slowly. Do it again. That's right. Yes, relax. Oooh, that's good! Go on down deeper."

As he relaxed, his face grew more serene and color returned to his cheeks. His breathing became deeper and slower.

"Now, Bill, I want you to make a picture in your mind of how role plays make you feel. I don't want you to make a picture of a role play, but rather how they make you feel. Do you understand?"

"I think so."

"Good. As soon as you have your picture, let me know."

About five seconds pass. "Okay, I have it."

"Good." (Now I am going for the submodalities—how Bill represents his feeling. As you will see, I don't need to know what is in Bill's picture or even what the picture is. That is irrelevant to the process!)

"Bill, put your hands on the lower corners of the picture."

He placed his hands about a foot apart in his lower right quadrant.

"Bill, is your picture a still shot or a video?"

"A still."

"Okay. Is it in color or black and white?"

"Umm, black and white."

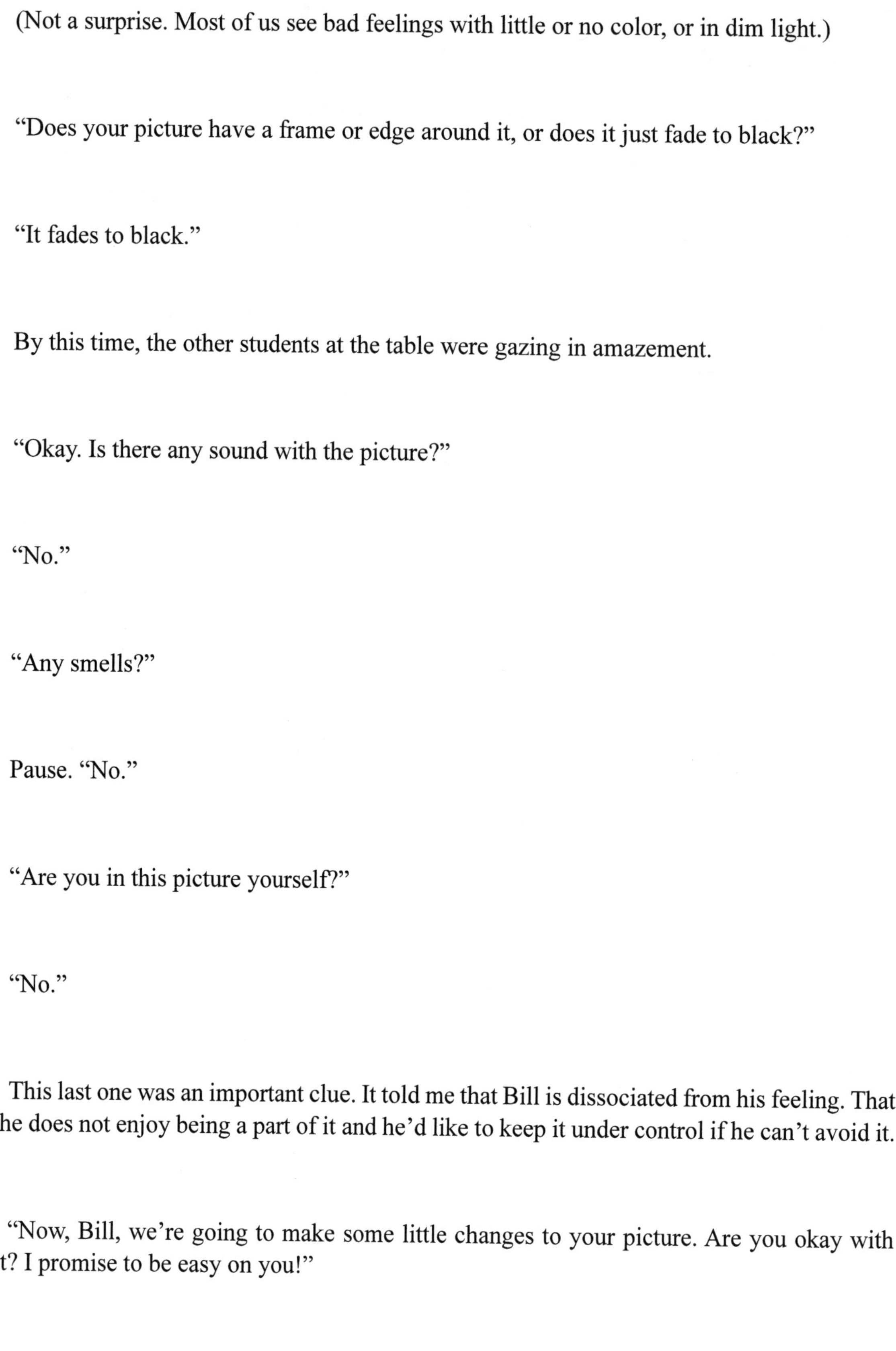

(Not a surprise. Most of us see bad feelings with little or no color, or in dim light.)

"Does your picture have a frame or edge around it, or does it just fade to black?"

"It fades to black."

By this time, the other students at the table were gazing in amazement.

"Okay. Is there any sound with the picture?"

"No."

"Any smells?"

Pause. "No."

"Are you in this picture yourself?"

"No."

This last one was an important clue. It told me that Bill is dissociated from his feeling. That is, he does not enjoy being a part of it and he'd like to keep it under control if he can't avoid it.

"Now, Bill, we're going to make some little changes to your picture. Are you okay with that? I promise to be easy on you!"

Pause. "Okay."

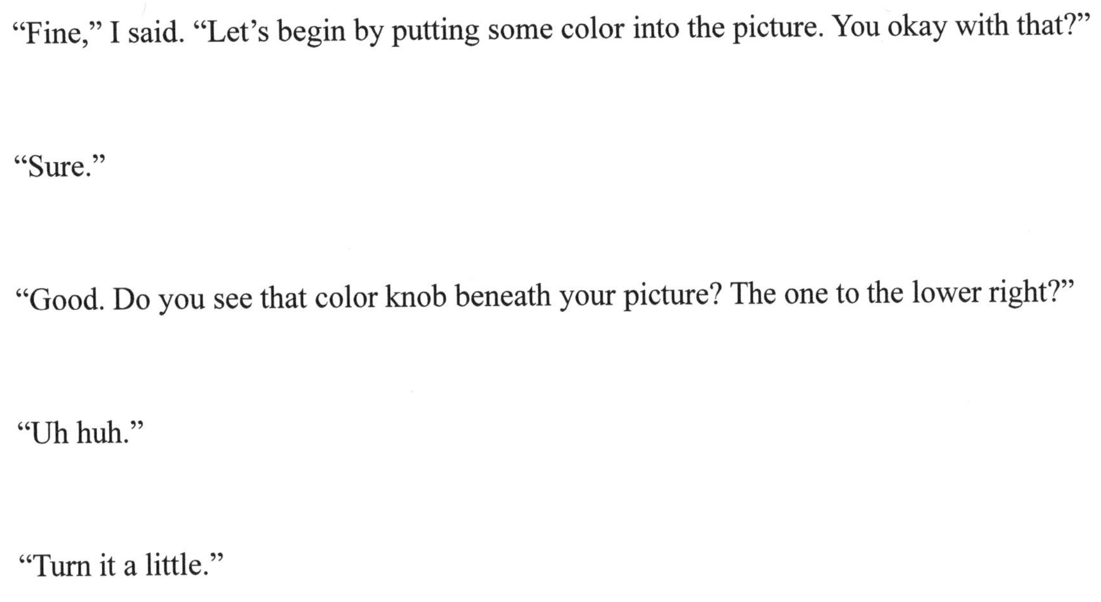

"Fine," I said. "Let's begin by putting some color into the picture. You okay with that?"

"Sure."

"Good. Do you see that color knob beneath your picture? The one to the lower right?"

"Uh huh."

"Turn it a little."

At this point, it does not matter where that imaginary color adjustment knob is. He will see it where I tell him to see it.

So Bill reached out into the air and turned an imaginary knob. The other students at the table dropped their mouths in silent amazement.

After he took his hand away, I said, "Is that better? Does it feel better now?"

"A little. Yeah, a little."

"Good. You can adjust it some more if you'd like. I want you to make the blues brilliant, the reds vibrant, the yellows warm, and the greens serene. Go ahead. Fiddle with the control until you get the maximum good feeling."

He turned his knob left and right until he stopped and took his hand down. He was smiling! I knew it was working.

"Next," I said, "Bill, there's a brightness knob to the lower left. See it? Turn up the brightness now, please."

He turned the brightness knob and grinned. I said, "Oh, that must have made it better!"

"It sure did," he replied.

"Well, go ahead and play with it some more until the feeling is about as good as you can stand it."

He dialed his brightness knob back and forth then stopped; there was a big smile on his face now. The other students could not believe what they were seeing.

"Bill, do you want to make it even *better*?"

"Wow, I… I guess so. Sure!"

"Good, because it can be a whole lot better, can it?" (Bill had a huge smile now.) "Do any particular sounds make you feel good? Sounds you don't mind sharing with me?" (Muffled laughter around the table, including Bill.)

"Yeah, I like the sounds of wild birds."

"Okay, let yourself hear wild bird songs in your picture."

His smile got even bigger.

"One more thing, Bill. Where is your picture right now? Please put your hands on its lower corners."

As I expected, he put his hands out about sixteen inches in front of his mid-chest. I took his hands in mine and said, "So your picture is right here? It's not up here?" (moving his hands up), "or down here?" (moving his hands down), "or here?" (moving his hands to the left then right), "or here?" (moving his hands front to back).

"No, it's right here."

"That's good. Now earlier, you said your picture did not have a sharp edge but just faded to black. How does it look now?"

He frowned and said, "Well, dang! It's got a sharp edge to it now."

"Interesting," I said. I then grabbed his hands and rapidly moved them to a full arm spread so his picture was panoramic and as I did so, I said loudly, "Bam! Now let's really enjoy this picture!"

Bill, with his eyes still closed, almost fell off his chair from the visual impact.

I let him collect his breath (and wits) and then said, "Hmmm, that's really good, isn't it? You like it better now?" As I said this, I gently laid a hand on his shoulder. (This is called an "anchor" in the reframing process, and I would come back the next day and use it again. You'll see in a minute.)

"This picture feels a lot different from the one you started with, doesn't it, Bill?"

"It sure does!"

This next part blew the minds of the other students at the table. I said, "And are you, by any chance, in this picture now?"

He looked stunned and said, "Why, yes!"

I said, "Can you see your face?"

"No, just the back of my head."

"Bill, we need a shot of your face for the evening news. Would you pick up that video camera there and walk around to the front of this picture and get a shot of it for us?"

The other students had to constrain themselves from bursting out with laughter as Bill, still seated, reached down and grabbed the camera, then moved his upper torso as if he was walking. He then lifted the camera to his shoulder and started to shoot the scene. As he did, his mouth dropped open.

I said, "What do you see, Bill? What surprised you?"

"I'm smiling!" he almost shouted.

I then told him to open his eyes and said, "Let me explain to you what just happened. Your brain started three minutes ago with a very bad picture about role plays. I did not know *what* was in your picture or how it was *composed*, but then I did not have to. What I had to do, and in fact did do, was teach your brain how to see your anxiety in a new way. Before, all you knew was dread. Now your brain knows that you can see role plays as peaceful, fun events that bring you joy.

Tomorrow, before you do your role play, you have a choice to make. You can look at your old ugly black and white picture and feel crappy, or you can look at your exciting new picture and be energized. It's your brain's choice. Now, Bill, I am going to talk to your brain for a moment. Bill's brain, tomorrow as you start Bill's role play, you're going to have this new color picture up because it feels so much better than that old crappy black and white one you had, right?"

"Yessir," said Bill's brain.

"And tomorrow, *after* you've done your role play perfectly, how *do* you feel?"

"I feel great!"

"In fact, if five months from now you are in another class and are asked to do a role play, you'll look back on this night and these five minutes at this table, and you'll knock it out of the park, haven't you?"

"Sure!"

I ended that evening by saying to Bill, "Go to your room and review your notes for tomorrow. Then, when you get up in front of the group, remember you have a choice in pictures now. You can feel like crap or you can feel like a king. It's up to you. Your brain already knows you can do it."

The next day, before starting his role play, I took Bill out into the hall and asked, "What picture do you have up?"

"The new color one!" he beamed.

"Hmmmm," I said as I laid my right hand on his left shoulder like I had done the night before in setting the anchor, thus triggering the emotional state he had when I set the anchor. "Great. Then go get 'em!" And he made one of the best role play presentations I have ever seen!

The Key

How was Bill able to do a virtually perfect role play? Because he was able to reframe his perception of the problem. What I did with Bill was some pretty heady stuff called *neuro-linguistic programming*. This is a powerful psychological tool. But it takes some intense training and lots of practice to become good at it. ***This is not for amateurs. I will not teach you in this***

manual how to become good at it. That is not your job. It can help you work with difficult cases, but it is not a requirement to be a good TM. If you want to learn it in more depth, learn it from good mentors. Do not try this on your own without proper training!

Would it be possible to take Karl through a reframing process like I did with Bill? Certainly. But even if you weren't comfortable with a neuro-linguistics approach, you could still help Karl reframe his feelings about Jefferson.

Would you be up to asking Karl and Jefferson to meet with you for breakfast at some restaurant with a quiet nook, or in your office, or some other neutral and mostly private area? Some may find this risky, but imagine what could happen if Karl gave vent to his feelings about Jefferson and Jefferson responded with something like, "Karl, I had no idea you were sore at me for hiring Tom five years ago! As you know, Tom did not work out, so I let him go after a year. If you really felt that way, I am surprised you did not hire him back!" What just happened? New information for *both* parties has been placed on the table and they can now work with it, if they choose to.

Conflict Resolution Styles

In the mid-1990s, I took a course on human resource management taught by Dr. Steven Sommer of the University of Nebraska. Dr. Sommer is now at the University of California at Irvine. In the course, Dr. Sommer gave us a powerful and simple little tool to help people figure out their conflict resolution style, and I will present this tool in this section (with Dr. Sommer's permission).

Have you ever noticed how different people approach a conflict? Some seem to cower in silence and hope the problem will just go away. Others are very quick to give in to the other party to avoid pain and struggle. Still others want to try to work out a compromise, and others seek the best solution for all involved. A few want it their way or the highway. Each of these styles is built on our own psychological makeup and if we know our style (along with its strengths and weaknesses), we can choose to work with others in a conflict situation and make better progress than if we are not aware of the different conflict resolution styles.

First, I want you to complete Dr. Sommer's little assessment tool (next page), and then I will explain to you what the different styles mean and their comparative strengths and weaknesses. In filling out the assessment tool, be as honest with yourself as you can. You may also want to ask your dealer to take the assessment the first time you find yourself in a significant conflict with him.

Sommer Conflict Mode Assessment[28]

Each of the following statements describes a method which individuals might use to manage differences with others. Please rate each question using the scale below in terms of how often you use each of these tactics to resolve conflict in your work setting.

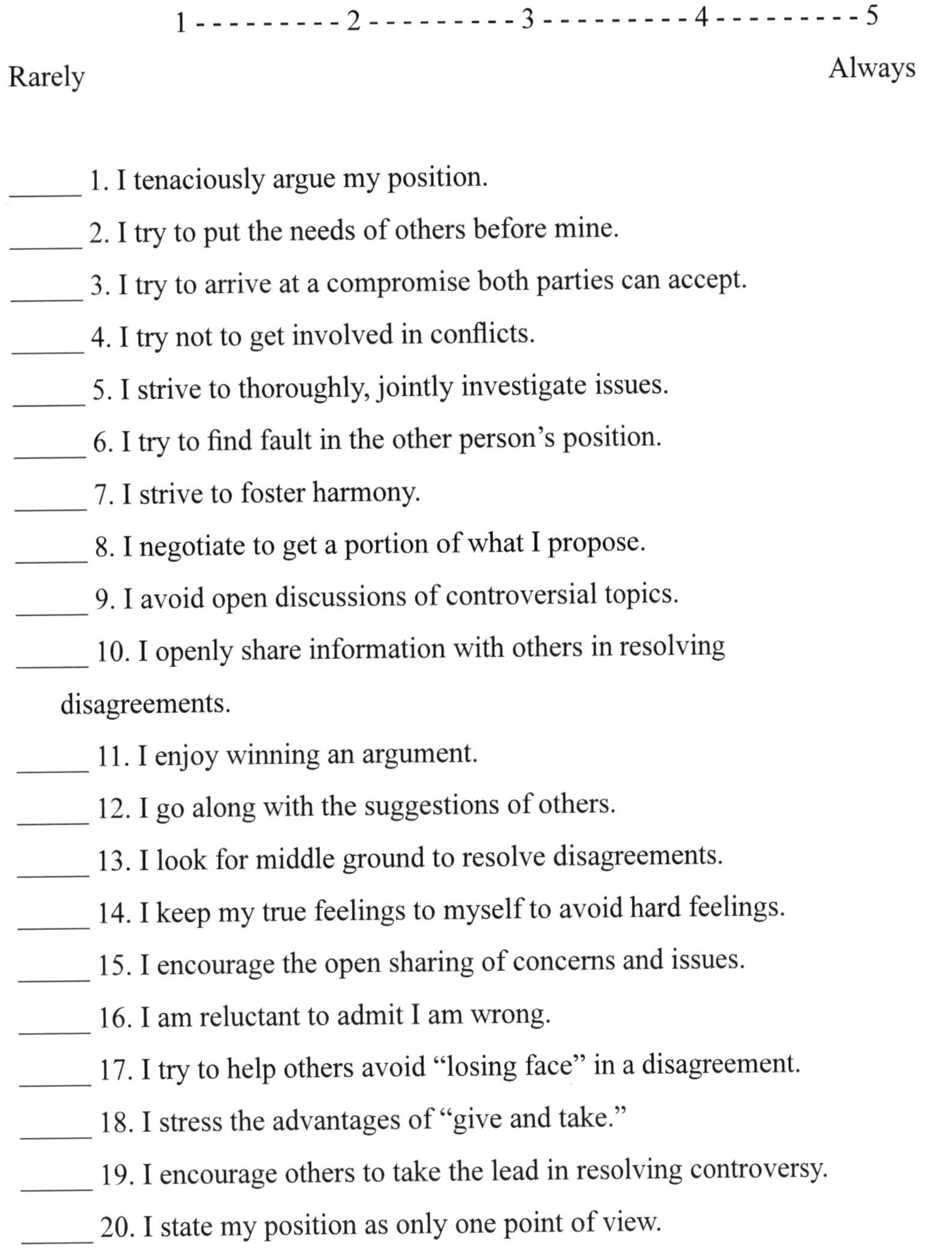

1 - - - - - - - - - 2 - - - - - - - - - 3 - - - - - - - - - 4 - - - - - - - - - 5

Rarely — Always

_____ 1. I tenaciously argue my position.

_____ 2. I try to put the needs of others before mine.

_____ 3. I try to arrive at a compromise both parties can accept.

_____ 4. I try not to get involved in conflicts.

_____ 5. I strive to thoroughly, jointly investigate issues.

_____ 6. I try to find fault in the other person's position.

_____ 7. I strive to foster harmony.

_____ 8. I negotiate to get a portion of what I propose.

_____ 9. I avoid open discussions of controversial topics.

_____ 10. I openly share information with others in resolving disagreements.

_____ 11. I enjoy winning an argument.

_____ 12. I go along with the suggestions of others.

_____ 13. I look for middle ground to resolve disagreements.

_____ 14. I keep my true feelings to myself to avoid hard feelings.

_____ 15. I encourage the open sharing of concerns and issues.

_____ 16. I am reluctant to admit I am wrong.

_____ 17. I try to help others avoid "losing face" in a disagreement.

_____ 18. I stress the advantages of "give and take."

_____ 19. I encourage others to take the lead in resolving controversy.

_____ 20. I state my position as only one point of view.

---

28 Developed by Dr. Steven Sommer, University of California, Irvine. Copyright 1992-1994. Used with permission. Lodestar Consulting Systems, Inc. 2009.

Scoring

FORCING STRATEGY

Win/Lose ("my way or the highway")

Item	Score
1	_____
6	_____
11	_____
16	_____
Total	_____

COLLABORATING STRATEGY

Win/win (listening + assertive)

Item	Score
5	_____
10	_____
15	_____
20	_____
Total	_____

COMPROMISING STRATEGY

Lose/lose (focus on give-ups, not mutual gains)

Item	Score
3	_____
8	_____
13	_____
18	_____
Total	_____

AVOIDING STRATEGY

Lose/lose (abdication of leadership)

Item	Score
4	_____
9	_____
14	_____
19	_____
Total	_____

ACCOMODATING STRATEGY

Lose/win (playing the Martyr)

Item	Score
2	_____
7	_____
12	_____
17	_____
Total	_____

My **primary** resolution style (the one with the highest score) is

____________________________________.

My **secondary** style (next highest score) is

____________________________________.

What the Styles Mean

The Forcing Strategy

The forcing style is sometimes called "my way or the highway" and results in a win/lose outcome. If you wish to maintain peace and harmony, it may not be the best style to use.

It does have its uses, though. For instance, when immediate action is required, we need someone who will stand in the flow of traffic and say, "This way! Go this way!"

It is also a good style to adopt if the course of action will not be popular but **must** be done. Example: the dealers must sign a semi-legal form in order to be a dealer. No form, no rights of dealership.

It is also a fair style to use when you **know** you are right and the alternatives are wrong. Example: your dealer argues for a large concession on a commercial job where the factory shipped 480-volt rooftop units (what the dealer wanted based on an email he sent you two months ago). Now he says he really ordered 230-volt units and wants you to pay the freight and restocking charges to take the units (he ordered) back and get the ones he needs delivered. The costs could run into several thousand dollars for you.

If you scored high in this style, you need to be aware of becoming surrounded by lackeys, people who say Yes to you to avoid fights in an effort to please you. That route often leads to lack of information and the eventual downfall of the one to whom everyone is kowtowing. You may also find your teammates reluctant to share bad news with you or pass along to you any negative feedback they picked up about you, fearing it will spark a nasty fight.

If you scored low in this style, you need to be cautious of feeling powerless in conflicts, or of being reluctant to take a firm stand. Again, sometimes yielding to the other person just to avoid a squabble does more damage than standing up to them and refusing to back down!

The Collaborating Strategy

This strategy is used to find a solution when both parties have concerns that are too important to be compromised. It is usually considered to be a win/win approach. Use it to learn about the concerns of the other party, or to blend your views and goals into a workable solution. Collaboration usually secures a deeper level of buy-in by the other party since they have a stake in the action now. It is also a great way to work through issues that may stir up bad feelings.

One of the downsides of collaboration, though, is that it usually takes a lot of time to reach agreement. If time is of the essence, the forcing strategy makes more sense. But if you have the luxury of time for coming to an agreement, collaboration is hard to beat as an approach.

If you scored low on collaboration, it may mean that you have a hard time seeing differences of opinion as opportunities for growth and gain. You tend to see the other side as opposed to you, not just different. A low score on collaboration could also mean that your co-workers and dealers don't buy into your initiatives with any real commitment.

But if you scored high on collaboration, be careful of burning up too much time to build an agreement. Also be aware that the exploratory and somewhat tentative nature of collaboration may be read by your opponent as weakness or dallying.

The Compromising Strategy

Compromising rarely leaves *both* sides feeling good about a settlement (which is why it is usually called a lose/lose approach), but it can be useful whenever the goals to be reached are of some importance but not worth the effort to use more disruptive approaches. "Is that really the hill you want to die on?" a former supervisor used to say to me when I sought her advice on conflicts with team members.

But compromise is also a decent approach if both parties are of equal power in the disagreement and both are strongly committed to *their* version of the desired outcome. It can also lead to fairly rapid decisions (but that is not always the best, of course).

A low score in compromising could mean that you may be too shy to take a stand in disagreements or that you find it too difficult to make a concession to the other side in an argument.

But a high score can mean that you are so focused on the tactics of compromise that you sometimes fail to see the bigger picture, and the fact that a more forceful strategy may be best in some cases. You must also be aware that a person who is known to be a compromiser may come to be seen as one who is all about gamesmanship, of back-room deals and logrolling. When you consider that these terms are generally reserved for members of the United States Congress, you can see where it can be negative strategy in the eyes of many people!

The Avoiding Strategy

The avoiding strategy is considered to be a lose/lose strategy because leadership is abandoned.

But the avoiding strategy actually has some good uses, as when the issue is not important enough to fight over. Example: your dealer wants to go to a pizza place for lunch and you'd rather go to a chop house. But since you also like pizza, you could easily avoid the conflict and go to the pizza place without disrupting anything in the relationship or business goals.

It is also a reasonable strategy when you think there is no chance you can get your concerns resolved by conflict.

> Example: you have a dealer who is just dead set against financing his inventory, preferring to pay cash for all his orders. This is his moral belief and you will probably have more luck air conditioning hell than changing his mind. So it would be wise to drop your plan of suggesting he use your factory's inventory financing system to fund his inventory.

Third, if the damages caused by a solution outweigh the benefits, it is probably wiser to avoid the disagreement altogether.

> Example: you could force your dealer to pay the service charges on a late invoice last month—his first late payment ever. But you sense that if you do, you will damage your trust more than the $137 the charge is worth. Drop it.

It is also useful to buy time to let the other party calm down (assuming that your silence does not just pour more gasoline on the fire).

> Example: your dealer just called you this morning mad as a hornet because a unit he needs for a restaurant job next week will not be shipped for a month. You know you have time to probably find a unit in some other distributor's stock or at least to work out a reasonable solution. For now, let your dealer rant and promise to look into it and take care of him.

Finally, it can be helpful when other parties are better equipped (or empowered) to handle the issue!

> Example: your management team has decided to cancel one of your favorite dealers (because he is now very late in his payables and started promoting a competing brand). Your friendship will probably make this a messy meeting, so you should let your sales manager be the bearer of bad news.

The down side of the avoiding strategy comes in the form of the avoider not being able to get his or her ideas on the table. There are usually two ways this is expressed outwardly: the avoider just resigns and walks away from the table (in which case they are viewed as weak and impotent), or they can explode emotionally in anger, attacking the other party in a bluffing routine that is designed to scare them off and thus avoid the dispute. In such a case, others may think they have to walk on eggshells and whisper in your presence!

The Accommodating Strategy

This strategy is called "playing the martyr" because the accommodating party usually ends up not getting what it wants and letting the other party have all it wants. It is a lose/win scenario.

But it does have its good uses too, like all the other strategies. For instance, if you suddenly realize that you are wrong, this is the strategy to use. Apologize to the other party and say, "You were right. I messed up. I am sorry. Let me make it up to you and then we can move on, okay?"

Another good time to use this strategy is when the issue is far more important to the other party than it is to you.

> Example: you have a dealer who wants to use co-op funds to sponsor a stock car at a local race track. This is not clearly against your distributor's co-op policy, but it is not exactly in the spirit of the program either. But the dealer is a die-hard stock car race fan and it means a lot to him. He will probably sponsor a car with or without your co-op, but he would sure like a little help from you. You should probably cave in on this one. You may need to set up a deal where this is a one-time event so it does not become an epidemic with your other dealers, but it is probably best here to let the dealer have his way.

Another use of this strategy is to build up a savings account of favors for use in future disputes.

> Example: the stock car fan dealer gets a win on the car advertising co-op. Later, he balks at using your brand's logo in his newspaper ads, so you can call in the stock car chips. "Mark, I gave in to you on the stock car co-op, right? Do me a favor now—use our logo in your ad this time." If he has any sense of decency, he probably will go along with you. (If he doesn't, you may have a bigger issue than logos in newspaper ads!)

Like the avoiding strategy, accommodating is also a good strategy to use when you clearly cannot win on the issue.

It is also an excellent strategy when preserving the relationship is more important than winning the battle. You probably have dealers you work with who mean more to you than almost any problem that could come up between you. This is especially the case when you have a high value account. Sometimes, you just have to take it on the chin and go on smiling!

Accommodating can also be a good strategy when you want the other party to learn a valuable lesson as they grow. Example: you have been assigned the job of breaking in a new rookie territory manager. He wants to set up a new account and is burning to nuke a competitor on pricing in order to get the account. You know that winning a dealer with a price approach means you will also eventually lose him with a competitor's price approach, but the rookie is deaf to your arguments. You should let him win this argument, set up the new account based on price, and then learn over the next six months just how bad a decision that really is!

The down side of this strategy is that you can start to feel like your views are not important in *any* disagreement.

Conflict Resolution Strategies: The Bottom Line

Steven Sommer presents five conflict resolution styles. You are probably strongest in one or two of them. So what?

By now, you should have seen that each strategy can be useful depending on the circumstances of the disagreement. As a wise human being, *you have the power to* ***choose*** *which strategy you will use to work out* ***any*** *disagreement.*

Did you get that? You can choose any strategy you wish to resolve any disagreement based on the level of the disagreement and the outcome you want. You can be flexible! You can change your style to get what is best for both parties. You can morph!

Let's summarize the five strategies in a matrix like this (next page):

Strategy					
	Forcing	**Collaborating**	**Compromising**	**Avoiding**	**Accommodating**
"Scoring"	Win/lose	Win/win	Lose/lose	Lose/lose	Lose/win
Use when	★ Immediate action needed ★ When the action will not be popular ★ When you know you are right	★ Concerns of both parties too important ★ You want a deep level of buy-in ★ To work through bad feelings	★ Both parties are of equal power ★ Both parties strongly devoted to their positions ★ When speed matters	★ Issue not worth the fight ★ You cannot win ★ A win causes more damage than benefits ★ Let the other party calm down (buy time) ★ Others are better equipped or empowered to handle	★ When you are wrong ★ Issue is far more important to the other party ★ Build up social "IOUs" for use later ★ You cannot win ★ The relationship matters more than a win ★ Let the other person learn a lesson
The Down Side…	★ Are you surrounded by "yes" men? ★ Are you shielded from bad news?	★ Takes a long time ★ Are you perceived as weak or wishy-washy?	★ Rarely leaves both parties feeling good ★ Do you miss the bigger picture? ★ Are you perceived as a "gamer"?	★ You can't get your views on the table? ★ Are people afraid to disagree with you?	★ Do you feel your views don't matter?

Other Conflict Resolution Tips

Sometimes, it helps to get a third party involved. It is no sign of defeat to do so! Often, a third party ("mediator" is the term) can bring a whole new perspective to the issue and help *both* parties see the issue in new light. This alone can often lead to a breakthrough. For example, don't be afraid to ask your sales manager or other management team member to step in when you have a serious dispute with a dealer and you are not sure how to proceed. Chances are, they have faced that problem before and can teach you a lot how to handle such problems in the future.

Early in a dispute, it can be helpful if both parties list all the possible scenarios that can fall out of the dispute, both the good and the bad. This can give both parties a better perspective of the importance of the issues and the consequences of a failure to resolve them.

Both parties in a dispute should stop early on and ask themselves, "What personal damage could come to me as a result of this dispute?" Answering that question often provides the motivation needed to work out a solution!

Recognize that whereas **anger** is often a justified emotion in a dispute, it is rarely directed at you *personally*. It is usually aimed at the situation, which is not tangible or visible. But you *are* both tangible and visible, so you become the lightning rod that draws the dealer's anger. Whatever you do, *don't respond to anger with anger*. Mirror and match, but don't cross the line into irrational behavior. You must learn to bite your tongue sometimes. As Mark Twain once wrote, "When angry, count to four. When very angry, swear."

Don't put too much hope in logic. Mr. Spock of the Starship *Enterprise* would be proud of you, but he was a Vulcan, not a human. He found human emotions strange and difficult to fathom. Conflict is emotional, not logical. Feelings are often stirred up, and strong feelings at that.

When speaking, avoid saying, "You" as much as you can. Say "I" instead. And state early on what you hope the outcome will be to the dispute.

Don't give advice to the other party. Period.

As you work your way through the dispute, it often helps to pause once in a while and check on where you agree and where you still disagree. Seeing progress can often help motivate both parties to press on to a workable solution.

Remember that a long and costly conflict is usually the result of both parties holding deep and strong belief systems that clash. Belief systems are difficult to change. It takes a titanic effort to change your own belief system, let alone that of someone else! Don't try it. Instead, try to understand their belief system so you can get a clue to how they see the conflict threatening *them*. Look for a workaround. Learn emotional Tae-Kwan-Do.

And remember the words of that famous bard and balladeer, Kenny Rogers: "You've got to know when to hold 'em, know when to fold 'em." If either party has a better solution *outside* the relationship, the relationship will probably dissolve, or at least be seriously wounded. If it comes to that, grant each other the right to go in different directions and change the relationship.

Review Questions for Chapter 23

1. The most important first step in resolving a dispute is to

A) lay your cards on the table so you can be sure your views are considered

B) find out what the other party wants

C) find out why the other party wants what it wants

D) choose a strategy that will give you a win

E) none of the above

Answer: ________

2. Sometimes ____________ a dispute can lead to a breakthrough.

A) ignoring

B) reframing

C) paraphrasing

D) redefining

E) none of the above

Answer: ________

3. When you know you are right and the issue is important, the best conflict resolution strategy is

A) forcing

B) collaborating

C) compromising

D) avoiding

E) accommodating

Answer: ________

4. When you are clearly wrong, the best resolution strategy is

A) forcing

B) collaborating

C) compromising

D) avoiding

E) accommodating

Answer: ________

5. Both you and your dealer feel strongly about your respective positions, and time is not critical. What is the best strategy to adopt?

A) forcing

B) collaborating

C) compromising

D) avoiding

E) accommodating

Answer: ________

6. For the upcoming dealer meeting, you think that blue paper tablecloths would work best, but Sharon, the office manager, wants red cloths. She is adamant about it, and to you it doesn't matter all that much. Which conflict resolution style would be best here? (Did I mention that Sharon is also the boss's daughter?)

A) forcing

B) collaborating

C) compromising

D) avoiding

E) accommodating

Answer: ________

7. One of your greatest tools for conflict resolution is

A) knowledge of the five resolution modes

B) the ability to flex your mode to the one that best fits the situation

C) the forcing mode

D) anger

E) use of a mediator

Answer: ________

Chapter 24: Doing a Good Show

A major part of being a Tier One territory manager is knowing how to do a superb presentation. Yet surprisingly few territory managers are ever taught how to do a good presentation. (This is not helped by the fact that the number one fear among Americans is that of public speaking!) Whether you are asked to speak as part of an annual dealer meeting or you are making a presentation to an account, you need to know how to communicate ideas clearly and effectively.

In this chapter, you will learn some of the skills that make for a powerful and effective presenter. After all, if the client does not listen to your presentation, what have you done to help him or her?

Good Selling Starts With Great Communication

Selling is really not much more than good communication—describing the course of action you want your customer to take in such a way that they want to take that course of action. To be sure, there are other elements too—like determining customer needs and aligning your value cluster to the customer's needs—but the whole thing succeeds or fails with good communication.

What you learned in Chapter 22 on Deep Communication you must use every day.

This chapter will focus on some tips to help you practically execute good deep communication on sales calls.

Match Your Show to the Client's Sensory Framework

If you are presenting to one or two people, this is not very difficult, once you decode whether they are visuals, auditories, or kinesthetics. But you will have to be on your toes if the two or three you are addressing are of different sensory channels.

For instance, what if you are speaking to a two-man partnership and one partner is visual while the other is kinesthetic? How can you make sure you address each in his comfort zone? By saying the same thing twice in different ways. The visual partner will hear your visual presentation and grasp it while the kinesthetic partner does not; then, when you say the same thing in the kinesthetic's frame of reference, he'll get it while the visual does not comprehend what just happened. (It is similar to how an AM radio won't pick up FM signals, and an FM radio won't play the AM stations.) Here is an example:

> SPEAKING TO THE VISUAL: "Tom, once you see the results of this pre-season promotion, I think you'll be glad you signed on."

> SPEAKING TO THE KINESTHETIC: "And Gary, when you start putting in all those extra jobs that came in from these new leads, you're going to be bone tired—and happy as a clam at high tide!"

While speaking to Tom, Gary won't pick up very much on the part about seeing the results of a promotion, but the word "glad" will strike a note in his heart. Then, while speaking to Gary, Tom probably won't connect with the bone-tired implication or the happy clam analogy. The funny thing is, even though you said the same basic thing twice—how good it will be for these partners to participate in the pre-season promotion this year—each will hear it stated only once (in *his* preferred sensory channel!).

But when speaking to a larger group (or to the audience at a dealer meeting) it is difficult to speak so personally and yet use all three channels with every major point you wish to make. Your safest bet is to use as powerful and flexible phraseology as possible that makes each major point in all three sensory channels. That way, everyone in the audience will understand your points in their own frame of reference.

For instance, this is one way you might convey how a new safety feature on an upgraded furnace might be stated in a dealer meeting:

> As you can see from this slide [appeal to the visuals in the group], moving the safety switch from where it was to here and going to the new XYZ safety instead of the older MNO safety makes it easier to service. Your service techs will just love how easy it will be to get to and how simple it will be to change out—it will almost change itself (but not quite!) [kinesthetic reference]. That will mean fewer complaints from the service techs about working on the new furnaces. It is just one more detail the factory has designed into this unit to make it the most efficient, safest, and reliable in the business [soft appeals to the auditories in the group through their detail side].

If you listen carefully to great speeches, you will notice how the speaker has a way of weaving all three sensory modes into the speech at each key point. Most speakers do this instinctively, not knowing that in so doing, they were going to address the greatest number of people possible. Therefore, the people would follow and do what they were being asked to do—making the speaker a leader with a following (which is the only true definition of leader that I know).

Fear of Speaking

Surveys over the last fifty years have shown that the fear of public speaking is always either first or second in the minds of most people, often ranking even higher than the fear of death! That's a pretty powerful fear to have to lug around!

Most people who have never spoken much in public are terrified of the idea of doing it and because of that, often do poorly. They stumble over their words, botch their delivery, miss their timing, or fail to convey the right amount of emotional punch in their messages.

The reason that so many people do poorly at public speaking is that they have the wrong reaction to the crowd!

There was a time when I was afraid to speak in front of people, but now I do it for a living and the size of the crowd does not matter. What did I do to get over my fear of speaking?

First, it helped me to *reframe the crowd*. By this, I mean get over the notion that they are a hostile lynching party just waiting for me to slip up so they can string me up from the nearest tree. In this regard, I found a small book by Ron Hoff to be of immense value. The book is titled *I Can See You Naked.*[29] It has a funny title but it conveys a wealth of ideas on how to overcome

29 Published by Andrews and McNeel; Kansas City, MO and New York, NY. ISBN 0-8362-7946-8

a fear of speaking before a group. I won't spill all of Ron's beans here—for that, you should get a copy of the book for yourself. But a few of his gems include focusing on *preparation* (a big reason so many people clam up before groups; they just aren't prepared well enough), the importance of the first ninety seconds, how to master your nerves, ramping up the energy level (but not too much), understanding your audience, and handling questions.

One of the things I really like about Hoff's approach is how he describes a presentation. In his words, "A speech [is] a free-wheeling **cannon**; it creates lots of smoke! [It] explodes a subject. It takes a subject of some interest and expands it. It is essentially an inside/out operation. A presentation [is] a **torpedo** that speeds precisely to its mark. [It] starts narrowly and gets sharper. It is essentially an outside/in operation."

Oh, I like that! That's why a good presentation tells the audience within ninety seconds of starting why the speaker is qualified to speak on the subject and how what he or she has to say will make their lives better. You do that in the first ninety seconds, and you'll have few problems with public speaking!

That, and imagining that your audience is naked. (That will conjure up some funny reactions in some cases, and some you'll need to get control of.)

Another mistake made by people who clam up is when they go inside their heads once they trip up. If you have ever flubbed a speaking assignment, you probably did something like this inside your head: "Oh, great! Now what do I do? I just blew it wide open out the kazoo this time! Hoo boy, where is there a hole I can crawl into?" And all this time I can bet where your eyes were pointed—up, toward the ceiling, as if you were looking for God to come down and rescue you.

Wrong place to put the eyes!

Remember what you learned in Chapter 22 (Deep Communication) about the eye accessing cues and where your eyes go during speech spooling? Looking up does you no good because the only things that are up are visual cues (both recalled and invented), and at that moment, your problem is not visual—it is verbal. When you need to re-cue the speech spooler, where *should* your eyes go? *Down and to your left*. That's where we have our normal eye position for internal dialog.

One of my pet peeves as a facilitator in territory manager training is when I give a group an assignment to prepare a presentation to the class. (It can be a product presentation, a presentation about a marketing program, or almost anything else a territory manager might be called upon to address in a meeting.) Invariably, at least one territory manager in that class will come back the next day to make his or her presentation and totally botch it because *they were not prepared.* Taking the time to thoroughly prepare yourself for a presentation shows you care and conveys to the audience the idea that you value them and their time. Preparation involves several steps (these are not all of them, but these are the basics):

- Knowing the subject matter (frontwards, backwards, upside-down, downside-up, inside-out, outside-in)
- Knowing how to relate that subject matter to the needs of the audience
- Knowing what sorts of aids to use (visuals, samples, drawings, charts, data, sound clips, etc.)

Any time you prepare a presentation and omit one of those three bullets, your presentation gun is not fully loaded.

This may sound tough, but if you can do it, you'll be a more powerful presenter for it—ditch the cue cards. A lot of speakers use cue cards (3x5 or 4x6 note cards with their comments on them) to help them make the presentation. You know what? It shows! (And sounds like it.) Instead, *learn your material so well that you can give it without note cards!* Your audience will love you for it and you'll feel better for having done it that way.

Another tip for preparing a presentation: *boil down the words to the bare essentials.* Too many presentations are too long and far too wordy. They are great for insomnia, but not for motivating people to take action. History's great orators (ranging from the Greek philosophers like Demosthenes[30] to modern day orators like Winston Churchill, Ronald Reagan and Billy Graham) tell us consistently that the greatest challenge they have in preparing a presentation is to boil down the words to as few as possible and the delivery to be as terse and potent as possible. Anyone can write a large number of words on paper; it takes inspiration to select the 20% best of those words and throw out the rest!

30 A countryman of Demosthenes, a man named Pericles, is said to have stated, "When Pericles speaks, the people say, 'How well he speaks.' But when Demosthenes speaks, the people say, 'Let us march!'"

What Aids to Use?

When giving a presentation, what kind of presentation aids should you use? It depends on the content of your message and the audience.

What sorts of aids can be used in a presentation? Here is a partial list:

- None at all (it's just you and the audience, baby)
- Flip chart
- Projection screen and projector (whether using slides or computer presentation programs like PowerPoint)
- Handouts
- Samples
- Models
- Charts
- Sound clips
- Video clips
- Dramatization (aka, live action, skits, mini-dramas)

Which of these aids is best for addressing the various sensory channels you learned about in Chapter 22 (Deep Communication)? This matrix sums it up:

Type of Aid	Visuals	Auditories	Kinesthetics
None	Vary your delivery and vocabulary		
Flip chart	Yes!	Sometimes	Usually not
Projection	Yes!	Usually	Usually
Handouts	Yes, if visual	Yes, if auditory	Yes
Samples	Sometimes	Usually not	Yes!
Models	Usually	Sometimes	Yes!!
Charts	Sometimes	Yes!	Usually not
Sound Clips	Sometimes	Yes!!	Sometimes
Video Clips	Yes!	Sometimes	Sometimes
Dramatization	Yes!	Yes!	Yes!

I find it interesting that Dramatization gets high scores across the chart, which is why so many people find plays, musicals, and movies so absorbing. If you can find a way to dramatize your concept, do it!

So which aid (or aids) should you use in your presentation? *As many as you need to convey your idea as clearly as possible.* For certain, you want to select aids that address all three sensory channels, and you will probably want to balance the mix to roughly reflect the makeup of your group. (If you don't know the makeup of your group, you can assume the average of 60% visuals, 20% auditories, and 20% kinesthetics. Some groups, however, would have significant changes from this distribution—for example, a convention of care givers might score more heavily in the kinesthetic area. If possible, do your homework before speaking.)

Any visual aids you use must be large enough to be easily readable from any seat in the house. If you are in a dealer's office making a presentation, this usually means any size at all would do. But if you are speaking before a larger group in a hotel ballroom or a large training center, size does matter. For really large rooms, you are probably better off putting the visual aids into a slide presentation and foregoing charts on an easel.

Likewise, if using a projection screen, use one that is sized correctly for the room you will be using! This guide should help you:

Room Depth	Screen Width
15'	4'
20'	5'
25'	6'
30'	8'
40'	10'

And so on as the room depth increases. (Use the general ratio of one foot of width for each four feet of room depth.)

Be careful when using tables of data. The font should be large enough to be readable from any point in the room, so again, in a large setting, a chart on an easel is a bad idea. Put it into your slide show.

Which brings me to an area that really irks me…

Where is the Power in PowerPoint?

Now before you call Microsoft and tip off their attorneys that I am about to libel them, hold off. I love PowerPoint. I use it every week and think it is about the greatest tool for presenters since the walls of the cave.

But I also find it irksome because so many gadgets are built into it and so many presenters have no idea how to properly use those gadgets. *Throwing together some pictures and charts in PowerPoint does not make it a good presentation*, even if you use Slide Animations, Slide Transitions, Animated Text, video and audio clips, and more.

There are a few basics I think you should keep in mind as you work with PowerPoint. (If you use prepared PowerPoint presentations from your manufacturer, you will find every one of these basics violated—because the people who prepare the PowerPoint shows don't understand how the brain learns.)

The Fonts of Life

First, let's talk **fonts**. No more than three different fonts per slide. I personally recommend you keep it to two or better yet, one. I have seen slides with as many as *seven* different fonts! Argghhhhh!

Generally, the cleaner the font, the better. Fonts like **Times New Roman** are generally excellent for printed material. But research reveals that in a large format like a projection screen, such a font can be tiring to read. The reason has to do with the serifs at the ends of the letters (those little lines at the bottom of an "l" or those little barbs at the top of a "T".) A *non-serif font* (like **Arial**, **Calibri**, and others, most of which come with Microsoft Office) are easier on the eye when projected onto a large screen.

Make the fonts *large enough* to be seen from any seat in the house. If in doubt, oversize the font!

PowerPoint comes with a good library of *slide backgrounds*, some of which are white or light in color and others which are dark. On the light backgrounds, the letters are dark (black, brown, blue, etc.) and on the dark backgrounds, they are light (white, yellow, tan, etc.). Which should you use?

It depends on the lighting levels in the room. If you are going to be doing a long presentation in a room with moderate to bright lighting (such as a training center or hotel ballroom), it is usually best to use the light backgrounds with dark fonts. This way, the eye is reading what to the brain looks like a huge sheet of paper. And we learned as kids that words should be printed on white or light colored paper, right? Using the dark backgrounds with light fonts in a well-lit room is very tiring on the eye and confuses the brain—words should be on paper, not the night sky!

If the room is dark, a dark background is usually fine (it causes less contrast for the eye, which means it is less tiring), but not if you have a great deal of text to show. Again, reading light text on a dark background is very tiring. In a dark room, you are probably better off using at least a light color background and dark fonts. If your presentation is mostly made up of images, though, and contains little text, use the dark background to your heart's content.

Don't Use Too Many Bullets!

During the American Civil War, the Union Army had available a new type of rifle—the rapid-fire repeater (models designed by Colt, Spencer or Henry). Such weapons gave a company (100 men) the firepower of 500 or more who were using muzzle-loading muskets. The response from the Union generals when asked if they wanted such wonder weapons for their men was "No! They'll fire too many bullets, use up too much ammunition!"

PowerPoint also allows you to create bullet points with a mouse click. But unlike the Union generals in the Civil War, you *can* actually fire too many bullets with PowerPoint! I suggest you use no more than *five bullet points per slide* and less if possible! If you need more bullet points than that, break up the subject into smaller pieces and address it with more slides.

You can also nest bullet points over three levels deep in PowerPoint. And if you do, your bullet points aren't bullet points—they are machine gun fire… from a Gatling Gun. As a general rule, bullet points should never be nested more than two deep, like this:

- Bullet point 1
- Bullet sub-point 1
- Bullet point 2

If you have to go to a third nesting level (or more), you need to break up your subject matter into smaller steps.

Bullet points should *summarize* the topic, not display your script word for word! How many times have you seen a PowerPoint show in which the bullet points (nine to a slide!) were complete sentences (with fonts too small to see beyond the third row)? Do you remember what I said about preparation? Here is where it pays off! A bullet list on a slide should only contain one word, or at most a few words. They are there to (a) remind *you* what to say, and (b) help your audience remember the *main points* you want them to remember.

Brevity is the Soul of Wit

Whether you use bullet points or not on a slide, your slide should contain as few words as possible. As a general rule, I like to see slides average seven words or less. (This means some slides will only contain two or three words or none at all, while others will contain twelve or fifteen, but the overall average should work out to seven or so.) Again, the slide is not there to be the script you read from (spare us from such dull PowerPoint shows!), but to *remind you of the points* you want to make and help your audience grasp the essentials.

If you try to keep your presentation limited to *one key idea per slide*, you should be able to use only a few words to convey the point.

Those Gosh-Awful Transitions and Sparklies!

I used to work for a distributor in Kansas City. We had a sales manager named Cass Cassing. Cass was a brilliant man, well ahead of his time. (For example, he had one of the first home computers in the area—they weren't even called PC's yet! And he figured out how to make it do things that are just now being done with today's powerful software.) He was also a fascinating presenter and talented photographer. He would often put together a short presentation to be given at a dealer meeting, a sales meeting, or local meetings of ASHRAE, using slides he had shot as background images while he spoke. (We call such images eye candy today.) Cass called his presentations "sparklers," and they really were! Like kids on the Fourth of July playing with sparklers, his audience would be spellbound and rapt, and on an emotional high when Cass got done.

PowerPoint gives you a massive library of sparklies (not sparklers—there is a *huge* difference!), and much of it should be banned from use on Earth.

You have probably been sentenced to endure a PowerPoint presentation by a sales person or manager who had to have every slide transition be one of those animated things, like the one where the words fly in from the top or bottom (or left or right, or who cares?), and the one where the slide looks like it is going down the drain when the speaker advances to the next slide (a little eddy forms and the text and graphics get sucked down the drain—like the speaker should do).

Those little creative sparklies can be a form of rescue when you are enduring a really bad presentation—at least your eyes get some fun! But as a general rule, they get in the way of conveying good information.

Slide transitions should be subtle and simple. And fast. My favorite slide transition is the "fade smoothly" set to fast speed. And I rarely use text animations (unless they are of the fade-in fast type—what I call a slide "build" where a bullet list is built one bullet at a time).

The PowerPoint sparklies probably have some value when creating a product presentation to run on automatic mode in a trade show booth. Here, you want to catch the attention of people walking by, and some of those sparklies do a great job of that. But please—not for a training program!

The same can be said for *text animation* (such as having little lights flash around the text like an old movie marquee sign). Text animations, if used at all, should be simple. One of the most effective I ever saw was done by a trainer who wanted to be sure a key word on his slide was remembered, so as he spoke his script, this word throbbed and pulsed on the screen by getting bigger and smaller, bigger and smaller, and changing color from black to red and back.

Also, be careful how you use *shadowing* with PowerPoint. The program gives you an awesome library of shadow palettes from which to select, but some shadow effects (especially with text) can make it hard to read the text—the text looks more like it was printed twice with a slight offset between printings! *Subtle shadows* are best, if used at all on text.

Don't Grate on the Ears

PowerPoint lets you embed audio clips in any slide and lets you dictate whether they play automatically while the slide is projected, or whether you must click an icon on the slide to play the clip. There is a fairly beefy library of audio clips in PowerPoint (ranging from a set of applause clips to bells, whistles, explosions, gun shots, and so on). You can also import an infinite number of audio clips from the internet and from CDs (but be careful you don't violate any copyright laws).

I endured a PowerPoint show one time where the presenter had to put a sound clip on every slide. I got so tired of ricochets and cannon shots and applause and bugles, I almost got up and left the room!

What goes for the other tips I've given about using PowerPoint goes here too: moderation! Use a sound clip if you wish, but try to make it fit the point you are making. A noise just for the sake of noise is an irritation, not a re-enforcer for an idea.

Too Much Eye Candy Rots the Brain

You heard it from your dentist when you were a child: don't eat too many sweets. You will get tooth decay if you do.

The same thing can be said for the use of visual graphics and videos in PowerPoint too. Again, the program gives you the ability to select from a large library of clips (both stationary and moving), and you can import any image or video you can download (assuming you have the rights to use it in a PowerPoint program). But that doesn't mean you *should* use them.

I have seen PowerPoint shows where every slide had some sort of picture or cartoon on it, whether it related to the theme or not. I call such stuff eye candy because it is fascinating to view, but causes brain decay.

Graphics (stills or movies) should be used with *moderation* too. I also suggest that any graphic you use should have some *thematic relationship* to the concept you are conveying.

For instance, if you are talking about making more money by using a particular marketing program, a small graphic of money, or a dollar sign, or a piggy bank might be fine in your presentation. But don't overdo it.

I have seen times when a presenter used a graphic *just to fill up slide space*. The graphic had no purpose other than soaking up some of the "white space" on the slide. Look, it is okay for a slide to have white space on it! In fact, I'd prefer a slide with only a few words of text and lots of white space to one with the wrong graphic art stuck on it like a bloody bandage.

Now if you are using a graphic as part of the concept development—say, you are showing a picture of a new condensing unit as part of a new product roll-out program—then the picture is necessary and vital. Try to use the *best picture available*—the right size, good color balance, good lighting, crisp resolution, etc. Often you will have no control over this (especially if using graphic images provided by the factory), but you can at least avoid dumb mistakes like using a picture that is too dark or out of focus. (What may look good as a small image in a previewer may look awful when blown up to fill a 12'x 18' screen.)

If you are going to show a close-up of a new unit and you want to draw attention to some component on the slide, use the PowerPoint shapes tool and draw a circle around it or have an arrow point to it. Make it easy for your audience to see what you are talking about.

You Aren't Darth Vader—Use Your Laser Saber With Care!

Too many times I have seen a person make a PowerPoint presentation and use a laser pointer improperly. I don't have a problem with using a laser pointer. I use one myself.

But I *do* have a problem with using a laser pointer to have a little red ball bounce across the screen (like one of those old sing-along movies) while the presenter reads the text word for word, or using the laser to punch the bullet as the speaker addresses it. There are times when I wish I could sneak up to the screen and place a small mirror on it so the laser bounces back into the eyes of the presenter and blinds them (at least temporarily).

Use a laser only to *point out a single word, graphic or component.* Don't draw with it or have it bob all over the screen like a ping pong ball in a hurricane.

The same can be said for PowerPoint's awesome on-screen presentation tools, like the ballpoint pen, felt tip pen, or highlighter. These can be useful tools to emphasize a concept, but done too much and they become distracting. Use them with caution.

And finally, learn how to use PowerPoint's B key during a presentation. If you have never done it before, pressing the B key on the keyboard causes the screen to go blank (black), and pressing B a second time causes it to come back. Likewise pressing W makes the screen all white, and pressing W again brings the show back on.

There is much more that can be said about the power and use of PowerPoint, but I have covered the points I think are most relevant for you as it applies to becoming a good presenter. If you want to learn more, get a good book on PowerPoint or enroll in a course on the program at a local training center or college.

Review Questions for Chapter 24

1. Boris is one of your contractors and is visual in sensory input. Which of the following phrases best explains to him a new product feature?

    A) Let me describe how this new gizmo works.

    B) Here, hold this gizmo in your hands and check it out.

    C) See this little gizmo in this picture? That's the new fusion switch.

    D) Any of the above

    E) None of the above

    Answer: ________

2. If you must address several people at once and have an important point to convey, your best bet is to

    A) Say it so the boss gets it and to heck with anyone else.

    B) Find a way to say it in all three sensory channels and say it three ways.

    C) Try to pick the slowest person in the audience and use his or her reactions to gauge your delivery.

    D) Say it at least three times.

    E) None of the above.

    Answer: ________

3. Seeing the audience as a bunch of cabbages in a garden is one way of…

    A) reframing the audience

    B) showing disrespect to them

    C) focusing on your presentation

    D) all of the above

    E) none of the above

    Answer: ________

4. Knowing the subject matter intimately, knowing your audience well, and selecting the best presentation aids are all steps in

A) using PowerPoint effectively

B) getting over your fears of speaking

C) preparation

D) all of the above

E) none of the above

Answer: ________

5. A room that is eighty feet long should have a projection screen that is about how many feet wide?

A) 25

B) 20

C) 16

D) 12

E) 8

Answer: ________

6. Which slide violates the fewest rules for a good presentation?

Slide A

- Mary had a little lamb
- SHE ALSO HAD SOME BEEF
- SHE THEN HAD CRAB CAKES
- She also had a plate of sushi
- She washed it down with a pint of Guinness
- Mar y got ver y sick

Slide B

- Jack be nimble...
- ... Quick...
- ... Candle stick

Slide C

- Mistress Mary
- Contrary
- Garden
- Cockle Shells
- Rows

Slide D

- Hey diddle diddle...
- The cat and the fiddle
- The dish ran away with the spoon
- The cow jumped over the moon!
- The little dog laughed
- To see such sport,
- And the dish ran away with the spoon.

Slide E

- Ring around the rosie
  - A pocket full of posey
    - Ashes to ashes
      - We all fall down

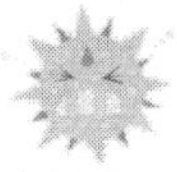

- Describes the Black Death of the 1400's

Answer: ________

7. The best word on using PowerPoint's vast library of special effects is

   A) The more the merrier!

   B) Avoid them like the Plague!

   C) Moderation.

   D) None of the above.

   Answer: ________

8. To suddenly go to a black screen during a PowerPoint presentation, you can press which key on the keyboard?

   A) Esc

   B) Q

   C) D

   D) B

   E) Backspace

   Answer: ________

Chapter 25: Prudent Etiquette

An idiot walks right along the edge of a cliff, every step possibly his last if his foot were to slip. A prudent person draws a line three feet from the edge of the cliff and stays on his side of the line. If his foot slips, he won't go over the cliff.

Likewise, there are certain things that a Tier One territory manager can (and should) do with regards to being a friend with his clients, and things that should not be done. This chapter will consider some of the do's and don'ts of being a Tier One territory manager.

Nothing More Than Common Courtesy

Most of good dealer relations etiquette is nothing more than good old-fashioned common courtesy. The trouble with that statement is today is that common courtesy is neither common nor very courteous!

I am not talking about a Miss Manners crash course here or a Dear Abby approach to life. But I am talking about what was once considered to be basic and valuable human relationship skills.

First, until you know a dealer well, I suggest you *use the title "Mister" or "Miss."* For example, call the dealer Mr. Smith or Mr. Wilson, or Mrs. Sandusky, or Miss Winters, rather than Bill, John, Veronica or Susan. If the dealer says to you, "Hey, just call me Bill," then go ahead and use their first name. Also, after getting to know the dealer well, you can say, "Mr. Smith, would you mind if I called you 'Bill?'" If Bill does not object, start using the first name. It's a small point, but using the title Mister or Miss conveys great respect to the dealer, and as the old song says, "R-E-S-P-E-C-T, find out what it means to me!" To most people, it generates a positive and pleasing aura.

You have two ears and one mouth on your head. Learn to use them in that proportion! The problem I have observed over and over is that most sales people talk way too much! They even talk *over* the dealer when he or she is trying to speak! I don't care how much the dealer walks all over your conversation as you speak. You don't do it to them. Let the dealer finish his or her statement before you address it. And while they are speaking, listen with all your being. Stay tuned in, stay alert, and stay in the flow of the moment. If you're thinking, "How am I going to counter THIS statement?" you won't get it. You'll be in left field all during the call.

Keep your appointments. For that matter, be sure to be in the top 10% of territory managers who *do* make appointments. If you are running late, call ahead and say so. Then ask if being late will be a problem or should you reschedule your call?

Leave your cell phone "off" or set to vibrate only on a sales call. Don't let it ring during your sales call. The appointment with your dealer should occupy 110% of your attention, and if your cell phone is going off during the call, you cannot devote 110% of your attention to the dealer. (Frankly, I don't think you should even have it set to vibrate, rather leave it in your car. However, I am not likely to win that one with the new wired and connected generation. You stay wired and connected during a sales call at your own peril!)

Keep your promises. If you tell the dealer you will get some information he or she requests, get it and get it in the time frame you promised. If you think it will take a lot of work and time to get the answer, promise long and deliver short. Always try to beat the date for which you promised an answer.

Play the hand you are dealt. This means that you learn to roll with the punches. For instance, if you make a mistake and order the wrong unit for a job for your dealer and he later tells you that the wrong unit showed up on the job, admit it. Tell him you screwed up but that you will make it right.

Buy meals on odd days; have your dealer treat on even days. This way, you build a partnership with your dealer and you share in the costs of entertainment. Any territory manager who allows meals and entertainment to be a one-way street is being set up to be the patsy. (As Warren Buffet says, "If you've been in the game for thirty minutes and don't know who the patsy is, you're the patsy.")

Don't drink alcohol on the job, even if your dealer does. This includes at breakfast or lunch.

(A drink with dinner is, though, acceptable.) It also includes calls at the dealer's office. (If the dealer offers you a drink at the end of the day, and all your business has been conducted, then it is your call whether or not to share a drink. Consider your drive home!) And if you accompany your dealers on an incentive trip, watch your alcohol consumption while with them. Some people can get very abusive and rude when they drink too much, and others can make stupid statements or get themselves into embarrassing predicaments when lubricated by too much liquor. I have no problem with a territory manager drinking with his or her dealers on an incentive trip, but I do have a problem when the drinking leads a territory manager to do stupid things.

Don't get romantically involved with anyone in the dealer's employment, especially his or her spouse. Don't get involved with the receptionist, or the service manager, or any other employee or family member (including available sons or daughters, nieces, nephews, and illegitimate offspring). The potential problems such relationships can generate far outweigh any advantages that may accrue to your sales career.

Always use the deep communication skills you learned in Chapter 22. Give your dealer all your attention; pay attention to his or her eye movements; listen to their language; unpack their thinking and decision strategies and speak to them within their wiring framework.

Always make sure your dealers come first. Let them go first in line. Let them get their plates filled at a banquet first. Let them eat first at a training class.

Never repeat gossip (or start it) about a dealer. I guarantee you; it will get back to your dealer. If you start a rumor, you should be drummed out of the territory manager corps in shame! But if you repeat a rumor, whether true or not, you are just as guilty. Don't do it. It's not worth the possible loss of business, trust, and friendship.

Always dress in a way that respects your clients. This means that you will normally dress one level above that of your client. If your dealer wears blue jeans and tee shirts, you should wear good casual slacks and a golf shirt. If he wears Dockers and a knit shirt, you should wear at least the same if not dress slacks and a nice knit shirt or cotton shirt. If he wears a jacket and slacks, you should do the same; and if he wears a tie, you wear one too. By dressing at or slightly above his dress level, you say to him that you respect him and want to look your best and most professional in front of him.

If you are a female, dress appropriately as well. This means neat and attractive, but not seductive. Halter tops are out, as are tank tops. Skin-tight pants are probably not a good idea either. I don't think it is a good idea for a female TM to ever wear shorts on a business call. (A casual outing, like a golf outing, is a different matter.)

Review Questions for Chapter 25

1. It's your first visit with a prospective dealer. Early on, he tells you his name is Ron Defflinger. What should you do?

A) call him Ron

B) call him Mr. Defflinger

C) ask him how he would like to be addressed

D) call him "Skeeter" and hope for the best

Answer: ________

2. You are in the middle of a sales call to one of your best dealers when your cell phone goes off. What should you do?

A) look at the caller ID and route the call to voice mail

B) take the call

C) leave the room then take the call

D) route the call to voice mail and apologize for having left the

phone on

Answer: ________

3. One of your contractors is installing a 50 ton rooftop unit on a school. You learned this morning that the truck carrying the unit was involved in an accident en route and the rooftop unit was totaled. The factory lead time is 6 weeks, too long for this job. You find a unit in stock at a distributorship 1,400 miles away, but you'll have to pay 20% more for it than the factory quoted you for the job plus you'll have to pay about $2,000 in freight. What should you do?

A) tell the dealer the unit will not be here for six more weeks and that he'll just have to live with it

B) tell the dealer the bad news and offer to bring in the unit from the other distributor and charge him what you quoted, arguing with the factory and its insurance company for the difference in costs

C) get the other unit and pass the costs on to the dealer

D) do "C" but give the dealer a free pair of seats on the next incentive trip

Answer: ________

4. You stop at a relatively new dealer for a 2:30 p.m. appointment. His day is mostly done

now so he opens his desk drawer and brings out a bottle of bourbon and two glasses. He offers you a glass. What should you do?

A) take him up on his offer

B) say you prefer Scotch

C) ask him if he has a soft drink you could have

D) tell him you're a teetotaler

Answer: ________

5. While on a visit to one of your mid-size dealers, he says to you, "Hey, I heard the other day that Jones is not paying his bills on time. Have you heard anything about that?" Jones is a good dealer in a town twenty-five miles away. What should you do?

A) say that you are not aware of it but that it does not have any bearing on your present sales call

B) get all the details you can and pass them to your credit manager

C) say you heard of it but thought it wasn't true

D) just ignore it

Answer: ________

Always Do the Right Thing

On one job, I had to order eighteen above-ceiling fan coil units for a commercial project. These particular units had to have hot-water reheat coils on the outlet end for humidity control, and the brand I sold at that time had a twenty-seven digit model number. There were two alphabetic characters in the model number (roughly positions eighteen and nineteen) which could be ordered as NO or ON. One code said it had a reheat coil. The other said it did not.

One day, I got a call from the contractor at the job site. He said, "Harshaw, weren't these boxes supposed to have reheat coils on them?" I said they were. He said they did not have them. I said I'd check into it and get back to him by the middle of the afternoon.

I got the job folder out and sure enough, I had transposed the NO and ON codes, and ordered the boxes without the coils. I called the manufacturer and asked how long it would take to get the coils made and shipped. They said eighteen weeks! Not acceptable! I called a coil manufacturer and they could have them on the job site within seven days. I gave them the purchase order and called the contractor back. I asked him to meet me on the job site next morning so we could discuss how he would field install the coils and what that would cost.

I prepared a concession letter with the dollar amounts as blank lines and asked our field service engineer what I should expect in terms of labor and parts to do the field conversions. I met with the contractor as planned and told him I had ordered the units the wrong way and that coils were already being built and would be here by next week. "How much," I asked him, "would it take for you in terms of labor and materials to install these eighteen coils?" He did some scratching on a legal pad and after twenty minutes told me his estimate. It was in line with what my field engineer had suggested, so I got the concession letter out and filled in the dollar blank, stating that I would issue a credit for that amount when the job was done and paid for, and gave him a copy of the letter. He read it and looked at me in disbelief. He said, "You'd really do that?" Sure, I replied, it was my mistake, not his. I owed it to him. It cost me thousands in gross margin dollars (and hundreds in commissions).

But in the long run, it paid off. On my next three negotiated jobs with this contractor, he got no other prices and did not care too much what I asked for my equipment. He knew that if it was not right, I'd be there to take care of him.

Take One for the Team

I recall a time when my wife and I were flying with a group of dealers to our annual dealer incentive trip. It was a long flight and they served dinner on the plane. Before the flight attendants started serving us, I overhead one say to the other, "I think we're going to be a couple short!" (The flight was fully booked and I suppose the caterer miscounted the meals they loaded before take-off.) I got out of my seat and approached the two flight attendants and said in a low voice, "Ladies, I don't mean to pry here, but I just overheard one of you say you may be two meals short?"

They nervously nodded their heads. I said, "Well, this flight is full of our company's good customers, so if you don't mind, please serve my wife and I last—we're in 16C and 16D. If we don't get any meal, that's okay with me. Just be sure our dealers get service, okay?" They smiled and nodded.

Sure enough, they were two meals short, so my wife and I did not get a meal. The dealers noticed it and offered to share their meals with us, but we said that was not necessary.

It was going great until the two flight attendants brought my wife and I meals of filet mignon served on real plates (the dealers were having chicken served on plastic trays). They said they were the crew meals and the captain and first officer agreed to let my wife and I have their meals to thank us for our willingness to help out. The looks of concern quickly turned to playful teasing about privilege!

Chapter 26: Expense Reports and Their ROI

Most territory managers have expense accounts. They are used to reclaim expenses incurred while conducting the business of the distributor. They can include such things as fuel, cell phones, pagers, and client entertainment.

Whereas it is impossible to defray some expenses, others are up to the territory manager to a large extent, and so should be analyzed with a view toward how much return the territory manager can expect to receive for the expense laid out.

It's the Paperwork, Dangit!

Like the cartoon of a kid on the toilet says, "The job isn't over until the paperwork is done."

That's true of your sales job too; whether it is completing an order form, a job quote, a sales call report, or your expense report.

Your expense report is a vital source document to your company's accounting department. Many companies track ratios involving sales expense (such as sales expense as a percentage of sales, or sales expense as a factor in the general return on investment—ROI—ratios). Your prompt and thorough completion of expense reports not only helps you get reimbursed for your out-of-pocket expenses faster—it also helps your company fine tune its asset management.

Expense reports are not fun things for most territory managers. Most territory managers are not energized by details and paperwork, and expense reports are big on both counts. Nonetheless, *never let your expense reports get more than a week out of date.* If you let them pile up, you will get so buried that by the time you do get them filled out and turned in, you will have been running off your own savings far too long, and your management team will have inaccurate measures to work with.

Some companies actually still use paper expense report forms or pads. Some use an Excel spreadsheet in lieu of the pad form. The advantage is that the Excel worksheet does all the math (mileage numbers and rates, meals, hotels, etc.) so there is less of a chance for errors. It is also much easier to read than the hen scratch writing some TMs have! Another electronic option is commercially-available sales management software.

You Are a Business Profit (or Loss) Center

One of the problems with traditional expense report systems is that it tends to encourage territory managers to think about their roles in terms of a company-insured cost cover. To me, that approach works against top tier territory management.

The most *progressive* distributors I know today do not use expense reports at all! Instead, they pay their territory managers a very handsome paycheck (based on commissions) and tell their territory managers, "We are not going to give you an expense report. Instead, we're going to pay you extremely well to sell. If you need to use your car to make that kind of money—or take your dealer to lunch—or buy a round of golf—that's your decision as a business person in your territory."

Such a policy virtually *forces* the territory manager to think of his or her role as an independent business, not a hired gun role for his or her company. Frankly, if you had the opportunity to make $300,000 a year (like most of the territory managers in these distributors do), why would you need an expense report?

The Impact of Expenses on Your Company's ROI

Let's suppose you have an account who is netting you 1.4% in net profit. (If that sounds low to you, it is, sadly, a very typical number!) Suppose now you also treated that dealer to a fishing weekend and it cost you (or your company if you have expense reports) $600. How does that affect your bottom line (or that of your company)?

To get the answer, divide $600 by 1.4%. The answer is almost $43,000! That could represent the dealer's total purchases for several months!

The big question is: did you get $43,000 worth of good will out of the fishing weekend? Sometimes, you will. If that's the case, the trip was a good investment. But most of the time, you won't. And you won't know until you try and know your dealer better. If it's your boss's nickel, the fishing trip is easier to justify than if it came out of your pocket.

The question then becomes, how can you get an idea of what a dealer is netting you in terms of profit so you can know how your expenses eat into that number? The calculations are not difficult to make, but you will need some details from your accounting department that may be beyond their present tracking capabilities.

There is a form on the next page to help you.

Account ROI Worksheet

Territory manager: ______________________ Date: ______________

Account being analyzed: ____

	A	B
1	This account's annual purchases from me (most recently completed fiscal year)	$
2	Gross margin generated by this account	$
3	My company's total sales volume last fiscal year	$
4	This account's sales as a percentage of the company's total sales (B1 ÷ B3)	%
5	My company's total overhead (including G&A) last fiscal year	$
6	This account's share of the overhead (B5 x B4)	$
7	This account's net profit (B2 – B6)	$
8	Claims credited to this account [1]	$
9	This account's net profit as a percent of its sales [(B7 - B8) ÷ B1]	%

Note:

1) Get claim data from your claiming department at year-end. Include your expenses.

Let's work through an example. Suppose Bubba is your dealer and last fiscal year, he purchased $376,459 from you at 18.6% gross margin. You would put $376,459 in box 1 and 18.6% times $376,459 in box 2 (the answer is $70,021).

Suppose that for the fiscal year of box 1, your company sold $46,200,000 in equipment, parts, supplies, and services. That number goes in box 3. To get your dealer's percent of this, divide box 1 by box 3 and put that result in box 4. (The number is 0.81%.)

From your accounting department, you learn that your company's overhead last year, *not counting expense reports, dealer claims and concessions*, was $8,131,200 (box 5).

To get the dealer's share of overhead (how much overhead his account must cover if you are to be profitable), multiply the number in box 5 by the number in box 4. Put that result in box 6. (In this case, the number is $66,257.)

Box 7 will show the dealer's net profit to you (before expense reports, claims and concessions) when you subtract the number in B6 from the number in B2. (The answer is $3,764.)

Next, get from the accounting department the total for this dealer for expense reports, claims and concessions. Let's say that co-op advertising claims, incentive trip expenses, your expense account, and a job concession from last year comes to $4,103. Enter that in box 8.

To get the dealer net profit, the form says to take (B7 - B8), or ($3,764 - $4,103) or (-$339), and divide that by box 1 ($376,459), which gives us a negative number: -0.90%. Here is the filled in form:

	A	B
1	This account's annual purchases from me (most recently completed fiscal year)	$376,459
2	Gross margin generated by this account	$70,021
3	My company's total sales volume last fiscal year	$46,200,000
4	This account's sales as a percentage of the company's total sales (B1 ÷ B3)	0.81%
5	My company's total overhead (including G&A) last fiscal year	$8,131200
6	This account's share of the overhead (B5 x B4)	$66,257
7	This account's net profit (B2 – B6)	$3,764
8	Claims credited to this account[1]	$339
9	This account's net profit as a percent of its sales [(B7 – B8) ÷B1]	0.90%

If your company has the ability to pull out of its ledger the costs incurred by expense reports, claims and concessions by dealer, it might be educational to run detailed ROI calculations like this for your key dealers. You may not like the results, though!

Review Questions for Chapter 26

1. Candace is a TM for a distributor. Last year, her expense reports came to $17,889. Her sales manager told her that her *net margin* on sales of $4,357,888 was 0.78%. How much net profit did Candace make for her company last year?

A) $33,992

B) $16,102

C) cannot tell without her gross margin too

D) cannot tell without the overhead data

Answer: ________

2. What should you do if you find your biggest account actually costs you 2.04% loss per year (on that account's sales)?

A) try to find a way to restore profitability to the account

B) live with it— the owner is a friend of the boss

C) cuts costs (including support) until profit returns

D) the account is a prestigious account; learn to live with it

Answer: ________

Chapter 27: Time Management

One of the greatest myths about time management is that it exists.

It does not. You cannot manage time. Time is a physical trait of the universe. You can no more manage it than you can the speed of light or the force of gravity.

All you can do is manage **yourself** as effectively as possible in the hours you have every day. That is the purpose of this chapter.

What is Your Time Worth (Reprise)?

In Broadway musicals, we call it a *reprise* when a theme from earlier in the play is played again as part of a new scene or for a transition between scenes.

In chapter three, we covered what your time is worth. Now comes your reprise.

Just to refresh your memory, flip back to page 35 and write down how much your time is worth per hour when you are with customers:

$______________

Do you remember the math you did on page 37 where you figured out how much more you could rack up in sales by spending more time with your customers? This is why time management skills are so important to a territory manager.

An Amazing Statistic!

Sales research conducted by a manufacturer I once worked for revealed a stunning thing about sales improvement.

If you take your account list and rank it from largest account down to the smallest (in order of sales dollars), you can do a quartile assessment. Take the number of accounts you have and divide it by four. This number is how many accounts are in each quartile of your list. Drop any fractions left over. (Example: 35 accounts divided by 4 is 8.75. Call it 8.)

Count down that number from the first name on your sorted list and draw a heavy line. Every one above that line is in your First Quartile.

Count down that many names again and draw another heavy line. This group is your Second Quartile.

Count down that many names one more time and draw another heavy line. This is your Third Quartile.

Everyone below the last heavy line is in your Fourth Quartile.

If you were to graph the total sales volume of each quartile, you would probably find that about half (or more) of your sales come from the First Quartile. The balance will be distributed among the other three in a rapidly declining manner. Your graph might look something like this:

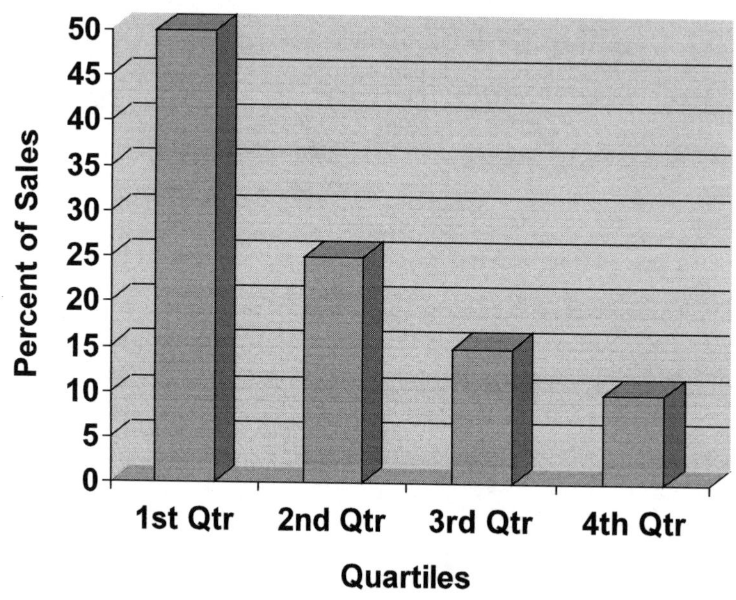

Research showed that when a territory manager spent just 15% more quality time with an account in any quartile (other than the 1st), the account could improve in performance enough to migrate to the next bigger quadrant. A First Quadrant account cannot migrate to Quadrant 0 (because there is none), but it will respond to more quality time by growing sales with you.

Look at the bar chart carefully for a moment. It should be clear that the biggest single jump in sales occurs when a dealer moves from the Second Quadrant into the First Quadrant. Jumps from 4 to 3 and 3 to 2 yield good results too, but not as much as the jump from 2 to 1.

Suppose you have ten accounts in the Second Quadrant. Five of them have no desire to work more with you, but the other five are open to growing if you can help them do it successfully and with a minimum of risk. What could the payoff be?

Let's suppose your average Second Quadrant dealer buys $50,000 a year from you while your average First Quadrant dealer buys $125,000 a year. A jump from 2 to 1 means $75,000 more sales (on average). With five accounts willing and able to make the jump, that could mean $375,000 more in sales.

So how much more call time are we talking about? I cannot tell you how much time to spend with an account in the Second Quadrant, but I typically spent about two hours a month (twenty-four hours a year) calling on such accounts. A 15% increase in call time means about 3.6 more hours a year—spread out over eighteen or so calls, this means about twelve minutes a call. (Some calls will be the same length as before; others may be half an hour longer—it all depends on what you have to talk about on your extended sales call.)

For your five targeted dealers, we're talking about eighteen hours more per year. An hour and a half per month.

Not a bad deal, is it? Investing eighteen hours of additional *purposeful* and specific call time to net maybe $375,000 more in sales. That's a rate of $21,000 in sales per hour invested.

But the key thing is that the extra time must be purposeful and specific, based on the dealer's needs (which you found out with excellent discovery questions), bringing your product and programs to bear where they can help the dealer grow past his present hurdles.

Where Do You Need to Focus?

Time management is nothing more complicated than figuring out where you are having trouble with managing your routines, then changing how you do your routines so more time is available for what is important. To help you do that, take a moment to fill out the following worksheet.

There are no right or wrong answers. This is not a test, and you cannot fail it. For each question, draw a circle around the number in the box that best represents how you think you handle the time management issue being addressed. For each section, total the numbers you circled.

	Strongly Agree	Mildly Agree	Undecided/Neutral	Mildly Disagree	Strongly Disagree
GOALS					
1. I write annual performance goals for my territory.	5	4	3	2	1
2. I keep a master list of all the smaller jobs and assignments that need to be handled over the next several weeks.	5	4	3	2	1
3. I review my long-range goals every day.	5	4	3	2	1
4. I constantly ask myself how what I am doing will help me achieve my goals.	5	4	3	2	1
Total Points for "Goals":					
PRIORITIES					
5. I start work each day with something that relaxes me.	5	4	3	2	1
6. I prioritize my jobs and activities.	5	4	3	2	1
7. I tend to do the quick, easy or enjoyable jobs first.	1	2	3	4	5
8. Constantly switching priorities is a big problem on my job.	1	2	3	4	5
Total Points for "Priorities":					

	Strongly Agree	Mildly Agree	Undecided/Neutral	Mildly Disagree	Strongly Disagree
ANALYSIS					
9. At least once a year, I keep a record of how I actually spend my time for a week or two.	5	4	3	2	1
10. I constantly analyze everything I am doing and look for ways to improve my performance.	5	4	3	2	1
11. I often have to spend ten or more hours a day to get all my work done.	1	2	3	4	5
12. Constantly recurring crises take up too much of my time.	1	2	3	4	5
Total Points for "Analysis":					
PLANNING					
13. I write out a to-do list every day (paper or electronic).	5	4	3	2	1
14. I write out a weekly plan, including specific goals.	5	4	3	2	1
15. At least once a week, I meet with others to coordinate plans, priorities, and activities.	5	4	3	2	1
16. I often think I should get better organized.	1	2	3	4	5
Total Points for "Planning":					
SCHEDULING					
17. I schedule a specific time each day for doing the most important tasks.	5	4	3	2	1
18. I often get distracted from my schedule and tend to jump from one task to another.	1	2	3	4	5
19. I have a quiet time every day so I can concentrate on important work.	5	4	3	2	1

	Strongly Agree	Mildly Agree	Undecided/Neutral	Mildly Disagree	Strongly Disagree
20. I maintain flexibility by allowing time in my daily schedule for unexpected things.	5	4	3	2	1
Total Points for "Scheduling":					
PAPERWORK					
21. I have a good systematic procedure for sorting and handling my paperwork.	5	4	3	2	1
22. I often analyze my paperwork and look for ways to eliminate it, simplify it, or improve it.	5	4	3	2	1
23. I use a tickler file to keep track of details and maintain good follow-up.	5	4	3	2	1
24. My desk or work area is fairly cluttered and could be neater.	1	2	3	4	5
Total Points for "Paperwork":					
INTERRUPTIONS					
25. I analyze my interruptions and systematically work on reducing or eliminating them.	5	4	3	2	1
26. I usually bunch items together and handle several things in one visit.	5	4	3	2	1
27. Distractions and socializing often keeps me from concentrating on my work.	1	2	3	4	5
28. Interruptions are a big problem on my job.	1	2	3	4	5
Total Points for "Interruptions":					
PROCRASTINATION					
29. I often put off tasks that are unpleasant for me.	1	2	3	4	5
30. I tend to wait until the last minute to get started on things.	1	2	3	4	5

	Strongly Agree	Mildly Agree	Undecided/Neutral	Mildly Disagree	Strongly Disagree
31. I often have to wait for the right mood or time to tackle creative work.	1	2	3	4	5
32. I often worry about making bad decisions.	1	2	3	4	5
Total Points for "Procrastination":					

Score your results below. Find the section scores you recorded in the survey and circle them on the chart below to reveal your "Effective Use of Time" condition.

Topic	A		B			C							D			E	
Goals	4	5	6	7	8	9	10	11	12	13	14	15	16	17	18	19	20
Priorities	4	5	6	7	8	9	10	11	12	13	14	15	16	17	18	19	20
Analysis	4	5	6	7	8	9	10	11	12	13	14	15	16	17	18	19	20
Planning	4	5	6	7	8	9	10	11	12	13	14	15	16	17	18	19	20
Scheduling	4	5	6	7	8	9	10	11	12	13	14	15	16	17	18	19	20
Paperwork	4	5	6	7	8	9	10	11	12	13	14	15	16	17	18	19	20
Interruptions	4	5	6	7	8	9	10	11	12	13	14	15	16	17	18	19	20
Procrastination	4	5	6	7	8	9	10	11	12	13	14	15	16	17	18	19	20

The more your line lies toward the E side of the chart, the better you are at managing yourself in that particular area. The more toward the A side, the weaker you are.

Here's a suggestion. For any area where you scored twelve or lower, go back to the survey and find that area and review what sort of things went into making it up. Make it your goal to improve how you handle each sub-behavior (moving towards a higher score).

The Behavior of Highly Effective People

In 1989, Steven Covey created a paradigm shift in business thinking with the publication of his classic *The Seven Habits of Highly Effective People*. Many people mistakenly describe it as a book on time management. It is not. It is a book about life management, and as such, is extremely valuable reading. If you have read the book, you already know that. If you have not read the book, make it your top priority to get a copy tonight and read it in the next seven days.

In his book, Covey writes about four quadrants of behavior that can be illustrated by a simple graph, like this one:

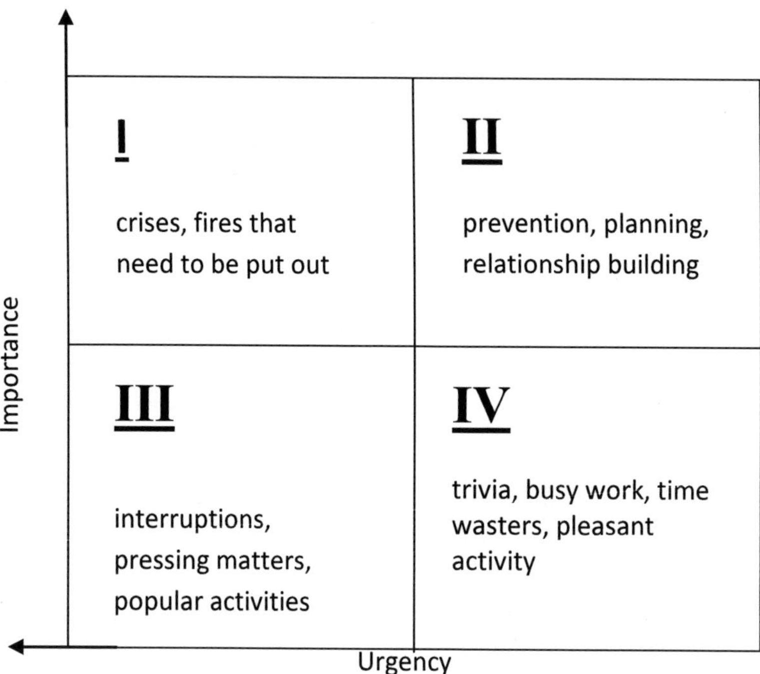

Covey advises us to think about our activity along two dimensions: importance and urgency. The two are not the same thing. Urgent things require our immediate attention. Important things require contemplation and planning.

Covey says that where an item is highly important and highly urgent, you have a Quadrant I scenario—crises and fires that need to be put out. Covey states that a lot of everyday people spend most of their days in this Quadrant because, frankly, some people feel good there. They like the stress and action of fire-fighting and see their role as vital to the organization. (After all, if *they* didn't put out those fires, who would?)

But Covey's research showed that whereas highly effective people spend *some* of their time in Quadrant I, they don't spend a majority of it there. They put out the fires when that is what is needed, but they spend *most* of their time in Quadrant II, an area I call fire prevention. Here, effective people work on relationships, planning and creating automatic systems that prevent fires in the first place (or, if they do flare up, they are easily knocked down by the fire fighting systems they create).

The rest of the population lives in Quadrants III and IV. They live life as busybodies, or waste it as drifters and what Zig Ziglar calls wandering generalities. Highly effective people tend to avoid quadrants III and IV as much as possible. (But they don't avoid them altogether—sometimes, an activity can migrate up the quadrants and by catching it early, you can often handle it before it reaches crisis status. Also, a pleasant pastime can recharge your batteries.)

Reframing How We See Time

One of the key breakthroughs of neuro-linguistic programming is in the area of how we visualize time and how that visualization process can help us manage ourselves in time better.

I want you to do an experiment for a moment. Read the rest of this paragraph before you do it. I want you to close your eyes and make a picture in your mind of how you see time. I want you to see time as something that has length to it, like a pipe, or a board or a rope. When you have your picture framed, open your eyes and answer the following questions.

- ❑ [1] I saw time as something running in front of me, roughly at eye level, and approximately level with the ground, with the past to my left, the present straight ahead of me, and the future off to the right.

- ❑ [2] I saw time much as the first case, but sloping slightly upward, either to the left or the right.

- ❑ [3] I saw time as an object that actually went through my body. It went through my torso with the past behind me and the future in front of me.

- ❑ [4] I saw time similar to the previous case, but it went through my head, almost between my eyes. The past was in back, the future in front.

- ❑ [5] I did not see it as any of these, but as something else entirely.

Most people—well over half—will see time as described in either case 1 or case 2. A significant few will see it as case 3. A minority will see cases 4 or 5.

So what does this mean?

There are basically two types of people on the planet—those who see time as external to themselves physically (what neuro-linguistic programmers call through time) and those who see it as passing through their body in some way (in time). People who are *through time* usually see time clearly and have a keen sense of it and where they are in it. If you tell a through time person that you will meet them at the country club at 7:00 a.m. for a round of Saturday golf, they will be there at 7:00 a.m., or even early. But in time people often get confused as they look at time because they can't always tell where their body is and where time is. If you tell an in time person that you'll meet for 7:00 a.m. golf, they may show up anywhere from 6:45 to 8:00 a.m., and not even be aware that they are not on time!

A dealer who is through time will usually keep his appointment with you pretty much on time. An in time dealer may (or may not) show up for the meeting at all!

And if that is how *you* are wired, there is not much you can do about it. Except reframe it.

I was speaking at a dealer meeting once where about 200 dealers and their wives were in attendance. We were discussing time management, and I asked everyone to stand and close their eyes and visualize time. I then asked them to place their left hands on the past and their right hands on the future. Most of the folks in the room placed their left hands on the past to the left of their faces; and their right hands to the right of their faces. A few had that pattern, but sloping from left up to right, and so on.

A small few had the behind me-in front of me pattern. Two of them were women and one was a man. I asked them if they would feel comfortable coming to the front of the room for a moment. They all came forward.

I asked them to close their eyes again and re-grab their time lines so the audience could see what I saw, and there were polite chuckles as people saw the unusual pattern. I then asked them to open their eyes.

I then asked them, "I'll bet you have trouble being on time for things, don't you?" All three nodded with grins and some embarrassment, one of the women even saying, "Sheesh!"

I said that was okay, but that I wanted to help them get better control of time. Would they like that? All three said they would.

I asked one of the normal time line people to come up front and had all four re-grab their time lines again. As they did, I asked them to look toward their futures. The normal person looked off to the right, but the other three wrinkled their foreheads as they squinted at what was in front of them.

The audience noticed this obvious difference in the two patterns. I asked the normal person how their future looked. "Clear," they replied, "like a stack of pictures, one behind the other." I thanked him and let him sit back down.

I then turned to the three back-to-front people and asked them how their futures looked. All three gave variants of "confused, jumbled, double-exposed." I pointed out to the group that this was due to a lack of depth perception. The normal time line person could see the future as a road that might have shrunk as it went off to the horizon, but at least he could see waypoints along the road. But for the three back-to-front people, since they were **on** their roads, they could not see clearly more than a picture or two into the future. I pointed out that for through time people, it is like looking at a box of slides on top of a lighted slide table. You can see all the slides as individual slides against the lit background of the table. But for the in time people, it's like stacking all the slides into one stack and then holding them up to the sun and peeking in at them. The picture is just too muddled!

"Now here is how you can get better control of time," I said. "Every morning, before you start your day, I want you to visualize your time line and hold it with your hands. Do so now, please." They all three closed their eyes and placed their hands on the back-to-front lines. "Now, for this next part, I want you to take your past and pull it around to the left of your head and push the future around to the right, like this." I then helped each of them move their hands. One of the women stumbled a bit and said, "Whoa!" I asked if she was okay and she said yes, just startled by the difference in the pictures.

I said, "Fine. Now look at the future. Do you see things you need to do now in perspective? Are some things closer to you in the stack than others?" All three said yes. I then said, "Good! Now I want you to make note of the three most important upcoming pictures and remember them, and when you open your eyes, write them down on a pad of paper. Then do this every day for the rest of your life, before you have breakfast, and see what happens."

The lady who stumbled and said, "Whoa!" gasped as she said, "Wow, that's so much more clear and easy to see now! Wow!"

I then asked them if this exercise was helpful and all three said it was.

Are they still using it? I don't know. That was five years ago and a lot of miles have passed by my airliner window since. But if they are, I'll bet they are doing a better job of managing themselves in time now!

Review Questions for Chapter 27

1. To be good with time management, you must become good at

A) getting up earlier

B) managing yourself in the present better

C) making lists of things to do

D) using a Day-Timer or similar planning aid

E) all of the above

Answer: ________

2. One of the biggest reasons territory managers have trouble with time management is their inability to

A) clearly state goals

B) plan

C) schedule their time daily

D) handle paperwork properly

E) all of the above

Answer: ________

3. Most people spend their days dealing with urgent and important things, but highly effective people spend much of their time working on things that are

A) urgent but not important

B) not urgent nor important

C) not urgent but important

D) all of the above

E) none of the above

Answer: ________

Chapter 28: Getting Your Sales Manager To Work for You

Some territory managers see their Sales Managers as the boss and try only to keep the boss happy and off their backs. Others see their Sales Managers as key partners in the factor-distributor-contractor chain and call on them regularly for help and assistance in building a powerful territory.

Which type do you think the Tier One territory manager is?

Not Every Good TM Makes a Good SM

I have seen many cases where a distributor had a superb territory manager who was promoted to sales manager (SM). Often this ends up being frustrating for the former TM and a source of consternation for the TMs who report to him or her. The job of being a Tier One TM is a lot different than being an overseer of a team of Tier One TMs!

There is a good reason for that: although some of the skills required for people to excel in either area are the same, there are significant— and critical— differences. Consider the chart on the next page.

As you can see, the common personality traits— self-confidence, professional image, listening, optimism— are the same. But there are also significant differences, as the list in the TM circle contrasts with the list inside the SM circle.

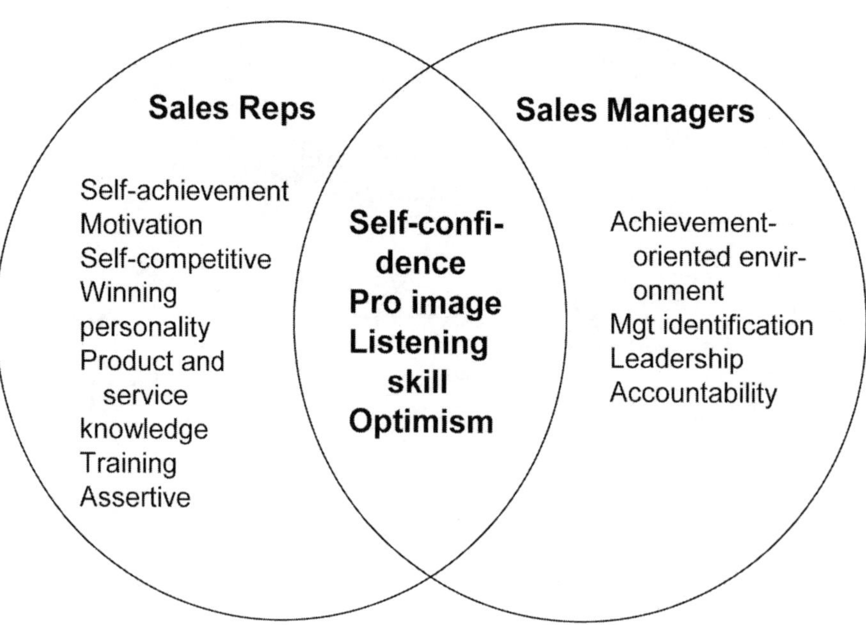

To this, add the skill differences required of each position:

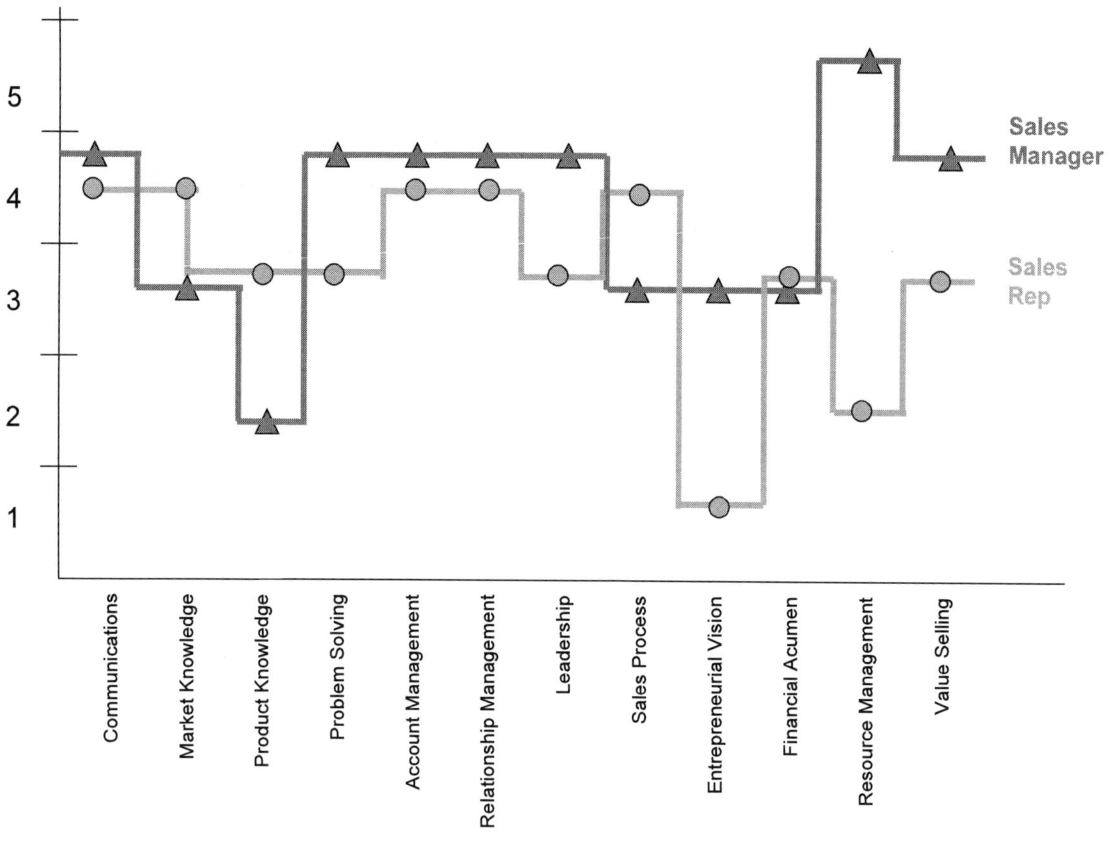

This is why I often cringe when a distributor tells me he is thinking about promoting his star TM to sales manager. Sometimes it works—most of the time it does not.

What If Your SM is a Glorified TM?

So what if you are reporting to a sales manager who was a good territory manager, but got promoted to a position over his head? What can you expect?

That depends on the individual.

Most adults find it very difficult to change their behavior. Their internal wiring is set and there is not a lot they can do about it, without tremendous effort or trauma. If your SM does not play the role of a SM (and more on that in a few paragraphs), you can't do much about it. You can complain, you can ask him to do what he cannot do, but don't bet the farm that he will comply. It is just not in him. He can make sales calls with the best of them, and prospect like a bloodhound, but he won't have the people skills required to be a good manager.

For you see, a manager is a person who is given the responsibility to get a team to work together in such a way that maximum results are obtained. They must manage their assets, human and material, to get the greatest return for the investment. All professional sports teams have coaches or managers who run the team during pre-season camps, practice, and the games. The coaches/managers don't actually play in the game. They call the plays and substitute players as needed to maximize the odds that their team will win. They may (or may not) be good leaders, but frankly, leadership is not a pre-requisite of being a good manager. Getting results is the main objective.

If your SM is a glorified TM, you can expect him to help you with your sales game, to get better at being a territory manager. But don't expect him to create powerful marketing programs, or implement sweeping and dynamic internal structural changes to streamline operations, or to be able to help a dealer work through a tough problem.

The Best World to Be In

Ideally, a sales manager is a special person who has the right skill set mix to be effective in the role. Looking back on the chart on the bottom of page 488, we should expect a sales manager to be…

- A superb communicator
- A good problem solver
- An astute account manger
- A positive relationship manager
- A pretty good (but not necessarily brilliant) leader
- A person with entrepreneurial vision
- A good manager of the resources charged to him/her

A champion of value selling

Let's look at each of these in detail to see what a Tier One sales manager would be like.

Superb Communication

A good sales manager is a master of Chapter 22 (Deep Communication) and Chapter 23 (Dispute Resolution). He (or she) has an ability to communicate with dealers that is amazing to an outside observer. He can read a dealer better than most people and can phrase his message in a way that the dealer understands it. He possesses good verbal skills (orally and written) and often goes out of his way to make sure the people he needs to communicate with get the message.

Problem Solving

Into every life a boatload of problems must crash. Some people make the wreckage worse by how they handle it; others soon get the mess cleaned up and everything back on track.

A good sales manager has an ability to solve problems that most territory managers would run from. He does not mind the challenge of a tough problem (but I would not go so far as to say he *enjoys* it).

These problems can run a wide gamut of possibilities. One day, he may be called up on to create a powerful pre-season marketing program. Another time he may need to find a way to negotiate a solution to a thorny but delicate problem with an account. Or he may need to find a way to either help a laggard territory manager perform better or reassign him (if necessary, making him ATI, "available to the industry"). He may need to come up with a plan to balance the distributor's inventory when stocks are imbalanced, or he may need to help create a huge and very complex sales and budget forecast for the coming year. He may need to find a good advertising agency that can deliver the leads without breaking the bank, or negotiate better pricing with a reluctant factory. The list is indeed endless.

Account Management

Like a good territory manager, a good sales manager has strong account management skills too. Sometimes this means the ability to bring an account on as a new customer; at other times, it means taking heroic actions to save an account from erosion to an aggressive competitor.

It may mean working with an account when the account is wrong and the company line must be held. There is a saying in business that the customer is always right. This is not true. Often, the customer is wrong. But even when the customer is wrong, he is still the customer. A good sales manager knows how to persuade an obstinate account to get on the company bandwagon, and— this is particularly important— knows when it is time to de-select a customer and make the customer ATI! (A Tier One sales manager knows that a company can make a very good living on 20% of the market when it knows what 80% to leave alone!)

Relationship Management

A good sales manager is an expert at managing relationships in many different directions at the same time.

First, he understands that *all* business is predicated on strong and healthy relationships. He understands what the legendary sales and motivational coach Zig Ziglar once wrote about this:

> *When we separate the word BUSINESS into its component letters, B-U-S-I-N-E-S-S, we find that U and I are both in it. In fact, if U and I were not in BUSINESS together, it would not be business! Furthermore, we discover that U comes before I in BUSINESS, and the I is silent. Also, the U in BUSINESS has the sound of I, which indicates it is an amalgamation of the interests of U and I. When they are properly amalgamated, business becomes harmonious, profitable and pleasant.*

He also knows another Zigism: *You can have anything you want in life if you help enough other people get what they want in life.*

A Tier One sales manager is adept at managing his relationships with his territory managers, of course. He is friendly, but not necessarily their friend. In fact, I have seen many times when a sales manager tried to be a friend to his TMs and ended up losing his job over not being able to get them to go along with company initiatives. Your sales manager should be friendly with you, but don't expect him to be your friend. You can dine together, travel together, plan together, work together, but don't expect him (or even want him) to be your buddy. He has to maintain a slight distance between himself and you so he can ask the difficult of you when it is necessary. He can be firm when necessary, relaxed when that is the proper course of behavior, humorous when appropriate, fearless when backed up to the wall.

He is good at working with his managerial peers in the distributorship, cooperating with them when he can, but not letting them run roughshod over his sales division. He can fight for what he needs, but also stand shoulder to shoulder with his peers to assault the market with a united front.

He is also a good manager of his family relationships. This means he knows when to go home and how to leave the job at the office. I have seen too many good men and women destroyed by a job that consumes them to the point that they lose their families and personal friends. No job is worth that! I have yet to see a tombstone with the epithet, "I wish I had spent more time at the office!"

Leadership

A good sales manager is a decent (not necessarily brilliant) leader. What does that mean?

There has been a flood of books on leadership over the last thirty years or so, from Wess Roberts' classic *Leadership Secrets of Attila the Hun* and Max DePree's *Leadership is an Art* to the powerful but pedantic works of Peter Drucker, Tom Peters, John Maxwell and others. I have read perhaps fifty books on leadership over the last twenty years and have observed leadership in every aspect I can observe it and I have come to a conclusion: *if you are a born leader, learning leadership skills can make you more effective; but if you don't have the leadership gene in your gene pool, you will never become an effective leader by learning secrets, twenty-one laws, or secret techniques.*

Does that mean a sales manager should not take courses on leadership and read books and magazine articles on it? Of course not! If he has that leadership gene, such studies can make him more effective. But if he does not have that innate trait, don't expect education to give it to him. Leadership is something that is extremely difficult to develop and I believe the forms into which our personal cement is poured are set up very early in life. A person who will mature to be a good leader is probably going to be a good leader in pre-school, elementary school, middle school, high school, college, and life.

There is a reason why 90% of the people are followers and only 10% or so are leaders. The right combination of genes, environment and experiences that produce brilliant leaders is rare!

Simply put, a leader has followers. A title of leader means nothing if no one is marching behind you.

But if you have that rare trait, books, seminars, and periodicals that deal with the subject can make you better at what you are already gifted at.

I am a student of the American Civil War. The Civil War was a horribly bloody conflict, creating some 440 or so deaths *per day* for four years. It is the costliest war in American history in terms of life. The Grim Reaper's bill for the conflict exceeds the total for all the other wars America has fought *combined.* So when I see people wringing their hands over a milestone like 4,000 combat deaths in Iraq and Afghanistan, I shake my head and think, "Almost 6,000 died in *one day* at Antietam Creek!"

The statistics on the Civil War are interesting to study, as such studies go. For instance, the Union (North) enjoyed about a 2 to 1 advantage over the Confederacy (South) in almost every criterion you could list: number of men in arms, number of guns, number of horses, miles of railroad, railroad engines, ships, people at home, and so on. The North enjoyed at least a 2:1 advantage, if not greater, in almost every category. As the southern historian Shelby Foote once remarked, "The North fought that war with one hand tied behind its back."

The 2:1 ratio holds for combat deaths and wounds too. The North had about twice as many killed and wounded as the South.

Consider now that the South won most of the major battles of the war in the eastern theater of Virginia, where its armies were lead by the brilliant and legendary Robert E. Lee. (The western armies, much farther from the seat of government in Richmond, Virginia, were much poorer armed and equipped, and suffered from weaker leadership.) The victory roster of the Army of Northern Virginia is impressive: First Manassas, The Seven Days (and its half dozen or so mini-battles), Second Manassas, Sharpsburg (or Antietam, tactically a draw), Fredericksburg, Chancellorsville (Lee's greatest victory), and the tactical but pyrrhic victories of the Overland Campaign (The Wilderness, Spotsylvania, Cold Harbor, and the awful trench warfare of Petersburg). Lee's opponent, the massive and superbly-equipped if badly managed Army of the Potomac could only count a few victories in that theater: Antietam (used by Lincoln to springboard the release of the Emancipation Proclamation), Gettysburg, and the strategic brilliance of the Overland Campaign.

So how was it that the Army of Northern Virginia, outnumbered in some cases 3 to 1 (as at Chancellorsville) and outgunned by better rifles and awesome Union artillery, managed to win most of the battles?

Look at one more statistic from the War and you get a clue: the 2:1 ratio of casualties of the North over the South breaks down in one vital category: deaths and wounding of high level commanders (colonels, brigadier generals, and major generals). Here, the South suffered a roughly 2 to 1 edge over their Yankee counterparts!

Why is that? I think it goes back to morale. The South fought with inspiration and raw courage when technology should have shredded them like rags (and it often did). But there is a crucial difference in the leadership of the two armies: in the Army of the Potomac, *most* (but certainly not all) of the colonels, brigadiers and major generals were political appointees or were seeking office after the war, so told their men to take an objective while they directed the action from the rear. But in the Army of Northern Virginia, the leaders said to their men, "Come on, my lads! We are going to take that hill!" And then they would run off at the head of their regiment or brigade to share in the danger and glory of the battle.

Yankee marksmen learned quickly that the men with the swords and gold braid on their collars and shoulder boards were the ones to shoot, so the South paid a terrible price in terms of leadership blood. But their men fought with inspiration, and often did the impossible.

To me, *that* is the measure of leadership. A manager directs the battle from his headquarters safely to the rear of the action. A leader gets in front, sticks his hat on his sword so his men can see it from afar (like General Armistead in Pickett's Charge at Gettysburg) and yells, "Come on, my lads! For your homes, for your families, for your sweethearts, and for old Virginia! Charge!"

Entrepreneurial Vision

Entrepreneurism is a word that is tossed around a lot in business. But few people really know what it means.

Most would say that an entrepreneur is a risk-taker, a person who amasses capital and risks it all on a single business venture.

That is not at all what makes a good entrepreneur! It makes for a good failure, but not a good entrepreneur.

A good entrepreneur is a business person who carefully studies a market and figures out a way to solve a problem in that market with an operation (a business) that makes more than it costs to create and run. Most entrepreneurs are not ardent risk-takers. They will take a risk when their calculations show it has a high chance of success and the returns are high, but most don't throw capital at a problem willy-nilly.

A sales manager with an entrepreneurial vision is one who will approach his job as if it was his own company. He will see his role not so much as an employee working for someone else as he will see it as running an operation that makes money. Lots of money.

He will study the market carefully and analyze it and find a way to solve a problem he identifies in it that no one else has thought of yet, or that someone else has thought of but executed poorly.

He will find a way to make his company, his sales operation, stand out in the marketplace so that customers gladly flock to him and pay his asking price for the things they need and want in life.

And it is in that order: needs and wants.

No one, in my opinion, is better at understanding this and bringing a powerful solution to the market than The Disney Company. I was privileged one year to sit in on a part of the training Disney gives all new cast members (they are never called employees). In driving home the core value of delivering entertainment that is not only better than anyone else but unique in the world, Disney has its cast members focus on the Disney Compass, a device they created to help cast members keep their perspective on what it means to be Disney.

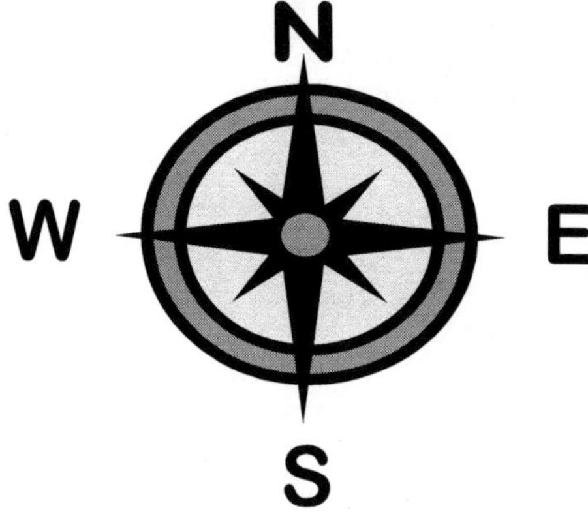

The cardinal points of the compass—N, W, S and E—all stand for principles that underlie the Disney experience.

The compass begins at north, where we find N—Needs. Everyone has needs. We need air, and water, and food and shelter. We need transportation, and certain tools to do our jobs, and so on.

Next is west, W—Wants. Everyone also has wants. Wants are more sophisticated than needs. They are also less vital to fulfill.

For instance, I need transportation. A basic car will provide it, but I may *want* the luxury of a BMW or a Ferrari. I need clothing. A basic pair of jeans and a T-shirt will do but I may want an Armani suit. Get the idea?

Disney tells cast members that between Needs and Wants is a chasm, and that chasm is gulfed by money. People will spend incredible sums to get what they *want* when the emotional power of attainment is high enough.

That's where South (stereotypes) and East (emotions) enter the picture. Disney knows that it cannot get people to come to Orlando or Anaheim and spend an average of $3,400 per visit if they are no better than a local theme park. To create that magic in the guests (never customers!), Disney knows it must shatter the stereotype of a theme park and touch the emotions of its guests in a deep and wonderful way.

If you have ever been to a Disney park as well as a local theme park, you know how they explode the stereotype. No one is better at that than Disney!

But they are also geniuses at touching people's emotions. Whether it is the look of awe and wonder in a five-year-old's face as she meets Minnie Mouse for real, or the moist-eyed gaze of a loving parent watching her daughter actually shake hands with a childhood hero or heroine, no one can grab the emotions of its guests like Disney.[31]

A Tier One sales manager knows how to break the distribution stereotype and grab the emotions of dealers in such a way that a premium for the product is not an obstacle to doing business.

Resource Management

A good sales manager has a solid ability to manage the resources committed to him. These resources are both human and technological. He hires good talent; he nurtures it so it becomes better; and he prunes dead twigs that aren't producing up to expectations.

He sees to it that his team has the technological tools they need to do their jobs efficiently and makes sure they know how to use them effectively.

31 When my oldest daughter was nine, we took her to Disney World. I will never forget the look of wonder on her face at the nightly Electric Parade. Disney has a unique piece of electronic music played during the parade, and my daughter just had to have that cassette when we left the park that night. Nineteen years later, she got married. What did she have the Dee-jay play as the wedding party filed into the reception hall? The Electric Parade march music. Talk about grabbing a little girl's emotions! On the happiest day of her life, she had the music played that made her the happiest girl on a balmy night in Florida!

Mastery of Value Selling

Finally, a Tier One sales manager is a person who knows how to work the value selling proposition to maximum effect. Value selling simply means finding out all the issues that plague a dealer and then providing mutually beneficial solutions to those issues. He is a master of carefully aligning sales talent to customer needs and expectations.

Consider the old equation for value, an equation that is taught in many business schools on the first day:

Value = Benefits — Costs

In this classic equation, the value a customer derives from a product or relationship is found by calculating the benefits derived and subtracting the cost to attain those benefits. If the result is a positive number—if perceived benefits exceed the cost—then the value is positive and the customer will be pleased to some extent. But if the costs exceed the perceived benefits, the value will be negative. The buyer will not be thrilled with his purchase.

This equation also, indirectly, gives us insight into the marketplace. Chapter 1 hinted at this when it discussed market segments. Those customers who are fixated on the costs are about 25% of the market. They want things cheap. The cheaper the better. They don't care for frills. Just make it cheap. They are *transactional buyers.*

Those who value the benefits of a business transaction are value-oriented customers. They will pay more to get something if they are convinced that the extra cost delivers a much greater benefit than a cheaper alternative. These customers make up about 20% of the market and are *value buyers*.

The balance of the market— about 55%— can go either way. Those who lie in the 55% slice of the market (thinking of the market as a pie with three slices, one large, two small) end up in the slice the salesman they buy from comes out of.

Every distributor has a decision to make— (a) to go to market with the lowest price product possible and sell a huge volume at low margins to the transactional buyers, (b) go to market with a premium product and matching service and then cater to the smaller value buyer segment, or (c) try to find a way to do both and cater to the entire market.

History teaches us that option (c) rarely works. It is difficult if not impossible to execute consistently and well. As the old slogan in customer service goes, "Our motto: the highest quality, the best service and the lowest prices. Choose any two.□"

So a distributor who goes to market on a low-price platform will probably never succeed with the value buyer because the value buyer seeks things beyond the product itself to provide the benefits—the relationship, expertise, guidance. None of these can be provided by a cost-driven distributor because it takes talent (expensive talent) to provide these.

Conversely, a value-driven distributor will do well with the value segment of the market, but will be overpriced for the transactional buyer because the pricing must be high enough to hire and keep good talent and provide dealer benefits besides a coil or furnace.

So a superior sales manager must align his distributor's go-to-market approach with the customer expectations and make sure the talent he assigns to cover the dealers is adequate to exceed the dealers' expectations. If the talent is too great for a dealer's low expectations, the distributor stands to lose money with an over-priced offer for a transactional buyer. If the talent is below the dealers needs, the distributor risks loss of the customers as better talent comes along and acquires the dealers.

A great sales manager has assembled a powerful and balanced package that fits the customer base the distributorship has chosen to work with to a tee. He also trains and equips his sales force to deliver that package to every dealer consistent with each dealer's needs and expectations.

Calling in the Cavalry

If you are fortunate enough to have a Tier One sales manager, you would be wise to use him and his knowledge every time you need him.

For example, suppose you are prospecting an account that you want to sign up badly, but the prospect has questions that you cannot answer on the spot and you always feel defensive in your courtship ritual. Why not ask your sales manager to go with you on a call and help you get past the obstacles in your way? Maybe he can ask the right kinds of questions— the ones you have not asked yet—to determine the customer's deeper needs and propel you along to a consummation of the deal?

Or let's say you have a dealer who is mad as a hornet because you want to set up another dealer in the same town. Your research shows the market can easily support two dealers with your brand, but the dealer has not bought into your proof. Maybe your sales manager can go on a call with you and help defuse the situation?

On another occasion, you may have to deliver terrible news to a dealer. Perhaps you are going to de-select him, or raise his prices. The situation is very delicate. Perhaps you should have your sales manager go with you to help deliver the message?

Or you can do what I did one time. I had an account who was playing us against a competitor, trying to beat us into submission to his ends which I felt were unreasonable. I had my sales manager go with me to a dinner meeting with this dealer and his two brothers and we played good cop/bad cop at dinner. The sales manager delivered the ultimatum to the dealer I wanted to deliver, but didn't know how to do at that time. Eventually, we ended up making the dealer ATI, but it was a great help having my sales manager there to play the ogre's role.

Any time you feel you need a tool to do your job better—anything from a laptop computer, or PDA, or cell phone, or other gadget, or software, or even training—go to him and ask how you can acquire it, if possible with the company's financial help.

When you don't understand a new product or a program, go to your sales manager and ask him to explain it to you so you can explain it to your dealers.

When someone back at the home office drops a ball you handed off and it causes you problems or embarrassment, let your sales manager know about it. (And be sure to tell the fumbler about it too, but be polite—at least, the first time!)

A Monthly Meeting Format

I strongly recommend that every territory manager meet at least once a month for a brief one-on-one meeting with his sales manager to go over the territory. To facilitate that meeting, I suggest you use a form like this one. (It is also on the CD-ROM that comes with this book as a PDF file.)

Monthly Sales Meeting Worksheet

Territory Manager: ____

Date of 15 Minutes Session: ______________ Time: __________________

1. Recap of My Sales Last Month and YTD

Item	Last Month	YTD
Total Sales	$	$
Gross Margin	$	$
Gross Margin Percent	%	%
Average Share of Wallet	%	%

2. Capture of My Targeted Accounts

	Account	Targeted Sales for Year	Sales Last Month	Sales YTD	Sales Going Rate[1]	Variance to Plan[2]
1.		$	$	$	$	$
2.		$	$	$	$	$
3.		$	$	$	$	$
4.		$	$	$	$	$
5.		$	$	$	$	$
6.		$	$	$	$	$
7.		$	$	$	$	$
8.		$	$	$	$	$
9.		$	$	$	$	$
10.		$	$	$	$	$

Footnotes:

1) Divide sales YTD by the percentage of business you normally have written by this month.

2) Subtract the Sales Going Rate from the Targeted Sales for the Year.

3. Prospecting Results

My current Five Prospects:

Prospects	Probable Annual Volume[1]	Status to date	Issues	Notes
1.	$	Strong Moderate Weak		
2.	$	Strong Moderate Weak		
3.	$	Strong Moderate Weak		
4.	$	Strong Moderate Weak		
5.	$	Strong Moderate Weak		
6.	$	Strong Moderate Weak		

Footnotes:

1). Multiply the employee count by $50,000.

4. Other Issues I Want to Discuss

____

____

____

____

____

____

How to Use the Form

In the Recap Section (part 1), use your monthly sales reports to get the numbers the form requests.

To compute the average share of wallet, you can take the dealer's employee count (count *every* employee) times $60,000. This is a good approximation of what the dealer buys every year from suppliers. Then divide this number into your annual sales to the dealer. That is your share of wallet.

> EXAMPLE: A dealer has nine employees and you sold him $160,000 last year. What is your share of wallet?
>
> Total wallet @ 9 x $60,000 = $540,000 in purchases
>
> Your sales = $160,000
>
> Your probable share of wallet = $160,000 ÷ $540,000 = 30%

In the Capture Section, list up to ten accounts you want to sell more to this year and put down how much you hope to sell to them this year. Then, from your monthly sales report, record their purchases for the month and year to date. Then convert the sales YTD to a going rate by dividing the sales YTD by the percentage of business you normally write by that month in the year.

> EXAMPLE: Suppose that by July 28, you normally write up 68% of your annual business. A dealer has sales YTD through July 28 of $48,500. His going rate would be $48,500 ÷ 0.68 = $71,323.

You should then subtract the targeted sales from this figure to compute the variance from plan.

> EXAMPLE: The plan for a dealer is $200,000. The going rate for sales is $175,000. The variance from plan is $175,000 - $200,000 = -$25,000.

In the Prospecting Section, list six prospects you are currently working on. (You should always have six on the burner at all times.) Estimate their annual purchases ($50,000 per head) and then rate them as you call on them— strong, moderate or weak prospects. Also record any issues the prospect seems to be having with you or your brand as well as any notes that come to mind.

Finally, in the Other Issues section, list any other issues you want to be sure to cover with your sales manager during your meeting.

Once you and your sales manager have set a date and time for your brief meeting, fill out the form and fax it to him (or deliver it if his office is near yours) at least three days prior to your meeting. (I advise the sales manager to review the form before the meeting and jot down some questions to ask the territory manager.)

Sales teams that I have trained to use this form find their sales significantly increase. Not because of the form, but because of a fundamental principle of business: people respect what their bosses inspect!

Review Questions for Chapter 28

1. True or False. A great territory manager will usually make a superb sales manager.

   A) True

   B) False

   Answer: ________

2. Which skill is needed by a sales manager more than a territory manager?

   A) communication skills

   B) resource management

   C) product knowledge

   D) market knowledge

   E) the sales process in general

   Answer: ________

3. Which of the following is *not* a trait of a superior sales manager?

   A) superb communication skills

   B) astute account management

   C) product application

   D) entrepreneurial vision

   E) value selling championship

   Answer: ________

4. You can have anything you want in life if you help enough other people get…

   A) what they want in life

   B) ahead

   C) good credit

   D) your product

   E) a good job

   Answer: ________

5. To cross the gap between Needs and Wants, you have to find a way to touch the cus-

tomer's

A) wallet

B) emotions

C) dreams

D) nerves

E) desire to go to Disney World

Answer: ________

6. You should call upon your sales manager for help when

A) you have a difficult issue to resolve with an account and you are stuck

B) you need help to nudge a great prospect along in the recruiting process

C) you need a tool to work smarter (laptop, PDA, etc.)

D) you have a problem with an internal company procedure

E) all of the above

Answer: ________

Chapter 29: Mentoring the Next Wave

Tier One territory managers have accumulated a body of knowledge and set of skills that is priceless. Often, a Sales Manager will hire a new territory manager and turn him or her loose in a new territory and cross their fingers that the rookie succeeds. Others understand that the talent and skills of a proven veteran can often help a rookie shave years off their learning curves and make them highly productive territory managers much faster than the sink-or-swim variety.

One of the highest compliments your Sales Manager can give you is to ask you to mentor a new territory manager.

In this chapter, we'll cover some of the things this may involve.

If You Are Just Getting Started

Maybe you are just getting started in your career as a territory manager— you are a rookie. Or still very young in your career. Great! Welcome to the club! I hope you develop the skills to become one of the country's best territory managers! But you'll need coaching to get there.

As you look at the other territory managers in your company's sales division, do you see individuals who really seem to have it together, who seem to really have mastered this business? If so, seek to establish a mentoring relationship with them.

To do that, I suggest you go to your sales manager and voice your concerns. Say something like, "I was thinking the other day about the people on our sales team, and I really look up to Margaret. She seems to really have this thing figured out pretty well. Do you agree with my assessment?"

Hopefully, your sales manager will agree with you (if he doesn't, your whole approach is in jeopardy!). Then say, "I'd really like to have her teach me all she can about this business. Would you mind if I approach her about mentoring me? Or would you prefer to talk to her yourself?"

Now if the sales manager disagrees with your assessment, you can say this: "Well, I kind of thought she could teach me some of the ropes. I'd really like to learn this business from a seasoned veteran. Who on this team could you suggest to me as a mentor? I want to learn this craft from the best we have!"

If the sales manager leaves it to you to approach Margaret, say something like, "Margaret, I have been watching you for several months now and I am always amazed at the numbers you put on the board and the glowing feedback I hear from those who deal with you. I would really like to get as good as you are. Would you mind becoming my mentor and teaching me the things I don't yet know and adjusting those things I do wrong?"

If Margaret Says "No"

If Margaret says "No," you can ask her why. Maybe she does not feel she can afford the time it would take to train you. Maybe she feels that is the sales manager's job. Or maybe she just doesn't feel that confident in her ability to teach you. She could have legitimate reasons!

Ask her if she would share why she is not willing to mentor you. Or, ask her who else on the team she could recommend.

If Margaret Says "Yes"

Thank her, and then ask her how she wants to do this. More than likely, she'll want you to travel with her, as she won't feel she can take time out of her territory to break in a newbie. That's okay. Agree on a ride-along schedule and do it. As you travel with her in her territory, take notes and ask tons of questions (in the car or at lunch—never in front of her dealers).

> How do you plan your week? How do you plan your day? How do you know what to bring to a dealer to help him grow? How do you prospect for new accounts? How do you do follow-up? How do you keep records? How do you handle various problems?

Watch her on her sales calls. Note how she communicates. Note how she defuses problems, how she praises her accounts, how she offers correction or negotiates a tricky problem. On the sales call, keep your mouth shut. This is *her* call and her customer. Don't step into it unless she asks you to. ***Just observe.*** You might see something! (If the dealer asks what you are doing here, just say, "Learning from the best!")

Between sales calls, talk in the car about what you observed. Ask her why she did what she did. Ask her how she felt when the dealer lost his temper halfway through the call. Ask her how she'll handle the next sales call based on what transpired on this call.

And feel free to ask her those difficult non-sales questions, like how do you think your sense of honesty and justice has helped you in your career? You will find as you observe more and more Tier One territory managers that ***character is at the center of their success.*** Zig Ziglar wrote a classic book for sales people fifty years ago called *See You At the Top*. It is about the value of character as the basis for sales. I highly recommend the book.

When you feel your mentoring is complete, tell her and ask her if she agrees. If she does, thank her for her work. I suggest you get your mentor a nice gift for the time and work they poured into you; perhaps a quality ball-point pen or a leather portfolio case. Something nice that says, "Thank you" in a professional way. If she feels your training is not yet done, acknowledge it and humbly stay under the mentor's tutelage.

What If You Are the Mentor?

Suppose, on the other end of the scale, you are the seasoned veteran and that your sales manger brings a rookie to you (or a rookie approaches you himself with the sales manager's permission) and asks you to mentor them?

First, recognize it as an honor. It is a sign that others in the trade recognize you as an outstanding performer in a business that judges cruelly on performance.

Second, recognize it as an awesome responsibility! You are being asked, in essence, to parent a youngster! It will not be easy. Your pupil will ask you a zillion questions, and will do things wrong time and time again. They will sometimes make you want to set fire to your hair. But in the end, if you stick with it and they grow with the work, you will have helped put a brilliant sales professional on the street working with you as a powerful ally. What a noble thing, to have secured the survival of your species by making a clone of yourself.

How you mentor the pupil will depend on how your company wants to frame the assignment. Unless you are being paid a stipend over and above your salary and commission to do the mentoring, you will probably want to have the TM accompany *you* on sales calls in *your* territory. If you feel you can afford a day off once a month or so from your territory, you can ride with the TM in his territory and watch *him* do his sales calls, but only if you feel comfortable with being out of your territory one day a month or so.

Feel free to state your conditions up front. For example, "I will be glad to mentor you, Paul, but there are some things that I will expect of you, and if you are not comfortable with these, let's get that out now. I will expect you to:

- Observe silently when you accompany me on sales calls; if I want you to participate I will tell you, or invite you to speak during the call.
- Accept my suggestions on how to improve your skills and not argue back with me or think your way is better; when we are finished with this process, you can do it your way all you want, but you are asking me to build your sales skills and I will do that the way I know best.
- I will give you assignments from time to time, and I expect you to have them done on time and without errors.
- I expect you to be on time for our appointments and phone calls, and if you cannot keep an appointment to let me know at least three days in advance, unless it is an emergency.
- I welcome any questions you want to ask me and want you to feel free to ask follow-up questions so you clearly understand why I do what I do. If you don't understand the why's, you'll never make it to the top of this trade.
- I will ask you to write a final report when this process is over and submit it to the sales manager, detailing what you learned and how you will use it to be a better TM.

Do you have any questions?"

From time to time on your sales calls with *your* customers, give assignments to the pupil. For example, you might say to your trainee, "On the call to Johnson this week, I want *you* to explain the pre-season marketing program and get Johnson to sign on at the 'A' level." (If Paul gets Johnson to sign at the "B" level, offer correction in the car later, then go back on your next call and get Johnson to go to the "A" level.) Or on a prospecting call, tell Paul, "I want *you* to cover the warranty process and co-op ad programs that Mr. Billings brought up on our discovery call last week."

As Paul gains experience, up the ante. Ask him to make the presentation on the first call to a new prospect. Have him write up the pre-season order from a major account. Have him do the submittals on a mall job you sold to a mechanical contractor. Have him fix a credit snafu that has the dealer ticked off. As he gains experience, give him harder and harder tasks to do, coaching him as you do, and giving him feedback when done.

As far as feedback goes, the best way to do it is as near to the event as time allows. Usually this means in the car between sales calls. If time permits (and you can plan for this on your ride-along days), stop for half an hour at a coffee shop and have a coffee or soda and discuss how the trainee did on the assignment. In feedback, try to use the ratio of three positives for every correction. For instance, remark on how well the trainee exhibited energy on the call, and how well he greeted the dealer and the dealer's staff, and how he took great notes. And suggest that the next time a dealer blasts your brand for a perceived product flaw, how could he have handled it better than the way he did.

From time to time, be sure to praise the trainee in public. For example, at a monthly sales meeting, report to the group how well the trainee did in handling a difficult claim denial at Joe's the other day. But ***never*** criticize the trainee in public. Remember the basic rule: praise in public; rebuke in private.

A Mentoring Program

Progressive distributors have formal mentoring programs in place. In such programs, the mentor is usually compensated for his work in training the understudy for a one-year program.

To compensate the mentor for time spent away from their own territory, a mentoring bonus of 1/4 to 1/3 of the rookie's commissions could be awarded to the mentor. Typically in this kind of arrangement, the rookie and mentor spend one day a week in the mentor's territory as the rookie watches the mentor do his or her job and one day a week in the rookie's territory in which the rookie applies the lessons he or she observed and the mentor debriefs after the sales call. The other three days of the week, each spends in their own territory doing their own business.

Suppose, for example, that your company pays sales commissions of 8% of the gross margin dollars a territory manager generates and that your company's mentoring program pays you 30% of the trainee's commissions for your year-long work. If the trainee racks up sales this year of $2,000,000 at 24% gross margin, he generates $480,000 of gross margin. His commission would be $38,400. The company would pay you your normal base and commissions, plus

30% of the trainee's commission, or an additional $11,520.

Don't Forget Dealer Mentors!

Not only do I suggest that young territory managers seek out a mentor (and Tier One territory managers serve as mentors). I also suggest to young territory managers that they seek out a dealer or two to mentor them in the HVAC trade.

There is a simple reason for this. The contracting business is a tough business, almost brutal. Contractors tend to highly respect territory managers who have a genuine and deep understanding of the trade, but that understanding does not normally come through the education that most territory managers receive (especially in college). Having worked for a contractor myself I could speak the language my dealers spoke and empathize with them when they faced struggles. I don't think I would have succeeded nearly as well as I did if I did not have that background, and many of the Tier One territory managers I have trained have similar backgrounds and enjoy similar levels of access.

You may not have a background in contracting, but you can learn a lot about it if you find a dealer or two who others in your company think has it together and then ask that dealer (or dealers) to mentor you. Tell him you want to serve him as best you can, and to do that, you need to know this trade as well as he does. Would he consider taking you on as a special project?

Your mentoring would include spending a day every two weeks or so actually working in the dealership. You might spend a day helping a crew install ductwork. (Wear tough work gloves if you do! I can just walk by a pile of sheet metal and start bleeding!) Or he may have you help a crew rough-in a job (if you don't know what that means, you really *do* need to be mentored). He may have you run with a service tech all day, or spend the day at the job take-off desk taking off jobs and preparing estimates. He may have you spend a day at the front desk with the receptionist helping take calls and even answering the phone yourself. He may have you go with him as he meets a client to discuss a design-build project. You might go with his comfort specialist on some sales calls to homeowners or builders. He may have you spend a day in the shop helping fabricate job materials. You might spend a day cutting in roof curbs on a shopping center, or helping install a chiller in the basement of a church. You may help hang unit heaters in a warehouse, or wire thermostats on a new condo project. You might help the bookkeeper do job costing one day.

Whatever it is, trust the dealer to assign you to tasks you need to know in order to master this trade.

And at some point, you should ask him to also show you how to manage a business with financial information and analysis. This means he will have to open his income statement and balance sheet to you, so you'll have to have really earned that trust to ask for this lesson.

And when you are finished with your lessons, thank the dealer by taking him and his key staff out to a nice dinner and give him and his key staff a nice gift, like a branded pen and pencil set or some other suitable gift. If you earned a company trip that year, it might be best to give that trip to your mentor.

Review Questions for Chapter 29

1. Mentoring involves

   A) having a more-experienced person teach you "the ropes"

   B) teaching someone less-experienced than you how to do the job well

   C) working closely with someone else

   D) all of the above

   Answer: ________

2. As a trainee in a mentoring relationship, you should

   A) butt in on a sales call being made by your mentor

   B) not take correction by your mentor seriously

   C) feel free to not keep a commitment if other things arise

   D) strive to do all that is asked of you

   E) none of the above

   Answer: ________

3. ________ is at the center of success for Tier One TMs.

   A) Pride

   B) Skill

   C) Character

   D) Perseverance

   E) Cunning

   Answer: ________

4. As a mentor, you have the right to ask your trainee to

   A) complete certain assignments

   B) carry the ball sometimes on a sales call

   C) keep silent on a sales call

D) prepare a job submittal

E) all of the above

Answer: ________

5. When giving feedback,

A) always do it at a restaurant, never in the car

B) praise three times as much as you correct

C) don't worry about giving correction in front of others

D) try not to hurt the other person's feelings

E) document everything you say

Answer: ________

6. Which of the following would not be an activity you should do if instructed to do so by a mentoring dealer?

A) hang ductwork

B) help prepare payroll

C) do a job take-off

D) go on a sales call with his comfort specialist

E) all of these are okay to do

Answer: ________

Chapter 30: Is Sales Management In Your Future?

In engineering schools, pre-graduate engineers are often told, "If you are still *doing* engineering ten years after you graduate, you are a failure."

The implication is that after a decade or so of practicing engineering, a good engineer will rise in the company he or she works for and enter management. Of course, they will still be doing some engineering, but mostly they will be coordinating the engineering output of others who report to them.

We would not say that if you are still selling ten years after you acquire your first territory that you are a failure, because the truth is a lot of Tier One territory managers have been working their territories for decades and are superb at it and still enjoy it.

But some start thinking along their career paths, "Hmmm. I think that someday I'd like a crack at being a Sales Manager."

If You Have the Dream

If you have no desire to become a sales manager, you may skip the rest of this chapter. You will not find it to be of much help to your present career situation. But if you think a career in sales management is something you may want to pursue, please continue.

First, if you have not already done so, read Chapter 28, "Making Your Sales Manager Work for You." That chapter contains some important distinctions between your present role as a territory manager and your future one as a sales manager.

Let's summarize the differences in the two roles in this table, where the numbers are relative weights on a scale of 1 (low) to 5 (high):

Trait	Territory Manager	Sales Manager	You
Self-achievement	5	5	
Motivation	5	5	
Self-competitive	5	5	
Winning personality	4	5	
Product/service knowledge	5	3	
Continually seeks training	4	3	
Self-confident	5	5	
Professional image	4	5	
Listening skills	4	5	
Optimism	5	5	
Achievement orientation	4	5	
Identified with Management	1	5	
Leadership abilities	2	5	
Accountability up the chain	3	5	
Good communicator	4	5	
Market knowledge	4	3	
Problem solving ability	3	5	
Account management skills	4	5	
Relationship management	4	5	
Sales process mastery	5	3	
Entrepreneurial vision	2.5	5	
Financial acumen	3	5	
Resource management	2	6!	
Value-selling advocate	4	5	
Totals	91.5	113	

To make it easier to visualize the similarities and differences, I have shaded the matrix with this shading code:

Skills are equal for both
Territory manager needs stronger skills
Sales manager needs stronger skills

The composite difference in skills scores is only 21.5 points, but that 21.5 points is the difference between a Tier One territory manager and a Tier One sales manager!

Look at that list for a moment and score yourself in the You column. The closer you are to 113 total points, the closer you are to being sales manager material. How did you do?

For every point you come short of 113, you have a skill area (or areas) that you should work on. Just look at those traits where you scored yourself low and decide that if you are going to be a sales manager, you are going to have to get good at that trait. Then go get good at it.

But how?

Setting Your Course Early

Begin by letting someone in management (distributor principal or general manager, your current sales manager, the manager of human resources, and others) know that you are interested in becoming a sales manager some day. Don't make the blunder of saying you want to be a sales manager right now— they will quietly think you are a fool, a braggart, or both (and may even tell you so). Just let them know that you'd like a career path in that direction.

If they recognize your potential of being a Tier One sales manager, they will probably confirm that with you and agree to work with you in developing those skills. If they don't, they may agree to your acquiring the skills and giving you a limited shot at the job, or they may tell you that it is just not in your cards. Don't get angry if they tell you that. They may be right— you may not have the right stuff to be a sales manager. Maybe a great territory manager, but not a sales manager.

I regret that in my career as a territory manager, I wanted to pursue a role as sales manager but did not tell my managers about it. I worked hard as a territory manager and consistently set sales numbers at the top of the ratings, but I never told anyone that I wanted someday to manage the sales division in our company. At a crucial point in my career development, I was approached by a major manufacturer with an offer to do on a regional level in the United States what I had dreamed of doing within our own company. I agreed to the offer and went to my home office to tell the president of our company that I was going to be leaving and joining another company. He was stunned and saddened to hear my news, and said, "I was going to offer you the job of sales manager next month. You wouldn't reconsider, would you?"

I was torn! I had no idea he was considering me for that role, and had I known it, I would have told the manufacturer thanks, but no thanks. But I had already given my word to the manufacturer and being a man of my word, I could not back out now. I told my president that I was flattered and really appreciated the offer, but that I had already given my word to work for the manufacturer, and that he knew me— true to my word no matter the cost. (That was, as I later learned, one of the traits he valued in me the most.) We parted, and it was bittersweet when we did.

I have no idea where my life path would have gone had I taken the job as sales manager at my old distributorship. Life has been very good to me in the path I did choose, so I don't know if it would have been any better or worse than it is now. But that is water under the bridge. I made a choice, I stuck to it, and I am glad I did.

Still, I wonder how it might have turned out had I done the sales manager job…

Where to Get the Skills

There are obviously some college courses that could help you. I won't say they are requirements—I have known many Harvard and Princeton MBAs who could not manage a lemonade stand. But there are certain technical skills you will find helpful and graduate schools of business are good places to find them—especially in the rough-and-tumble grind of researching, writing, presenting and defending position papers on business topics assigned to you. I took several courses from the University of Phoenix (because of the flexible scheduling and on-line collaboration that was necessary since I had a full-time job already) and spent probably hundreds of hours in small group study, research, work and coordination as our teams tackled business problem after business problem. It was frustrating, but it also taught me a lot about how to get people to work together to meet a deadline, and pull off what sometimes looked like magic.

You'll find courses on organizational behavior helpful, as well as business law, finance, and statistics. It will be especially useful to have a course or two on good writing (oh, how I learned to love that hated *The Little, Brown Compact Handbook*). Whether you go the whole distance and earn an MBA or just pick up certain courses is up to you— an MBA does not make you a better sales manager in and of itself. But it certainly helps open doors for future assignments with your present (or future) employers.

Become a master of office software (whether it be the Microsoft Office suite of programs, or Apple's Mac OS suite, or the open structure of Linux). Learn how to create powerful spreadsheets, captivating multimedia programs, and good-looking mailings and brochures. (You may never be as good at it as an advertising agency, but learning how to compose a powerful brochure or mailer is a great lesson in what works— and doesn't— in media.)

Take a course or two in public speaking (like the famous Dale Carnegie courses), or join an organization like Toastmasters.

Join civic clubs (like Rotary, Sertoma, Lions Club, or Optimists, to name a few) and get active. Take on leadership roles; lead committees; get results.

Coach a Little League team. Be a Scout leader. Get active in your church, synagogue, temple or mosque and take on tasks when they are looking for volunteers.

Serve as a volunteer teacher at adult night schools sponsored by area junior colleges. Teach English as a second language to immigrants. Go abroad and serve for a few weeks in a humanitarian project, like building homes or providing medical services or food to the poor.

And don't forget one of the most important sources you have: your present sales manager. Ask him or her to mentor you. If that does not work out, ask your distributor principal or general manager if he knows a top-notch sales manager at another distributor and see if he could set up a mentoring program between you and their sales manager. (This will involve travelling, but will be worth the effort if the other sales manager is really good.)

Earn Your Wings

As you acquire your skills, expect to earn your wings in steps. You may be asked, for example, to lead some internal committees at your distributorship. This may include fact-finding committees, or process improvement teams. Learn how to lead a group of your peers and show you can do it well.

Eventually, you may be asked to manage a branch for your company, if it has branch locations. This will be a live-ammunition test of your skills. Can you do the job and do it well on your own? Do you get results? Do you build and maintain a strong sales team there?

If you do well in your small assignments, the day will come when you will be called to the main office and told by the president or general manager, "We would like you to take on the job of sales manager for the company. We think you're ready for it. What do you say?"

And you will smile and say, "By all means! When do I begin?"

Review Questions for Chapter 30

1. One area where you'll need stronger skills as a sales manager than as a territory manager is

A) identification with management

B) leadership ability

C) accountability

D) resource management

E) all of the above

F) none of the above

Answer: ________

2. If you desire to pursue a role as sales manager, you should tell

A) your best friend

B) your company management team

C) your dealers

D) your spouse (if married)

E) none of the above

Answer: ________

3. True or False. In order to be a Tier One sales manager, you need to get an MBA from a well-respected business school.

A) True

B) False

Answer: ________

4. Which of the following would *not* be a good place to pick up valuable skills for your role as a future sales manager?

A) your local homeowners association (if you belong to one)

B) military service

C) volunteer work

D) civic clubs

E) coaching young people in a sport

F) in a fishing tournament

Answer: ________

(Footnotes)

1 The company manual should be called an Employee Handbook, not the Employee Policy Manual. The term "policy manual" is pregnant with legal implications, whereas "handbook" allows for a much more loose legal restriction.

2 It does not have to be long or elaborate, but it does need to be on paper.

3 See Chapter 15.

Do you need a speaker?

Do you want Richard Harshaw to speak to your group or event? Then contact Larry Davis at: **(623) 337-8710** or email: **ldavis@intermediapr.com** or use the contact form at: **www.intermediapr.com**.

Whether you want to purchase bulk copies of *The HVAC Territory Manager's Field Guide* or buy another book for a friend, get it now at: **www.imprbooks.com**.

If you have a book that you would like to publish, contact Terry Whalin, Publisher, at Intermedia Publishing Group, (623) 337-8710 or email: twhalin@intermediapub.com or use the contact form at: www.intermediapub.com.